OFFICIAL NARRATIVE OF

AND PAPERS CONNECTED WITH

THE EXPEDITION

TO EXPLORE THE TRADE ROUTES

TO

CHINA VIA BHAMO,

UNDER THE GUIDANCE OF

MAJOR E. B. SLADEN,

POLITICAL AGENT, MANDALAY.

RANGOON:—PRINTED AT THE BRITISH BURMA PRESS—1869.

MEMORANDUM

BY THE

Chief Commissioner of British Burma.

From Major General ALBERT FYTCHE, C. S. I., Chief Commissioner, British Burma, Agent to His Excellency the Viceroy and Governor General, to W. S. SUTON-KARR, Esquire, Secretary to the Government of India, Foreign Department, Foreign (Political) Department, dated Rangoon, June 30th 1869.

I have the honor to submit, to be laid before the Right Honorable the Viceroy and Governor General of India in Council, Major Sladen's Report of his Expedition to explore the old trade routes between South Western China and Burma viâ Bhamo, together with its appendices, and ten plans of towns and remarkable buildings visited by the expedition, and two manuscript maps. A report by Mr. Robert Gordon, C. E. attached as Engineer Officer to the expedition is also annexed, together with a lithographed map of the routes surveyed by the party between Bhamo and Momein, drawn up by Mr. Gordon, and containing information regarding the country beyond the latter city and in other directions, compiled from all reliable sources that were available. The delay in the submission of the report is to be regretted. It has been caused by Major Sladen's illness since his return to Mandalay, and the delay in getting Mr. Gordon's map lithographed in Calcutta. Major Sladen's Report reached me on 15th April last.

2. I have in my several letters to the Government of India (contained in the Appendices) described the progress of the Expedition from time to time as reports reached me from Major Sladen; and as the accompanying Report of Major Sladen's speaks for itself, there is no occasion for my going into the subject at length, and little more than a brief resumé of what I have already written is required.

3. There are three principal routes from Bhamo, which, leaving the town of that name on the Irrawaddy, run in a North Easterly direction to Talifoo, the present Capital of Western Yunan, passing over the Kakhyen hills, then through a narrow belt of Shan States, and, joining together at Nantin,

proceed on to Momein the border town of Yunan, whence by Yunchan (the centre of the trade in Western Yunan) the route passes on to Talifoo. Major Sladen succeeded in reaching Momein, and I consider, under the circumstances described by him, that he was right in not proceeding beyond that town.

4. The chief objects for which the expedition was sent, was to discover the cause of the cessation of the trade formerly existing by these routes, the exact position held by the Kakhyens, Shans, and Panthays with reference to that traffic, and their disposition, or otherwise to resuscitate it; as also to examine the physical conditions of the routes. All these have, I consider, been satisfactorily obtained. Considerable delay occurred in the Kakhyen hills, prolonging the period of absence of the expedition beyond that which was anticipated, but this is, I think, not to be regretted, as it has enabled Major Sladen to obtain considerable information regarding the Kakhyens, who, holding the hills, must always form an important element in any scheme for re-opening the route, and has given them an opportunity of learning our real intentions, regarding which they would appear to have been falsely imbued by designing persons. Major Sladen throughout the difficulties he experienced from these people shewed great tact and command of temper, and wisely chose to wait patiently at Ponsee, despite the disadvantages in some respects of the delay thereby necessitated, until he received a reply to a communication he had, with much judgment, despatched to the Panthay Governor at Momein, and which, when obtained, enabled him to advance with all the prestige of the direct support and encouragement of the Panthay Government, whose predominance was at once manifested by their rapid occupation of the route up to the base of the Kakhyen hills, and the altered tone towards Major Sladen of the Kakhyen and Shan Chiefs as soon as they became aware of his friendly relations with the Panthay Government.

5. The trade by the Bhamo route as late as the year 1855 (the commencement of the rebellion of the Panthanys against the Chinese Authorities) was nearly half a million of pounds Sterling, and all previous history of this line of commerce with which we are acquainted proves beyond doubt that there exists an important field for trade in these localities,

The knowledge, too, acquired by the present Mission assures us that the parties most interested in this commerce desire a revival of the trade. It is of course useless for the Kakhyens to hold trade routes through which no trade flows, and they are quite alive to this fact. The Shan Chiefs, also—apart from some local jealousies caused by a wish to secure for themselves the advantages of having the route through their individual territories—would gladly see the old interchange of commodities renewed. The Shans are an enterprizing race, and the unsatisfactory position they have occupied for the last few years, disunited and preyed upon both by Chinese and Panthays, and all the trade stopped, make them anxious for any arrangement which would be likely to lead to a more satisfactory state of affairs, and enable them to develope their natural industry. It would, doubtless, have been very interesting from some points of view had the party succeeded in reaching Talifoo, the Head Quarters of the Panthay Government; but it certainly appears that the Panthay Authorities whom Major Sladen met at Momein were of sufficient importance and position to render their views and opinions a safe criterion of the favorable feeling of the Panthay Government towards the resuscitation of trade.

6. The Panthay rebellion was no doubt the primary cause of the cessation of trade by the Bhamo routes, but Major Sladen considers that there is some reason to believe that during the last five or six years, or since the comparative consolidation of Mahomedan rule within the Province of Yunan, the non-resuscition of trade by these routes is due to the King of Burma, who for political reasons has restricted the trade to a long overland journey of two months viâ Theinnee to Mandalay. He states "what Burma has always dreaded" (from our occupation of Pegu) "is that British interests would not" "be confined to British possessions, but that contingencies" "might arise which would give the foreigner the right of ex-" "tending his influence to Upper Burma, and to a point" "above and beyond the limits of the present Burmese Capi-" "tal. Such a contingency was always imminent as long as" "it could be made demonstrable in any way that Bhamo" "might again become the natural emporium of a direct" "overland trade between Burma and China. The same ob-" "jection did not hold good provided *Mandalay* could be"

subsidy will be granted to the above mentioned company to induce them to extend the voyage of their steamers on to Bhamo. The open navigation of the Irrawaddy river has been held in view by the Supreme Government since 1862, and the Treaties of that year and of 1867 will be largely inoperative if the Government do not take every opportunity of pushing on the commercial policy which promises so much both for the King's Territories and for British Burma. If we aim at binding up the interests of the two countries by the free interchange of commodities, and by the impetus thus given to the producing power of the territories, rather than by Political compacts, which from the constitution of the Burmese Court cannot have, at least for a far distant period, that complete and substantial security which attaches to Treaties with European Powers, we should use our best endeavours rapidly to extend trade with Upper Burma, and especially in the shape which will appeal most forcibly to a comparatively backward nationality. Our trade with Burma Proper is already two and a half millions Sterling—what need to hesitate in adopting the most liberal view of any scheme which will develope trade that has doubled in four years? The vast political importance of all means of rapid locomotion is now practically conceded. They break down prejudices; they create new wants; they quicken and liberalize the national opinion; they lead to a peaceful rather than a warlike phase of thought; and all these useful objects are precisely what we should desire to see having effect in Upper Burma.

9. The Expedition having only reached the frontier town of Momein, Major Sladen has been precluded from speaking with any authority regarding the trade statistics of Yunan, and I think he has acted wisely in refraining from any attempt to do so. The great mineral wealth of the country is, however, known, as also the enormous wealth of the neighbouring provinces of Sechuen and Kwei-chow the most populous in China, and their gigantic trade in tea, silk, rhubarb, tobacco, sugar, hemp, oil, varnish and other commodities, and that vast capacity of all those Provinces to comsume European manufactures, a large proportion of the whole of which trade we shall gain when once the route by Bhamo is fully re-opened. Mr. T. T. Cooper in his late endeavour to traverse the through route from China viâ Thibet to India, in a letter to *North China Daily News* from a place named Tai-Tsian-loo on the extreme Western frontier of China,

fully corroborates the importance I have attached to the resuscitation of the trade by Bhamo. In it he states that the "present trade between Chung-King and Yunan and Kwei-chow, is only temporary" (with Hankow) "on account of the closure of the Bhamo and Tali route, and as sure as this route is opened, so sure will Burma take to herself the trade of these two Provinces, and if, as is probable, British Merchants establish themselves at Ava" (this has already been done) "then a rivalship for the trade of Sechuen between China and Burma Merchants seems almost certain, the result telling probably in favor of the latter, both in Exports and Imports. Trade by this route has flourished before without European enterprize, and as soon as it is re-opened, the trade between Hankow and Chung-Caing will be lessened one-third."

10. The good effects of the visit of Major Sladen and his party should be promptly and vigorously followed up, and the Assistant Agent (whose appointment has been sanctioned) be despatched to Bhamo without delay, to strengthen the belief in the reality of our intentions, and to maintain communication with the Shan Chiefs, and Panthay Government; and continue also to influence the Khakyens towards giving facilities for safe transit of goods. I feel certain that on the prompt action of Government depends a question of the very highest Imperial importance. Our Seaborne trade with China is being actively competed for by America. The hot haste with which the Government of Washington have pushed on the completion of the Atlantic and Pacific Railroad, and the dominance they have lately advanced in China's diplomatic relations with other Courts—all point to a determination on the part of America to secure if posible the command of the Chinese market. The present obstacles of difficult communication they have solved or are in a fair way of solving, and the necessity now remains only of adopting their exports to the Chinese requirements. Will this be possible without vitally affecting our Commercial superiority? Further will America long submit to our holding the commanding position we derive from our Opium Exports, and the hold we thus have on the Exchange? It is here that the question touches India in a tender point. The derangement of our Opium Revenue means a most serious crisis in Indian Finance, and

were American interference to affect our Seaborne Opium, the routes through this Province would become on this account alone, of the highest importance. In the case of such a contingency, and for obvious collateral reasons in themselves, I consider it highly prudent on Imperial grounds that we should be in a position to substitute a Western ingress to China, for the present Sea-board approach, destined to be disproportionately shared—if not entirely absorbed by America. I observe, also, that the American Government, not content with the Pacific railroad, has Officially recommended to the European States, the great enterprize of a Ship Canal to be constructed across the Isthmus of Darien.

11. The Engineer Officer originally attached to the expedition was Captain J. M. Williams of the Madras Army, who thought fit to return from Ponsee—or after the expedition had proceeded a distance of only forty miles from Bhamo. His conduct in quitting the expedition will be remarked upon hereafter. His report on the Northern route as far as Ponsee has already been submitted to Government with my letter No. 39-37 dated July 10th 1868. It contains a very meagre report on a portion only of one route, and any importance which it might have possessed has been nullified by the accompanying report of Mr. Robert Gordon c.e., Executive Engineer of the Upper Pegu and Arakan roads, an Officer of well-known active habits, and great personal energy, to whom, immediately on information reaching me from Mandalay of Captain Williams' abondonment of the expedition, I telegraphed to proceed as rapidly as possible to Bhamo and follow the track of Major Sladen's party. Every assistance was given by the Burmese Government (whom I addressed on the subject) to facilitate Mr. Gordon's advance, and he came up, in an extraordinarily short period, with Major Sladen at Muangla or Maingla on the return of the expedition from Momein. His report is succinct and clear, and is as full as can be expected under the circumstances; his journey being a hurried one throghout, did not admit of careful surveys being made. Had Capt. Williams remained with the expedition his opportunities would have been far greater, and during the stay of the party at Momein (which Mr. Gordon did not reach) he would have had the advantage of making full enquiries regarding the through routes from Momein to Talifoo, Eastward to China

Proper; as well as Westward to India:—as also regarding any East and West routes from China to India to the North of Talifoo, and which, according to the written instructions issued to him formed one of his principal duties, apart from the report on the physical condition of the routes actually traversed by the party.

12. Mr. Gordon explains in his report that between Bhamo and Momein lies a range of hills lying in a North and South direction, and forming a spur from the Himalayan range of mountains. Bhamo is on the West of the spur and Momein on the East. In travelling between the two places it is obligatory to cross this range, which is pierced by three valleys through which traffic has been conducted between the two towns. The Northern, Sanda valley, or Ponlyne route is formed by the Taping river, a tributary of the Irrawaddy, into which it flows a few miles above Bhamo, the general direction of the rivers being from North East to South West. On its North side it is bounded by high hills, and on the South by the Shamaloung range, which separates it from the centre valley. The Centre, Hotha valley, or Embassy route is formed by the Namsa river, a tributary of the Taping, into which it flows at a point about forty five miles East of Bhamo. Its Northern boundary is the Southern boundary of the Sanda Valley, and its Southern boundary is a spur of hill from the Shamaloung range, which spur forms also the Northern boundary of the Muangwan Valley, Southern, or Sawuddy route. Through this last named valley runs the Nam-wan river, which apparently takes its rise in the Shamaloung range. The Southern boundary of this valley is formed by the Myne-won mountain range. The three rivers running through the valleys have all one general direction, that is from North East to South West.

13. Mr. Gordon in the first instance marched from Bhamo through the Northern or Sanda Valley as far as Muangla or Maingla, a distance of ninety miles from Bhamo. Leaving Bhamo, he crossed the Taping river near its junction with the Irrawaddy and kept along its right bank for a distance of about twenty miles. The road then left the river, the distance between them varying until the village of Ponlyne was reached, distant thirty miles from Bhamo, and about four miles from the Taping. The elevation reached was 1814 feet,

being at the rate of a little more than sixty feet per mile from Bhamo. The next place reached was Ponsee forty miles from Bhamo and not far from the river, the elevation being 2719 feet. About half way between the two villages the Namphoung stream, an affluent of the Taping, was crossed, necessitating a descent from Ponlyne of 1241 feet, and an ascent to Ponsee of 2127 feet. Three miles beyond Ponsee the Sanda Valley commences, and at a distance of eleven miles Manwyne with an elevation of 1,900 feet was reached. The route lay apparently near the river up to this point and was still on its right bank. The next place reached was Sanda situate about six miles North of the Taping river. It stands upon an affluent bearing its name, and which flows into the Taping river at a distance of ten miles from the town. The affluent is crossed close to the town. This town may be presumed to be the central town of the valley. Its elevation is 2912 feet or about 100 feet above the elevation of Manwyne. Beyond Sanda and at a distance of about sixteen miles Muangla is reached with an elevation of 2091 feet. Beyond this point, Mr. Gordon did not go as he was met by Major Sladen returning from Momein.

14. The general impression derived from Mr. Gordon's report on the Sanda Valley is not an unfavorable one. With the exception of the steep descent and ascent from the Nampoung stream between Ponlyne and Ponsee, there seem to be no difficulties of any magnitude, and what difficulties there are, appear to be within the first forty miles from Bhamo. Mr. Gordon points out that by removing the line of road from its present crossing of the Nampoung stream, the steep gradients would be avoided by passing over the affluent some miles higher up.

15. The line of road marched over by Mr Gordon apparently runs, for the greater part of its length, over high ground adjoining the Taping river, and after leaving Ponsee would seem to pass over fairly level ground. He states that dry weather roads follow each bank, and he would recommend any new line of road, if narrow, to follow the course of the river. The length of such a line would possibly be much greater, and the cost of bridging for the purpose would be heavier than on the high ground, but then the rise throughout would be gradual. The relative merits of a line along the foot of the

hills, and bordering the river, and of a line carried on the existing track are not easily determined in the absence of more data than are available, though Mr. Gordon seems to think a road running on the high ground could be constructed for £1,000 a mile, or between Bhamo and Momein for £90,000. The cost of a road on the rivers edge would probably be greater, as much blasting would be necessary, together with extensive bridging. Perhaps the Government of India from the experience gained in the construction of the Simla and Thibet road might be able to approximate to the probable cost. One advantage of the high level road would be in the opening out of the country it would lead to, tending to increase cultivation and population. These results would directly affect the extent of the Merchandize carried along it. On the whole, I am disposed to think that the advantages are in favor of the high line road. There seems to be abundance of material for the bridges and metalling of the road.

16. On his return from Muangla to Bhamo, Mr. Gordon came through a portion of the Hotha valley. He appears to have marched from the former place back to Manwyne and then to have crossed the Shamaloung hills to Hotha, 3749 feet above the town of Bhamo, and 1749 feet above Manwyne. Between Hotha, which from the map appears to be about the centre of the valley, and his next halting place, Namboke, both of which have nearly the same altitude, the distance is about twelve miles. The exact character of the country passed over is not clear from Mr. Gordon's description. Between Namboke and the next halting place Ashan, a distance of about seven miles, the country appears to be very mountainous. One point of the road was recorded as 4650 feet above Nantin, which is equivalent to 7218 above Bhamo. Between Ashan and the Namphong stream, a distance of about five or six miles, there is a descent of 958 feet, and from this there is no record of the intermediate places reached until arrival at Hotone, the elevation of which is 2450 feet. This place appears to be in nearly the same parallel of Longitude with Ponlyne in the Sanda valley, which is less in elevation by about 600 feet than Hotone. Between the Namphong stream and Hotone the ground is described

as hilly though easier than the ground over which the usual journey is made. From Hotone the descent towards the Taping is described as rapid and difficult.

17. It seems clear from this description of the portion of the Hotha Valley marched through, that the advantages for traffic purpose are all on the side of the Sanda Valley. The elevations to be crossed in the Hotha Valley far exceed the elevations met with in the Sanda valley and furthermore it seems certain that ground higher than that in the vicinity of Momein would have to be passed over. The population also is much less and owing to the rugged nature of the country is not likely to increase. Mr. Gordon has summed up the demerits of the Hotha valley route very carefully in the 36th paragraph of his report, and also as far as can be judged, he shows fully why this route is not an advisable one.

18. Of the third or Muangwan valley, Mr. Gordon reports but little, and that only on hearsay. I doubt the expediency of dwelling upon his remarks.

19. The remaining paragraphs of the report are taken up with the consideration of the country lying between Momein and Yunchon. The exsting traffic crosses the Salween river by an iron bridge, which testifies to the commercial activity that must have formerly prevailed. Even now Mr. Gordon is able to report that 30,000 mules pass yearly between the two cities. Of course no engineering opinion can be formed on the country lying to the East of Momein, as nothing as yet is known regarding it.

20. From Mr. Gordon's report it appears that he considers the Northern route along the Sanda valley to be the most advisable one as far as physical difficulties are concerned, and that the central, Hotha valley, or Embassy route for the purposes of a road constructed on scientific principles, cannot compete with either the Northern or Southern routes. He does not speak so confidently of the latter as of the former route, as he had not the same opportunities for observing it; but on the whole he is of opinion "that a good road with " easy gradients can be made without great expense through either the Sanda or the Muangwan valley." No difficulties greater than are ordinarily met with in constructing hill-roads exist in the Kakhyen hills, and the country compares favora-

bly with the Arakan Mountains opposite Prome over which a twelve foot road has been constructed one hundred miles long, ninety of which are in the mountains. Mr. Gordon has had this road under his charge for three years, and can affirm that in the thirty or forty miles of hilly ground necessary to pass over to reach the Sanda valley from the plains, there are no greater difficulties than are met with on the Prome and Tounghoo road.

21. Major Sladen in his remarks regarding these routes states that "it would be immature to puzzle ourselves which" "is the most practicable in an engineering point of view," "until we are prepared to entertain a definite scheme of" "road improvement, or even railroad communication—that" "trade to an almost unlimited extent is now possible by" "any of the present existing routes without reference to" "their engineering capabilities, and that the determination of" "either of these three routes as a through-route for gene-" "ral traffic must depend for some time to come on questions" "of policy and general expedience, rather than of special" "adaptability or Physical disqualification;" and prefers the Hotha valley, Central, or Embassy route to the other two for all present purposes of commerce and communication.

23. From both the reports of Major Sladen and Mr. Gordon we gather therefore that the present routes are available for traffic by means of Mules as formerly, that between Bhamo and Momein no physical difficulties of any kind exist to the construction by one or other of these valleys, of either a road built on scientific principles for wheeled carriages, of a tramway, or of a railway; that the length of such, would only be 130 miles, or probably less, and that labor and good material for road making are available in the country to any extent that may be required.

24. The vitality of the Bhamo route for traffic which it maintained for centuries among all the disturbing influences of the flow and ebb of the Chinese and Burmese power indicated that, somehow or other, the line in that direction possessed some practical advantages over other through routes, and induced me to press the subject of its Exploration on the Government of India. So much however, has been written regarding the route proposed by by Captain Sprye from

Rangoon to Canton viâ Kyang-Hung, that the present papers might perhaps be considered incomplete if all mention if it was omitted.

25. When I proposed the expedition to Bhamo a survey had just been completed from Rangoon as far as the borders of our own territory for a line of Railway from Rangoon to Kyang-Hung, and thence on through the mythical City of Esmok to Canton. It was with no intention of interfering with this survey that that proposal was made. My proposition to re-open traffic by the Bhamo route with the Provinces of South Western China stands upon a different footing altogether, in fact the two schemes are perfectly distinct. The object of the Bhamo expedition is to re-open a temporarily closed trade by a line of country already known and from which, if successful, the most advantageous results must *at once* flow; whereas the object of the survey is to discover a route by which a Railway *might* be constructed, and even if pronounced feasible and advisable it would take at least a generation to complete. I have myself always looked on the Kyang-Hung line as a most Quixotic scheme as a route for trade; but as the survey of the country from Takau ferry on the Salween river viâ Kyang-Tung on to Kyang-Hung on the Cambodia river, a distance of about 200 miles, would be of great scientific and poltical value, I would still advocate its continuation at any rate as far as that city. We have already a fair general knowledge of the country from the British Frontier through the Shan States tributary to Burma up to the Takau ferry but the tract of country lying between the Salween and Cambodia rivers is unknown.

26. When Captain Sprye's scheme was *first* proposed there was something in it both plausible and attractive—to connect Rangoon with Canton by a railway running through a country with, as it was supposed, no insuperable obstacles very naturally commended itself to notice. Canton was then, and had been for many years, the great centre of foreign trade with China. From that port nearly all the tea, silk, and other valuable produce was shipped, and there all the European goods were imported. It was naturally believed in consequence, that Quangtung and Quangsi were the great producing and consuming districts of the Empire—but on the opening of Shanghai to foreign trade this fallacy was exposed,

and it was completely dispelled by the opening in 1860-61 of Hankow and the other ports on the Yangtse river, which showed that the Foreign trade that had centred in Canton, had been flowing, not in its *natural, but in a forced or artificial* channel, and that the great bulk of what was shipped from Canton, was really produced in Sechuen, Kweichow, and other provinces drained by the Yangtse, and that this produce had actually been carried up that river in boats, to a point where it is separated from the Canton river or one of its affluents, by a steep range of hills, through a pass in which the produce was carried by porters down to the Southern stream, and from thence to Canton in boats. By the same route also imports found their way to the place of consumption. So soon as the Yangtse ports were opened all was changed; trade began to flow down the Yangtse and nearly the whole trade of Canton ceased, except what may be considered its legitimate trade, that is, exporting the productions of Quangtung and Quangsi, and the supplying of these Provinces with European goods. The trade of Canton at one time sunk so low that it was, I believe, seriously proposed to abandon it altogether as a place of European trade.

27. I will now glance rapidly at the bearing which these facts have upon the routes viâ Kyang-Hung and Bhamo. First then as regards connecting Rangoon and China by a railway viâ Kyang-Hung and Esmok, the only Chinese markets of importance that would be reached by such a line of railway would be those in the extreme south of Yunan, in Quangsi, and Quantung; but as has been shown, the foreign trade of the last two named provinces is comparatively small, and as they are well known to have already such easy and cheap communication with Canton, it would be in vain to hope that commerce could be diverted to what must be a much more expensive outlet. The Southern portion of Yunan too is very poor compared with the Central and North Western portion of the province; and the trade with the Shan States, also, by this route, would be less than by the Bhamo route, the States to the Northward being wealthier than those to the Southward. Turning now to the route viâ Bhamo, Momein, and Tali, we find that there is a commercial highway used by Burmese and Chinese merchants from time immemorial, leading through the richest part of Yunan, and tapping Sechuen

and Kweichow which, as has been said before, are the wealthiest and most populous provinces in China. Although Sechuen is bordered by the Yangtse, still the difficulties of the route towards Chung Ching, the great Central mart on its banks, are said to be great, and the mouth of the river is so far distant that the carriage of goods is very costly. The navigation of the river between Chung Ching and Hankow is moreover extremely disastrous to trade on account of the total loss of many Junks and their cargoes in the dangerous rapids and whirlpools, and besides which, goods passing through such a great number of separate districts, (in each of which heavy taxes are levied,) the cost of the produce is greatly enhanced before it finally quits the country, and we may very reasonably suppose with Mr. Cooper that we may share at least one-third of this vast trade, when the Bhamo route is fairly re-opened.

28. The desertion at Ponsee by Captain J. M. Williams of the Expedition has already been alluded to, and is referred to by Major Sladen in paragraphs 179 to 191, and 491 to 494 of his report. The circumstances connected with his leaving, and Captain Williams' own explanation have been previously communicated to the Government of India. Major Sladen generously takes the onus of Captain Williams' departure in great part on his own shoulders, but paragraph 491 fully explains the reasons why he was anxious to get rid of such an unwilling and, to say the least, lukewarm coadjutor. It appears that Captain Williams endeavoured before even leaving Bhamo to persuade Major Sladen to give up the Expedition and return. His attempt to explain that it was from lack of funds that he abandoned the Expedition, and that he would expedite the progress of the party by so doing, is not borne out by facts; for all the difficulties that had hitherto beset the Expedition were in a great measure removed previous to his leaving by the receipt of a communication from the Panthay Governor of Momein, guaranteeing carriage, escort, and all expenses of the party through the Shan States to Momein; besides which, on his return, between Bhamo and Mandalay he met a strong Burmese escort under a confidential Officer of the King of Burma conveying Rs. 10,000 which I had despatched from Rangoon for Major Sladen, and if want of funds was alone the reason, why did he not return

with this escort? and to whom his services, having just travelled over the road by which they would have to proceed, would have been most valuable. Moreover if a reduction in the number of the party was obsolutely necessary, Major Sladen under whose orders every one connected with the Expedition had been distinctly placed—would have doubtless sent back Lieutenant Bowers together with the other mercantile representative Mr. Stewart, or even the Medical Officer Doctor Anderson. His conduct regarding the Photographic apparatus described by Major Sladen was petty, and his taking away with him the Government surveying instruments mentioned, and his refusal to send them back, when a special messenger was sent after him for them by Major Sladen, was most reprehensible. Captain J. M. Williams has shown himself to be altogether unfitted to accompany any expedition of this description, and his services will doubtless never be availed of by the Government again in any such capacity.

29. Dr. J. Anderson, Conservator, India Museum, whose services as Surgeon and Naturalist to the Expedition were placed at my disposal by the Trustees of the Museum, is highly spoken of by Major Sladen. Dr. Anderson has, it is understood, made a large collection of valuable specimens of natural history, and of the products and manufactures of the several localities visited, the whole of which were sent to Calcutta as I was unwilling that his cases of specimens should be opened at Rangoon, for they might have been injured in repacking; and the different specimens were not then arranged. They have, however, no doubt been all classified by this time, and I would suggest that a complete series of his collections may be sent me for deposit in the Phayre Museum at Rangoon. I have not yet received Dr. Anderson's Official report. On its receipt it will be immediately despatched to your address.

30. Lieutenant Bowers R. N. R. attached to the party as Commercial Agent, appears to have been of great assistance to Major Sladen, and his varied knowledge and experience of special utility to the expedition.

31. Major Sladen himself is deserving of highest commendation for his skillful conduct of the expedition. He has shown throughout sound judgment and discrimination in his

intercourse with the various Authorities with whom he had to deal, and in the many novel and delicate positions in which he was placed; and it is owing to his great tact and judgment that the expedition was brought to the successful termination it has been.

CAPTAIN SLADEN'S REPORT.

From Captain E. B. SLADEN, Political Agent, Mandalay; to Major General A. FYTCHE, C.S.I., Chief Commissioner British Burma, and Agent to His Excellency the Viceroy and Governor-General, dated 24th February 1869.

I do myself the honor of informing you, with reference to your letter No. 12 M, of November 1867, that the exploring party which was ordered to proceed under my command viâ *Bhamo* to the borders of South Western China, commenced its journey from *Mandalay* on the 13th January 1868.

Captain E. B. Sladen..................Leader.
Captain J. M. Williams..................Engineer.
Dr. John Anderson....Medical Officer and Naturalist.
Captain A. Bowers }
T. Stewart, Esq. } ....Mercantile Representatives.
F. N. Burn, Esq. }
One Native Doctor. One Police Inspector. Fifty armed Police.

2. The narrative of the expedition has already been told, in a somewhat fragmentary form, in my several letters (as per margin), private and demi-official, which were despatched from time to time as opportunities offered, during our protracted absence beyond British Territory. I shall endeavour, in the present official Report, to beat out the whole of the material at my disposal, into the form of a simple and consecutive Record, by which to reveal the objects of the expedition and to trace out its progress and results in the order they occurred, without any studied attempt at classification, and with a seeming disregard, perhaps, of the mere conventional restraints of ordinary official correspondence.

LETTERS DATED.
Bhamo, 22nd January 1868.
Do.   23rd   do   1868.
Do.   27th   do   1868.
Do.   31st   do   1868.
Do.   2nd February 1868.
Do.   15th   do   1868.
Do.   25th   do   1868.
Ponsee 29th April 1868.
Do.   10th May 1868.
Bhamo 5th September 1868.
Do.   12th   do   1868.

3. It will be necessary too, as the narrative proceeds, to quote to some extent from my rough diaries; and in many places, I may be led to adopt the diary system altogether. But all matters of a purely evidential or explanatory character will be submitted in the form of an appendix, so as to interfere, as little as possible with the consecutive nature of the report itself.

4. I may further state once for all, by way of introduction, that I have carefully abstained from all scientific

and statisctcal details which did not appear to come within the scope of my duties or relationship to the expedition. All such information may be looked forward to with confidence in the Reports of those members of our party to whom the scientific details of the journey have been happily entrusted.

5. It has long been a matter of special notoriety to those acquainted with the affairs of Upper Burma, that its commercial prosperity has depended, for many generations past, on the means afforded of prosecuting overland trade with the Southern and Western Provinces of the Chinese Empire.

6. Most of the Gold that for centuries past has been lavishly expended in the decorative arts of this country, and in the adornment of its interminable pagodas; and all the silk which from time immemorial has helped to feed the looms of it's principal industry, found it's way from China to Burma by an overland route from Yunan, which struck the Irrawaddy at the old central mart of *Bhamo*.

7. In return for this wealth, Burma exported raw cotton from amongst her indigenous products; and supplied woollen cloths and piece goods, imported yet sparingly, from a British market.

8. But for more than a dozen years past or from a time which is somewhat remarkably coincident with the British occupation of Pegu, internal trade with China had either entirely ceased, or was prosecuted only to an extent which was inappreciable in estimating the wealth, the capabilities, or the requirements of the countries to which that trade naturally belonged.

9. It is no new theory at the present time, as regards the origin or design of the present expedition, to have ventured upon a solution of causes, which from their very apparency (it would seem) have hitherto baffled or deterred every attempt to account for the cessation of trade by the old caravan route between *Bhamo* and the Chinese Province of Yunan.

10. Every Merchant who has ever been led to speculate on establishing himself in Burma, since the British occupation of Pegu in 1852, has had his attention keenly fixed for several years past on vast fields for commercial enterprize in the

fertile openings of Upper Burma, the Shan States, and Western China.

11. But when a substantial scheme had been set on foot for penetrating this same Western China by a route or railway which was to be projected from a Rangoon terminus, it became a matter of very significant import to consider whether the direct route from Rangoon, so energetically advocated by Captain Sprye, was the route par excellence which was to be made practicable at any cost,—or whether special means were not available for arriving at precise data upon which to justify and consummate the idea of reviving an old overland trade route, which had always been recognized as the natural outlet by which the commerce of China had hitherto worked a channel for itself into the Provinces of Burma.

12. Hence originated the expedition of 1868; which involving as it did the exploration of unknown Territory lying within and beyond the Northern confines of Upper Burma, could only have been prudently undertaken by a party of British officers, under a full assurance that they enjoyed the confidence of the Burmese Government, and would profit by its active support in removing the primary difficulties of a somewhat hazardous and tentative undertaking.

13. Having concluded a second treaty with the British Government, the time seemed to have come when the King of Burma and his Ministers had been led by experience to renounce for ever the primitive state of exclusiveness by which they had hitherto hedged in their country and denied themselves the benefits of free commercial intercourse with neighbouring states. It was, therefore, an opportune moment for making known the requirements of the British Government, and of obtaining the consent of the king of Burma to the despatch of a party of British Officers to explore the old caravan route between the upper waters of the Irrawaddy, and the South Western confines of Yunan. This consent was given with a cordiality which called forth the thanks and acknowledgements of his Excellency the Viceroy and Governor General of India, and afforded an indubitable ground for belief that that cordiality would be continued, and that those acknowledgements would not be too lightly esteemed.

14. For several weeks before the expedition left Mandalay, the King, the Chief Minister, and other officials of the Burmese Government, had been repeatedly urged to bear in mind the great importance of the expedition; and, at my special solicitation, written orders were despatched to the Governor of Bhamo, and to the Heads of the several towns and villages which lay in our route, to anticipate our arrival and make provision for several known requirements.

But irrespective of these outward assurances of support, held out by the officials themselves, other indirect evidence was not wanting of an apparent desire on the part of the Burmese Government to place no direct obstacles in the way of our progress, as long at least as that progress lay within Burmese Territory.

15. In my several interviews with the King, previous to my departure for Bhamo, the subject of the approaching expedition was alway referred to in a way which was intended to convince His Majesty that the eyes of the World were then directed towards Burma; and that the ultimate success of the expedition—depending as it did, in a great measure on the guaranteed support of the Burmese Government—had connected itself very intimately with His Majesty's interests, and probably also with the permanence and stability of His Majesty's Dominions.

16. There were times when the King wavered so far as to yield temporarily to certain jealous influences which were secretly fomented with the object of proving to him that he had acted unwisely in giving his consent to a British expedition which was to penetrate China through Burma, and produce an objectionable influx of foreign intruders into Burmese Territory. The King himself made known to me the existence of this secret opposition, and spoke in particular of a petition presented by an European resident of Mandalay, which warned him that if the expedition started and succeeded in its object, a death blow would have been levelled against Burman supremacy and the perfect independence of His Majesty's Government.

17. But, knowing as I did that the king felt his interests in this undertaking to be bound up with our own, and relying upon this fact with more confidence than all the other out-

ward evidences of Royal support and co-operation, I had persuaded myself into a belief that Burmese opposition, beyond the ordinary petty restrictions of travel in any half civilized country, would not have been seriously attempted, so long as the expedition remained within Burmese limits, or was subjected to Burmese influences.

18. In this, as in other instances of misconception in our estimate of the facilities attending this expedition, we are now proved to have erred; and I simply instance this one fact in particular, at the present state of my narrative, because it shews, I think, that no provision, however complete, could have warded off a difficulty which not only defied anticipation, but grew, as it were, out of what we were bound, in our friendly relations and intercourse with the Burmese Government, to rely upon as a chief fundamental element of success and encouragement.

19. It can hardly be wondered at then, that the expedition took its departure from British territory under a very erroneous idea of coming events, and with a despatch which would have indicated undue haste and an absence of all effective preparation, had the realities of the adventure or the political difficulties which every where encompassed it, been recognized as conditions or contingencies which had not already been amply provided against by the cordial assent and guaranteed patronage of the Burmese Government.

20. In arranging for the despatch of the expedition from Mandalay to *Bhamo*, His Majesty the King of Burma had volunteered the services of one of his river steamers; and in spite of much conflicting testimony to the contrary, there was every prospect of our reaching a starting point on the Irrawaddy, without any of the delays incidental to boat transit during a somewhat unfavorable and uncertain period of the year.

21. On no former occasion had it been deemed prudent or advisable to despatch steamers beyond a well defined distance above the capital at Mandalay. Those whose experience entitled them to be heard on a matter of so much general import, openly affirmed, with a great deal of assurance and ingenuity, that no steamers, then available on the Irrawaddy, could possibly proceed as far north as Bhamo during the

months of January, February, or March. Others, whose opinions were equally entitled to consideration had expressed themselves in favour of steam traffic on a river which they declared to be as navigable at all seasons above the capital as it was between Mandalay and the British frontier.

22. The King, taking advantage of this conflict of opinion, and being swayed moreover from time to time to a variety of beliefs which appeared to him to interfere injuriously with his own interests if he admitted the feasibility of steamer traffic above the capital, withdrew temporarily from his engagements, and gave me to understand that he did not think it advisable to risk a royal steamer in the cause of the expedition.

23. Neither the King nor his Government could have been in any real doubt as to the capabilities of the river for steam navigation, above the capital; but the policy of the Government has always been jealously opposed to the spread of British influence, and nothing it was believed would tend more directly to extend that influence than the fact that English steamers had passed up beyond the capital, and come into direct commercial contact with races and people over whom the Burmese Government had often pleaded its inability to exercise efficient authority or control.

24. It became necessary therefore that I should make known to His Majesty my own belief in the possibility of reaching Bhamo with a steamer of moderate draft, under skilful superintendence. I thought it right moreover to notify my intention of procuring the service of such a vessel in which I hoped to make a successful survey of the River, and prove its navigability for all practical purpose of trade as far at least as the frontier station of Bhamo.

25. This was a contingency little expected. The king had now worked himself, so to speak, into a political corner from which there was no retreat. However great may have been his desire to restrict British Steamers to the lower waters of the Irrawaddy, it was an undoubted fact that the right of navigating that river, throughout its whole course, had been already guaranteed and secured to us by Treaty stipulations The Government had been led to infer, from my avowed intention of employing a British steamer above the capital, that

the question had resolved itself from one of policy into one of right. No reference was now made to the capabilities of the river for steam navigation, but the simple point for consideration was—shall a Burman or a British steamer be the first to reach Bhamo?

26. The king did not hesitate in selecting what appeared to him to be the least of two evils; British steamers had not as yet passed beyond the capital, the policy of exclusiveness would not be infringed by despatching his own steamer to attempt the passage to *Bhamo*, on the contrary his doing so would secure for himself honorable recognition, not only as a pioneer of trade, but as a Sovereign who had exerted his power and his resources in furthering the special interest of the British Government.

A royal steamer, the "Yaynan-Sekia," better known as the "Honesty", was immediately placed at my disposal; and although there was some cause of satisfaction in the knowledge that an important point had thus been secured, I was nevertheless subjected to the unpleasant reflection that my significant allusion to the employment of a British steamer above the Capital had unintentionally reduced His Majesty to the neccessity of a somewhat ungracious and conpulsory loan.

27. There is perhaps an appearance of undue adventure, in having attempted at the outset of an undertaking, (although that undertaking had been devised for exploration purposes) to arrive at the solution of a question, which if unfavourable would have involved the whole party in a serious complication of delays and difficulty. But I accepted the king's steamer without hesitation, I knew her draft of water to be only three feet; her engines were powerful, and she would be lightly laden. There was little reason therefore, to attend to prognostications of evil, which took their rise, no doubt, in a pure Mandalay conception; that a king of Burma's steamer, could be controlled, under Burman superintendence, into a means of obstructiveness, irrespective of the uncertainties of river navigation altogether.

28. The "Honesty," with the Expedition party on board, left Mandalay on 13th January, and arrived at Bhamo on 21st of the same month. Her passage up the river was signalized by an absence of every thing like difficulty, in or-

dinary river navigation. On one occasion only was it necessary to make any serious effort to discover a navigable channel. A steamer of greater draft than the "Honesty," might at this point have been subjected to prolonged detention, but though the channel through which the Royal steamer found a way did not exceed a depth of three feet it was by no means certain that deeper water might not have been discovered had search been made with that skill and diligence which would have guided Europeans, but which could not be looked for in a slovenly crew of uninterested Burmese.

29. It may however be laid down as a general deduction from our experiences on the Irrawaddy between Mandalay and *Bhamo*, that no steamer is justified in attempting the passage during those months of the year when the water is at its lowest, whose draft of water exceeds four feet. Captain Bowers who accompanied the expedition as Mercantile representative, and whose nautical and professional experiences have been of great value, has been at some pains to complete a chart of the river, which cannot fail to be practically useful to British steamers as soon as they elect to make *Bhamo* their terminus instead of Mandalay. Captain Bowers has promised to place his chart at my disposal for the information of Government, and a copy of the same if received in sufficient time will be appended to this Report.

30. On 22nd January, the day after our arrival at *Bhamo*, the two Tsitkais or headmen of the town and district, paid us a visit on board the steamer. They were courteous but exceedingly reserved as regarded the subject of the expedition. They professed an entire ignorance of all orders from the capital, which directed that preparation should be made for our reception at Bhamo.

31. No expedient could have been more opportunely contrived to meet the circumstances of the time, and the natural proclivity of a Burman in power, with or without reason, to make himself recklessly obstructive in his dealings with Foreigners, than the reality which presented itself in the recent murder of the old Governor of Bhamo, and the late Shan disturbances at the town of *Momeit*. Both events were unfortunately facts, which had immediately preceded our own arrival at Bhamo.

32. The old Governor of Bhamo had held also the title of Governor of *Myadoung*, an important district south of, and adjoining the district of *Bhamo*. The Shan town and district of *Momeit*, which had always been under the immediate Government of it's own Chiefs, was now placed under the *Bhamo* Governorship, so far as to give the latter the power of collecting and remitting the annual revenues of the district to Head Quarters at Mandalay.

Shans and Kakhyens joined to resist such an innovation on national rule and custom. The Governor of *Bhamo* proceeded to *Momeit* with three hundred armed men, and tried to restore order; but his force was surrounded by the insurgents; and cut off himself from all his reserves the Governor was compelled, after several days of helpless endurance, to attempt to retreat by cutting a way through his implacable opponents. In this attempt he lost his life, and a large number of the gallant 300, who had originally accompanied him from *Bhamo*, became victims to the hatred which Burman oppression had naturally inspired in the minds of despised Kakhyens.

33. These were events which had occurred within a few weeks previous to our arrival at *Bhamo*; and it required a well studied gravity and control of temper, to listen to the disheartening but plausible and hypocritical utterances of the Tsitkais, as they dwelt pathetically upon the recent murder of the Governor, (making it a reason for inattention to instructions from Mandalay,) and quietly informed me that no effective preparations could then be made, for the prosecution of our journey onward across the Kakhyen Hills towards Yunan.

34. It was not less discouraging to be informed further, by these officers of the Burmese Government, that the principal routes eastward across the Kakhyen Hills, were effectually closed against transit of every kind; or to learn two days later, after notices had been sent to the Chief Saubwa of the only supposed practicable line via *Ponlyne*, that the chiefs refused to recognize the summons of the Burmese Tsitkais, and required written orders from the Governor himself, before they consented to come to Bhamo, or enter into preliminary engagements relating to our journey across their Hills. The old Governor having been killed, the advent of a new one

depending as it did, on Burmese caprice, became a matter of very great uncertainty, and was especially awkward, as regarded ourselves, whilst assured that the Kakhyens required the direct orders of a veritable Burmese Governor, before they could be induced to bestir themselves in our Expeditionary interest.

35. There was cause also for discouragement in the fact that, owing to the unsettled state of the country, and the severe retaliatory measures which Kakhyens and Burmans were mutually inflicting on each other whenever the opportunity occurred for doing so, Kakhyens were positively interdicted, by order of the Burmese Authorities, from entering *Bhamo*; and that thus the very people whom we had come to conciliate, and by whose friendly assistance alone it was possible to carry out the the purposes of the expedition, had been induced, by our unfortunate connectionship with Burman Officials, to look upon us as something akin to national or natural enemies.

36. On the 23rd January I returned the official visit of the two Tsitkais or Magistrates, who were appropriately designated or distinguished, by the prefix to their official title of *North* or *South*, according to the position and extent of their respective jurisdictions. It was during one of their visits that I made the acquaintance of an old Chinaman, who was allowed by the Burmese Government to exercise special jurisdiction over his Chinese brethren located in *Bhamo*.

The officials were kind, and received we with as great a display of dignified hospitality as the impromptu nature of the occasion admitted. But however impressive this may have been, in one sense, the interviews disclosed with painful apparency that no effort was being spared by which to discourage, and destroy if possible, by plausible arguments, every hope we might already have etertained of succeeding in the undertaking we were then committed to.

37. The Kakhyens were described as treacherous, and disinclined to allow transit of any kind across their Hills. Though nominally subject to Burma, they professed an independence of their own, and lived principally, it was said, in a state of indiscriminate conflict amongst themselves, and by general depredation on the villages or property of their immediate neighbours.

38. The country beyond the Kakhyen hills, as well as the whole Chinese frontier in the direction we proposed travelling, had lapsed into a state of dangerous disorganization, and was preyed upon by large bodies of marauders, who having first succumbed, during a state of anarchy, to being despoiled themselves, were now compelled in turn to seek retaliation and livelihood by a reckless spoliation of others. The Head Chinaman asked repeatedly with bitter significance "How do *you* expect to succeed when kings even have tried and failed?"

39. But in the midst of many vexatious and discouraging statements, which were suggestive of every thing evil if we attempted to advance, the Tsitkais, when directly urged to action, were careful for their own sakes to make certain vague promises of assistance, which results have proved it was never their will or intention to fulfil. On them however depended for a time my only means of settling certain preliminaries, which were indispensible before a single step could be taken in prosecuting the journey beyond Bhamo.

References to Mandalay were virtually forbidden on account of the delay which would have been involved in making them. The Tsitkais were on the spot, and it was necessary to keep up a friendly bearing and intercourse with them, in spite of all that was harassing and disagreeable in their secret opposition and forced reserve.

40. A point of primary and essential importance, as connected with my instructions, related to the possibility of effecting a safe and liberal understanding with the Kakhyen Chiefs, who occupied the mountain route through which the expedition would pass, whilst yet within what is nominally termed "Burmese Territory."

41. I have already stated that the Chiefs on the *Ponlyne* route, to which we had been committed by the advice of the Burmese officials at *Bhamo*, had refused to attend to orders which were not transmitted to them by the Governor himself. The written instructions of the Tsitkais had been forwarded by their own Burmese messengers, and I also despatched, along with them, a half Chinese half Burman scribe, (Moung Shwe Yah) who had journeyed to *Momein* more than once, and whose services had been given over to me by

the king, as a man who was to prove eminently useful on account of his local and varied experiences.

42. I desired Moung Shwè Yah to mention privately to the Kakhyen Saubwas the true reasons which made me long for their acquaintance and friendship. On the 29th January he had returned from his mission to *Ponlyne*, (the head quarters of the Kakhyen chief of that name) and brought word that although the Saubwa had declared he would not attend to Burmese orders, he was willing nevertheless to visit me privately, if a meeting could be arranged without Burmese interference.

43. The fact was, I afterwards learned, that these same Burmese officials, (although they had gone through the form of despatching written orders to the chiefs, to come and confer with me at *Bhamo*,) had indirectly expressed, through their own private messengers, that the presence of the chiefs was not really desired: on the contrary, a ready means had been actually improvised for these chiefs, whereby to excuse and even justify their absence.

44. But although the chiefs had promised in anticipation to award me a private interview, it was necessary, they said, to hold a consultation with the nats or minor deities, who rule over the destinies of Kakhyen land, and obtain their previous sanction to the proposed interview. Thus the fate of the expedition was made for a time, to depend on the eventualities of a ceremonial, in which the blood of bulls, and the peculiar markings on chicken's bones, would play a prominent and perhaps a decisive part.

45. On the same day (29th January) that Moung Shwè Yah returned from *Ponlyne*, the Tsitkais also appeared, and entered into a string of particulars, by which to convince me that the absence of the Kakhyen Saubwas was a natural proceeding, which could be easily explained. The orders in force were, they said, that no Kakhyen should enter Bhamo. The Nükhandaw, a very lively official, subordinate only in name to the Tsitkais, but more active in his obstructiveness than any of his brethren in office, acted as spokes-man on this occasion, and publicly declared that if any Kakhyen was caught by Burmans inside the stockade he was liable to be shot down as an enemy. He concluded as follows, "The

" Saubwas will think that we are sending for them for the
" sole purpose of getting them into our power. It is not likely
" that they will come with the certainty, in their own belief,
" of being put to death; but even supposing the Ponlyne Sau-
" bwa and others in his vicinity, come and agree to escort
" you into their hills, this will be no real help to you, since
" there are numerous chiefs at a distance who are independent
" of our power altogether, and who will never consent to allow
" you a free passage into the Shan States. In some places
" in the Hills your route will lay through narrow defiles, above
" which means are taken to command and prevent all chance
" of approach, unless with previous consent."

46. It can hardly be deemed a mere coincidence, after these several attempts to thwart and deter us from further enterpise, that the principal Chinese inhabitants of *Bhamo* should have selected this day to invite us to take part in an entertainment, specially provided for the members of the expedition. Nothing could have exceeded the hospitality of our new Chinese friends. We sat round a table on which a very complete desert of twenty five dishes had been previously arranged. Tea was handed round, and each guest, in addition found a veritable teapot at his side, filled with the strongest samshoo. The desert being removed, fresh and substantial signs of hospitality evinced themselves in the appearance of nine separate dishes of cooked meats and vegetables, which we were forced by good breeding to attack with chopsticks.

47. In my diary of the day previous I find the following entry. "I am informed on good authority that the China-
" men of this place are much opposed to the expedition. They
" believe, it is said, that we are leagued by caste or race with
" the Panthays and are about to make common cause with
" them, to the detriment of the Chinese Government. The
" Chinese residents here are in active correspondence with
" their brethren at Mandalay. The Panthays of Yunan have
" only partially subjugated that portion of the province of
" Yunan which is in their possession. There are still it is
" said, several towns and villages this side of *Momein* which
" do not acknowledge any master, and in some instances the
" malcontents are confederated into large bands of dacoits
" who are ready at any time to act against the Panthay Go-

"vernment. These are the dacoits who block up the way
" between *Bhamo* and the Chinese frontier and it is with
" them, I hear, that the Chinamen of this place are in corres-
" pondence, with a view to obstruct our passage to *Momein*.
" They think only of their own petty interests, and would
" neutralize the objects and success of our present undertaking,
" for the sole purpose, if no other existed, of keeping to them-
" selves their present petty earnings, instead of allowing them-
" selves to be entirely swamped, as they suppose, by opening
" out to all the overland route between Bhamo and South
" Western China."

48. It soon became evident, that the object of the China men, in awarding us so much good cheer, was about to be disclosed in a plausible attempt to second the obstructive and deterrent pleas already insinuated by Burmese officialism. With all the courtesy in the world I was definitely given to understand that the expedition was proceeding on a wild goose chase. The old argument was again adduced. " How " can you possibly succeed in accomplishing that which even " Kings have striven for but failed to attain.

49. This state of affairs lasted until 31st January, when the Kakhyen Chief of *Ponlyne* arrived and paid me his promised visit. He was dressed as a Chinese mandarin, and carried a golden umbrella, which had been presented to him by the King of Burma. Contrary to Burmese etiquette in *their* dealings with Kakhyens, I received the chief with the respect due to his position, and the Police escort was drawn up under arms, for his peculiar benefit and edification. But, half Burman half Chinaman as regarded his externals, the hang-dog-expression of his countenance (different in every respect from the Kakhyen type, or from any type I had ever seen) was an ugly feature in the proceeding, which did not augur well for the results of our proposed conference.

50. The whole of the Burmese Officials of Bhamo attended in full strength, and the interpretation in the Kakhyen language was conducted by a Burman Tamon of the village of Nanlyan. The Kakhyen Chief and his followers were stern and obstinately silent. They hardly condescended to answer the few questions of greeting and salutation by which I tried to enlist their sympathies, and pave the way to busi-

ness communications. But as soon as I commenced to make enquiries regarding our route and the practicability of transit, the interpreter above referred to suddenly warmed with the subject, and became so demonstrative in his over eagerness to communicate all that boded difficulty or evil, that I saw at once he was improvising statements of his own, and was obliged therefore, after a time, to disown his services in toto and to ask rather energetically for a man who would take less interest in the subject matter of the conference, and confine himself, simply, to truthful interpretation.

51. The Saubwa remained intractable, but I could see that the position he had assumed was in a measure forced, on account of the presence of the Burmese officials. After a time I was enabled to speak to him a little more privately, and with more promising results. He was able to guarantee safe transit through his portion of the Hill route, but would not be answerable for the conduct of other Chiefs beyond the range of his authority. I distinctly asked, whether it was his real wish, or the wish of the Kakhyen people generally, that we should pass through their country?

He answered at once, "Yes, and we will take care of " you." Then, why did you say just now, that supplies were " not procurable, that mules would be charged for at treble " their usual cost, and that you would not be answerable for " the conduct of other chiefs?"

He was significantly silent, and I was not slow to see that he secretly desired a more private interview.

52. On the following day Ponlyne again presented himself; and after a good deal of haggling conversation, in the presence of several Burmese Officials, an arrangement was entered into for the supply of one hundred mules, to convey us from a point on the Tahpen river, above Bhamo, to Manwyne, the first Shan town of importance met with on descending the hills which slope into the Sanda valley at it's western extremity.

53. The Kakhyen Chief subsequently accompanied me into a private room, and Moung Shwé Yah acted as interpreter in Chinese, a language, with which most Kakhyens seem to be familiar, more so at least than with either Shan or Burmese. The sullen stupidity of the savage at once merged

into a genuine expression, of reason and intelligence. He acknowledged that his backwardness in coming to see me or to provide facilities for our journey had been prompted by a disinclination on his part to offend the scruples of his Chinese friends in *Bhamo*, who had written and advised him to keep out of the way altogether.

He too had Chinese friends he said in the countries eastward, and it would ruin him if they believed that he alone of all the Kakhyen Chiefs had been instrumental in affording a European expedition the means of entering their country. He made it a sine-quâ-non on this account that I would insist on Burman support and co-operation; so far at least as to ensure the attendance of a small Burmese party who would accompany the expedition from Bhamo for appearance sake only, and thus relieve him of the onus of being considered our sole conductor.

54. Nothing could more clearly indicate the state of the Chief's feelings, and his knowledge of the obstacles which Burmese Officials were insidiously and persistently throwing in our way, than this simple desire, when all chance of active interference on their part was at an end, that these same Burman officials should be asked to take a demonstrative part only in our proceeding, and act as dummies, in a way which openly belied their own wishes, and the very limited scope of their real intentions. Had Ponlyne openly accused them of downright hostility to our undertaking, his words would not have been so innocently effective or naturally convincing as the simple consistant requisition, that Burmese officials should contribute, by a mock show of reality, to a proceeding which it was well known from the first they had indirectly thwarted and opposed.

55. It required but little explanation on my part to give the chief a Comprehensive idea of the object of the expedition, or to convince him of the advantages which it offered to the inhabitants of the countries through which the Bhamo trade route would eventually pass. I had not at the time discovered the peculiarities of the Kakhyen mind, or realized to its full extent the avaricious greed of this chief in particular. There could be no harm, however, in promising rewards for faithful services, or in making a show of certain finery which

it was my wish to present to the chief, as an earnest of present gain and future emoluments.

The chief viewed the gifts with inexpressible delight, but requested me to keep them till I reached his village. Much as he coveted them, their acceptance by him at the present time, he said, would give offence to Burmese officials of Bhamo, and interfere moreover with his own arrangements to serve me as effectually as he desired.

56. The next day (2nd February) Ponlyne took his departure from Bhamo with the promise to procure mule carriage and make all other requisite preparations for a start in ten days from date. There was no longer any difficulty as regarded the consent of the Kakhyen chiefs. He (Ponlyne) boasted of his relationship with and superiority over all the Saubwas on the route we were to take. He was in a position, by his own statement, to guarantee safe transit through Kakhyen land, as far as *Manwyne*, the first Shan town met with, on the Yunan side of the Kakhyen Hills viâ Ponlyne.

57. The same afternoon, the *Nanlyan* Tamon (the man whom I had so summarily got rid of for false interpretation on the occasion of Ponlyne's first visit) came to me, in a very abject condition, and confessed that he had purposely exaggerated difficulties and raised imaginary sources of opposition to our intended journey, having been advised to do so, by those whom it would have been a crime in him to disobey. He was faithfully attached, he said, to Moung Shwe Yah, my Chinese interpreter, and supposed that I would perceive the awkwardness of his position, and make allowance for obligations he was under to his Burmese masters.

58. He further stated to me that he was present with the Ponlyne Saubwa at the time letters were brought to him from the Chinese residents of *Bhamo*, who wrote to dissuade the Chief against visiting that town, or from giving us his assistance. The Tamon though cunning and shrewd in his duplicity, was truthful, I believe, in the present instance, because he knew that I had found him out, but his subsequent dealings, prove that the excuses made for false interpretation and hostility to our cause on the 31st January, were mere attempts to gain my confidence, and acquire greater facilities for working out the ruinous designs of his Burmese superiors.

59. But to continue the account of Burmese petty obstructiveness, I may mention, even at the risk of extending my narrative indefinitely, that the embarrasments of our position were not improved by a forced and unnatural restraint on the part of the Burmese inhabitants of the place, which compelled them to be silent and uncommunicative on all points in which it was essential to procure truthful or reliable information.

This reserve on the part of the people contrasted very unmistakeably with their true instincts. Their real disposition we know to be friendly and unobstructive. They had repeatedly assured us that the presence of the English expedition at Bhamo gave confidence, and secured them against the frequent raids of hostile Kakhyens. For months past, previous to our arrival, their nights had been spent in fear and watching. But the protection afforded by our presence had given relief, and placed them under obligations which, in the ordinary course of human nature, would certainly not have resulted in unfriendliness of disposition or a desire to be uncommunicative on matters of general and social interest.

60. The population generally had been terrified into a belief that any familiarity with members of the expedition, or information afforded relative to existing trade routes between Burma and the south western provinces of China, would subject informers to a Government prosecution, a mode of proceeding which had terrific signification in its practical application to the unofficial masses of an outlying Burmese Province.

61. Numerous proofs were soon given of this Official interdiction to friendly intercourse between ourselves and the people of *Bhamo*. The officials themselves evaded all such causes of complaint, until forced into a conviction of their reality. Extenuation was then sought, in the announcement that the officials themselves were at logger-heads with each other, and could not be held individually responsible in the absence of a Governor or other Chief controlling power. The consequence was that, whether by design or otherwise, the part taken by the officers of Government at this time had assumed a course which coincided exactly with the well known Burmese policy of exclusiveness, by which it was

intended to bar for ever the right of way beyond the Burmese capital to foreign traders or intruders, whatever their claims or the introduction under which those claims were presented.

62. Thus the officials from whom alone real assistance was due had become our steadiest opponents. Redress could hardly be expected from those who were principally concerned in instigating the several wrongs complained against. My frequent reference to the patronage under which the expedition originated, and the direful consequences of offending against royal promises of support given by the King of Burma to Her Majesty's Government and confidently acknowledged by that Government, were not likely to be regarded by men who drew their inspiration and belief from Burmese Head Quarters at Mandalay.

63. I will illustrate the above remarks by another passage taken at random from my rough diary under date 9th February.

"Other instances have occurred of Burmese little mind-
" edness and cruelty. An old Munipooree woman, who had
" occasionally interpreted for me in the Kakhyen language,
" was yesterday dragged out of her house into the public
" Streets and severely beaten at the instance of the Nakhan-
" daw, a petty officer under the Tsitkai. The reason given
" for thus publicly chastising this poor female is that she
" had burned a light in her house the previous evening after
" hours. The real cause of her offence happens to be that she
" assisted us to be kind towards a small party of despised
" Kakhyens. The woman has complained to me privately,
" but begs that I will not invite further trouble and suffer-
" ing by making a direct grievance of her case. Many others
" have come forward and complained of the restraint put
" upon them and the fear of punishment which precludes the
" proffer of their services. Amongst the crowd of candidates
" who are eager for employ if left to their natural inclinations
" I find it is impossible to procure the services of a Kakhyen
" or Shan interpreter. To-day a common Shikaree, who had
" promised to shew us game, has been obliged to excuse him-
" self on the plea that he was in danger of provoking official
" censure by contributing in any way to our wants &c., &c.
" The north Tsitkai called this evening whilst we were at

"dinner and I explained to him our detestation of the Na-
"khan's behaviour, in having publicly chastised a poor wo-
"man whose only offence was that she had helped us in our
"communications with inoffensive Kakhyens. The Tsitkai
"did not attempt to refute my complaints, but excused them
"on the ground of misunderstanding and disagreement
"amongst the officials with whom he was associated. The
"orders of one were nullified or exaggregated he said by the
"envy or design of another. This could not be helped as
"the officials acted independently of each other and Bhamo
"was without a controlling Governor. I mentioned the cir-
"cumstance of the Burman Shikaree.

"*Tsitkay.*—Never mind I will give you a man.

"So I suppose he would. It simply amounts to this that
"we are forced into an unnatural dependence on these officials
"for every want however trivial, and even then with very
"little chance of success because the officials pretend to be
"divided amongst themselves and submit to the disgrace
"of openly admitting the trecherous cancelment of each other's
"orders.

"They are stupid enough to think that this nonsense is
"believed in, and that I fail to perceive that the alleged dis-
"agreement amongst themselves is a mere pretext, by which
"they rely on their ability to continue a Policy of obstructive-
"ness with credit to themselves and to the complete satis-
"faction of their Mandalay masters." &c. &c.

64. On the 13th February the Tsitkais called upon me with letters from a Burman Officials at Tahpen, which reported several recent attacks on villages in his neighbourhood by large numbers of marauding Kakhyens, who were said to have taken up a position on the direct route by which the expedition would pass in its progress towards the Shan States.

65. These letters and the reports they contained were anything but veritable or genuine in themselves, but the emphasis and enthusiasm with which the Tsitkais dwell upon their contents, as means of giving additional zest to the many other deterrent stories in circulation at Bhamo which related to the dangerous opposition which the expedition would of a certainty encounter, made it at length inevitable that I should come to a complete understanding with them in this and

other instances of official interference in the affairs of the expedition.

66. As a further reason for plain speaking I may mention that my information at this time made it evident that the Tsitkais had cognizance of certain communications from the Robber Chief Lees-hee-ta-hee who in reply either to their requisitions or the requisitions of the Chinese residents of Bhamo had signified to them his readiness to cooperate in our extermination by threats of armed opposition, as soon as we appeared within the limits of his supposed jurisdiction.

Moung Shwè Yah, my Chinese interpreter, saw one of these letters and entered the Burmese Yon or Court of justice at a time when a discussion was being held regarding it: but the letter was folded up and the discussion ceased as soon as it was known that my interpreter or a person then supposed to be in my confidence formed one of their assembly.

67. Subsequently a writer of the Court, in conversation with a Burman clerk in my employ, not only admitted the receipt of letters from Lees-hee-ta-hee but declared that they were favourable to tha cause of the British Expedition. Lees-hee-ta-hee had merely stipulated, he said, that the English party should advance alone without any Burmese accompaniments.

This stipulation is hardly intelligible unless we bear in mind the ambiguous style of writing which would naturally be adopted in a secret correspondence carried on between officers of the Burmese Government and a friendly Robber chieftain of a foreign state!

68. The following has been suggested to me as the correct interpretation of that portion of Lees-hee-ta-hee's letter, which provides that the English party should proceed on its journey, without a Burmese escort.

The Chinese dacoit-bands, which were pledged to annihilate the British Expedition, felt scruples of conscience which did not allow of their acting on the offensive towards Burmese subjects for whom as brethern in crime they were supposed to entertain a profound friendly regard They therefore intimated to the Tsitkais, in polite and suggestive terms, that it would be as well if Burmans did not form a portion of our party. The truth is that the presence of a Burmese guard would have implied that we were under Burmese official protection, and this fact alone, considering the nature of Lees-hee-ta-hee's relationship with and confessed subservience to the Court of Mandalay, must have secured us against much active opposition.

69. It was now late in February. More than the allotted ten days had elapsed since Ponlyne's last visit and still there was no news of the Kakhyen Chief or of his promised succour. Rumours had reached Bhamo in the mean time that the new Governor had left Mandalay by boat and might be expected daily.

By degrees I realized what might have been apparent from the first, viz. that the officials then in power at Bhamo had never intended that we should leave that place before the new Governor's arrival. I had worried the officials and myself for nearly a month to no purpose. Their impassiveness was now accounted for, for to all intents and purposes they had simply been acting within the scope of their instructions, and felt secure against all prospect of censure or rebuke at Mandalay Head Quarters.

70. With the full conviction that the Tsitkais had given up every idea of furthering the cause of our expedition at Bhamo, my only chance of success was to push our interests with the Kakhyens and disregard all prohibitory orders, which made it penal on the part of Burmese subjects to afford us their assistance.

71. It had been necessary, from the date of Ponlyne's last departure from Bhamo, to keep up communication with that chief by means of my own messengers, and I was thus enabled to disprove the false reports relating to raids and disturbances in and about the vicinity of our proposed route through the Kakhyen Hills.

72. My messengers were further enabled, in their intercourse with Ponlyne, to learn and note the endeavours which were being made by adverse interests to bring ruin on the expedition, even though it might eventually succeed in making a fair start from Bhamo. The opposition most likely to be effectual and even dangerous in its results was that which related to a correspondence which I have already referred to

between certain Chinese residents of Bhamo, and the famous Robber chief Lees-hee-ta-hee. It was not within my means at the time to obtain direct proofs by which to test the real nature of this correspondence, but the Chinese themselves spoke openly of their confederate Lees-hee-ta-hee, and frequently alluded to him as an irresistable barrier to any attempt we might make to reach Momein.

73. Ponlyne too was reported to be wavering in his fidelity. He could not help recognizing the fact of formidable Chinese influences, which were the more dangerous to himself from the fact that the Chinese were seconded in their hostility to the expedition by the support and countenance of the Burmese Government.

At the same time the Tsitkais, taking advantage of the state of helplessness to which they themselves had mainly contributed, advised me, with well feigned earnestness, to await the Governor's arrival, and be guided by his counsel in determining upon a further prosecution of my journey.

74. The position then at this time may be briefly recapitulated as follows.—

The Kakhyen Chief was supposed to await the expedition with mule carriage at *Tahpen*. I was disposed to trust his services, in spite of calumnious reports of bad faith and an insidious rumour to the effect that he was known to have leagued himself with those who were then engaged in conspiring our discomfiture.

The Bhamo officials had been persevering in their efforts to discountenance the expedition, to make it unpopular throughout the province, and to discourage every attempt to advance beyond the cordon of Bhamo.

If I proceeded and met with reverses the Burmese Government would have it in its power to declare, with some show of reality and truth, that I had neglected advice, or disregarded consequences, as foretold by its own officers. My instructions were distinct and imperative. The Government would "*prefer to see the expedition return, without accom-*
"*plishing the object for which it was undertaken, than learn*
"*that the safety of the party had in any degree been compro-*
"*mised.*

75. It had thus become an unavoidable necessity, under all circumstances, to abide by my instructions, and submit to the further delay of awaiting the new Governor's arrival, rather than allow the Burmese Government the power of making it appear that I had acted with undue haste, or without a just regard to official admonition.

Such delay was inevitable from the first, but the vile duplicity to which we had been subjected was such, that the facts of the position were only realized by a gradual developement of unpleasant disclosures, after the expedition party had reached Bhamo.

These discloures were, for the time, a grave contradiction to all the imaginary facilities of opening out the old overland trade route through Burma to China. Plans which had all along appeared practicable and facile in theory presented in practice a series of obstacles, which were not only perplexing at the time but promised to be eventually insurmountable. Patient endurance and forced submission were the more irksome and oppressive because provoked by breach of faith and a wanton departure from international obligations.

76. It was not until I had fully comprehended the magnitude of the dangers to which a British expedition would be exposed, in consequence of the Chinese confederacy at Bhamo and the professed inability of the Burmese Government to be of any service to us beyond Burmese territory, that an expedient presented itself of counteracting the intended evil by a direct appeal for assistance to a power over which the Burmese Government was then supposed to possess no controlling influence.

77. The City of Momein was well known at the time to be the Head quarters of a *Panthay* Governor, who exercised sovereignty also over the Shan States bordering on Upper Burma. The Panthays themselves have shown an inclination of late years to revive the old caravan trade with Burma, and there was reasonable ground for presuming that their interests would lead them to disfavour the pretensions of a Chinese Freebooter like Lees-hee-ta-hee, whose very existence and means of livelihood were persistently opposed to every legitimate effort to promote either friendly intercourse with neighbouring states, or commercial Freedom within their own possessions.

The Chinese of Bhamo were confederated with this Lees-hee-ta-hee for the purpose of keeping to themselves the profits arising out of a petty trade, as it then existed, between that place and the States and Provinces lying Eastward in the direction of China.

The cessation of trade between Burma and China had become dependent rather on a system of recognized freebooting on the frontiers of Burma, than on disorganization produced by a period of devastating civil war within the Province of Yunan.

78. In 1866 Lees-hee-ta-hee had gained so far on Burman credulity as to head a deputation to the King of Burma, in which he passed himself off as the representative of certain Shan Chiefs, who were desirous, he said, to make over their country to the Burmese Government. His deputation was successful so far as to have been well received by the King of Burma; but his Majesty, in referring to the supposed Shan Deputation in his conversation with me before the expedition started from Mandalay, had made it appear that the late rebellion in his own country prevented active interference on his part in the affairs of the Shan States. Lees-hee-ta-hee nevertheless received two gold umbrellas as a mark of vassalage, and in appreciation of the disinterestedness with which he had acted on behalf of certain Shan States, with a view to their becoming a component part of His Majesty's dominions.

With these distinctions he returned to his stronghold on the Mauphoo hills, where for years past he had so far controlled the caravan route between Bhamo and South-Western-China as to put an effectual stop to all legitimate traffic.

79. It will be seen from the above that there was a sufficient connectionship between this Robber Chieftain and the authorities in Burma (Chinese or Burmese) to make him a useful tool in effecting either the ruin or the accomplishment of any proposed object.

Had his services been utilized by the Burmese Government (as they most assuredly might have been) for the purpose of opening the old overland trade route with Momein; or had they even been enlisted in our behalf as a means of furthering an advance towards the Chinese frontier, the success of the expedition, as regards exploration within the Shan States, must have been considerably expedited, and we should in all probability have avoided detention on the Kakhyen Hills. But in as much as that it had been openly announced and declared at Bhamo, that Lees-hee-ta-hee was himself hostile and had been made the tool of our enemies to oppose British influences beyond Burmese Territory, it became a matter of very serious moment to frustrate designs which set at naught every reasonable hope of successful enterprise in the direction of our proposed exploration.

80. Hence originated the idea or expedient of making application to the Governor of Momein, by the despatch of letters which, whilst they stated the true object of our mission and were intended at the same time to escape the action of our supposed friends in Burma, were designed also to further our own interests and invite the assistance of the Panthay Government.

I was particular, however, in affording some sort of proof that although we had met with opposition at Bhamo the Burmese Government was with us in our undertaking, and had recorded its assent to the same in a Royal Proclamation; a copy of which, together with printed copies of our treaties with the Burmese Government, were forwarded with my letters to the *Momein* Government (vide appendix).

81. The letters were forwarded from Bhamo by private Kakhyen scouts on the 19th February; and their concoction and despatch were contrived with a secrecy which, either by chance or miracle, defied the surveillance of even Burmese detectives.

I subsequently learned beyond all doubt that the Bhamo Governor, when informed of the means thus successfully used to secure Panthay assistance and defeat the designs of his own subordinates, was savage beyond measure, and commented on their supineness and want of vigilance with an animosity and force which resulted in the subsequent despatch of those Officials in irons and in disgrace to Mandalay.

82. It is only fair, perhaps, to mention that the alleged reason for the dismissal of the Bhamo Officials was their infamous treatment of the British Expedition. But to give credence to such an announcement appears to me to outrage alike justice and common sense. The Officials were retained

in office for months after my own letters condemning their conduct had been delivered to His Majesty. Their removal from office took place only after the return of Captain Williams and Mr. Stewart from Ponsee, and after it had become manifest that we had outwitted our opponents by the despatch of letters to Momein. It is moreover an offence against Justice to assume that men should have been ignominiously dismissed from office and kept in irons for an indefinite period for a faithful discharge of duty in carrying out the orders and Policy of their own Government or of their immediate superiors in Government employ.

83. But the Governor of Bhamo is now himself on the scene at Bhamo. He arrived by boat on the 20th February, and sent to tell me the same evening that it was not his intention to land until the 23rd, as the intervening days were unpropitious and unsuited to so momentous an undertaking.

This determination he stuck to, in spite of my written protest and entreaties that he would not allow private considerations of convenience to delay, for even one day, matters of great urgency, which could not be disposed of until after he had landed and installed himself in Office as Governor of Bhamo.

84. The following is a short account of my first interview with the Governor, as extracted from my rough Diary of 23rd February 1868. "Greetings over I referred with
" surprise to the Governor's protracted stay at Mandalay in
" excess of the time which had been stipulated for by himself
" and allowed by the King. I spoke of the unwonted time
" occupied en route, and my own difficulties during the inter-
" val of his absence, in combating the obstructiveness of his
" subordinate officers at Bhamo.

"The Governor tried to justify the delay as well as the
" other annoyances I had experienced, on the ground that
" the Officials at Bhamo had not fully comprehended the or-
" ders issued at Mandalay, and were moreover, he said, at va-
" riance amongst themselves. Supposing such to be the
" case, it is not satisfactory, I said, after having waited a
" month in vain attempts to rouse the Officials to energy and
" a sense of their duty, to find that the Governor himself had
" allowed four days to elapse since his arrival without evinc-

"ing any desire to avoid further procrastination, and make
"up for the miserable shortcomings of his blundering subor-
"dinates. The Governor said that, being a *New Man*, he was
"ignorant of local customs. He professed to be actuated by
"a zealous interest in our undertaking, and promised to facil-
"itate our departure by every means in his power. But
"take my advice, he said, and do not start until I have time
"to superintend all your arrangements, and satisfy myself
"personally that there is nothing amiss."

85. The Kakhyen Chief Ponlyne arrived the next day, and paid me an early visit before proceeding to see the Governor. He particularly begged that I would not forget his former reasons for urging upon the Governor's notice the advisability of sending a small Burmese escort with the party, as far as the Shan town of Manwyne. I accompanied Ponlyne on a visit to the Governor, and the whole day was spent in conferences and explanation. As soon as the subject of the Burmese escort was touched upon the Governor turned to the Kakhyen Chief and asked him in rather browbeating style. "Why do you want a Burmese guard?"

Ponlyne.—A guard was allowed when the King's cotton was sent for sale a year or two ago.

Governor.—Yes; that was a different matter altogether; (angrily) no guard is required now!

Ponlyne.—(rather staggered) Oh! I understand."

86. What Ponlyne understood, or was intended to understand, was that the sale of the cotton was a matter in which the Burmese Government had an intimate concern but that the Bhamo Expedition was a British undertaking, and might therefore be allowed to take care of itself!

I interfered peremptorily, and begged the Governor to explain matters clearly. I also called the Kakhyen chief near me, (he had been hustled into an inferior position at a distance amongst the Governor's menials) and told him not to be afraid but speak out his mind. The king of Burma (I continued to the Governor) had formally recognized and supported the present enterprise. He had encouraged the English Government to embark in it, in a full and confident reliance on that support. Did the Governor wish the Kakhyen Chiefs and others to understand that the Royal commercial speculation, in the matter of a few bales of cotton was of greater Political importance than the well being of an undertaking on which the king had staked his reputation and word?

87. This sensational outburst had its effect, and raised me at once in the estimation of the Kakhyen chief. To speak so authoritatively and without fear to the Governor of Bhamo evidenced to his mind the fact of my being a person of influence and position. But Ponlyne had already been so unmercifully badgered by the Governor because he had dared to make mention of a Burmese guard, and had moreover been so clearly made to understand that he was condemned solely on account of this unpalatable requisition, that he elected to forego the guard altogether, and told the Governor, under evident compulsion, that he would undertake to conduct us in safety to Manwyne without Burmese aid or intervention of any sort.

88. I came to the rescue at this crisis of affairs and said that Ponlyne's reasons for specially requiring a *Burmese* guard were good, and would be explained by and by, or as soon as the Governor would allow the chief to confer with him in private.

Shortly afterwards the Governor dismissed his numerous attendants and I sent away mine, we were therefore alone.

The Kakhyen Chief now spoke out, and said that it was his fear of Chinese influences at Bhamo and on the frontier which caused him to ask for a Burmese guard, to save appearances only, so that mischief-makers might not have it in their power to say that *he* alone was to blame for having brought English interlopers into a Foreign state.

89. I too had all along complained of these same Chinese influences and was glad of the open testimony thus vouchsafed to the Governor, by a comparatively disinterested Kakhyen chief, who had himself only recently been bound to Chinese interest and was even then inclined to abandon us to serve their cause.

The Governor said that he was aware of the Chinese opposition, but could not as yet discover whether the mischief arose at Bhamo or at Mandalay where the Merchants were desirous for their own sakes to keep the Bhamo route closed, so as to profit to the full extent by the Southern route viâ Theebo and Thainee. He promised that the head Chinaman should be called upon for an explanation. He would himself make full enquiries &c., &c.

90. Ponlyne called again the same afternoon, and seemed ill at ease and disheartened.

He was evidently much hurt at the Governor's refusal to give tangible proof of a willingness to assist the expedition. I could see that he was personally anxious on his own account. The drift of his remarks was as follows:—

"Both the Chinese and Burmese are against you; but "never mind, leave this place quickly and depend on me. "The Chinese give out that you are going to join the Pan-"thays against them. They really would not care if you did. "This is not their real grievance. Their chief reason for "wishing you evil is, that they may monopolize trade them-"selves and keep all outsiders at a distance."

91. The Kakhyen chief had openly announced in the presence of the Governor his ability to conduct the expedition as far as the Shan town of *Manwyne*. He had been forced into abandoning a point which affected his private interests very considerably, viz the desire that Burmese Officials should enter an appearance in the affairs of the expedition, and not withdraw themselves as unconcerned spectators only.

Nevertheless Ponlyne agreed to conduct us himself as far as Manwyne without Burman aid or support. He had formally guaranteed the good will and cooperation of all other Kakhyen Chiefs, and I saw reason at the time to confide in his powers, rather than abandon ourselves to the procrastination of the Burmese Government.

92. I was still, however, dependent on the Governor for the services of interpreters in the Kakhyen and Shan languages. Numbers of men were available for the work, and would accompany me anywhere, but the fear of offending by disobeying Government orders which placed us beyond the pale of communication with Burmese subjects, overcame their own instincts and paralized every effort I had hitherto made to

procure assistance of any kind by a recourse to ordinary expedients.

93. When I explained my difficulties in this respect to the Governor in person, an order was given to the Tahpen Cheoung-oke to accompany the expedition himself, or make over to me, two of his subordinate peons, or Tamons of villages, who spoke either the Shan or Kakhyen languages. The Cheoung-oke in my presence openly told the Governor that he would rather forfeit his position as Cheoung-oke than be under the necessity of obeying orders which compelled him to accompany the expedition on so perilous an undertaking. The Governor smiled instead of rebuking the official and enforcing his own orders; but two Tamons were afterwards told off, and directed to place themselves under my orders as interpreters to our party. The Tamons belonged to the villages of *Manlyaw* and *Hentha* and the understanding was that they should join me on our arrival at Tahpen.

94. Only one more slight hitch and we shall have turned our backs on Bhamo and the hateful incubus of its Burmese belongings.

All the money in my possession consisted of India coined Rupees, which, it was said would not pass current amongst Kakhyens or within the Shan states. The Rupees must be changed for silver Bullion of peculiar standard, readily procurable at Bhamo, and current everywhere. Such at least was the information tendered at Mandalay; and yet on arrival at Bhamo silver had become, for some unaccountable reason, an unknown commodity altogether. I would gladly have changed five thousand Rupees. It was our all, but no amount of solicitation was of any avail in procuring as many hundreds in Bullion. I importuned every one. The Chinese said they were poor, and did not possess silver. The Officials excused the emptiness of their Treasury by assuring me that remittances had only just been made to the capital on account of the previous year's tax collections.

95. The South Tsitkay sent his wife to me who said, that if I would give her time and pay out Rs. in advance she might possibly get me (200) two hundred Rupees worth of change in the indefinite Burmese period of four or five days,

The Tsitkay's wife was a garrulous old lady of 60, who boasted of her near relationship to a Woongyee at the the capital. She had evidently assumed the privileges of a Burmese *Woongadaw* (Governors's wife) and to all appearances conducted a large percentage of his Official duties. The alleged inability of such a woman, backed as she was by so much official status and authority, to procure a small amount only of what on an ordinary occasion would have been forthcoming in abundance, was a convincing argument against the futility of my attempting a bullion business on a large scale, and I persevered in the work so far only as to let the Governor know my wants and receive his stereotyped reply in this as in all other petty emergencies, that being a *new man* he found it out of his power to afford me any assistance.

96. There was no help for it, we must start with *Rupees* or not at all. Had bullion been procurable the exchange would have involved, by Burmese calculation, an estimated loss of (30) thirty per cent. My own idea was that Rupees would not be valueless, even in the Shan States, and that as a last resource, if the coin was refused, the Rupees might be melted down as required at less cost and trouble than the labour and vexation of making Burmese give in when once the determination had been come to of sending us on our journey minus cash and as they supposed minus everything.

97. No silver, no interpreters, the evil influence arising out of stremuous Burmese opposition; and yet a British expedition was about to advance through a country which even Burmese Missions had failed to penetrate.

Well might the officials chuckle over the utter state of helplessness to which they conceived the expedition had been reduced by a wanton disregard to Royal Promises and international obligations.

98. It was evidently beyond their powers of calculation to take into account that our worldly short comings were more than out balanced by the possession of qualities which, however, alien to Burmese conceptions, would probably gain for us a larger amount of success than was procurable by wealth or it's more material accompaniments. Honesty of purpose, a good cause, friendly conciliation, and perfect truthfulness, were likely in the long run to be steadier allies

and more certain aids to success, than all the resources of Bhamo, tinged as they must have been by elements of deceit.

99. But it is time to start. The 26th of February is a day to be remembered in the annals of the expedition. On the 25th our baggage had been despatched by boat, and would be conveyed up the Tahpen river to a village where mules were in waiting to convey it across the Hills to Manwyne.

The land journey from Bhamo to this said village was the most convenient to travellers relieved of their baggage, but as the route led through jungle and was intersected at short intervals by branch roads which diverged in all directions and led no one knew where, a guide was an absolute necessity. It was necessary too, to provide against other contingencies, as implied by the fact that a broad, rapid, unfordable river would be encountered on our first march, and that the means for crossing it could not be depended on without contrivance and a certain amount of Burmese pre-arrangement.

100. On the 25th the Officials (I was still made to depend on them for every want) had assured me that efficient arrangements had been made for our start the next morning, and that guides, with the requisite number of porters, should be in early attendance to accompany us on the first march out of Bhamo. They failed in their promises to the last; and it was with difficulty that we got off at 10 A. M., with very incomplete attendance and no guides.

It would have been more baneful to our proceeding to have remained on this account, and hazarded the delay of obtaining a guide, than to have started without one and trusted to accident. I chose the latter alternative and was right. A petty Burmese official, known as the *Toung-mhoo*, met me as I rode through the town, and was persuaded into accompanying the party; after carefully stipulating that I would use my interest at Burmese Head Quarters in screening him from the liability he incurred by giving his services to the British Expedition. The man in fact was pressed into our service; and it is right perhaps that I should admit (on the principle only of giving the devil his due) that the Toung-mhoo, though a Burman official, proved on this occasion, an essential aid in forcing the start from Bhamo, and providing the means which were otherwise unavailable of reaching a destination on the proper (right) bank of the river Tahpen.

101. We arrived at the village of *Tahmeylon* at 2 P. M, and occupied a deserted Shan Phongyee house, on the bank of that river. The priest had fled or become defunct, but the paraphernalia of his office were everywhere in abundance. We settled down into comfortable quarters, amongst model shrines richly carved in wood and inlaid with coloured glasses, a library of Religious Books, Sacred Alm's Bowls, and complacent images of Gaudama in every variety of shape and profusion. They remained intact, for it would have been sacrilege to have disturbed ought before the advent of a new incumbent.

The baggage boats, which left Bhamo the day previous, passed up the river during the afternoon towards our proposed destination at the village of *Sitkaw*, which we reached ourselves on the following morning (27th February.)

102. Our Mules and Mule-men were assembled at *Sitkaw*, and at this starting point had also arrived a few Kakhyen Chiefs (with their Pawmynes or deputies), who were afraid to trust themselves within the dangerous precincts of Burman Bhamo.

The *Ponsee* and *Tahlon* Saubwas were present in person. The *Saray* Saubwa was represented by his two grown-up sons, and several Pawmynes or deputies. The route viâ Ponlyne to Manwyne was virtually in the hands of these three Saubwas, *Ponlyne*, *Ponsee* and *Saray*. They had all contributed mules and men for the expedition, and their willingness to serve, and allow free transit through their respective Hill tracts, was signified without hesitation, now that no further occasion existed for fearing or being influenced by Burmese restraints.

103. It is true that the Tahpen Cheoung-oke and a few Tamons or heads of villages on the banks of that river were still present; but the villagers referred to are a hybrid race known as Shan Burmese, who pay taxes but receive no protection from the local Government at Bhamo. Their Head men find it necessary, therefore, to come to a private

understanding with the Kakhyen Chiefs who occupy the adjacent hills, to be mutually forbearing to each other and purchase exemption from kidnapping raids to which Kakhyens and Hybrid Shans, as a rule, are by no means (by nature) indisposed.

The villagers thus become subservient rather to the Kakhyen Chiefs than to their more lawful masters at Bhamo, and the presence of their headman at Sitkaw, even in a Burman capacity, could no longer act with undue restraint on the relations of these chiefs towards the expedition party.

104. Mule-men are as intractable, and far more restive than mules themselves, unless properly understood or under well trained management. First experiences at Sitkaw verified this fact to an insufferable extent.

The mules generally belong to petty proprietors, whose stock may consist of from one to a dozen animals. Each proprietor is a sort of irresponsible agent, and though his mules may be herded in a caravan with the mules of other proprietors he will not be regarded as a collective whole, but looks for and demands separate recognition, in all that relates to the hire and use of his particular property.

105. As soon as our baggage had been made over to the Kakhyen Chiefs, and past in review by the several mule proprietors assembled at Sitkaw, an incessant clamor was raised as to its apportionment into parcels, for allotment to the several claimants for carrier employ.

I was obliged to depend a great deal, at this time, on the Ponlyne Chief and my Chinese Interpreter Moung Shwè Yah. Both were occasionally drunk; but this seemed to be of no consequence, as drunkenness is the normal condition of Kakhyens when on duty, and is not regarded by them as any real interruption to love or business.

106. I find the following note in my Diary of 29th February.

Diary.—"Ponlyne visited me at 12—a volley of Muskets on entering the Village.

He is suffering from a night of drunken debauchery.

I offered him Brandy as a sedative, it was nectar as compared with his native Shamshoo. He evidently thought so, and seized the cup, but vomited in the attempt to gulp down its contents. He looks vacant, and woe-begone, but talks *business* nevertheless. Moung Shwè-Yah has been drinking too, and is useless—little or nothing can be done with either in their present state. Orders are given for mules to be brought, to try their loads. Panniers come first, and each muleteer seizes upon an allotment of boxes and binds them securely to the panniers. All is noise and confusion; but order comes out of it after a time. The panniers with their loads are subdivided again into lots and arranged in front of our residence. But there is a superfluity of mules, and the surplus proprietors quarrel amongst themselves, and fight with those who have already secured a baggage allotment. Panniers are unslung, and there is much angry dispute about their readjustment.

Ponlyne has recovered a little, and says I must leave all to him and not interfere. The panniers must be re-arranged tomorrow morning, and a fresh apportionment of baggage made before we can start. The mule-men are principally Shans, with a sprinkling only of Kakhyens. They are inclined to be quarrelsome and discontented on account of their long detention at this place. Every little dispute calls for an appeal to arms. The hand is instinctively led to grasp the sword handle on the slightest provocation. But the weapon is not often drawn. The act is demonstrative, rather than real. There is a good deal of cowardly bluster, but it very rarely happens that blows are struck or that actual damage is the result.

The Tahlon Saubwa promises to take us anywhere if I will only pay him well. But he is not be trusted. I am told that he suggested to his Brother Ponlyne the advisability of levying an arbitrary Customs duty on our baggage on account of mule demurrage.

Ponlyne replied very staunchly that I was his friend, and threatened his Brother Tahlon, with immediate extermination if any thing was done to cause me annoyance. There was an earnestness in the threat which must have been irresistible, for Tahlon has now become affable again and is both friendly and useful."

107. We were to have left Sitkaw on the morning of the 1st (March) but the Burmese Cheoung-oke re-appeared on the scene with certain of the Kakhyen chiefs, and all affirmed that the day (being the 9th of some imaginary Kakhyen Month) is altogether unpropitious as a day on which to set out on a journey or commence any other important undertaking. Other trivial causes were assigned for delay. The mule-men were said to be dissatisfied and quarrelsome, but the cause of their dissatisfaction was not explained or explainable. I expostulated strongly, though determined not to provoke a quarrel. There seemed greater need than ever for conciliation and forbearance. No other line of action would have been possible in the present state of our dependance on Kakhyen friendship. Up to that very moment Burmese Officialism was doing all it could to make itself obnoxious and obstructive. But we shall get off after all. The Cheoung-oke tried to discourage me by saying that the Kakhyen Chiefs were at variance with the mule-men and that there would be open strife before long. I warned him against interference and at the same time sent for the Chiefs, and said that I would abide by any arrangements they might choose to make as to the distribution of mules or carriage generally. They were satisfied. I praised them openly for friendly assistance and they as unreservedly declared that we were their relatives and friends and that they would be true to us for ever.

108. Demands for money were pressing and continuous. Phoongyees even, seemed to have turned beggars. A Shan Priest called upon us at Sitkaw, and as I treated him with becoming respect he became communicative. Shan Phoongyees are admitted to be very lax and unorthodox in their religious observances. Our guest on this occasion appeared to be an exception to the general rule. He possessed a large comfortable Monastery at this village, but his Missionary duties take him, he says, to rude villages in the interior, where he hoped in time to convert the half Shan population into civilized conformity with Budhist teachings.

109. The Phoongyee was wonderfully shrewd, and gave us the following good advice at parting. These are almost his own words:—

"We have met before in a former existence; and it is by virtue of meritorious acts then done that I am privileged to meet you again in the present existence and advise you for your welfare."

"Let me tell you then that wisdom and prudence are necessary ingredients in the performance of all worldly undertakings. Use special care and circumspection in your present expedition. Your enemies are numerous and powerful, but do not believe that they are either Shans or Kakhyens. Do your best. We shall all hail the re-opening of overland trade with China. The happiness and prosperity of the Priesthood depend on the wealth and condition of the country and its inhabitants. What is good for the country is good also for religion &c. &c."

110. The Expedition did not get away from Sitkaw until 2 P.M. on 2nd March.

Late at night on 1st the Ponlyne Chief came to tell me that Moung Shwè-Yah my Chinese Interpreter had colluded with the Chinese, and was as much our enemy as any Burman of Bhamo. I sent for the man but found him too drunk to be intelligent or intelligible.

111. On the 2nd a delay arose in taking lists of our mule-men, and in ascertaining who they belonged to, and what particular Chiefs were responsible for safe conduct and protection en route.

In the midst of this confusion the Ponsee and Tahlon Saubwas discovered, in an interval of sobriety, that the Ponlyne Chief had received a present of a musket whilst in attendance on us at Bhamo. Moung Shwè-Yah had urged them to claim similar consideration and reward as independent Chiefs who were as powerful if not more so than the Ponlyne himself. It was not in my power to satisfy them. They were under evil influences and the musket difficulty was a mere prelude to further obstructiveness. At the last moment they refused their services and prowled about in sneaking silence taking lists of ourselves and of our baggage and implying or intending to imply thereby that they were measuring our strength and resources with a view to opposition as soon as we commenced the march into their Hills.

112. It was long after mid-day therefore before mules were brought and finally loaded. The arrangements were that the first day's march should take us to Ponlyne's village, which was said to be not more than 4 koss (or 8 miles) from Sitkaw. Although therefore the day was already far advanced, and our arrangements for the journey by no means so effective as they might have been, the necessity of making a start was imperative and could not have been delayed without endangering our enterprise. It would have been prejudicial to every hope of success at this time to have allowed mere considerations of time or distance to stand in our way, when the opportunity of an actual advance of any kind had at last become even remotely practicable.

113. Up to to the last moment I was not sure that secret influences might not yet prevail to cause the desertion of our mule-men, and make our advance from Sitkaw as remote and impossible as it had been for a whole month of harassing in-action within the hated precincts of Bhamo.

114. The state of my feelings and opinions at this time is best described by a short entry in my note book which was jotted down on the morning of 2nd March under pressure of anxieties and whilst surveying in suspense and impatience the circumstances of our unfriended and somewhat forlorn situation.

" Whatever reasons Burmese Officials may have to dread our success in re-establishing the old trade route between Burma and China, and however much we may congratulate ourselves on the discomfiture of their present plans of opposition and distrust, there is nothing encouraging in the admission that, if this resistance is continued with the same morbid pertinacity which has thus far characterized its connectionship with our undertaking, a very effectual restraint will have been put on all British commercial enterprise through upper Burma, as long at least as that country is allowed to be a separate Kingdom and glories in the excesses of a faithless and effete Government."

115. But we are all off by 2 P. M. Three Kakhyen Saubwas lead the way, the mules follow and certain men of the Police escort are told off to ammunition and cash chest.

There was something outrageously wild even to romance in the manner of our start. The Kakhyens on the contrary from *their* point of view might probably have been discussing the conpleteness of the arrangements, whilst we, in our ignorance of their peculiarities and in the absence of Interpreters or of a single Burmese adherent who either possesed the requisite knowledge himself or dared to volunteer information as to the correct mode of marching at the head or bringing up the tail of a Kakhyen convoy, were unable to enforce order ourselves or to distinguish any sign of arrangement in the irregular programme of our exodus from Sitkaw.

116. The route lay in a Northerly direction, through paddy or grassfields for a distance of three miles as far as the small village of Sehek, from which point the ascent commences rather abruptly at the base of the Ponlyne hills. We had here headed our baggage and a temporary halt took place.

The three Kakhyen Chiefs, who had preceeded us from Sitkaw, were seated by themselves at a point where the road branched off almost at right angles from the village of Sehek towards the base of the Ponlyne hills.

They were evidently in deep counsel and much excited, but as I came up the Ponlyne ran towards me and pointed out the road up the hill exclaiming at the same time as if to excuse himself for not leading the advance " all right! go on don't be afraid."!

117. It puzzled me at first to know what he meant by the expression *"don't be afraid ;"* for hitherto there had been no cause to apprehend danger at all.

But on we went, my pony was a good climber and was a-head. After ascending the hills some two miles a shot was fired a long way in advance. The mule-men shouted like fiends and urged me to fire off my guns. I waited until Dr. Anderson had joined me, a second shot, then four shots all at once but no sound of a bullet. Capt. Bowers and Mr. Stewart came up almost immediately and we went on as if nothing had occurred. At least 50 of our mules were a-head. The Kakhyens of our party were many of them in liquor and though they vociferated frantically they did not exhibit the slightest sense of fear or misgiving.

118. One of them was mounted on a mule and became more dangerous at close quarters as a friend than any number of our Jungle enemies in the bush. In his excitement he occasionally flourished a long sword, in reckless disregard of every thing and every one but himself. He became a still more formidable animal when the sword was sheathed and his matchlock brought into earnest operation. Drunkenness seemed only to steady his movements, for although the road was rough and a steep incline in most places, the matchlock was nevertheless loaded and fired with wonderful precision as regards time but with utter recklessness as regarded direction. The man was both friendly and quarrelsome at the same time. A word or suggestion out of place would have converted him on the instant into a foe, and the only means of keeping him in good humour with himself and with us was to praise his dexterity and promise to renew his exhausted powder-flask as soon as we arrived at the village of Ponlyne.

119. Soon after the firing commenced Mr. Stewart picked up a spear which is supposed to have been hurled against some of our party with hostile intent. But the evidence on this point is not very convincing, as it rests solely on the testimony of a Burmese horse keeper, who said he saw the spear alight in the ground when first thrown from the jungle. My belief is that the spear incident, as well as the shots which were fired in advance of us as we ascended the first projections of the Ponlyne range, had no real purpose beyond a mere *show* of hostility, contrived most probably on the one hand under Burmese direction with the object of terrifying us into a return to Bhamo, and assisted on the other by certain of our own Kakhyen party, who no doubt required very little pressing in a matter which promised to make them masters of our baggage and property.

120. But as we are now on the march it is advisable I think for the sake of more concise elucidation to confine my narrative for the present to a selection of quotations from my rough notes and journal.

3RD MARCH 1868.

"Did not reach Ponlyne village until nearly dark last evening. The Pawmyne conducted us to a Kakhyen house which had been swept and set apart for our accommodation.

The building, like all Kakhyen houses, consists of an elongated Bamboo shed, the front portion of which is open and forms a portico in which the live stock of the proprietor (Pigs, Fowls, Ponies and Buffaloes) are fed by day and herded at night. The remainder of the house is floored with Bamboos, and is divided longitudinally down the centre, with transverse partitions on one side only, so as to form rooms or cells in which the separate members of one or many families finds a habitation. The other side is open throughout and is used as a general lounge, but the whole exterior of the building is closely matted in with a single opening or door-way at the back, through which it is a sin for any one who is not a member of the family to enter, although egress is allowed through it to all alike.

Very few of our mules had arrived last night, but there is a novelty about the scene and occasion which atoned in some measure for the absence of bed and supper.

We stroll out and admire Kakhyen women pounding Paddy by moon-light. An old lady of the party beckoned me to follow her, and I was conducted, with a thrill of ambiguity as to results, to a house at a little distance, where I found Ponlyne himself in the midst of his family.

The old lady was his wife and I was most hospitably entertained. The Chief made me sit down by him on his own carpet, and the family attended on us with successive relays of Kakhyen Beer, a very good substitute for an English original, provided of course nothing better is to be had.

This morning there is a report that a portion of our mules and baggage have been looted by the Tahlon Saubwa. As the day wears on matters improve. We find that numbers of our mule-men, who were supposed at first to have decamped altogether, had simply herded for the night in small groups at their own pet halting places in and around Ponlyne. Missing baggage turns up most opportunely in various out-of-the-way localities.

The Jemadar with the escort arrived at 1 p. m., and reports that he remained for the night in charge of the ammunition and cash chest, at a village some three miles distant from Ponlyne; a number of our mules are also congregated there, with my Chinese Interpreter Moung Shwè yah. The

Pawmyne of the village, for some unaccountable reason, refused to let them come on. The Ponlyne Chief has sent his own son to bring them. When they arrive we shall have lost nothing of any consequence.

The Chief's wife has paid us a visit in great state, with her family and a retinue of female attendants. She brings presents of geese, boiled rice, eggs, and Kakhyen beer.

She is a fine intelligent matronly looking woman; her get up is perfect in its way, and though a little outré at first sight is by no means unbecoming.

The head dress consists of a black cotton scarf which is wound round the head so as to ascend a foot or more above it in the shape of an inverted Pyramid. The upper garment is a loose black velvet Jacket, ornamanted with large silver button-embossments which encircle the neck from behind and are brought forward towards the breast. Circular plates of chased and enamelled silver, each three inches in diameter, are arranged in lines down the front seam of the Jacket on either side and a similar line down the centre of the back and continued all round the skirt. The lower garment is a single dark blue cotton cloth about a yard and a half in length, which passes once round the body from the waist to the knees, and is fastened in front with a simple tuck. It is edged with a red woollen border, one end being tastefully worked with silk embroidery a foot in depth. This attempt at decoration is not lost sight of but dangles on one side with a captivating effect which is as much a study amongst the women of the Kakhyen hills as it is the right and privilege of the female sex every where.

Sounds of Kakhyen music are heard in the distance, and going in search we arrive at a house full of men women and children, who are dancing vigorously to a rattling accompaniment of gongs and sticks, played by themselves. They do no not object to our presence, and Anderson and I enter the house and take an active part in the festive proceedings. The dance is a measured side step with side movement, crab-fashion. We go round in our proper places and are enjoying a certain wild novelty in the arrangements, when suddenly the male dancers become more than usually excited and rush madly out of the house like demons. We remain inside with the women.

The scene of rejoicing has turned into one of mourning and lamentation. Two of the women retire and cry piteously over the corpse of a child which has been carefully concealed in an out of the way corner of a side apartment. Horribile dictu! We too have joined in the death dance, and contributed our aid in the propitiation of Nats and in driving away from its late tenement the hovering spirit of the departed! Other women bring us logs of wood to be used as stools and we sit down for a time, whilst our hosts hand round Kakhyen Beer in conical cups of plantain leaves, which have been ingeniously improvised for our especial benefit.

If our object is to familiarize ourselves with Kakhyen manners and customs we shall soon become proficients with a vengeance! We paid our footing in Rupees and left the house with feelings not altogether unpleasurable, but shadowed perhaps by a tinge of sadness and a sense that death dances do not add to the personal dignity or moral elevation of European adventurers who have unconsciously indulged in them in the wilds of Kakhyen land. The Saubwa's wife has come again with her Suite whilst we are at dinner, and brings more fresh brewed beer.

A number of our muleteers also congregate round us, and are inclined to be rude and even insolent but quiet down when properly spoken to.

They ask whether our Country is a hot or cold one: "Cold."

"Oh that is why you are good people like ourselves! but "you must pay well as you go along and there will be no "difficulty. There are three Chiefs who have still to be "conciliated one of them is your friend but two promise to "oppose you. We cannot mention names."

4TH MARCH 1868.

The cash chest arrived at 12 o'clock mid-day. The mule-men have commenced to filtch out of our cases in earnest.

They are considerate too in some respects. In one of Stewart's cases they discovered a bottle of Port wine and got at it's contents by pushing in the cork, but the liquor proving unpalatable they made a wooden cork and replaced the bottle in its original place, with a very innocent and laudable desire to prevent waste.

I have assembled the Chiefs and Ponlyne to day and made them all suitable presents of cloths &c.

The Ponlyne makes a speech and exhorts all to faithful service.

He informed me however privately that the Nats look unfavorably upon us and will require propitiation. This communication was followed during the evening by an announcement that he was about to consult the spirits of good and evil, and obtain their consent or dissent to a continuance of our journey on the morrow. I am invited to attend.

This implies another demand for Rupees. We proceed to the Saubwa's new house. The Kakhyen Priest (Meetway) separates himself from the rest of his companions and occupies a dark corner at one end of the house. Here he crouches down and works himself into a fury of attitudinizing, strokes his head and face with both hands, tears his hair, sighs, moans, groans and finally his legs from the knee downwards quiver with a reverberation which repeats itself on the bamboo flooring with a sharp castanet commotion of sound which is kept up throughout the ceremony. We now know that the man is possessed and beyond self control. His utterances are henceforth those of Demons and Nats. There is anger and fury in his voice.

The Chief whispers and asks me if I have brought a propitiation. I am prepared for the worst: but bargain to be let off for 15 Rupees.

The money is laid on a new cloth and offered on a platter of plantain leaves, but in a moment platter and Rupees are kicked to a distance in scorn. The Chief approaches with reverence and supplication and begs that the offering may not be rejected. No reply, but deeper groans and more piercing shrieks. I am appealed to and add five Rupees to the offering which now finds favor and is duly brought to account. Benedictions follow and all that is good is prognosticated in our future travels.

The effect of all this would be ludicrous and uninteresting in the extreme were it not for the reverence and devotional earnestness with which the Chiefs and people regard the ceremonial from begining to end. There is no doubt that their faith is firmly bound up in the prognostications for good or evil which emanate from the being who, to their ideas, becomes thus miraculously inspired or possessed.

No work of importance or even necessity is ever undertaken without his approval, or rather the approval of the minor Deities who speak through him.

But the respect and dignity due to his office cease with the moment of inspiration. When unpossessed the *Meetway* sinks into the common-place reality of an ordinary Kakhyen layman. The man to whom Chiefs bent in reverence, and upon whom perhaps the fate of the expedition principally depended whilst under spiritual influence in the recent ceremonial, was in ordinary life a common labourer, and carried one of my boxes on the march from Sitkaw to Ponlyne.

The embryo *Meetway* in early life, or as soon as he begins to evince evident signs of a connectionship with the world of spirits, is subjected to an infallible test, which passes him at once into the recognized status of a full blown Kakhyen Priest.

The test is simple but awkward: a ladder is provided (the steps of which consist of sword blades with the sharp edge turned upwards) and leads on to a small platform which is thick-set with the sharpest spikes. The Novitiate takes his degree and becomes forthwith ordained to the office of a Kakhyen Meetway by climbing this ladder and seating himself upon the spiked platform, not only without personal inconvenience to his nether parts at the time, but with freedom from all after traces of visible or apparent injury.

The faculty of becoming possessed has thus been proved, and whether such faculty has any real existence beyond mere momentary phrensy and excitement it is certain that the Meetway becomes a recognized medium, and possesses a kind of inspiration which for want of peculiar training perhaps, our limited ideas fail either to conceive or comprehend.

After the ceremony the Ponlyne spoke to me in confidence and said that if I wished to succeed in my travels no help would be so powerful as a large expenditure of the precious metal.

He says that the Shans and Kakhyengalays have fraternized for the purpose of opposing us, and that conciliation will be a difficult matter in the face of all the evil reports which have already been circulated with the avowed object of putting an end to the expedition.

5TH MARCH 1868.

Up at day light.—The mule-men come early and ask for their loads. We are prepared to start but now comes the inevitable hitch. The Saubwa (Ponlyne) will not shew himself.

I am told he is asleep or at breakfast but in reality he has assumed a fit of Diplomatic Sulks, and obstinately refuses to leave his house or afford explanation.

I understand the indisposition and go to him. More Rupees! This system of silent extortion is ruinous. It is a repetition of last night's story.

"Unless you are prepared to pay well you had better go "back."

Rupees 600 are demanded and I pay down 300 which are accepted. I had already given him and his wife rich cloths and carpets as well as a flint musket, a valuable present in itself. The Rupees 300 now given are intended as a further advance to the mule-men who had already received Rupees 500 before we left Sitkaw.

It is far more probable I think that the money will find its way into the Chief's own private hoard.

The cash chest is another difficulty. Rupees 300 are demanded as the sum to be paid for its conveyance as far as Manwyne.

I offer one Rupee each per diem to 20 men as long as they are employed.

No.

Then I must break up the chest altogether. This involves delay. If the money is distributed and placed in our boxes they will of a certainty be looted.

We eventually count it out in allotments of Rs. 300 each to be carried alternately by men of the Police escort.

Did not get off till half past nine. Our route to-day lay along the valley of the Tahpen. The view now and then is glorious. On either side hills tower up into mountains and range after range succeed each other indefinitely till lost in the blue distance.

Ponlyne itself (the village) is about 2,500 feet above sea level. The immediate descent from Ponlyne to the bed of the Nambouk river is steep and difficult for a distance of about three miles; but the next four miles is occupied in crossing a succession of lofty spurs which abut into the valley from the main ranges.

Kakhyens keep to the high ground as much as possible, and their roads seem to be purposely designed with a view to reaching the most elevated points on any given route. My theory is that the first trace is made in ignorance of locality, and that high points are selected as places from which to look out and espy a way to any desired destination.

The track once made may be any thing but a direct route; but it serves as a guide and is perhaps rigidly adhered to ever after. The Tahpen river is constantly in sight. At times we descend nearly to its bed and anon it is roaring two thousand feet below us. It is a broad rapid torrent, or rather a continuation of rapids down which the water rushes with unceasing roar and with a force which nothing could withstand, if we except prodigious boulders of granite, which lie occasionally across its bed, or hang suspended on its immediate banks with an inclination which suggests a gradual but inevitable downfall.

Halted at 2. p. m.—The mules are fagged and cannot go further although "the wheel" has only registered eight miles in six hours!

I have no faith in "the wheel" over this kind of ground.

The "wheeler" is obliged to carry it over a great portion of the road, which remains accordingly unregistered or unaccounted for.

We encamp in the Jungle and call the spot *Likhon* which is the name of the largest range of hills in our immediate vicinity.

6TH MARCH 1868.

The Ponlyne Saubwa says that we must proceed with caution to-day as the Ponsee Saubwa is offended with me for not having presented him with a Musket.

The Kakhyen Deities had spoken, he said, through the *Meetway* and ordered us always on commencing a march to fire a volley.

He inserted a slight amendment however to, the effect that double charges of powder were advisable, so as to make as great a report as possible.

Started from Lakhon at 8-45 A. M., and reached Ponsee village at 11-30.; the wheel only registering four miles. Road comparatively easy and good the whole way.

The Ponsee Saubwa has not provided us with accommodation, and we encamp in a hollow at the foot of the village.

A Pawmyne with his wife and female relatives paid us a visit this evening with presents of Beer and vegetables. One of the young women was inclined to be merry and communicative in the hope of attracting attention and securing Beads. Her hair was cut straight across the forehead (*a more virginorum*) and allowed to hang down mop-fashion behind.

She was married nevertheless, although the Puggery or head dress which Kakhyen married women ought by right to wear was absent. I offered to supply the deficiency, and raised a burst of modest merriment which took the Pawmyne quite by surprise. He reproved the levity of his young relative and evinced dislike to innocent flirtations.

One of my Burmese followers was struck this evening by a Kakhyen in the employ of the Ponsee Chief.

Ponlyne interfered and said that he would resent an insult offered to any of my people as if offered to himself. He has shewn himself our friend thus far, but it would suit the reduced state of my finances better if he was less covetous and exacting in his pecuniary requirements.

7th March 1868.

The Ponlyne Saubwa has come to me early this morning to say that a small Army of Shans and Kakhyens have collected on the road we intend proceeding by and threaten opposition. He thinks they may be bought over for Rupees 2,000!

I do not mince matters, but say at once that I must give up all idea of proceeding further unless Ponlyne can let me off at a cheaper rate of black mail than that which he now advises.

It is necessary to be particular on this point, for I have already been twice asked since we ascended the hills what pecuniary arrangements I had made for our return journey Homewards.

The Ponlyne rather significantly remarks that the Panthays have lots of money and will be glad to accommodate me.

This is another instance of an unvarying belief in our connectionship with the Panthay cause; and our determination to assist it to the exclusion and confusion of all other interests in Yunan.

But a more serious difficulty is at hand, and threatens to be an obstacle to our further progress, at all events for some days to come.

Our Muleteers, without a word of complaint or even misunderstanding, have suddenly struck work and I see them streaming out of camp with their animals and empty panniers. I appeal to the Saubwa (Ponlyne) but he merely sends back word to say—"All right; let them go they will come back by and by."

He will not come to me so I go and find him seated in the Ponsee Saubwa's house, in as complacent and collected a state of mind (though in liquor) as if nothing particular had occurred.

The Muleteers, he informs me, have left on account of private messages which have been conveyed to them from the Saubwas of Sanda and Mynela, who threaten death and extermination if they afford us the means of entering the Shan states.

Ponlyne advises me to write to these Shan Chiefs and warn them that if they object to my visiting the Shan States *we* too will close the roads leading towards Burma and prevent Shans from attending the annual fairs at Bhamo.

I stop him rather rudely by saying that my object is to conciliate strife rather than foment new causes of misunderstanding.

I have no objection I add to write to the Shan Chiefs in the same friendly and explanatory sense in which I have lately addressed the Governor of Momein.

Ponlyne becomes very communicative in his cups and volunteers to tell me the truth about my Chinese Interpreter Moung Shwè Yah, who is accused of having deserted us at Ponlyne (village) as soon as he found that he could not succeed in making the Kakhyen Chiefs take part against the expedition.

His advice all along had been to murder me at a convenient season, and take possession of the cash chest and other Government presents of which I had charge.

This story is not improbable (in vino veritas) and bears out my own suspicions. Shwè Yah had behaved like a villain ever since we left Bhamo and even there I began to suspect him. It was on this account that I did not take him into my confidence in despatching letters to Momein.

His private efforts to thwart and confound my plans having failed at Bhamo, he bethought him of the dastardly expedient of robbery and bloodshed, (so Ponlyne says) but in this too he missed his mark, and, fearing exposure, chose rather to return in confusion to Bhamo than let it be supposed by the Burmese Government that after all he might have been secretly aiding in the fulfilment of our undertaking. This is Ponlyne's opinion and it agrees in all respects with my own observations.

So much for a man who was specially told off to our assistance by the King of Burma.

Ponlyne informs me that the Chief of Saray, who occupies the next range of Hills in our advance, has been sent for and refuses to come in. It is out of the question, he says, to think of moving without his previous sanction.

Political Agent.—Very true but provided we get sanction what about mules for our baggage.

Ponlyne.—I have a few mules of my own. We will take what baggage we can with them and send back for the remainder.

Ponlyne is inconsistent. The mule difficulty may turn out after all to be a ruse of his own for the purpose of covering another extortionate demand.

It is whispered in private quarters that the muleteers left because they objected to being kept in inaction with their animals.

They were willing, it was said, to take on our baggage and did not fear Shan threats of extermination, but it was unreasonable to expect them to remain at Ponsee after their stock of provisions had been consumed and when they found that they were being uselessly detained with the sole object of serving Kakhyen purposes.

Rumour is very conflicting but it would have been dangerous to move without the Saubwa's concurrence or contrary to his advice.

I do not agree with Sir Samuel Baker in the pleasure he finds at being in a downright difficulty.

This is now my position and I should regret it the less on my own account were it not for the incubus of responsibility to others, and, in a more remote degree, to my own Government. We have impatient spirits too amongst our number. A has boils—B is not in good spirits—C. is silent and anxious—D. is jolly under all circumstances, and regards difficulties as things to be overcome rather than growled at in lanquid inactivity.

The sky above is gloomy and overcast, clouds pregnant with rain threaten a discharge which will damp the little ardour or Romance that might otherwise attach itself to a residence on the far famed Kakhyen Hills at Ponsee.

We are now encamped on the upper terrace of a tumulus shaped hill, which has been cultivated to its base in a succession of terraces, generally regular and equidistant in their gradations of descent. The camp consists of three small sepoys palls or tents, which are sufficient to give cover to the Europeans of our Party. The escort and followers are busy hutting themselves on the several ridges which surround the encampment. There is little to grumble at beyond the anxieties of delay and our own impatient eagerness to be again on the move.

Ponlyne has just came into camp and sits himself down in my tent. He is in liquor, but seizing me by both hands swears fidelity and friendship. I fire off my guns and revolvers at his request. The bullets will not hit a particular bamboo which is an eyesore to him in his drunkenness. He becomes a savage instanter and abuses me in foul Burmese. Forbearance is necessary otherwise he is sure to commit himself to some reckless act of violence. I quiet him down by degrees, and he assumes his old show of friendly familiarity. But the animal is not to be trusted. He is true to his savage instincts and treachery underlies every look and action.

The chiefs of *Ponwa*, *Nyoungen*, and *Wacheoon* have came in with small presents, for which I make a suitable return in cloths. They occupy separate Hill tracts on the route between this place and the Shan town of of Manwyne.

The Ponsee Saubwa's mother called during the afternoon with a number of female attendants. They are bearers of Kakhyen delicacies. Beer, cooked rice, eggs, and vegetables. I made a general distribution of Beads, but they beg for Rupees which are in greater demand, I find, and more acceptable in these parts than any other presentable commodity ; so much for Burman duplicity or ignorance which made it appear that coined silver would not pass current or be accepted as an article of exchange when once we had left the vicinity of Bhamo.

Ponlyne tells me, with a look of serious reality, to make up my mind to the payment of two baskets (Bushels) of Rupees before I quit Ponsee.

8th March 1868.

It rained heavily all last night; the single fly tents afford but a poor protection against either wind or rain; so violent were the gusts of wind it became necessary to hold on to the Poles to prevent the tents being blown away altogether. As the wind abated I got snatches of sleep, but in the absence of a bed my mattress, which was on the ground, had bcome clammy and wet; we are better off after all than some of our followers who are without shelter of any sort.

I have just heard of the arrival of the Nanlyaw Tamon, with written orders from the Governor of Bhamo directing both the Chiefs of Ponlyne and Ponsee to return forthwith to Bhamo, for consultation on the subject of the Ponsee silver mines.

This is mysterious! What reason is there for such urgent haste in ordering the immediate return of these chiefs, whilst it is known that they are our only guarantee of protection in these wild unknown regions? The pretence too for requiring their services at this particular juncture is palpably and ridiculously false. The Ponsee silver mines have been worked for many years past by Burmese and Chinese, and their condition and circumstances are already well known.

I suspect this Nanlyaw official. He is always selected when dirty work has to be done. He denies now that orders were ever given to him to accompany me on the present expedition. Yesterday I was informed that five houses had been accidentally burned by a jungle fire which is said to have originated at our last encamping ground. I was in no way held responsible and the matter was satisfactorily settled for a bottle of whiskey. To-day (since the Burman official's arrival) a serious demand is made for 300 Rupees. The Tamon chuckles. He knows that the demand is false and will be resisted, but this is just what he wants, as it affords a pretext for our detention until a compromise of some sort can be effected. I am afraid to yield to this claim, as compliance to-day would lead to double demands to-morrow, or be supplemented, without loss of time, by other equally false and unjust means of extortion.

The Saubwa refuses a compromise and predicts difficulties. He begins to find out that I am not to be squeezed to the extent he at first imagined, and talks about returning to Bhamo and leaving only his Pawmynes with me. I remonstrate but he says the Governor's orders are imperative and that he cannot afford to disobey them &c., &c.,

9TH MARCH 1868.

The Ponlyne Saubwa is both sulky and angry. He has become really obstructive and insolent since the arrival of the Nanlyaw Tamon with orders from Bhamo. I am given distinctly to understand that unless I at once pay down 600 Rupees as black mail and 300 Rupees as compensation for the village fire he will no longer be answerable for our safety, but return forthwith to his native village.

Of course he knows that I cannot and will not pay. He will thus have a ready excuse for breaking off connectionship with us, and absolve himself from the danger of open rupture with the Burmese Government for having thus far contributed to our advance.

I argue at length against the unreasonable nature of the demands now made and conclude my interview in the following strain.

"The village fire did not originate with me any more
" then it did with you. The houses which are said to have
" been burnt lay at a very considerable distance from our line
" of march. I do not believe that our march had anything to
" do with their destruction, further perhaps than the simple
" idea that any evil which takes place at present will be
" connected in the Kakhyen mind with our presence in
" their hills and be ascribed to us accordingly. Having
" come as a friend it is far from my wish to offend against
" Kakhyen scruples or custom. I will pay all reasonable
" demands and am even willing to make reparation in the
" present case to the full extent of the damage done. But
" if the Kakhyens wish us to be their friends they must
" deal fairly and believe that we will do the same by them.
" Neither can I pay you the 600 Rupees which you have just
" asked for, but I agree to send on valuable presents

"to the chiefs through whose territories we are to pass,
"and will pay them the customary dues as soon as we
"arrive at their respective places of residence. I shall regret
"your departure very much, for on some occasions you have
"been a true friend to us. It is not in my power either to
"detain you by force, but remember that you are under an
"engagement to conduct the expedition in safety as far as
"Manwyne, and although the Governor of Bhamo has sent
"(with what intent I cannot say) and ordered your immediate
"return, I still beg of you to remain and rely upon my assur-
"ances of support against any oppressive acts to which the
"Governor may try and subject you as a consequence of your
"compliance."

This speech had its effect, the Saubwa did not again allude to his intention of leaving me, but simply asked for 100 Rupees as a means of settling the village fire dispute. This I agreed to pay partly in money and partly in cloths.

It was at this stage of our interview that I was suddenly made aware of the presence of three men dressed up in all the wonderful apparel of Chinese Officers of Rank.

I knew their faces at once and they recognized me; but beyond this I was as much mystified as Ponlyne himself in trying to imagine who the men were; and how I could ever before have held communication with Chinese officers of their stamp and appearance.

The mystery is soon solved, Lanboo strips off a portion of his trappings and discloses himself as the Kakhyen scout whom I sent from Bhamo with letters to Momein. He takes from his waist a small bundle, which, when unrolled, reveals a letter and envelope of prodigious dimensions, scored over with Chinese superscriptions and a variety of Chinese seals in red and blue devices. Ponlyne is silent and uneasy. He is seized with anything but pleasurable feelings at the style of the newcomers, and appears hurt at their friendly recognition of all our party without a word of explanation or ac-
knowledgement in recognition of his own presence and authority.

The envelope contains two letters, one in Chinese the other in Arabic. Our native Doctor is able to interpret a portion of the latter very imperfectly. The Chinese epistle cannot be read for the present but Lauloo explains its contents as favorable and in the highest degree encouraging.

The Governor of *Momein*, he said, expected us by the central or Ambassador's route (which leads direct from Bhamo into the Shan State of Hotha,) and had arranged accordingly to assist and cooperate with us on the march.

I am advised not to advance for the present viâ Manwyne, unless we are strong enough to fight our way through the Blockade established by Lees-hee-ta-hee at Mauphoo.

The Governor of Momein received my Kakhyen scouts with every mark of friendly respect, and has sent them back as an Embassy in the costly dresses which have just contributed to our amusement and surprise. Each man has a silk cap of blue satin embroidered with gold, a thick padded superfine cloth jacket highly ornamented, a long silk coat and Chinese gold embroidered shoes. They are Kakhyens of the Rowlee tribe and carry their new honors with wonderful self composure. Altogether seven men have come in from Momein, one of them, *Shatoodoo*, is a (Kakhyen) Panthay Officer of some rank and recommends himself to our notice by a display of good breeding and gentlemanly attainments which are far in advance of any preconceived ideas of semi-barbarous civilization.

The arrival of letters from Momein and the manner of their delivery by our own messengers, who had met with so much favor at Panthay Head Quarters, is an event in the fate of the expedition which not only promises well for the future but is pregnant also with encouraging influences in our present emergencies &c. &c.,

The Shans of Manwyne are coming in and establishing a small bazaar in our lines: rice is selling at 8 measures for the Rupee. Yesterday it was only three; an empty bottle was bartered for fourteen to-day and attained therefore to an estimated money value of nearly two Rupees.

But when gain or game offers Kakhyens are insolently exacting on their own Hills, and openly persecute our Shan bazaarmen with an overbearing amount of injustice which is ridiculously irritating to unpractised observers.

The Shans are too mild or too much afraid to retaliate. They will either forsake us or the Bazaar prices must rise considerably, so as to cover extraordinary loss caused by Kakhyen excesses. It is out of my power to interfere much with the customary rapacity of these Kakhyen Hill tribes. Other considerations are too pressing just at present to justify the risk of dispute on points which, though they sadly try our power of endurance, are not so absolutely urgent as to require an immediate remedy.

10TH MARCH 1868.

Ponlyne is savage with my Kakhyen scouts for having handed me letters from Momein direct, without previous consultation with himself. I cannot afford to make advances to him or try other means of conciliation as long as he remains in his present temper, otherwise he will at once fancy himself in the ascendant and fall back upon the old demand for Rupees 600.

The Nanlyaw Tamon has gone off to Bhamo without leave or intimation of his intentions. Ponlyne assured him in my presence yesterday that his villainy had become notorious and that I had found him out. He was undoubtedly sent here as a fit agent to add, if possible, to our difficulties and has returned in haste to Bhamo to report the arrival of letters from Momein.

It is now an undeniable fact that this said Tamon incited the Kakhyens to re-open the village fire question after it had once been settled. We cannot blame the Kakhyens for having become unruly and extortionate when they thus found themselves backed up by powerful Burmese influences at Bhamo.

But under all circumstances it is desirable to show that we are not over anxious or disconcerted at the unavoidable detention at Ponsee. I therefore send to tell the Ponlyne, with feigned unconcern, that having made up my mind to an indefinite stay on the Kakhyen Hills it is as well that we should pass the time pleasantly, and I am in favour therefore of an excursion to the silver mines on the opposite bank of the River, if he will accompany me or supply guides. He is astonished but not out witted. His message was *"wait a little and I will come and see you."*

That is all I wanted, as, combined with Whiskey, it will afford the means of a temporary reconciliation.

11TH MARCH 1868.

A few mules belonging to Ponlyne, which had been kept in reserve for a start as far as Saray if all other supplies failed, have left Camp this morning.

The Saubwa presented himself shortly afterwards looking very foolish. He asked with an assumed air of effrontery and in a taking-the-Bull-by-the-Horns-style.

"What I intend to do?"

"How did I intend to get on? &c., &c., &c."

I replied by a ferocious *Tu quoque* placing as much, emphasis as possible on the *Tu*. How, I asked, did he reconcile the unnecessary delay here with the promises of safe conduct as far as Manwyne. Of what avail was it to make the village fire a pretence for opposition when it was *patent* to all that our mules had been taken away with his knowledge and approval, and that the possibilities of our further advance had been effectually destroyed (for a time at least) without any reference to the fire question at all?

Ponlyne was at last hard up for a reply but fell back as usual on his old craving demand for Rupees. You must pay me down 900 Rupees at once or I cannot undertake to assist you further; of this sum I will pay Rupees 300 towards the village fire and send 600 for distribution amongst the Chiefs in our advance.

I firmly refuse both demands. *First* because I have not the funds to spare; *secondly* I know that the money if paid will be simply appropriated by *Ponlyne* to his own uses; and *thirdly* I feel certain that a compliance with unjust exactions of this kind, without assisting our advance, will give me so notorious a reputation amongst Kakhyens as a fit subject for squeezing that other unjust demands will be made and pressed with an urgency which must lead either to riot, insolvency, or inevitable failure, &c., &c., &c.

12th March 1868.

Money difficulties do not cease, but the Kakhyens are pleased at hearing that I regard their love for Rupees as a good omen in our future dealings and intercourse.

Hitherto we have all believed, I said, that a few Beads or pieces of Redcloth were more precious in their sight than any amount of silver and gold. Had I understood their real wants before I left Mandalay I might have provided myself with money in abundance, and more than satisfied all reasonable demands. It was my wish I added and the wish of the Government I served to give freely and concede liberally to the wants of a new people whom we wished to reconcile as friends rather than irritate into enemies by resisting any demand which had the slightest semblance even of reason or justice. But however liberally inclined they might rest assured that I would never yield to pressure, when once convinced that the demands made were neither reasonable in themselves or consistant with justice. Even now, in reference to the village fire, it was not my intention to act in opposition to the advice of those Chiefs who had asked me to award suitable compensation, although I was still of opinion that the demands made were exorbitant, and that the origin of the fire could not be justly set down to me at all.

The Ponlyne retired for a short time to consult with other chiefs and afterwards came to tell me that 100 Rupees had been agreed upon as a sufficient sum to cover all losses and allay further dispute.

The money was then and there paid and accepted, but returned the next evening with an insolent intimation to the following effect.

"Pay the original demand or stand the consequences!"

There is mischief in all this; and if I could spare the money I would pay up at once and defeat one of the schemes of our Burmese oppositionists. As it is I am obliged to appear unconcerned; and having done all that reasonably lay in my power, with the approval of the chiefs, to come to a settlement, matters under this head must now be left to take care of themselves.

Yesterday I despatched messengers with presents and letters to the chiefs of *Saray* and Poogens or headmen of *Manwyne* and Manhleo. Ponlyne not only advised this course but took part in it by despatching two of his own Pawmynes with my messengers &c. &c.

Ponlyne is sober to-day and makes some shrewd observations as follows—The only effectual means by which the old trade can be revived between Burma and China depends upon a reconciliation of Chinese and Panthay interests in Yunan. He asks me to concentrate all my best efforts towards this one point in preference to all others.

He also begged I would speak well of him to the chiefs of the Shan States; and dispel any evil effects arising out of an impression that *he* was alone to blame for having conducted the British expedition so far on its journey.

I said that the English and all other Governments which had any interest in our present undertaking would owe Ponlyne a debt of gratitude if he faithfully carried out the promise which had bound him to our service at Bhamo.

He was flattered by this and other allusions to his personal merits, and informed me openly without any reserve that he was giving us his assistance at the present time in direct opposition to the wishes and injunctions of the Burmese Governor. The Tamon of Nanlyaw (the official who conveyed to him certain messages and letters from Bhamo) had not ceased, he said, from the time of his arrival to the time of his departure, to persuade and even order him in the name of the Governor to desert the Expedition and return with the Ponsee Saubwa to Bhamo: all that Burmans desired, he said, was that we might be lost or made away with so effectually as to prevent the possibility of our return to Burmese Territory.

I felt convinced, from the earnestness with which the Chief spoke and from my own general observation of facts, that he had in no way exaggerated the tenor of the instructions conveyed to him in the letters or messages from the Burmese Officials at Bhamo.

Those letters however were not forthcoming. They were only shewn to him, he said, and retained by the officials who brought them. He laughs at the shallowness of the pretext for requiring his return to Bhamo, and alludes to it only as another proof of the unscrupulous action of the Burmese Government in its endeavour to frustrate our purposes and progress.

He adds "you did wrong Ayeybyne in sending your "Burmese clerk with the letters and presents to Manwyne. "Dont you know that all Burmans have been against you "from the first? Even your own Burmese servants are not "to be trusted, as it is in their power to work infinite mischief "by misrepresentations which may seriously retard your "further advance."

The Burman clerk was sent by me as a check on the Kakhyen Pawmynes, who would otherwise have helped themselves to the presents and made distribution of them as they pleased without reference either to justice or my wishes.

I note the circumstance in my diary because Poulyne's remarks are an apt illustration of the readiness with which even Kakhyen instincts have grasped and are able to account for the petty designs of our obstructive Burmese associates at Bhamo.

14TH MARCH 1868.

The Messengers who were despatched with presents to Manwyne returned today and report that none of the presents have been accepted. The chiefs are not hostile, but they have been induced by evil report to doubt the character and intentions of the Expedition: I am advised by them to put myself in direct communication with the Shan Saubwa of Sanda.

The Saray Saubwa too has arrived, and called upon me to-day with a large following of Pawmynes and other Kakhyen attendants. He is respectable in manner and address, and sensible in his remarks when he makes any, but his curiosity in all our foreign appurtenances, guns, dress, saddlery and general equipment is too great for the present to admit of ordinary attention being given to mere matters of business!

---

§ *Ayeybyne*.—My Burmese title.

The Ponlyne is present and has altered his tone again to one of downright hostility. This is a sample of his delightful conversation.

"What do you intend to do now A'yeybyne? all are "against you, you cannot go back and the Shans will not "allow you to go forward. You *must* listen to me and "pay 500 Rupees on account of the fire and 600 Rupees "to be distributed *as I like* in presents, I speak for your "good. Shans Burmese and Chinese are all leagued against "you. For one man who would dare to assist you there "are hundreds who are ready to cut off your head. (Here "he suited the action to the word by holding an ima-"ginary head by imaginary hair in his left hand, and drawing "his right hand backwards and forwards with a sawing motion "at an imaginary neck.)

My reply is that I do not believe that the Chinese and Shans are against us.

The Chinese petty traders of Mandalay and Bhamo do not certainly wish us well; because they are afraid our success as an expedition will interfere with their own profits and livelihood.

The Shans will be our friends as soon as I can make them comprehend the true objects of our mission: all will yet find that we are present amongst them as friends, however much they may now fancy that we are separated by race, religion, or national interests.

Ponlyne "True; The Big Chinese are not against you, "but it will be difficult to overcome all the evil which Burmans "and Chinamen of Bhamo have done by misrepresentation; and "more especially by making it so apparent that the Burmese "Government is against you. Why did the Shans send "back your presents? They are ready to oppose you if you "go on. Lees-hee-ta-hee has received letters from Bhamo and "is determined to stop you. You ought to have given me "the money I asked for. The Panthays may be your friends; "but Lees-hee-ta-hee is very powerful, and is not only guided by "Burmese advice, but receives supplies in money and arms "from Bhamo. He visits that town sometimes, and his "mother resides there. The Panthays are his enemies; but

" he is strong enough to be independent and to altogether
" disregard them."

The Saray Saubwa listened to this conversation with great attention ; but as I spoke to Ponlyne in Burmese, he could only understand a portion of what was said.

The village fire question was again brought up. My object was to let the Saray Saubwa see that I had acted throughout in this matter in fairness and with reason.

He said that if I would come quickly to a settlement in this matter, he would conduct me by a direct Hill Route to Momein, without any necessity for entering Manwyne or the Sanda Shan States.

I said that the affair had already been settled *three times* with the approval of the Ponlyne and Ponsee Chiefs. The villagers were satisfied themselves, and only feigned disaffection because they were under Burmese influences. The Ponlyne Saubwa had already made me pay him 480 Rupees on account of mule hire; and not a fraction of that sum had been honestly distributed. What security was there now if I paid the present demand that other claims of the same kind would not at once be urged against me?

The chiefs all leave, but make their appearance again in full force at 7 p. m. The Ponlyne is spokesman. He commences by insisting on the payment of the balance of mule-hire from Sitkaw to Manwyne.

Yes, I say. If you will take me on to Manwyne according to my original agreement I am willing to pay this balance, although the Mule-men of our party have forfeited all honest claims by desertion and breach of contract.

The sum of 900 Rupees, which I have already paid in hard cash, is far in excess of the usual rates, and had the money actually reached the pockets of the Mule-men they would be more than compensated for their labours.

The conversation was then carried on as follows:—

Political Agent.—Where are the Mule-men? whom shall I pay the money to? Will you hold to your engagement of taking me to Manwyne if I *do* pay?

Ponlyne.—Dont talk of Manwyne; you cannot go there.

Political Agent.—Then why did you promise to take me there?

Ponlyne.—The Manhleo Poogen is your enemy and his people have conspired to murder you all.

Political Agent.—We are not afraid!

Ponlyne.—(Angrily) dont be afraid; but listen to *me*—you know as well as I do that Burmans, Chinese, and Shans are at present opposed to your proceeding.

Political Agent.—I am proceeding under the patronage and protection of the Burmese Government and have a Royal proclamation in my pocket to that effect.

Ponlyne.—(Angrily and in derision at my apparent want of gumption). True; but you know that the Burmese Government never intended that you should profit by it. We have all been secretly ordered to oppose you by every means; even to the extent of murder or assassination if other means failed to deter you from proceeding beyond Burmese Territory. I have remained your friend throughout. Three written summonses have reached me since I left Sitkaw to desert you and return to Bhamo.

Political Agent.—The Bhamo Governor cannot reasonably expect you to return until your duties are first fulfilled to the expedition.

Ponlyne.—Yes; the orders are to return at once. Your Burmese clerk has seen them. I have taken care to keep the last letter and will shew it to you.—*(Diary ends).*

120—(*a*). This written order was sent to me the same day by Ponlyne and after I had convinced myself that it was a genuine document—that it bore the seal of the Governor of Bhamo—and that it really did contain an order to the Kakhyen Chiefs to desert the expedition, and proceed themselves without delay to Bhamo; I delivered it to my Burmese clerk and directed him not to return it to Ponlyne without my express orders. My intention was to have obtained Ponlyne's permission to retain the document and exhibit it at some future time as one of the proofs of unfair dealing on the part of the Burmese Government. My plans were defeated by this very clerk, who himself turned traitor and deserted me a few days afterwards, under circumstances which verified Ponlyne's suspicion of bad faith amongst my own Burmese followers. The box of records of which he had charge remained in my possession but on examining its contents, the Governor's letter to Ponlyne was nowhere visible. I have not the slightest doubt that it was designedly removed or made away with, and it is not at all improbable that the desertion of the clerk was prompted as the readiest means of depriving me of this letter, and of avoiding on his part the responsibility of its loss. On our return from Momein I learned for a certainty that this same Burmese clerk, after he had deserted us at Ponsee, was well received by the Governor of Bhamo and treated with even kindness and familiarity. On reaching Mandalay he was immediately taken into the King's private employ and promoted to the position of a Royal detective: a reward no doubt for meritorious services whilst attached to the British Expedition!

120—(b). The probabilities are that he was in the pay of the Burmese Government and had leagued himself against us from the first. Such an admission suggests the question "why were men of this stamp employed by the leader of the expedition"? and I reply once for all, for the benefit of those who may never have resided at an Asiatic or more especially a Burmese Court, that no Burman subject in Upper Burma dares to have a will of his own as opposed to that of his Government. The indirect mode of reaching him offensively for slights or offences, which the Government could not possibly resent at the time of committal, are too numerous and too certain, both as regards himself and probably also his whole family, to obscure the consequences of free and independent action as opposed to Government wishes or policy. His training too from infancy has been so abject and servile that Government bondage becomes a second nature, and marks every man as an instrument to its own purposes either for good or evil.

120—(c). Under these circumstances the fidelity to our cause of any Burman dependent, who had once recognized the position and contrary action of his own Government as regarded ourselves, would have been much more a matter for surprise and bewilderment than the natural play of infidelity to which his training, his instincts, and possibly his (supposed) duties to his own Government must almost of necessity have inclined him.

120—(d). It is this unseen power in the hands of the Burmese Government that intensifies the difficulties of diplomatic contact, and gives it the vantage ground in all contests which are not at once reducible by honest straightforward plain speaking. A recourse to extraordinary argument or diplomatic subtleties of expression is fatal; for then the unseen powers come in as aids and outnumber or overmatch all honest opposition. A Burman diplomatist right or wrong concedes only to fear. This will continue to be his distinguishing characteristic ad infinitum or ad eternum!

Diary (continued) 14th March. The Saubwas take their leave, and we are some of us sullen, and perhaps a little dejected. Visions of treachery and throat-cutting as designed by Burman intrigue present themselves too palpably to certain imaginations to produce a healthy or pleasant train of ideas &c. &c.,

15TH MARCH.

I have determined to despatch messengers to Momein, and let the authorities there know the true state of our present situation. My messengers are the men who arrived lately from Momein and they are well provided with money and presents, and may be expected to return in about ten days. In the meantime the position here is one of disagreeable helplessness. I can neither advance nor retreat without sacrificing all our baggage. The Kakhyens have cut off the usual Rice supplies from Manwyne; and common necessaries are at a premium. The Ponlyne exults in having got me into a fix. I am obliged to put up for a time with his taunts and extortion, but he knows my mind.

He became furious last evening because I told him that we were not afraid of the murderous reports which predicted our speedy annihilation. He is evidently disheartened as well as discomfited at having failed to carry out with effect the mercenary purposes which first drew him into our meshes (or us into his) at Bhamo. He has been at times sanguine and earnest in his professions but always lukewarm and reserved in real action.

I have now the use of his Burmese and Kakhyen interpreter Moung Mo. He is a Cheoung Zau or Tamon of Hentha, a village on the Tahpen. The man wishes to serve me but is afraid at present to let it be openly known that he is one of my employees.

Manhleo is a Shan Township beyond Manwyne. The Poogen or Headman who is referred to by Ponlyne as our greatest enemy is known to be a man of great influence and authority in the Shan State of Sanda. About five years ago he attacked a Panthay Caravan and committed indiscriminate slaughter. The Panthays it is said have never been able to retaliate with effect. It is believed that the Poogen will not be superior to the attractions of presents and Rupees when he once realizes the fact that we have come as friends and that he has no real cause to regard us as enemies.

The fire question is at last settled. I bound myself to abide by the Saray Saubwa's decision; and he has advised me to pay 260 Rupees. This is not extortionate, but my reasons for holding out were imperative. The claim had at one time risen to 500. All parties are now satisfied, and it is thoroughly understood that the onus of further dissatisfaction, should any arise on this account, rests with the chiefs and not with me.

Notwithstanding this settlement I am warned at 9 P. M., both by Ponlyne and Saray to be on the alert during the night and look out for an attack, as a number of malcontents are known to have assembled and intend mischief.

The Saubwas declared that they had done all they could to quell the unruly feelings of these obstreperous Kakhyens but to no purpose. Finally they confess to having incited them to action with taunts and encouragement of rather a negative kind, which implied that they (the Saubwas) would look on from a distance and see how many of the attacking party fell to our Bullets and became victims to their own folly.

16TH MARCH.

I did not neglect the Saubwa's warning but we passed a quiet night and are still unmolested.

Threats of injury and molestation used to be unpleasant at first, but they naturally lose much of their effect as the various intimations of danger remain unfulfilled. The only anxiety they cause now is the evidence of secret opposition and enmity, instead of hearty friendship and good will, which would have been secured to us if freed from the trammels of Burman interference.

The Saray Saubwa has asked me how many mules I require, and promises to secure 80 animals without loss of time.

Wrote and despatched letters to the Manhleo Poogen and the Saubwa of Sanda. Enclosed also copies of Treaty with Burma, along with other general information which may assist in furthering our expeditionary prospects.

There is something suggestive in the fact that the Governor of Momein should have selected the Embassy or central route as the one by which to expect and assist our advance. This is the route by which all Political Missions to and from China have hitherto travelled, and it may be almost inferred from this fact that the object of the Burmese Officials at Bhamo, in denying us the Embassy route, was purposely contrived as a means of ignoring our Embassadorial character, and thereby detracting from the honorable notice, which the mission might otherwise have profited by in its travels beyond the Burmese Frontier.

One thing is pretty evident, and that is that to all appearances we have been consigned to a route which is most impracticable, and under Burman superintendence the most inhospitable of all known routes in existence.

Ponlyne has informed me this morning of his intention to return forthwith to his own Saubwaship. He asked for the balance of mule hire. I say that he has already received Rupees 630 irrespective of 300 Rupees paid as demurrage at Sitkaw. The engagement was that the mule-men hired at Sitkaw were to convey me as far as Manwyne. They had deserted and forfeited any balance of mule hire even supposing that such balance was a reality. The amount already paid is in excess of the average rate of hire between Sitkaw and Ponsee.

Nevertheless I tell the Saubwa that if he will make up his accounts they shall be duly considered and attended to. He left but returned shortly afterwards to say that all advances already made on account of mule hire ought to be regarded as *subsistence* only and not *hire*. An account was provided in which two hundred mules were charged for at the rate of 20 Rupees per mule.

I could only laugh at this barefaced attempt at imposition. Ponlyne looked grave and had recourse once more to the old system of intimidation (murder and stoppage of supplies.) When this failed he got up in a huff and swore that he would leave Ponsee instanter and consign us to certain destruction.

The Saray Saubwa is accompanied by a Chinese Interpreter who speaks the Kakhyen language. He reads and interprets my letters from Momein, and promises to be generally useful, but having friends at Bhamo he is not at present to be depended on. From his conversation and remarks he evidently believes our Expedition is a Military demonstration in favor of the Mussulman population of Yunan as opposed to Chinese interests every where.

17TH MARCH.

Difficulties increase. The Saubwas come early and pass several hours in small talk. The demand for old mule hire has risen from 20 to 25 Rupees per head. The Saubwas would be glad, they say, to come to any terms, but their followers have cast an avaricious eye on our cases, and would hail with delight a crisis or collision which would give them a pretext for the acquisition of loot.

I offer 500 Rupees in addition to the hire already paid if carriage is procured as far as Manwyne.

Chiefs.—You cannot go to Manwyne. The roads are guarded by armed men who have been sent to oppose you.

Political Agent.—This is not true. My own messengers travelled by this road a few days ago and saw no one.

Chiefs.—It is generally believed that you have got 16 Baskets of Rupees.

Political Agent.—This is mere idle report. The Shan Chiefs will protect me against robbers in search of loot.

Chiefs.—They will have nothing to say to you.

Political Agent.—You are wrong again. The Momein Authorities are already on my side. The Chief of *Manwyne* is anxious to receive me, but wishes first to consult with the Chiefs of *Sanda* and *Mynela*.

Chiefs.—True; but Lees-hee-ta-hee holds the passes at Mauphoo. He has sent orders to the Sanda Chiefs and told them on no account to let you pass. The Sanda Saubwa is in doubt and cannot act without offending the Panthays or Lees-hee-ta-hee. He is afraid of both.

Political Agent.—I shall await the reply of my letters to *Sanda* and *Momein*. The Panthays may be induced to send a guard to escort us through the passes at Mauphoo. I shall not advance beyond *Manwyne* without the full consent of all the Shan Chiefs. (The Chinese interpreter here suggested that I should write to Lees-hee-ta-hee who could be restrained to any extent in his conduct towards us by a threat of retaliation on his mother, who was a Burman and resided at Bhamo under the protection of the Burmese Government.)

This is very true but we are not Burmans. There is no doubt however that the Burmese Government, which considers itself privileged to visit the sins of the Father or other male or female relatives upon any number of present or succeeding generations and to the remotest degree of consanguinity (if necessary or rather expedient), has perfect control over Lees-hee-ta-hee, and can mould him at will into any course of action or inaction.

But whilst engaged in conversation alternately grave and humorous, a shot was fired from a house in the village which almost overhung our encampment, and whilst one bullet or slug was heard to whiz over the tent we were sitting in, another struck the head of a camp cot inside the tent. We were surprised, but no one believed that the firing was in earnest, until after the lapse of a few moments when a second shot was fired, and this time also the bullet whizzed close over the tent.

Ponlyne got up and vociferated like a madman. The Saray Chief was perplexed, but shewed no signs of alarm. The state of his feelings may be presumed, however, from the fact of his having informed me not five minutes after the firing that it was his intention to return forthwith to his own dominions, and take leave for ever of Ponsee and its uncertainties.

The shots hurt nobody and were traced to nobody. It is not improbable that Ponlyne may have innocently designed them as an aid to his pecuniary negotiation. The ruse was without effect. I promised to abide by my engagements faithfully and even liberally, but it was now evident to all that I would never submit to wrongful extortion.—*(Diary ends.)*

REPORT PARA: 121. But the inordinate length to which this report is growing and the endless matter which has still to be touched upon warn me that I must drop the diary system for a time, and confine myself to a more concise form of abridged narration.

122. True to his word the Saray Chief left Ponsee on the 18th, the day succeeding that on which the two shots had been fired into our camp. His message to me on leaving was that he would probably return as soon as I was relieved of the Ponlyne incubus. It was impossible he said to come to any fair settlement or make provision for our onward journey so long as Ponlyne himself or his rapacious Pawmynes possessed any influence in the conduct of our affairs.

123. On the same afternoon it was announced to me that Ponlyne too had left without any intimation of his intentions, and had taken away with him the only man upon whom I was dependent as an Interpreter in the Shan and Kakhyen languages. He had further appropriated and carried off all the presents which had been entrusted to him for delivery to the officials at Manwyne and Manhleo.

124. A Ponlyne Pawmyne who remained behind assured me the next day that the Ponlyne and Ponsee Chiefs had quarrelled violently, and that the latter had used threats which were dangerous and unmistakeable to Kakhyen comprehensions. Ponlyne had therefore deemed it prudent to beat a retreat and seek ease and safety within his own territory.

125. It was now time for the Ponsee Saubwa to come to the front and explain the new state of affairs which had deprived us of Ponlyne's aid, and made him (Ponsee) Chief Arbiter in our (exploration) destinies. Ponlyne had not only robbed me he said; but had interfered moreover with the rights of all concerned, by appropriating to his own purposes, the several advances which had been made on account of mule hire, as well as presents which were intended for general

distribution. Before his departure he had suggested and made arrangements that our supplies of provisions from Manwyne should be stopped; and that the Kakhyens of the neighbourhood should cease to hold any kind of communication with us.

126. The Ponlyne has been actuated throughout by an inordinate greed for Rupees. *Avarice* is his ruling passion. He had occasionally rendered valuable service, in the certainty (as he thought,) of securing an exorbitant recompense. But beyond this, there has never been any real sincerity in his feelings or actions. His object was to bleed me as effectually as he could; then throw me over at all risks and fall back on the Burmese officials at Bhamo, whose friendship could easily have been regained if only he could shew that we had been reduced to a state of inextricable difficulty.

127. But with all his avarice I feel positively convinced that, had Ponlyne been quite free from the ties or the fears of Burmese influences, he would have aided us to the last; not without haggling and extortion, but in a spirit which would have been above cowardly meanness and treacherous desertion.

128. Several days passed in the consideration of a variety of Plans, by which the *Saray* and *Ponsee* Saubwas had mutually engaged to afford us aid in pushing on towards our destination. The *Saray* Saubwa had made his appearance again on 21st March and brought letters addressed to himself and other Kakhyen Chiefs from the Governor of Momein, who solicited assistance in our cause and guaranteed to pay the expenses of our journey. Our prospects brightened. The chances of an onward move seemed in a fair way of being realized as the Saray Chief, under Panthay persuasion, had himself agreed to become our escort, and to provide the necessary requirements in porters and mule carriage. A settlement had been come to, as regarded mule hire past and present, and the Chief left Ponsee for Saray under promise to return in two days, and conduct us onward in triumph Manwyne.

129. It was unfortunate, however, that, he should at this particular time have despatched his Chinese Interpreter to Bhamo, under a plea of effecting a settlement of accounts between himself and some Chinese merchants of that place.

His real object was to learn the true state of affairs at Bhamo, and realize the consequences for good or evil, in which he might be involving himself by aiding an expedition which was being undertaken, to all appearances, in direct opposition to the wishes of the Burmese Government. The proofs which I was able to produce, in the King of Burma's written proclamation, and the letters* given to me by the Burmese Government previous to my departure from Mandalay, were as waste paper compared with facts as disclosed by Burmese officials themselves in our immediate neighbourhood. A hitch had certainly occurred somewhere, for the Saray Chief not only failed in his agreement to return to us with mule carriage in *two* days, but had not made any appearance himself or explained his absence or intentions up to the 29th March.

130. Early on the morning of that day it was known in our camp that two Chinamen from Bhamo, with a party of armed Burmese Soldiers, had passed through *Ponsee* and were making their way to Saray, distant only four miles from our own encampment. On the same evening the Saray Saubwa's Chinese writer arrived, and informed me, with well feigned regret, that his master was deeply concerned at having to state that he could no longer be bound to his agreement of providing carriage for our onward journey.

131. The Saray Chief appeared himself the next morning (30th), and assured me that with all the best intentions in the world he was precluded from serving us, in consequence of a dispute with the *Ponsee* Saubwa, who had quarrelled with him in particular, and threatened destruction to any neigh-

---

*The Burmese Government had given me two letters addressed in the name of Governor of Bhamo to the Panthay or Chinese authorities whom we might meet with during our exploration into Yunan. I did not make use of these letters beyond transmitting a copy of one of them from Bhamo to Momein, because I discovered, only when it was too late for remedy, that the letters merely purported to be sent by a Provincial Governor, instead of being addressed in the name of the Burmese Government. I do not think that it was ever the intention of the Government that we should proceed far enough to make personal delivery of either letter, neither did it calculate upon the probability of my forwarding on copies of the letters to pave the way to our own introduction and arrival within Panthay territory. I have elsewhere been led to express an opinion that the arrival of this letter at Momein afforded evidence of Burmese co-operation and incited the Panthays to the attack on Mauphoo. I now further incline to the belief that the secret mission from Mandalay to Yunan, which could not have been despatched till late in April, was intended, in one material respect, to counteract the use I had made of the Burmese letters and explain, as far as *we* were concerned, the mysterious working of Burmese State Policy.

bouring Chiefs who either interfered with us whilst in his territory or helped us to quit our encampment at Ponsee.

It was in vain that I proved to him that the Ponsee Saubwa had been working with him throughout, and that the agreement to provide mules had been shared in by Ponsee as well as by himself. Expostulation was useless. I recognized the Chief's difficulties, and he nodded an assent when I attributed them to private messages and secret instructions which had been sent to him from Bhamo.

132. But if the advent of these messages had been productive of difficulties in alienating the offices or the good will of the Saray chief, a much more serious evil threatened us, in the arrival of a party of fifty (50) armed Burmans under a Tsayay-daugyee (secretary) from Bhamo; who had been despatched, it was said, with the ostensible object of working certain silver mines on the part of the Burmese Government.

These far famed silver mines had been worked at fitful intervals for several generations past by Shans, Burmans and Chinese alike, until finally abandoned some years since when the precious ore had become exhausted beyond all hope of remunerative production.

133. Was it a *mere* coincidence that the Burmese Government, after so long an interval of tardy inaction, should have *now* sent an armed party of fifty men to renew mining operations at Ponsee, at the precise time of our own unfortunate detention within Ponsee bondage? From the time of its arrival the Tsayay-daugyee in charge never came himself or allowed any of his party to visit me. Everything was done to convince the Kakhyen mind that Burman and British interests conflicted, and that the party was hostile to us both in purpose **and** interests.

On one occasion proof was afforded of a bribe having been given by the Burmese Secretary to certain Kakhyens to induce them to steal and carry off our ponies.

Parties of three and four of the armed party were constantly being despatched into the Shan States with damnatory reports of our mission and intentions. The Tsayay-daugyee terrified the only Kakhyen interpreter we had with threats of Burman vengeance; and when other means failed to deprive me of his services he wrote to the Governor of Bhamo and framed charges which resulted in the imprisonment of the interpreter's wife (as security for the interpreter himself), pending his absence in the service of the expedition.

134. And what became of the silver mines? The whole project may justly be censured as a mere flimsy contrivance, under cover of which it was intended to watch our action at *Ponsee*, and defeat by an overwhelming preponderance every honest endeavour to force our exit and our interests beyond the limits of our Kakhyen encampment.

135. Their success was certain, had we not anticipated them by securing the support of the Panthay Government.

It only remains to be told that the mining or undermining operations of this shallow confederation naturally ceased with our own departure from Ponsee. Left as it was, without purpose or resources, the party return baffled and disheartened to Bhamo, to recount there the history of its own failures and the marvel (as it must certainly have appeared to them) of our success.

136. But the expedition is still at Ponsee. I must go back to the first week in April. The Saray Saubwa had left us in consequence of an alleged quarrel with the *Ponsee* Saubwa, who is said to have threatened the former with a lifelong enmity if he assisted us to leave his jurisdiction and Saubwaship. The *Ponsee* Saubwa had been our friend for one short week, or from the time the Ponlyne Chief left us until the arrival of the Burmese armed mining party at *Ponsee*. He was now our avowed enemy, and had openly conspired with neighbouring Chiefs and invited them to attend his sacrificial offerings to the minor deities, whose propitiation was a preparatory measure only to our own intended immolation.

137. The Saray Saubwa himself brought this fact to my notice and dwelt upon it in his own defence as evidence of the hostility which threatened not only ourselves but all who aided or befriended our cause. I told the Chief that he as well as the Chiefs of Ponlyne and Ponsee had guaranteed me safe conduct as far as Manwyne, that if evil befel the expedition the probabilities were that force would be despatched from Mandalay to afford assistance and seek redress. The old chief replied with a smile. "You will get no assistance

"from Burmans; they have repeatedly sent to tell me that you "are not to go on. If you persist we have been advised to "make away with you in any way we please, and the reward "offered is the appropriation of your property."

138. It will be remembered that the Ponlyne Chief on a former occasion spoke much in the same terms of the Burman influences by which he and other Kakhyen Chiefs had been instigated and even ordered to assume a state of enmity towards us. It is important and perhaps instructive to mark the course of that enmity, as instanced in the case of the Ponsee Chief's sudden hostile demonstration.

139. Some days had passed in assembling Chiefs and maturing means for an effectual onslought. The sacrificial buffaloe had been slaughtered and the usual revel was being kept up in a manner dear to Kakhyens as long as they are assured of a plentiful supply of Beef and Shamshoo. The night of the revel was no secret and we were well prepared for eventualities. Only two Chiefs of any note had joined *Ponsee*. His principal Pawmynes held aloof and rejected the conventional pound of flesh which had been sent to invite their attendance at the domestic festival. The Pawmynes had already signified to me their dissent from the Saubwa, and stigmatized his conduct as that of a madman and his actions as dangerous and beyond all control.

140. I assured them of passive resistance only on our part as long as the Saubwa confined himself to threats and demonstrations. If, however, an actual attack was made upon our position I should assume the offensive and the consequences might be disastrous.

It was necessary to deal somewhat in mysteries. A month's residence at Ponsee had caused our fame to be noised abroad as a people whose knowledge and powers exceded even that of Demons and Deities. Breach loading Rifles, Adam's and Colts Revolvers, Photographic apparatus, Bryant and May's Patent Vestas, which "ignite only on the box" and defy both wind and rain, had all helped to create and maintain a practicable belief in our connectionship with supernatural agencies.

141. On the day of the expected attack the Police escort had been drawn up under arms, and the opportunity was taken of entertaining our friends for the first time to the sound of a volley. The firing was good and the effect salutary and imme-

diate. The Pawmynes were alarmed and prayed that their houses might not be included in the general destruction which now seemed to await all who were foolish enough to belong to the number of our enemies. I simply referred them to their own Chief, who was the immediate cause of present misunderstanding. My own strong desire, I said, was to live on friendly and peaceable terms with all; but even Kakhyens must not expect that any number of Englishmen would ever quietly submit to an attack which threatened them with annihilation, without some effort to save themselves and retaliate on those who had forced them into hostility.

142. But Ponsee now had come to his senses. The morning's volley had penetrated the scene of his convivial rioting, and the pugnacious confederates cooled down very considerably under a formal introduction to fifty muskets which would all *go off*. It was soon hinted to me, as a preliminary to reconciliation, that the *Nats* had looked with disfavor on the Saubwa's intentions and failed to give him any encouragement in his evil designs against the expedition. (This was only to be expected as the *Meetway* or Nat-oracle was my friend and *in my pay*.)

My Pawmyne friends next intimated that they had come to terms with the refractory Saubwas, who were now anxious to be introduced to me and secure our friendship. This meant that I was expected to receive and give presents to the men who for a week past had been sitting in council against us and plotting our destruction.

143. Nevertheless I was prepared to secure peace for the present, at any cost, and pave the way to a better understanding for the future. It was difficult, however, to restrain a burst of either indignation or laughter when the Chiefs presented themselves, and I was openly asked to pay a money indemnity to which the *Ponsee* Saubwa had become liable for having cut down a Shan petty trader who had committed the crime of bringing supplies to our encampment!

Thus I was not only to receive with open arms those who had an hour before been conspiring against our lives, but to pay a heavy ransom for acts of hostility committed against ourselves, and which threatened, as they did, the very means of our existence!

Still there was nothing extraordinary in all this to the people we were dealing with. They could not be elevated in a day to a just appreciation of our principles, either in punishing crime or rewarding virtue. Nor when I exceeded even the limits of Christian charity, and submitted to the necessity or inclination of doing good to our revilers, did I calculate upon developing all at once in the Kakhyen intellect a proper appreciation of its own folly or of our magnanimity. The Chiefs tendered their friendship and received ours—and presents into the bargain. Their minds may not have grasped the soundness of a moral code which enjoins us to love our enemies and do good to those who despitefully use us, but certainly were not backward in seeking immediate application of the principle in their own case, and profiting by it, it may be hoped, in their future estimation of Christian friendship and British conciliation.

144. They left rejoicing; but the Ponsee chief sat silent and sheepish. Much had been urged on his account or in extenuation of his hostility towards us, because that hostility is said to have taken its rise in anger at my supposed neglect of him on the one hand and Ponlyne's rapacity on the other. But strange to say this animosity did not manifest itself in any very dangerous form until after the departure of Ponlyne; and until the arrival of the armed Burmese party from Bhamo. One of the buffaloes which was offered up as a propitiation for sins or as an enticement to the Gods to favor the means of our destruction was provided by this Burman party; and the official in charge, understanding well the purport of such a gift, had accepted the pound of flesh which was to bind his interests against us and array them on the side of the refractory Saubwa.

145. The demonstration had failed: we were masters of the position and the significance of this superiority was the more valuable because it rested on the acknowledgments of the Hill tribes that we lived under the auspices and protection of their own presiding Deities. Another source of satisfaction was that a reconciliation had been come to between the Chief and his Pawmynes. The latter had sided with me throughout, and it was at their instigation on a renewal of friendship that I was induced to pay Ponsee 100 Rs. to make up in some respects for our own supposed neglect and the loss sustained by *Ponlyne's* misappropriations.

146. The Saubwa in swearing friendship vowed that he had always regarded us as his friends and relations.

"Save me from my friends" I exclaimed laughingly "if "connectionship with them is supposed to carry with it the pri- "vilege of being assassinated at will to suit the love or the ca- "prices of the Saubwa's relatives!" The Saubwa grinned uncomfortably. I tried his temper still further by asking why he had omitted his new relations in the late distribution of Beef at Ponsee? He understood the allusion and left somewhat awkwardly but in good humour.

147. During the first few days of April matters were hopeful and exciting. The great drawback was that the Saubwa and Pawmynes had been reconciled only as regards conventionalities, but their interests jarred at once as soon as any reference was made to the affairs of the expedition or the means required for our further progress. On both sides there was an over zealous desire to be of service. The Pawmynes were willing to supply porters in any abundance. The Saubwa volunteered to go and procure mules. The object of either party was to secure to itself the whole, or as large a proportion as possible, of our valuable baggage. Privately the Saubwa advised me to have no dealings with the Pawmynes and described their intentions as evil and dishonest. To his face and to mine the Pawmynes accused the Saubwa of entertaining a design against our property. Each frustrated the other in any attempt to be useful. Their united or rather disunited friendship was thus rendered as unprofitable and futile as their joint enmity. I had paid 100 Rupees for a mere outward show of reconciliation which seemed only to have widened the breach of their greedy disunion.

148. Early on the morning of 6th (April) the Pawmynes brought a small crowd of Kakhyen coolies and asked for our boxes. I was ready to move I said but not without a previous understanding.

1. The Saubwa must be a consenting party to our proceeding.

2. The Pawmynes must convince me that they had sufficient men to carry the whole of our baggage at one time.

On the first point the Pawmynes said that the Saubwa was a nonentity and need not be consulted. On the 2nd that though the coolies were not all then present they would come in gradually in sufficient numbers to make the start that day. "Let them come I said and we will make arrangements for an immediate move." But they did not come. Overtures however were made to the Saubwa during the afternoon, and a temporary reconciliation was agreed to on the understanding that the Saubwa and his party should be privileged to carry forty mule-loads of our baggage.

149. The events of 7th April must be taken from my rough Journal of that date.

"This has been an eventful day. In promise big, in effect an abortion. Up at daylight. Tents struck and baggage arranged for an early start. The Saubwa and Pawmynes appear by turns but the coolies only begin to assemble at 8 A. M. The parties are still at logger-heads about the appropriation of baggage. Time and patience reduce matters to something like order, but there is still a strong party spirit at work. The opposite factions regard each other as implacable foes, both being intent only on loot and each vying with each other for the lion's share. The existence of dishonest intent is palpable in the barefaced rivalry which is displayed by either party in seizing upon the most *promising* packages, regardless of their weight or size. My small japanned tin cases bring on a crisis. The Saubwa's men have secured them and "Death's-Head" Pawmyne is in a fury of madness and drink. I have told off the escort into detached parties, to prevent the exit from camp of any baggage until all is in readiness for a start. The small circumference of our encampment is filled with armed Kakhyens. They are our porters and friends. It would be awkward in this scene of confusion if they turned out to be enemies! The Pawmyne seizes my gold dah which is in the hands of a Burman. Williams is standing near and wrenches it from both with a twist which was irresistible.

Pawmyne is at bay for an instant but rushes away excitedly and suddenly reappears with his slow match in a blaze. He advances to within three paces of me and is priming his piece preparatory to fire. Before I could move he had fired it into the air with a loud report. There is consternation for a moment but no immediate movement. All would have been quiet again but unfortunately an assistant surveyor with our party carried a Revolver, and fired it off in the air with unmeaning effort. Again tumult and confusion. The Kakhyens shew that they have no fight in them and fly in all directions as if panic stricken. There is no movement on our side. The Saubwa too is quiet and behaves with a just appreciation of events. He calls upon the Kakhyens not to fly, and at the same time makes us understand by word and gesture that the Pawmyne's anger has no reference to ourselves but is directed against him. Order is restored after a time and the coolies return to their respective loads.

I had taken the precaution of telling off the escort for the march in such a way that when the start was made each set of coolies would be under surveillance, with a chain of communication between the advance and rear guards. The japanned tin cases, or rather the coolies who were to carry them, were placed under the immediate supervision of armed followers and could not bolt without creating an alarm.

The precautions were disagreeable to both factions, and rather confounded their schemes of bolting with our baggage under the disguise of porters. Time wore on. It was noon. The coolies had arranged their loads and a start might even then have been made when it suddenly occurred to the Chiefs that being late that day we had better remain where we were and make an early start on the morrow.

This proposition was irresistible because it had come from the Saubwa and Pawmynes, whose disinclination to move without solid advantages to themselves or when they saw that their plans for wholesale robbery had been to some extent frustrated was an argument per se which it would have been in vain to oppose. I was therefore bound into acquiescence—a grievous disappointment to say the least of it, after six hours exposure to a hot sun and a month's captivity at Ponsee. Shall we start tomorrow?

That is the question and a very doubtful one too if we are allowed to judge by this morning's experiences of Kakhyen treachery and caprice &c. &c. &c."

150. We did not leave! The morning of the 8th was ushered in by a demand for money. Up till 9 A. M. not a cooly had presented himself in camp, at half past nine the Pawmynes appeared and informed me that as the Saubwa had withdrawn his support they could not assist me single-handed. I must consider their promise to forward me on to *Manwyne* as already at an end. Shortly afterwards the Saubwa came in person and laid the onus of our false start on the Pawmynes, who he again accused and condemned as men who were intent only on robbery and imposition.

151. I soon discovered the real source of mischief and miscarriage in the presence of the Nanlyaw Tamon, who had already held a conspicuous place in our Burmese experiences. The last trip he made to Ponsee had been undertaken with the express object of inducing the Ponlyne and Ponsee Saubwas to desert us on the Hills and return with him to Bhamo. His influence and advice had now been enlisted on the side of the Burmese armed party of miners at Ponsee; and having been successful on his former mission it is only reasonable to suppose that he would again be armed with authority to negotiate with the Chiefs and assist them to the utmost in our further discomfiture. He can hardly have been instrumental in the 'abortion' of 7th April; but I attribute our disappointment on the succeeding day to secret influences of which he (the Tamon) had become by tuition and intuition a most inflexible agent and promoter.

152. Happening to meet the man in our camp on the 8th I caused him to be arrested, and would henceforth have detained him as a spy and a prisoner; but the Pawmynes, with whom he was on particularly intimate terms, interceded so forcibly in his behalf that I was obliged to concede to their scruples rather than be subjected to interminable dispute or additional misunderstanding. The Tamon was dismissed with a warning not to cross our path again, and I have never seen or heard of him since.

153. At this juncture, or rather on 9th April, letters reached me from Momein, and I was informed therein that Tah-sa-kon, the Governor of that place, had taken the field in person and had resolved upon the extermination of Lees-hee-tahee who then held the passes and heights of Manphoo, situa-

ted half way between the Shan State of *Mynela* on the one side and the Chinese or rather Panthay town of Nantin on the other. This Mauphoo had been a place of considerable note during those days of commercial prosperity when, as the people themselves describe. "Trade flourished to such an extent that the caravan fires at the successive halting stations were never extinguished."

154. It is just matter for surprise that the Panthay Government had so long submitted to allow this stronghold, commanding as it did the high road between the Shan States and Momein, to remain in the occupation of a robber chieftain who utilized it indirectly in the cause of Burma, partly because it served as a buffer to the Panthays by closing the direct means of inroad to Bhamo, and partly on account of the convenient means it opened out to himself for safe retreat and successful Brigandage.

155. Lees-hee-ta-hee may have often been disturbed in his possessions at Mauphoo; but on no former occasion had the Governor of Momein so deliberately determined on securing his downfall. It had now been made apparent to him that Foreign interests were at stake, and his assistance was invoked in the cause of an expedition which promised once more to put the Province of Yunan into commerical intercourse with the old trading mart on the Irrawaddy at Bhamo. The letters which brought the intelligence of Tah-sa-kon's intended attack on Lees-hee-ta-hee warned me further not to advance beyond *Ponsee*, until further advices had reached us of a settlement of affairs at Mauphoo. Their arrival raised me at once to a position of superiority, from which advice and admonition could be the more readily exercised in still temporizing with our Kakhyen associates and rousing them betimes into active adherence.

156. On one point in particular it had become a vital consideration to give vent to firm and decided plain speaking. Kakhyens, Burmese and Shans alike had conceived extravagant ideas as to the value of our baggage; and frequently suggested by their behaviour and speech that the hope of some day making it their own was one of the indirect inducements which aided in our detention on the Ponsee Hills.

I began therefore at this time to proclaim on all sides that though we had cheerfully submitted to privations and delay in conciliating the Hill tribes and ingratiating ourselves into their favour and good will, they were not to suppose that this state of long suffering would continue for ever; or that we would patiently endure perpetual isolation. "Extremis malis extrema remedia." I told them that any extremities to which we might be reduced would not involve an abandonment of our baggage; for I did not intend that there should be anything left to abandon. All that we could not take away with us for want of carriage would be piled up en masse to set fire to, and blaze forth in flames the cause of our departure. If to their own disappointment in loosing this supposed source of wealth they added the probabilities of future demands in compensation for losses sustained at their hands or through their neglect, they would find small cause, I said, for after triumph in having alienated those who now had desired above all things to be considered their friends.

157. It will of course be understood that in making known to the Kakhyens the determination to destroy our property rather than allow it to fall into their own avaricious and unworthy possesion I had not desired to exhibit in myself or to illustrate to their detriment a Dog-in-the-manger principle, which would have been no less degrading to British character and civilization than ruinous perhaps to our safety and future interests. The Chief comprehended and believed what was said and I thought then, as I think now, that the practical removal from their minds of one grave temptation to err was a subject for general satisfaction, as it contributed in no small degree to generate in them, and probably also in ourselves, the elements of future confidence and mutual understanding.

158. The burden of their reply was as follows:—

" Do not altogether blame us (Kakhyens) for your mis-
" fortunes; we have always been in doubt how to act towards
" you on account of the many warnings we have received to
" withold assistance and oppose your progress. *Now* we
" know you; and will no longer attend to bad advice. You
" have been always kind to us and are a powerful people, only
" give us *Rupees* and we will procure carriage at once."

The gist of the speech is in the *Rupees*. Mules we did not then require, since our instructions from Momien negatived an advance until further advices.

On the whole the position, though surrounded by uncertainties, was nevertheless more hopeful and promising than it had hitherto been since our arrival at Ponsee.

There was a satisfaction in feeling that Burmese stratagem was so far on the decline as to force Kakhyens into an acknowledgement of our superiority and a tacit dependence on powers which could neither be trifled with with impunity or affronted without retaliation.

159. The determination to make a bon fire of our property and then seek reprisals at some future date when the expedition had returned to recount the history of its losses to its own Government, was a spec on the political horizon which even to Kakhyen comprehensions contained the elements of interminable enmity. On the other hand they could not help perceiving that under just treatment we were harmless as friends, and promised in our future intercourse as pioneers of trade to open up to them old sources of wealth and prosperity. Added to this the uniform kindness with which we requited all just services were valuable recommendations in themselves, and contrasted in a marked manner with the treatment to which they had hitherto been subjected in their dealings with other races.

It is not to be wondered at then that the delay at Ponsee has been productive of at least one great advantage, in having worked out for us an ascendancy in the Kakhyen mind, the importance of which will be manifested in time to come by the facilities of future action and intercourse in the same rich field of civilizing enterprise.

160. Nearly six weeks had elapsed since the desertion of my Chinese interpreter Moung Shwè Yah at Ponlyne. The manner of his flight, without cause or warning, at a time too when his services were of the utmost urgency to the well being of the expedition, was dastardly and inexcusable. Now in the middle of April I am all at once made aware of Moung Shwè Yah's whereabouts, and received a written explanation of the causes which are said to have necessitated his flight from Ponlyne. These may or may not be true and consistent

in themselves, but the sources from which my information comes are so divergent in themselves and at the same time mysteriously coincident as to invite special reference and examination.

161. On the evening of the 10th April, two Kakhyens arrived in camp, with letters which purported to have been written by Shwè Yah himself, from some halting place on his journey through the Shan states. The Kakhyens could give no consistent account of themselves, and contradicted each other in trifling matters of detail, without being able to state how long the letters had been in their possession, or from whom they had been received.

162. The next morning one of the Burmese armed mining Party stationed at Ponsee, brought me a letter from Moung Shwè Yah, which he said had been given to him 14 *days before*, at the house of the Kakhyen Saubwa of *Suddan*; but instead of bringing me the letter, he had taken it to Bhamo *by mistake*, and only *now* remembered that it was in his possession, and that it would be as well to deliver it.

The flight of Moung Shwè Yah, serious as it was at the time, had long since lapsed into comparative insignificance, and for five weeks or more he was a thing of the past and deservedly forgotten. *Now*, however, for a whole day previous to the delivery of his letters, Moung Shwè Yah was in every one's mouth; and the subject of his desertion and whereabouts was forced upon me, usque ad nauseam, by my Burmese followers, who had private friends amongst the Burmese armed mining party from Bhamo.

These reports I afterwards ascertained reached me under special Burmese instigation, and it was Burmese stratagem which planned that I should receive on the same date letters from Moung Shwè Yah himself, written on different dates from widely distant destinations and brought by directly opposite routes.

163. My solution of the affair is as follows:—

Moung Shwè Yah, after his shameful desertion at Ponsee, either returned direct to Mandalay to report progress or made his reports at Bhamo and awaited further orders from Mandalay. The King could not have heard with indifference that his own special Deputy with the expedition should have behaved towards us in a way which would compromise himself and lead to complications with his Government. Moung Shwè Yah too would have naturally heard, during his five weeks stay at Bhamo, that a diversion had been made in our favour by the Governor of Momein, and would be led to believe in the probabilities of our successful advance into China without Burman aid or in spite of Burman interference. The same reports would have reached Mandalay and have given rise to similar apprehensions. Hence I conceive arose the necessity of despatching stringent orders to correct so glaring an abuse, and remedy past defaults by a mock show of zeal and a superabundance of courteous deception.

164. Moung Shwè Yah had evidently only just started for Momein when the two letters reached me, and their arrival through a Burman source is accounted for by a sudden and excessive desire on the part of the Officials to carry out their master's instructions, and save his reputation by making it appear that Moung Shwè Yah had never wavered in his service to the expedition.

The clumsiness of this contrivance places it on a par of apparency with other shallow expedients of a similar kind, whenever patchwork is resorted to as a means covering and concealing an old and dirty piece of jobbery and wrong-doing.

165. On the 11th of April the *Choung Zan Moung Mo*, whom I had formerly used as a Kakhyen interpreter but was treacherously carried off by the Ponlyne Saubwa on the 18th of the preceding month, returned from Bhamo and offered me his services. I had formerly held out to Moung Mo every inducement in my power to make him disregard mere Burmese threats, and he had at length agreed to attach himself to the British expedition, if I would afford protection against the Burman Officer then in charge of the mining party at Ponsee: Moung-Mo pleaded that he had ceased to have any Official connectionship with the Burmese armed party or with the Government, and that his services were at my disposal for any appointment to which I might choose to appropriate them.

166. I have already said that Moung Mo was one of the village headmen who had been specially made over to me

by the Governor of Bhamo as Shan and Kakhyen interpreter to the expedition; and I had every right to claim his services from the date of our departure from Bhamo. But the Governor proved insincere in his promises; and Moung Mo only at length joined me under private pecuniary inducements, and after he had freed himself from Official restraints by breaking off all former connectionship with the Burmese Government.

His disinterested account of affairs at Bhamo at the time he joined me may be briefly recorded as illustrative of much that has already been said in describing the peculiarities of our present position on the Kakhyen Hills.

Moung Mo loquitur.

A. Orders have been received from Mandalay concerning the expedition. The officials are directed to be careful in their obstructiveness and not to allow the *Royal ears to be ashamed* by reports of shallow half measures. The King was displeased with the complaints which reached him of our detention at this place. The Ponlyne Saubwa has been written to and told *that he may take you* as far as Manwyne in accordance with his original agreement. His reply was that he would willingly have carried out his engagements from the first had he not been tampered with by Burmese Officials, and ordered to abandon the expedition almost before the journey had commenced. Having been led thereby to compromise himself with you he now positively refused to attend futher to the Governor's orders or to conduct the expedition on its journey to Manwyne.

B. The Governor was suprised and enraged at hearing that you had been able to despatch letters from Bhamo to Momein without the knowledge of any of his subordinate officials.

He threatened them with dismissal from Office as soon as the necessary reports could be made to Mandalay.

C. The idea of working the Silver mines was a sham from the commencement. The party came to Ponsee with 50 men and already orders have been given not to continue the work. The object of that party is to watch your proceedings, and prevent your progress by disseminating evil reports of your intentions. The Kakhyens are afraid to assist so long as they see amongst them an armed party of Burmans with orders not to allow you to enter the Shan States.

D. Do not go on to Manwyne until you hear again from the Panthay Governor at Momein or until they send to meet you. I hear all that goes on and I know that Lees-hee-ta-hee has sworn to oppose you if you attempt to cross into the Shan States. Not one of your party is to be *left* alive. Depend on what I say and mind do not leave, although the Kakhyens agree to conduct you, until you are assured all is safe.

E. Numbers of Shans and Burmese are anxious to accompany you as interpreters or in any other capacity, but they are afraid to do so. The Officials know that if they can prevent you getting an interpreter your position is comparatively a helpless and dependent one. Their object is to add to your difficulties in the hope of making them insurmountable.

F. When you sent a packet of letters a few days ago to be forwarded to Bhamo the Sayay dawgyee would not allow any Burman to take charge of it, although he communicated daily with Bhamo. Do not send letters at all, they will never reach their destination.

167. So much for the confessions of a man who, being a Burmese Official himself, has been behind the scenes from the commencement. He has since rendered me faithful services and I am indebted to him for subsequent disclosures which will be recorded in their proper place as my narative proceeds.

168. Moung Mo had no sooner established himself in my service than further light was thrown upon the subject of his confessions by the arrival of the Toung-mhoo of Bhamo, a man who it will be remembered acted as my guide from Bhamo to Sitkaw and then rendered us most valuable assistance.

This Official now informed me that he had been specially deputed to examine and report upon the practicability of continuing operations at the silver mines. If his opinion was unfavourable he was vested with authority to stop the work and order the withdrawal of the Burmese armed party.

Considering that the party had not at this time commenced to mine (for silver at least,) and that its original organization and equipment was that of soldiers and not of miners, it was rather premature to talk of relinquishing the undertaking and of withdrawing the party altogether from Ponsee. Another ridiculous phase of the affair (enough in itself to expose its mere equivocal character) was that the Toung-mhoo, according to his own confession, knew nothing of mining and less of silver ores, so that his opinion can really have had no practical or professional weight by which to decide on terminating so momentous an undertaking. As Moung Mo had already stated the whole affair was a snare and a delusion.

169. Although time has become a matter of very serious import, both as regards our detention at Ponsee and (to descend to trifles) the exceeding length of this laborious narrative, I must digress for a moment to note a hail-storm which occured on the 12th April.

The most observable feature of the storm, as apart from its violence, was that each hailstone was composed of a *flat* piece of clear ice with a small opaque nucleus at its centre. The pieces were of all shapes and some of them exceeded half an inch in breadth or diameter.

170. For several days subsequent to the hail storm heavy rain-clouds had been coming up from the South West, and showered down their contents in copious profusion, although North Easterly gusts still blew furiously at times over our camp as if to keep up an appearance of being the prevalent monsoon. But the rains had set in to a certainty, and apart from the inconveniences of very imperfect shelter it was a serious reflection to think that an expedition, which started under apparently fair auspices and with a reasonable conviction that its employment and occupation would not extend beyond the limits of a single dry season, should find now. whilst on the threshold only of its operations, that that season has passed and that further efficent progress would only be attainable (if attainable at all) by prosecuting exploration in the face of a South West monsoon.

171. On the 15th April messengers again arrived from Momein with a Chinese interpreter who spoke Burmese fluently. They did not bring letters but were privately des-

patched by the Governor to make further personal enquiry into our circumstances at Ponsee and the purposes of our mission to Momein.

The ordeal I was subjected to was not a pleasant one, as the deputation had arrived under a suspicion that the expedition had been despatched with sinister designs, and that we were mere political spies who were preparing the way for a vast army which was to follow and sweep all before it into British possession.

172. The messengers commenced fairly enough, by stating that they had been sent to clear up certain points touching the objects of the expedition. Doubts and contradictions had arisen, they said, in consequence of evil reports which had reached Momein both from Bhamo and Mandalay.

I submitted out of courtesy and for reasons of policy to a rigorous cross examination, although the members of the deputation were given to understand from the first that they could not expect me to treat with them as real accredited Agents, because they had failed to furnish me with written proofs in support of their right to act in an Official capacity.

173. In my subsequent conversations with this deputation I learned the following facts.

1. That the Governor of Momein had received letters from Bhamo in which he was warned against us, on the ground that we represented a formidable nation and that our real object was to side with the Chinese (our allies by Treaty) and drive the Mahomedan population out of Yunan.

2. That we were not Mahomedans but had always been aliens and foes to the Mahomedan race all over the world. Both statements were discredited it was said, in as much as they directly contradicted the first reports which had been sent from Bhamo to Lees-hee-ta-hee and which plainly gave out that we were foreigners and were allied in race to the Panthays (that is to say we were neither Burmese, Shans, nor Chinese), and that our object was to join with our Panthay friends in securing to the latter the full enjoyment of their Yunan possessions.

174. It is worthy of notice that the new doubt which it was intended to establish in the Panthay mind, relative to the evil purposes of our mission into Yunan, is coincident as regards

Ponsee. The man was in earnest and it was evident at the time that he had yielded to Panthay influences.

195. I replied encouragingly and with a small money douceur which sent him away in a state of joy and exultation. In a short time afterwards we had the satisfaction of seeing him actually start in company with his head Pawmyne on the road which led towards Manwyne, and the barometer of our hopes rose under an earnest expectation that the Saubwa's journey would be productive of results, and lead to a deliverance from our Ponsee imprisonment.

But day by day fresh evidences affirmed that our stay in Kakhyen-land had given rise to attachments which Kakhyens would cling to as a means of continuing our detention rather than assisting in (to them) a disadvantageous separation. That detention however had not as yet affected the actual progress of the expedition as regards its arrival at any given destination in Yunan. Had we descended earlier from the Hills into the Shan State of *Manwyne* we must still have been detained there or at some other Shan town as long as *Mauphoo* remained in the hands of *Lees-hee-ta-hee*.

It is with a feeling of proud satisfaction that I turn to our sojourn on the Kakhyen Hills, and prove the possibility of forming friendships with mountain tribes, many of whom (to our misfortune) had learned to love us so well that they would not exert themselves to aid our departure.

To quote from my Diary.

197. "Chiefs and people swarm in from distant villages, women and children are ever present with gifts of rice, tobacco, vegetables and beer."

"They testify, in a variety of unmistakable ways, that the Foreigner is a valuable acquisition to their Hills, and will ever be welcome as long as he behaves himself with moderation and treats *them* with justice. The general observation amongst our more distant visitors is. 'Why did you not 'come *our* way? We should then have been the recipients 'of favors which are so freely enjoyed by the inhabitants 'of Ponsee.'"

"It speaks well for Kakhyen instincts and intelligence that, although this hitherto despised people has never experienced anything save oppression and injustice at the hands of time with the arrival at Momein of the Burmese deputation, which passed through Ponsee on the 28th March, with the avowed object of hiring Chinese coolies to aid the working of the silver mines.

It seemed evident to me at the time that the men who formed that deputation were the bearers of letters or reports which were intended to interfere mischievously with our own progress. The fact that such letters reached Momein from a Burmese source at the time they did warrants the belief, though founded at first on conjecture, that Burman intrigue was still alive and would impede our objects long after they had ceased to have any connectionship with Burmese Territory.

It was at first hoped to ruin our enterprise by making common cause with the Chinese, and exciting their enmity under an impression that our interests were identical with those of the Panthay Government.

But when the Panthays replied with cordiality to my protests against Chinese intrigue, and had promised assistance with which we must have triumphed in spite of Burmese duplicity and opposition, it was time for Burmans to shift their ground of Political tactics and affirm, with a recklessness which did not even escape Panthay observation, that the expedition which was once proclaimed to have been got up in the Panthay cause had become exclusively Chinese and threatened destruction to Mahomedan Government in Yunan.

176 But why anticipate events at Momein? Burman intrigue was still with us at Ponsee. Up to as late a date as the 16th of April I was appealed to by the Saubwa to contradict a report which made it appear that we contemplated reprisals, and were about to retaliate on the Kakhyens for the delays and annoyances to which they had subjected us during our stay on their Hills.

The * *Red* Pawmyne affirmed most positively that the Burmese officer in charge of the armed mining party had personally told them that we were about to burn down the village and make an indiscriminate slaughter of its inhabitants. He spoke feelingly and begged I would not forget the numer-

---

* Pawmynes are an hereditary class of Kakhyen officials subordinate to the Saubwa. Those at Ponsee belonged to one family, the two principal members of which we had nicknamed for sake of distinction *Red Pawmyne* and *Deaths—Head Pawmyne.*

ous obligations I was under to himself and to the Kakhyens of the neighbourhood with whom I had always been on terms of friendly and social freedom. The man was excited and in earnest through more or less under the effects of liquor. I laughed at his misgivings and referred as *he* had done to past kindnesses as an earnest of future good understanding. There had been an excess of friendship on either side. Disputes may have occasionally arisen with the chiefs but they related to business only; and had resulted in an increase of good feeling as soon as the injurious influences which inspired them could either be explained or altogether removed. What cause now existed for supposing that our feelings had changed or that we contemplated a vicious retaliation on those whom it was still to our interest to conciliate and retain as friends?

177. The Pawmyne relented and confessed to a too hasty judgment. The apprehensions he had indulged in now appeared to him visionary and unfounded, but to us there was a stern reality in the fact that Burmese intrigue remained illimitable, and was still insatiably at work to inspire animosities of a very dangerous tendency.

178. I now approach a time in the History of the expedition when a multiplicity of considerations impelled me, in the cause of success and the interests of Government, to advise a reduction of our party and a return of some of its members to British Territory.

179. These considerations and the responsibilities attaching to them (and to myself in particular) for having consented to or encouraged in any degree a breaking up of the expedition, as compared with its original efficiency, are so fully disclosed in a series of letters (which will appear in their proper place in the appendix to this Report and in my Demi official letter to the Chief Commissioner dated Ponsee 27th April 1868) as to obviate the necessity of a separate Report or of further lengthened explanation. It is only by a close attention to facts as they stand disclosed in those letters, and at that particular period, that it is possible to appreciate the motives or make allowances for the necessities under which an extraordinary course of action may have been either suggested in practice or warranted in execution.

180. It will be generally admitted as a self evident fact that at the time I addressed the circular letter of 18th April to the members of the expedition the probabilities of an advance beyond the limits of Ponsee were both remote and uncertain.

The rains had set in and exploration surveys in a strictly engineering sense had ceased with the dry season and were virtually impracticable.

181. The funds at my disposal had become sensibly reduced by unforeseen delays both at Bhamo and Ponsee.

Five months had been named as the probable time during which the expedition was expected to complete its operations, *and for that period accordingly its funds had been apportioned*.

Four months had elapsed in comparative inaction but not without an expenditure which seemed to be multiplied and increased in an inverse ratio to expeditionary progression.

182. To have sent back for funds and have awaited for three months their arrival at Ponsee would have amounted to an assumption, which I had no right to make, that the expedition regarded neither time nor season and would prosecute its plans with indefinite limitation.

It would have become incumbent, under that assumption, not only to have provided against pecuniary deficiences but to have solicited a complete refitment or an entirely new organization on a scale commensurate with our altered conditions.

183. For it will be borne in mind that we were not free trevellers living alone on our zeal and dependent only on individual responsibilities. Our party numbered nearly a hundred Government servants and the change implied by waiting for funds or extending the scope of our enterprise over an illimitable period involved the consideration also of a corresponding provision not only in funds but in food, pay, clothing, medical stores and general requirements.

184. Such a consideration led moreover to the inevitable question: whether the refitment which the expedition must undergo could be carried out at *Ponsee*, or whether it was not rather desirable that we should return en masse to British Territory and make a new start under new auspices, more perfect preparation and a new dry season. The latter no doubt as an unpleasant alternative which could not be contemplated

even, as long as it appeared feasible by reducing our strength and economizing resources to devise a means towards the accomplishment of our object without incurring the odium of a primary failure, or risking the doubt of a renewal of our undertaking.

185. The determination I had come to, of remaining at Ponsee until a favourable opportunity offered of continuing the journey into Yunan, was based upon the immediate prospect of securing political and commercial advantages, which were so promisingly held out at the time by the friendly attitude and assurances of the Panthay Government.

But I had no means of forming a positive opinion as to the time which must elapse or the further delays which might be incurred in accomplishing the desired object. The rains had set in; and the Engineer's department was practically of no further use (as it then appeared to me) for purposes of either exploration or survey. My funds were low and a rigid regard to economy had become an unpleasant but imperative duty. There was no immediate prospect of a speedy delivery from present bondage. In fact it was very questionable, in certain points of view, whether the expedition had not already come to an abrupt termination. Such a contingency however had never been contemplated; on the contrary it had become a fixed resolve for some time past, apart from pecuniary considerations altogether, to abandon our baggage and trust for shelter to the resources of the country, rather than submit to failure and ruin the hope for a generation at least of all further successful efforts in so fair and cherished an enterprise.

186. But I deemed it a natural question enough, in determining the course which then seemed to me the most effective and desirable in serving the interests committed to my keeping, to propose what appeared to me under the circumstances an immaterial reduction in the strength of our party, and secure by so doing to those who remained a more certain prospect of eventual success than would otherwise have been available had the whole party been kept together according to its original composition.

187. It must not be supposed that in dispensing with Captain Williams' services I underrated the importance of engineering science as an essential aid to our expeditionary adventure; but it was reasonable, and I may add imperative

in the position I then found myself, to disregard all mere subsidiary accompaniments, and limit our enterprise to means which not only provided against *total* failure but held out in the distance a hopeful promise of complete success.

188. Both Captain Williams and Mr. Stewart, in electing to sever their connectionship with the expedition, were actuated by a conviction that they thereby added to the means of my progress. Their departure from Ponsee was a matter of convenience which originated with myself and for which I alone am held solely responsible.

189. I may be pardoned therefore for expressing a hope that the Chief Commissioner, as well as the Government of India, in reviewing the circumstances of the case as they are here set forth in this report (as well as in the correspondence which took place at Ponsee between myself and the members of the expedition during the month of April last) will approve of the measures which were necessarily adopted by me when a reduction in the strength of our party had become an indispensable expedient, which not only tended to our own advancement but conduced to the best interests and welfare of Government.

190. It must be obvious throughout that the onus of Captain Williams, return from Ponsee rests entirely with myself as leader of the expedition. It is a duty therefore I owe that officer to bring his conduct to notice and to suggest that his willingness to comply with my wishes, at a personal sacrifice to his own material interests, ought to secure for him the thanks of his departmental superiors and invite also the favorable notice of the Chief Commissioner of British Burma.

191. Captain Williams left Ponsee on 29th April.

On the 19th, the day after the issue of my circular letter of the 18th of the same month, news reached me of the fall of Mauphoo; and on the 20th I received letters from the Governor of Momein in which he informed me of his successes, and invited us to advance under the protection of the several Kakhyen and Shan Saubwas en route, whose co-operation was ensured as loyal subjects of the Panthay Government.

Assurances were also given of pecuniary support and I was even informed by the messengers who brought the Governor's letter that the mule-hire was a matter of secondary importance and that all expenses of this and every other kind would be borne by the Government as soon as we reached Panthay Territory.

192. But the original difficulty of procuring mule carriage was as prominent as ever. Mules were known to be in abundance everywhere, but their proprietors were restrained by a multitude of misgivings against hiring them for a purpose which would ensure Burmese enmity without gaining the approval of their own Shan superiors.

193. Another party of armed Burmese had passed through Ponsee on the 20th April, under the guidance of that arch-offender the Nanlyaw Tamon; and although their avowed object was said to be the collection of rice supplies for the party at Ponsee, their departure into the Shan States was full of ominous significance to those who had already realized the mischievous results of similar Burmese excursionists.

Happily however Burmese intrigue was beginning to wane.

It was inevitably succumbing to its own falsity and the realities of our conciliatory demeanour and continued moderation.

194. On the 22nd April the Ponsee Saubwa presented himself before me in penitential mood; and expatiated upon the obligations he was under for having been raised from a state of careless boy-hood into a masterly sense of his duties as a powerful and hereditary Kakhyen Saubwa.

Our kindness and consideration to himself and his people had produced a feeling of gratitude which he confessed it was impossible any longer to disregard. He had now brought himself, he said, into complete obedience to my advice, and for several day's past had rigidly abstained from drink and debauchery.

The English were his friends and had taught him to esteem himself as a ruler and chieftain. It was his duty to befriend us to the utmost of his power. He would proceed himself to Manwyne in conjunction with the Saray Saubwa, (who had already repaired to the same place) and concert measures which would at once relieve us from the irksome position which we had so long been placed in at his head quarters at cognate races on the plains, it should now so readily appreciate and esteem the exercise of disinterested kindness and friendly conciliation. It is not to be supposed that Kakhyens are free from certain evidences of degradation which are innate in savage instincts all over the world."

"The more prominent of these are treachery and ingratitude; but most of the races we have come in contact with possess nevertheless, in compensating abundance, many of the finer sensibilities of human nature, which raise them considerably above the supposed level of ordinary Hill Tribes in a state of semi-barbarous civilization. Numbers of Kakhyen women are in the habit of daily visiting our camp with small presents, for which they hope to receive a return in looking glasses, beads or other finery, which will immediately be converted into a means of female decoration."

"The women form in lines, and each clasps her neighbour in an embrace which is at once affectionate and provoking. The time spent in conversing with and observing these interesting groups is well repaid by the insight afforded into their domestic relations and the state of civilization they may have collectively attained to."

"My Interpreter Moung Mo is a rip and goes in strongly for love making. His object is to give us an opportunity of verifying his former statements relative to the freedom observed by Kakhyen maidens in their daily intercourse with their male admirers. If conversation is to be accepted as a test of manners some of the young ladies we were introduced to exhibited a freedom of speech and gesture which certainly went far to prove the easy and promiscuous state of relationship in which they stand towards the other sex."

"Promiscuous intercourse is the rule amongst Kakhyen lovers of every degree."

"Marriage rarely takes place until the parties have come to a very complete and practical understanding on the natural temperament and physical capabilities of those most concerned."

"An unmarried woman is but lightly esteemed until she is proved to be a child bearing reality. She then acquires a corresponding value in the matrimonial market; and a total revolution takes place in her former ideas of maiden morality.

The marriage code punishes unchastity with death and Kakhyen males are as jealous and unforgiving in a case of adultery as savagery and civilization can combine to make them."

"Moung Mo makes love for us all, and the conversation is animated and I dare say *naughty* if we could understand it all. It is a pardonable diversion perhaps in the interests of scientific research to herd even with savages and gain an insight into their habits and mode of thought by a temporary submission to forms of speech which most effectually smooth the way to native affections."

"After all it is only a game not for love but for beads. The women are sure to be the winners. There are insuperable obstacles to intimacy beyond a mere fanciful play of words and a complete absence of all fine sentiments."

198. But this is a digression. We must go back to the Ponsee Saubwa, who returned from Manwyne on 30th April with the news that certain of the Shan Chiefs have met in Council and awarded their consent to our progress through the States.

The Panthays were reported to be busy in collecting taxes and regulating assessments, consequent upon their recent successes, and the expulsion of Lees-hee-ta-hee from his stronghold at Mauphoo.

The Shans were described at this time, by the Saubwa, as delighted with their freedom from the Lees-hee-ta-hee incubus; they paid heavy exactions to this predatory Chief without being absolved from their dependency to the Panthay Government.

In either case the exactions were arbitrary; and the sensation of present relief is said to be satisfactory and complete. The Panthays were spoken of by all with whom I then held communication as kind and lenient masters, and their late success over the predatory band whose existence at Mauphoo implied the interception of all healthy communication between Burma and China, could not but be considered at the time, by all of us, as an event which was full of good omen to our own cause, and to future commercial intercourse with an enlightened Government in Yunan.

199. It was not however until the return of my Kakhyen messengers, with letters from the Governor of

Momein (on 5th May) that the least certainty existed of a speedy deliverance from Ponsee captivity. Lauloo, the Kakhyen who had first conveyed my letters from Bhamo to Momein, had just returned from Nantin, where he had remained for two days in the suite of the Governor of Momein, at a time when active operations were being carried on in the vicinity of Mauphoo.

Tah-sa-kon, the Governor, had determined upon coming himself as far as Sanda to meet the expedition, but the Shan Chiefs waited on him in deputation, and begged that they might be allowed to escort us themselves.

They knew what was meant by the march of a Panthay force through their respective territories, and understood that Tah-sa-kon's threat of proceeding to meet us in person was intended as a rebuke against dilatory action, as already manifested in their continued neglect to co-operate with his friends. The Chiefs guaranteed their assistance; and the Governor having conquered Mauphoo, and otherwise arranged for our advance through the Shan States, sent us word of his triumphs, and returned himself to his head quarters at *Momein*.

200. In accordance with their guarantee, the Shan Chiefs elected certain high officials from each of their States, and requested them to meet us at Ponsee with the means of transit from thence to Momein.

The deputies arrived at Ponsee on 18th May, and their manner and bearing at once declared them to be men of superior civilization and ready intelligence. Had the Shan Chiefs been left to follow the bent of their own inclinations, it is not improbable that recent political adversities and the discouragement to action imposed under the false tutelage of Burman and Chinese emissaries from Bhamo may have estranged them from us for a still further indefinite period and left us in a state of perpetual isolation.

201. But the kindred offices and congenial efforts of the Government of Momein intervened in our favor to expedite a union, and when the deputies from the Shan States arrived at Ponsee they professed a genuine sympathy in our undertaking, which at once compensated for all former shortcomings and proved that they had been produced by varying uncer-

tainties rather than engendered in a spirit of neglect or opposition.

The Deputies alluded to a feeling of regret, which was shared in, they said, by all Shan Chiefs, on account of their inability to hold intercourse or treat with me personally during our residence at Ponsee, but as a plea for neglect and dilatory inaction they let me understand that individual Chiefs were restricted in such matters and could only treat with Foreign Agents after all interested Saubwas had met in council and expressed a general assent to questions which concerned them as a collective confederacy.

Two days were spent in pleasant intercourse with the Shan Deputies; whilst effectual arrangements were being made for an immediate advance into the contiguous Shan States.

202. The Ponsee Saubwa and his Kakhyen Pawmynes were in constant attendance and in no way concealed from their Shan superiors the kindly regard which had won their goodwill and leagued us to them as allies.

This manifestation of Kakhyen good will was an incalculable advantage as an introduction to a race which had been taught at a distance to regard us as foes, but now learned by practical experiences at close quarters to estimate us as friends.

The Kakhyens expressed eternal devotion. They asked me significiantly not only to consider their hands at my service but their whole bodies; a figurative form of speech which meant a good deal I fancy in Kakhyen conceptions and was received with applause by the Shan Deputies. The Saubwa affirmed that our departure would be a source of regret not only to himself but to all his people. There was not a man or woman far or near within the limits of his Saubwaship who had not profited by our stay and whose houses did not testify to our liberality and friendship.

203. But so persistently unstable are Kakhyen impressions that in spite of all past manifestations of friendship and regard the very Pawmynes who had blessed us on the 10th had turned to anger and were implacable on the 11th.

So complete was the reversion and the severity of their threats that the Shans became terrified and we were in danger at one time of losing their services.

The 11th was fixed for our departure from Ponsee, and the start, which would have been made at a comparatively early hour, was delayed by a wrangling argument with the Kakhyen Pawmynes who deemed the opportunity a good one for urging at the last moment a multiplicity of demands, which were extravagant in their nature and defied all settlement. The most outrageous pleas were put forward as a means of extorting money or of aiding in our detention.

At one moment it was urged that some of our party had set up instruments (a Photographic Camera) in front of the chief Pawmyne's house and had thereby deliberately bewitched his family and household.

I was called upon to make restitution for such demoniacal practices.

Then the subject of mule-hire was brought forward and I was asked to make good the amount of Ponlyne's defalcations.

204. The last monstrosity was a demand of 2 Rupees per head for each mule which the Shan Deputies had just brought with them to convey us from Ponsee. Unless this was paid I was warned that no member of the Expedition would be allowed to leave our encampment. "Deaths-head" Pawmyne was in his most bullying and offensive mood. The Kakhyens about him were pertinacious because they saw a prospect of Rupees. The Shans naturally hesitated and were alarmed for their own safety. It was evident that decided steps must at once be taken by which to control at once the offensive action of the Kakhyen's and inspire confidence into the wavering Shans.

205. All reasonable endurance had come to an end. Turning to the Shan Deputies I forcibly asked them to get ready their mules and at the same time declared in the presence of the Pawmynes that it was my determination to start and that whoever opposed me would do it at his peril.

The Shans understood me and acted with vigor. The Kakhyens perceived an earnestness of intention which plainly told them that their plans were a failure. Their opposition had been nothing more than the brag and bluster of cowards. The Shans brought their mules and the Pawmynes relapsed as naturally as possible into a kindly state of inoffensive action and even friendly acquiescence.

206. But we did not get off till after mid-day. The actual fact of having made a start seemed like a dream too pleasant for reality.

The scene presented by a monotonous train of loaded mules, as they toiled with our baggage up the Eastern slope which led from Ponsee, would have been insignificant in itself without other improvised accompaniments which formed to the mind's eye an agreeable back ground of varied prospective.

I called out to a clerk in my employ who was about to return to Bhamo and exclaimed, perhaps with more enthusiasm than prudence.

"Look at this scene; describe it to the Governor at Bha-
" mo, and tell him that you saw us leave Ponsee under the
" patronage and protection of all the Chiefs of these Free
" Shan States. Tell him especially from me that the two
" months persecution which has followed us into the Hills has
" resulted only in *his* disgrace and our advantage. Say that
" the expedition started in a good and benevolent cause, and
" by God's help it has prospered and will prosper still in spite
" of all that Burmese man can do to frustrate it &c."

207. On leaving Ponsee a gradual descent for nearly four miles brought us to the foot of the larger spurs which slope down in irregular projections between the main ranges of the Tahpen valley. We are now on the minor undulations which merge, so to speak, into the vally of Sanda and the eye roams over a narrow expanse of plain, stretching away in an Easterly direction into space, but bounded laterally by two lofty parallel ridges of mountain, with an average intervening area of about 4 miles.

This valley is richly cultivated throughout, and presents an endless succession of villages which either skirt the bases of the high land on either side or nestle within clustering Bamboos on the margin of the Tahpen. The Tahpen itself has become a broad placid stream, with occsionally well defined banks and anon shelving reaches of shingle and sandbank, which limit its mid valley windings through the plain.

208. Several small villages are passed ere we reach the town of Manwyne, formerly a dependency of the Sanda Saubwaship but ceded to Mynetee as the dower of a Sanda Princess who married into the Mynetee family. The Town lies on the

right bank of the Tahpen, and is a succession of villages which are more or less detached or separated from each other by luxuriant enclosures of lofty bamboos. There is a mixed population of Shans and Chinese, who enjoy the semblance of a prosperity which is characteristic of all Shan communities which are fortunate enough to escape the notice of Foreign Governments.

209. Our own arrival at Manwyne was a disappointment. The mule-men with our baggage had preceded us on the march and on reaching the precincts of the Town had thrown down their loads in reckless confusion on a portion of the dry bed of the river at a very inhospitable distance from habitation or shelter. But this distance was no security against the curiosity of several hundreds of the inhabitants, who quickly formed a wall of humanity round any given spot where a European member of our party might choose to locate himself. Chinese have always been accounted a notorious nuisance in this respect from the time that Foreigners first gained a footing in the Celestial Empire, but I will back the Chinese Shans of the Sanda valley to be more eagerly uncouth and wondrously curious in their first acquaintanceship with European travellers than the rudest village community any where in Asia.

210. On the river's bank the human or inhuman blockade was so effectually maintained as to shut us out for a long time from every thing save our own individuality. When at length the officials had cleared a road to us and were induced, after considerable entreaty, to provide us quarters within a religious building adjoining the town, the curiosity nuisance had in no way abated. Neither Priests nor officials had power to check it. There was absolutely no relief, in eating—drinking —reading—writing—washing—dressing and undressing (to say nothing of other equally ordinary domestic arrangements) it was in vain to attempt privacy. The glaring curiosity of these unsatisfied gazers was a positive affliction, forgotten happily for a time though by no means terminated even in sleep.

211. On 13th May I visited the Dowager Saubwa who ruled at Manwyne as the widow of its late Chief. She is a portly, dignified old Lady of some 50 summers, evidently well

bred and of refined and even gentle manners. A friendly conversation ensued in which I entered fully into the cause and objects which had brought an English expedition into the Shan States and thanked the Saubwa-gadaw for the consideration which she had shewn us whilst at Ponsee, as well as for the kindly reception within her Manwyne territories.

Manwyne was so situated, I said, at the foot of the Kakhyen Hills on the direct highway to Momein as to make it a place of very considerable importance in the restoration of the old trade between Burma and S. W. China. In spite of all the drawbacks, caused by a comparative cessation of trade, the people of Manwyne, I was glad to see, were happy and prosperous. This shewed that they were well governed! To what an illimitable extent would their well-being be increased under a state of affairs which made *Manwyne* a central depôt for merchants and merchandize between two great and powerful Empires.

212. The Saubwa-gadaw replied with pleasant affability.

She was delighted to see us; regretted that she could not converse with us in our own language; hoped that we might succeed in our undertaking; begged that I would make effectual arrangements with the Governor of Momein for future tranquillization of the country; being only a woman she could not interfere in politics. Advises us to stay a whole year in the Shan States and not return until after the close of the rains. Hopes that we will not be offended at the rudeness of her people, whose curiosity in crowding round new comers cannot be controlled. People who travel through a new country with the object of opening out trade relations must be patient and forbearing &c. &c.

Would Dr. Anderson prescribe for her daughter (a nun) who had been for some time past in a delicate state of health? &c. &c. &c.

Tea was handed round during the conversation in true Chinese style, and the general impression which a novice would derive from the occasion and its surroundings would be that he had suddenly dropped from the Kakhyen Hills, *not* into the Shan States, but into veritable China.

214. The Saubwa-gadaw's house or Haw or Palace is situated in a central position within the town, and like all

other "Haws" is built on the Chinese plan of a succession of telescopic courtyards, four or five deep, which lead into each other by a communication of arched door ways, with an exterior wall surrounding the whole. The inmost recesses are devoted to the Saubwa's Harem (if he has one) and his family.

The penultimate forms his reception room for guests. The ante-penultimate may be used as a caravansery, stables, barracks or accommodation for attendants and menials.

215. The prosperity of the Shans of Manwyne was a perplexing fact for a long time, until explained by their comparative immunity from taxation at home or the arbitrary interference of an alien Government. It is a lawless unsettled community no doubt, and to a casual observer there is an apparent absence of any controling authority of sufficient force to keep in subjection the evil proclivities of an unchecked mob. Yet it is this very lawlessness amongst Shans (anomalous as it may appear) which produces order. Men live under an instinctive sense of right and wrong, and their individual interests are or seem to be a mutual guarantee against unneighbourly practices.

Religion too is by no means unrepresented, for although Shan Budhist Priests are lax and unorthodox when viewed from a Burmese stand point of Buddhism they nevertheless exercise a moral effect for good, as instanced in the large congregational attendances at their "Kyoungs," and the devotion to ceremonies which daily fills the alms-bowls of the Priesthood.

216. The population of Manwyne and its adjacent villages does not probably exceed 5,000 Souls. It fortunately escaped the desolation which a greater portion of the Shan States was subjected to at the outbreak of the Mahomedan rebellion in Yunan, and received too an accession to its population by becoming an asylum of refuge to those who were driven by poverty and invasion from the more disturbed districts on the Chinese frontier. Its proximity to a large productive area of the Kakhyen hills, and its own fertile resources in soil and climate have conduced to an almost superabundance of creature necessities, by which poverty and want have become unknown entities in a Manwyne existence.

217. The visit to the Saubwa-gadaw was an event which produced a decided improvement in our social relations with the Manwyne population. I had made her a few presents of cloths from amongst our stock, and return presents were forwarded in the shape of rice, fowls, eggs and a variety of Shan comestibles, which gave bulk and substantiality to our table luxuries without perhaps commending themselves in other respects either to the sight or palates of, even hungry, Europeans.

But the demeanour of the people had sensibly changed, and the mutual return of courtesies between ourselves and their Chief had placed us on a familiar and friendly footing with her dependents and subjects of every degree.

218. Our friends too, the Kakhyen Pawmynes of Ponsee, had accompanied us to Manwyne and were solicitous only about extorting promises of a speedy return to the scene of our late sojournment on their Hills. They volunteered their services and promised to meet us themselves on the return journey and provide full means of transit betweeen Manwyne and Bhamo.

219. These new evidences of hospitality and welcome formed a bright contrast to the monotonous void of three months inaction at *Bhamo* and *Ponsee*.

The 14th May was the day fixed upon for the march from Manwyne, and much argument and consultation had been carried on between the respective deputies of Sanda and Mynela as to the route which the expedition should now proceed by. A large portion of the Mynela district lay on the left bank of the Tahpen immediately opposite to Manwyne. The Sanda States occupied the whole extent of the right bank from Manwyne to beyond the town of Sanda itself. A small saving in distance might have been effected by crossing the river at once at Manwyne and proceeding direct to Mynela along its left bank, but this would have cut us off from all communication with Sanda and have defeated one of the express objects I had in view of treating personally with all the principal Saubwas on the route towards Yunan.

When therefore I was appealed to by the contending parties to decide between them as to the route to be taken on leaving Manwyne I affected indifference and merely stipulated that we should enter Sanda. The Sanda officials accordingly triumphed and their victory would have been a simple one as regarded ourselves had it not roused the jealousy of Mynela and led indirectly to resentment and hostility.

220. Some 3,000 men, women, and children were assembled on the outskirts of Manwyne to witness our departure. The Camp was crowded to excess with all the élite and fashion of a mixed Shan, Chinese and Kakhyen community. The population was well dressed and the female portion of all races scrupulously neat and cleanly in their attire. Men wore loose jackets and trousers of dark blue, but the women enjoyed a pleasant variety of gaudy dress coloring. Their jackets were white or pale green slashed with red at the sleeves and collar. The skirt is dark blue with a variegated silk embroidery, a foot in depth, from the knee downwards. Fanciful leggings or gaiters of rich design cover the ancles. The tout ensemble was rich and effective. Exception must be made in the case of the Chinese, who, as a rule, wore patched clothes and evinced signs rather of penurious thrift than of absolute poverty. The elaborate head dresses of the women, and their cramped apologies or substitutes for feet proved equally attractive to novices on account of certain exaggerated proportions from head to heel at either extremity.

221. Several Shan Officials led the way, mounted on ponies with huge saddles of red cloth and padded coverlets, which raised them at least a foot above their animal's backs. The route lay in a North Easterly direction along the right bank of the Tahpen. Road making had only been attempted at rare intervals, in places where a bridge was indicated rather than a roadway. When such a bridge occurs it is built of long slabs of granite, which are laid laterally side by side so as to form a semicircular arch over the channel to be crossed. So true is the semicircle in most instances that it is impossible to resist an inclination to look down for the other half which is below high water mark and exists rather in imagination than reality.

222. At a distance of a mile from Manwyne we passed the Village of *Onlen* or *Nyounglen*, which belongs to the once notoriously hostile Poogen or Chief of Manhleo. Opposition is a thing of the past, for the villagers now turned out in hundreds and evinced a hearty interest in our undertaking by

spontaneous expressions of welcome and good cheer so manifestly genuine as to invite in ourselves an indescribable thrill of silent ecstacy.

223. But anon there is cause for annoyance and disappointment, for it suddenly became evident, during one portion of the march, that the left bank of the river was occupied by an armed party of Shans whose gesticulations and shouts were unmistakeably hostile. At first I was inclined to believe that the demonstration was unmeaning, until it became evident that the Shans of our own party had commenced to indulge in return manifestations of threat and defiance.

224. We were proceeding along a portion of the river's bank, which was high and precipitous. The opposite shore was a wide reach of sand bank along which the hostile party consisting of about 50 armed Shans, were keeping pace with us in a state of furious excitement. Their actions can have been intended to be demonstrative only, otherwise it was an easy matter, had the party been really intent on active opposition, to have crossed at any of the river fords previous to our own arrival and have disputed our advance.

As it was when they found that gesticulation was of no avail in retarding our progress a shot was fired, and a spent bullet whizzed at an uncomfortable proximity to my Pony's head, which caused *him* to plunge and *me* to "duck"! The "Shan" shouted and throught I was hit. Two more shots were fired and the demonstration was at an end.

225. But being a short distance in advance of our carriage my proposition was to halt until it came up and make all secure against further attack. But the Shan deputies with our party begged me to go on and treat the Dacoit party with the contempt it deserved. They could do us no harm it was said and would never dare to cross over to the Sanda side of the Tahpen river. The deputies were right and we went on as if nothing had occured. Our foes were satisfied with a mere demonstration and evidently deemed it imprudent to come to close quarters.

226. A Mynela Deputy by name Kingen was with us at the time of the hostile demonstration, and I have reason to believe that he secretly abetted it.

As soon as it was over he crossed the river and rode off alone in the direction of our supposed enemies.

But no satisfactory explanation was ever given of this imbecile opposition, beyond the fact that the malcontents belonged to a disturbed portion of the Mynela district which for many years past had declared its independence and boasted of its allegiance to no Chief or Government.

227. The Sanda Deputies treated the matter from first to last as a mere empty demonstration which was intended to punish our want of discrimination in having selected the Sanda Route in preference to that which led through Mynela. The true facts of the case will probably never be known, for I failed to ascertain them after our return to Manwyne, when we passed over the very portion of the disturbed Mynela District in which the demonstration had been originally got up.

228. The whole day's march, from Manwyne to Sanda, disclosed fresh scenes of pleasurable interest. As apart from the personal gratification of a Shan ovation, or the temporary excitement of a hostile attack, the monotonous grandeur of this endless valley, with its sublime ridges towering up on either side to a height of five thousand feet, and running in straight parallels into boundless space, was in itself a source of infinite admiration. But to this estimate of its interest and its sublimity I may add the fact that the whole valley area teemed with villages, and was alive with a population which had laid out and conjoined every available acre into one vast garden of fertility and wealth.

229. Half way between Manwyne and Sanda is the Chinese Town of Karahokha, which is important as a central mart at which periodical fairs or market days are held in common with all other towns in the northern Shan States. The Bazaar is a mere broad road which is flanked on either side by Chinese shops, but on market days the intervening space, or rather the whole road-way, is occupied by a succession of stalls in which butchers, bakers, druggists, and jacks of all trade do a thriving business.

With the exception of buttons, needles, and an occasional piece of woollen-cloth I did not notice that British Manufactures were represented here or at any of the bazaars or fairs within the Shan States.

230. The interest of the fair at Karahokha is centered in the fact of its being essentially Chinese in the midst of a large Shan population. A market was being held on the day of our arrival, and the concourse of people was so great and their curiosity so intense that our Shan friends advised us not to go through the Town but simply to skirt it on one side and avoid all chance of collision with those who, as the sun declined, would have indulged to the full in Chinese stimulants.

231. This never ending supply of strong drinks throughout the States we have traversed bordering on China ought, according to ordinary ideas of political or social economy, to be the bane and scourge of any community of people in the world subjected to its influences. But somehow or other it does not interfere with the well-being or prosperity of Shans and Kakhyens, who exist and thrive in a figurative sea of beer and shamshoo.

Five cash or the hundreth part of a rupee is sufficient to purchase a small tea cup full of a spirit which approaches in taste and potency to Scotch whiskey. This is drunk freely and probably to excess, though it must be supposed to be "the cup which cheers but not inebriates" as little interruption is caused thereby to trade or to the general tranquillity of a Shan market day.

$231\frac{1}{2}$. In our case however we were always advised not to visit a fair during the afternoon, when the bulk of those present were already supposed to have imbibed their modicum of *solvents,* and any latent animosity towards strangers would then if ever be very readily evoked. Caution was required, *not* as regards the mass of the people, for the "In vino veritas" principle would I believe have been verified to our advantage, but a few evilly disposed emissaries always lurked in our train, and with them a collision whilst in liquor was a contingency at all times imminent.

232. Karahokha was passed without incident or accident, and the road, leaving for a time it's mid-valley course, turned away northwards and brought us to the foot of one of the many projecting spurs which abut from the counterslope of the western range. The peculiarity of these spurs is that they are for the most part barren whilst the main ridges are clothed with a dense vegetation.

The soil is a bright red which can be discerned for a distance of several miles. At present these spurs would seem to belong only to the western range, though their former prolongation and connectionship with the eastern range is often traceable at certain corresponding points where the red soil crops up in unmistakable relationship.

233. Our route is continued in a northerly direction to Sanda itself, which lies at the foot or rather occupies the base of one of these red spur-projections and is close within the border of the main north western range.

Sanda, or as it has hitherto been known in our maps *Santafoo* (having the designate termination of a second rate Chinese City,) is poor and insignificant both in appearance and reality.

There are neither towers or temples, or minarets or pagodas or any of the outward evidences which proclaim the approaches to a provincial capital. The remains of an old defensive brickwall may still be traced round a portion of the suburbs, but within its enclosure all is ruin and dilapidation.

234. In 1863 Sanda was subjected to a Panthay irruption. The Town was first gutted by Panthay soldiers and subsequently handed over as a prize to any number of Kakhyen adherents who professed to favor the Panthay cause.

The town contains perhaps 800 houses with a population amounting to about six thousand souls. The apparent poverty of its dejected inhabitants is a sad contrast to the independent bearing of the Shans of Manwyne. Fire and sword have been ruthlessly applied. Their most lasting evils are in the check which has been given to private thrift and national industry. Nothing has been done during five years of retrogression to repair former losses or provide for further resettlement. The houses represent ruins. The kyoungs or monasteries are mere bamboo erections of the most flimsy construction. All bears evidence of doubts and uncertainty, the origin of which may be traced to Yunan and the evil effects of a neighbouring rebellion.

235. On the 15th of May I visited the Sanda Saubwa in company with Dr. Anderson and Captain Bowers. We were conducted from our Phoongyee house residence to the palace of the Chief by a retinue which comprised the elite

of the Sanda Officials. The approach to the *Haw* is somewhat imposing and consists of a triple arched gateway with one principal and two side entrances, the architecture throughout being essentially Chinese. We passed through two court yards which communicated with each other by roofed arch ways and side enclosures. Our reception took place in the vestibule of a penultimate building which led directly into the the Saubwa's private apartments. Here we found a fixed number of high backed arm-chairs, Chinese in form and therefore unaccommodating and impossible in construction. The open space or court yard in front of the vestibule was crowded with respectable visitors, who had been invited to the interview and note our communications with the Chief of Sanda.

236. The Saubwa made his appearance in due course and placed himself upon one of the impossible seats which was nearest the door by which he had entered.

He was evidently unaccustomed to ceremonial visits and glared at us for some time in impotent idiocy.

I was obliged to break ground by a few introductory remarks of greeting and salutation to which the Chief replied by vacant noddings.

But his Prime Minister or Factotum, a steady clearheaded old Shan who was evidently recognized as the Saubwa's duplicate, took up the conversation and responded to me with a genial good sense which was both pleasant and encouraging.

237. After I had generally explained the objects of the expedition and the benefits which would be realized by a reopening of the old Trade route between Burma and China the mouth piece informed me, with a good deal of earnestness, that the Saubwa himself with his subjects welcomed us heartily and sympathized in our undertaking. If our efforts succeeded we should be hailed as deliverers and saluted everywhere with shouts of "*Thadoo*."

The immediate cause of present anxiety did not depend so much, he said, on Trade stagnation as upon the uncertainties produced by the war in Yunan. Owing to the various phases of that conflict and the varying successes of Chinese and Mahomedans the Shan States had been subjected to hostile irruptions three times during a period of twelve years and its towns laid waste by fire and pillage. There was neither security for the present or hope for the future. The one thing looked forward to was further disturbance and probably further invasion.

238. In reply I said that one of the principal objects of our mission was to ascertain the present causes of disturbance, and exercise our power as a friendly neutral in the restoration of order and the conciliation, if possible, of some, at least, of the contending interests. The unsatisfactory state of affairs in Yunan had attracted the notice of the British Government and had sensibly affected British Merchandize. Our interests in China were represented by a British Minister who resided permanently at the Court of Pekin. It was not impossible, in course of time when our acquaintance with Yunan had been more clearly developed, that representations would be addressed to the Imperial Government and an effort made towards the restoration of trade.

The Panthays had ruled for 12 years in Yunan, and if by any legitimate interference on the part of other Governments their sovereignty was confirmed and recognized at Pekin, the Province would be tranquillized and the Shans restored to former prosperity. I too would strive to secure these advantages and favour the cause of conciliation and commerce. The Panthays were known to be interested in my visit and would listen to propositions which held out so many promising conditions to themselves and secured the possession of their recent acquisitions.

239. The whole of this reply was listened to with an attentive interest which now and then exploded in murmurs of assent and approbation.

But I had not finished. My next effort was to let the Saubwa and his Officials thoroughly comprehend our present circumstances and the position we were placed in as regarded themselves.

Having come to them as friends we did not feel satisfied, I said, with the idea that Shan support and assistance had been reluctantly proffered under a compulsory requisition on the part of the Panthay Government.

The object which the British Government had at heart, in seeking to resuscitate trade with China through the Shan

States, could only be accomplished with Shan assistance. The Shans must come forward boldly of their own free will, and believe that they are serving their own best interests in seconding the efforts now made by us on their behalf.

The Saubwa and his people must not believe mischievous rumours which ascribed evil intentions to our mission and a desire on the part of the British Government to extend its dominions in the direction of the Shan States.

Shans were shrewd and could reason for themselves. Let them be guided by facts and give credence to nothing derogatory to our Mission until duly assured by the evidence of their senses.

We too had numerous Shan subjects in British territory. They had emigrated in great part from their own free states and settled down in a country where they found security for their persons and protection against injustice.

It was not uncommon, I said, for the Shan Saubwa of any state adjoining British Burma to make an application to place himself and his territory under British rule.

Several Saubwas had even applied in this manner to the British Government, and solicited its interference to enable them to throw off their subjection to Burma. With our permission they promised to wage a war against Upper Burma and deliver over the country to British rule.

The Government had replied that it did not require an extension of territory. That as friends of the King of Burma we were bound to respect his rights and abstain from acts which might tend to foment strife or discord within his dominions.

The Saubwa and his people, if they believed in these instances of our moderation and forbearance, would learn thereby that we were more concerned in the observation of Treaty rights than the mere gratification of territorial aggrandizement.

This led to the subject of our treaties with Burma, and I spoke at length on that portion of them which related to the amount of export duties on goods passing between British Territory and the Provinces beyond Upper Burma.

240. The conversation had taken a decidedly political turn. There was a satisfaction in feeling that what I said had

an interest for the people and was credited in spite of the damning reports which had preceded the expedition into the Shan States.

The most encouraging assurances were given of friendship and co-operation. I was even asked in a tone of confidence, which was almost too genuine to have been assumed for the occasion, to use my influence with the Governor of Momein and prevent if possible another Panthay invasion.

241. The good effects of this visit were soon manifested in a multiplicity of minute attentions which had hitherto been either negligently overlooked or purposely disregarded. Since our arrival at Sanda the Saubwa had sent abundant supplies of rice and firewood for our whole party. They were now supplemented by delicacies which comprised ducks, fowls, bacon, eggs, and dried salt-geese, the latter quite equal in taste and flavour to the best English cured bacon.

During the evening the old Minister or Medium also made his appearance with other Shan Officials, and passed the night in friendly conversation. I now learned by their apologies that the Saubwa has ever been singular as a man of few words. His tact and ability however, in other respects (and possibly also in the art of *thinking*) were very favorably reported on and gained him the confidence and esteem of his people.

242. I was agreeably surprised to find the next morning, (16th May) whilst making provision for a start from Sanda, that a deputation had arrived with presents from the Saubwa.

I had given him a few cloths and carpets which were esteemed of great value on account of their rarity in the Shan States. In return the Saubwa sent me 3 handsome Shan pillows, one for each member of the expedition, and a very dandy satin cover-let or counterpane of Shan manufacture which I was told was intended for my personal use at Momein, where I should find the climate cold and inhospitable as compared with that of the valley of Sanda.

243. A very extraordinary message accompanied these presents. I was asked to adopt the Saubwa's grandson a boy who was recommended to my protection as being next heir to the Saubwaship.

It was at the same time notified that certain Shan Astrologers, who had been consulted during the previous night, had given out as the result of their divination that the young heir to the Saubwaship would neither prosper in health or acquire social position within his own estates unless I consented to consider him my son. The earnestness of the request was matter for surprise, and could only be accounted for by making full allowance for the reverent credulity with which charms and spiritualism are everywhere regarded throughout the Shan States.

244. Shortly afterwards it was casually made known, as if the result of an after thought, that the Saubwa himself would visit me before we started and I had only time to make a few hasty preparations for his reception when his arrival was announced. He was accompanied by a goodly retinue of attendants and two large umbrellas one of red silk with a heavy broad curtain and the other a veritable gold Chatta of Burmese manufacture.

I received the Saubwa at the door of our monastery and rather took him by suprise by seizing his hand and leading him in my grasp towards a seat specially prepared for him. The object of the Saubwa's visit was one which naturally called for a display of diplomatic reserve. But in the present instance his anxiety and impatience were so great that almost before he would allow himself to be seated or exchange the usual salutation of greeting with the members of the expedition he had introduced me to his grandson and begged, as if his life depended on it, that I would adopt him into my family and treat him as my own child.

At the same time another silk counterpane and a long silver pipe were presented to me in the young Saubwa's name, and I was urged to bear in mind that their use was intended to recall old memories and make the child's interests identical with my own.

245. It is difficult to convey a correct idea of the earnest and importunate manner in which the request for the adoption was urged upon my notice. The fates had been consulted and some sage astrologer, strong in the Shan cause and with an intuitive foresight into a political Shan future, was led to predict that the well-being of the heir presumptive

to the State of Sanda depended on a close family alliance with a representative of the British Government. The old Chief was sensibly affected by the willing courtesy with which I accepted the charge entrusted to me, but the youthful scion was shy and would not be reconciled to his new connectionship. I made a few return presents and the interview passed off with becoming cordiality.

246. It was arranged by the Saubwa that our departure from Sanda should be honorably signalized by a public demonstration. The route we were to take was made to pass the Saubwa's palace, and as our procession advanced up the street leading to the front entrance a salute was fired and a flourish of trumpets heralded our approach. We dismounted for a final hand-shaking with the Saubwa and I took the opportunity of giving my newly adopted son a few shining four anna pieces which won his affections and probably made him my friend for life.

247. If to wear Rupees is a sign of livery it may be truly said that a large number of influential Shans, Phoongyees included, have already donned Her Majesty's uniform. There is a greed on the part of all Shan swells for four anna pieces and the coveted possession is no sooner gained than Her Majesty's coin is turned into finery and becomes an article of ornamental equipment. The novitiates of the Monasteries and even the Priests are the supreme leaders of fashion and indulge in a mass of varied ornamentation which would prove a study to even Buddhist ritualists.

248. But to return to the Saubwa, it is due to him to say that he was no longer afflicted with nervous incapacity and had lapsed into a state of positive cheerfulness. He grinned with delight at my recognition of his grandson whom he nursed and tended with almost silly devotion. We parted with many expressions of mutual good will. The trumpeters in advance heralded us onward with repeated blasts of most brassy intonation. Sanda was alive with a concourse of people, who must have gloried in knowing that the present procession betokened peaceful promise and presented in this respect a marked contrast to recent exhibitions of hostile triumph.

249. The road led through paddy fields for a distance of some two miles across or athwart the valley, in a direc-

tion South of East, and brought us to the foot of another red hill projection, which we cross and descend on its eastern slope to the right bank of the Tahpen, when the route again assumed its North easterly course through the centre of the valley.

250. Unlike Sanda, the town of Mynela lies on the left bank of the Tahpen, at the base, or along the lower ridges, of a central spur which divides the main valley longitudinally into two separate gorges without causing any material deviation in the direction of the Sanda valley itself or the general parallelism of its high flanking ridges.

251. The Tahpen is crossed at the ford of *Nammon*, which in addition to its being a convenient ford is also at this season a vast expanse of sandy desert two miles in breadth, which represents between well marked banks the dry bed of the Tahpen and Tahaw rivers at the particular point of their apparent confluence. As we proceed and approach Mynela the Tahpen is lost in an amphitheatre of hills which form a noble back-ground to that ancient metropolis. It has entered the Western of the two gorges into which the valley is here divided and its source is traced to the town of *Rooyon* some three days journey North from Mynela. The Tahaw keeps to the Eastern gorge and marks our route as far as Momein.

252. Mynela including its suburbs contains about 1,200 houses, with a population of from 8 to 10,000 inhabitants. Like Sanda the town is defended by a loopholed brick wall, from 8 to 10 feet in height with watch-towers which overhang the wall at intervals and do the duty of bastions. The position with regard to the valley we have been traversing is similar in most respects to the position of Sanda. Both towns are built on rising ground or on small spurs which abut a short distance only into the valley from the main western range. The houses rest on a ground floor and are built of unburnt bricks without any upper story. With the exception of the main street, inhabited by Chinese and in which the daily bazaar and weekly fairs or market-days are held, no attempt has been made to lay out the Town into streets. The various roadways leading through the Town are mere connecting lanes flanked alternately by the backs of houses on the one side and by walled enclosures with small covered gateways

leading into petty court-yards on the other. The appearance of these Shan towns is disappointing as regards cleanliness and the evidences or rather absence of household wealth or domestic economy.

The evidences of former prosperity are perhaps more strongly marked at Mynela than at Sanda and the difference is to be accounted for by a very palpable infusion of Chinese blood which has permeated the old Shan stock and left traces only of Shan originality.

253. On entering the Town at 3 P. M. on the 16th May we were escorted by the officials to a Chinese temple which had been newly roofed and otherwise put into repair for our accommodation. Chinese temples on a first introduction are no less a study as regards their laborious structure and variety of design than in the illimitable play of their interior decorations. Demigods and Heroes are personated in all the grotesque exaggeration of a mythical period. Each temple may possess and doubtless professes to have a history of its own, but four intepreters and the sages they consulted were only able to form (or at least to impart) a very faint idea of the conceptions of those celebrated artists whose graven images and laborious designs were nevertheless a subject of adoration and praise to a host of ignorant but self satisfied worshipers.

254. The temples at Mynela are costly stone buildings and the interior decorations have been carried out with a lavish expenditure of gold-leaf and labour which proclaims the wealth of the people at large and are evidence also of their artistic attainments.

255. The number of these temples as compared with purely Budhist monasteries is proof also of the predominance of a Chinese element at Mynela, and determines the fact that geographical position has had its influences on religion and given to the Budhism of these parts a variety of forms which stultify its pure tenets and are the reverse of orthodoxy. It would be a work in itself of labour and research to attempt the barest nomenclature even of the various images of Buddha and the never ending series of Demigods and deified representations of brutes and heroes which go to make up the the sum of Shan-Chinese Theology. My note book contains a few observations on certain scenic decorations with which

the temples abound and which illustrate the mode of disseminating scriptural truths amongst the manifold worshipers at a Chinese shrine.

256. I must be excused for making two short extracts.

1.—"The floor of one room (inside the Temple) contained a model on a large scale which was intended to be typical of a man's journey through life, and represented in practical development the allegorical paths which lead respectively to life or destruction.

A broad deep river separates man from eternity. On the one bank is misery and human affliction on the other Paradise and heavenly liberation (nikeban). The River is spanned by a solitary bridge which all must cross who hope for salvation. There is a double roadway one broad and seductive. The other tortuous and intricate.

The paths to seduction are pleasant and manifold. They are brightened for a time with the allurements of sin, and the temporary attractions of vice and immorality. But they lead to destruction.

The haunts of vice though partially concealed are typically represented by their dangerous position on the extreme edge of the bridge, with an abyss below which yawns forth death or rather life in death in most terrorizing propinquity. Removed from these seductive pathways is a narrow road which winds its way through a labyrinth of difficulties. The good and the virtuous are seen bravely threading its mazy intricacies and striving to reach the haven of their desires, a paradise teeming with all that is estimable in man's conception. Those who strive with steady purpose with their minds intent only on piety and religion and dead to the allurements of human existence cross the bridge and enter a region of heavenly enchantment, whilst others who have recklessly followed the broad road to ruin have fallen into the abyss and are seen underneath the bridge struggling in billows of molten lead or wound in the coils of monster serpents.

Altogether the scene is one which once looked upon by a true believer in the hideous reality of such after punishments is intended to cure him of all wandering propensities and guide his inclinations to the narrow road which leads to life and everlasting happiness.

257. (2).—In an adjoining apartment was another model which illustrated the Buddhist belief in transmigration and the inflexible laws which guide and direct the living principle or vital force into certain grooves which have been expressly contrived or cut out for its passage from one state of existence to another. In one cavity which has the appearance of a hollow tomb the living principle is symbolized as an embryo fœtus in a state of quiscence. From this hollow tomb a number of grooves or branch roads are seen to diverge in all directions and each groove is illuminated by pictorial designs which typify the peculiar existence into which the vital force may or may not enter in its passage from the cavity in which it first became matter. Certain rules and conditions are supposed to exist by which direction is given to these inert forces in their transitory stages, and it seemed evident that the model was intended to teach and inculcate these conditions and afford "a wrinkle" as to the readiest mode of hitting off a particularly happy groove, but my interpreter, like all Chinamen when religion is on the tapis, professed a pardonable ignorance of details which seemed to suggest that even Chinese theology does not bear questioning but that simple faith without reason or enquiry is a fundamental principle also in the creed of even Mynela worshipers.

258. Whilst on religious subjects I may here mention as one of the peculiarities of Shan Buddhism that it seems to create a strong desire in the female mind to assume the garb and duties of wandering Priestesses or in other words incites them to become peripatetic female Phoongyees. These Phoongyees or Nuns shave the head, dress in white and have separate monasteries or rather convent Nunneries of their own. But here the anology if there is any with the European order ceases, for a Shan Nun is a migratory animal and is never content to remain for any length of time in one place. It seems to be one of the duties to make annual pilgrimages to the most celebrated Buddhist shrines whether in China or Burma and in this respect she is a person of political importance on her return to her own native states, where she becomes the sole dispenser of foreign intelligence and a well tested authority in the political status of the countries she may have visited.

259. I was forcibly reminded of this fact during our stay in the Shan States by frequent personal communication with these Nuns, and a careful observation into their habits and the social position held by them amongst their own native communities. Whilst at Mynela I was visited on several occasions by a gathering of eight or more Priestesses, some of whom spoke Burmese fluently and had even resided a portion of their lives in British Territory at Rangoon.

Rangoon is a kind of Budhist Mecca to certain Shan old ladies, who will not believe that they have perfected themselves in their religious calling until a pilgrimage has been made to the shrine of Dagon. It is doubtless owing to this fact, and the itinerant habits of Shan Nuns in particular, that the English occupation of Pegu has both been acknowledged and appreciated in the Shan States. One of the old Nuns who visited me, spoke in rapturous and familiar strains of *Rangoon Mahamengyee-Phayyah* (Colonel Phayre,) and the esteem in which he and other English officers were held by our Burmese subjects in Pegu. I could *now* understand and account for the almost spontaneous display of good feeling with which Shans who are left to their own inclinations have always welcomed British enterprise although directed towards their own dependencies.

260. The Shan nuns who have been in the habit of making pilgrimages to Rangoon have returned from time to time to their several States filled with the fulness of their own good works, and carrying with them a lively and grateful sense of the power, the justice, and the toleration of the British Government. It is not too much to say that the present Expedition is indebted for much of its success in the Northern Shan States to the veritable dicta of these female divines, whose presence at Rangoon, with shaven heads and long white robes, is a pleasant or unpleasant momentary attraction, but whose political powers for good or evil involve us in a problematic conception too fanciful and far fetched, perhaps, for the most visionary of diplomates.

261. As I have before said the Chinese element was proportionately in greater force at Mynela than at Sanda. The close proximity of the Robber Chief Lees-hee-ta-hee at Mauphoo had a terrorizing effect over the Shan population.

and kept up a divided allegiance between their old and new masters. Lees-hee-ta-hee had been powerful enough for some time past to levy tax contributions at Mynela, and his presence in the neighbourhood with a band of Chinese marauders not only favored Chinese expectations but produced doubt and distrust in the Panthay Government. His recent defeat and the dispersion of his associates at Mauphoo had of course somewhat destroyed his prestige at Mynela, but I was painfully reminded nevertheless, on a first acquaintanceship with Mynela officials on their own soil, that as friends of the Panthay Government we are not altogether desirable visitors and that the Chinese yoke was preferable as a permanency than the seeming instability of their pretentious conquerors.

262. The effect of repeated conversations with these officials disclosed to them that the English Expedition was not pledged to any particular party or people, and its sole object was centred in a desire to ascertain with precision the present causes of trade obstruction between Burma and China, and with the assistance and co-operation of the intermediate races and people to devise a remedy and urge reconciliation of all adverse interests. The people of Mynela had gradually become polite and courteous in their manner, but there was an absence of that extreme cordiality which had marked the conduct of their Shan brethren of Sanda.

The old Saubwa was dead; and his son, a lad of 15 years of age, was hardly in a position to guide the affairs of the province under the regency of a mother, already known to be in her dotage.

263. It had been arranged on the day after our arrival that I should pay a ceremonial visit at Government house, and (although the Dowager Regent excused herself for not seeing me on the plea that she had no teeth and did not care about exposing her deficiencies,) the young heir apparent received me with all due formalities, and with a large concourse of his family and officials. An opportunity was thus afforded of entering into an explanatory discourse on subjects which have been already recorded as having formed the basis of my conversation with the old Chief of Sanda.

264. My desire was to push on towards Momein without any unnecessary lengthened detention in the Shan States

but the officials of Mynela were inclined to demur at the responsibilities which would attach to themselves provided harm befel us on the route between Mynela and Mauphoo. The road was still infested, they said, with Dacoits, and only a day or two previous to our arrival a caravan of more than 30 mules which was proceeding with rice to *Nantin* had been attacked and several lives were lost. If I pressed for an immediate start they were bound to attend to my wishes, with the proviso however that they were absolved from whatever responsibility might arise out of accident or misadventure, and that all such responsibilities rested solely with myself.

265. It was at this juncture of affairs that the Shan Saubwa of Hotha arrived, and his superior intelligence and bearing soon asserted itself in the councils of the timid and undecided officials of Mynela.

The Saubwa was himself proceeding to Momein with a caravan of 150 mules laden with cotton which had been brought from Bhamo by the central or Ambassador's route via Momouk, to Hotha. He had been instructed by the Governor of Momein to join our escort and give us the benefit of his assistance on the marches below Mynela and Momein.

He declared decisively that he was not prepared to leave Mynela until assured that the route via Mauphoo was in all respects safe and practicable. His information led him to believe that large bands of Lees-hee-ta-hee's Dacoits were still at large with the avowed purpose of disputing our right of way and of looting our baggage.

266. Under these circumstances I found it necessary to write and forward a letter to the Governors of *Nantin* and *Momein*, and as three or four days must elapse before replies can be received it may be as well here to glance cursorily at the affairs of a Shan State either as a separate principality or as one of a group of states which combine in the formation of a separate Province.

267. The Northern Shan States, with which we are now concerned, have been hitherto known in Burmese nomenclature as the *Shan Sheet Pyee* or eight Shan States whereas the Shans themselves divide this same territory into ten states in the following order :—

	Eastern			Western
1.	Mynechai *		6.	Hotha
2.	Mynechon		7.	Latha
3.	Sayfan		8.	Mynela
4.	Mynemaw		9.	Sanda
5.	Mynewun		10.	Mynetee

We have explored and acquired a pretty accurate geographical knowledge of five of these states which form the western group. *Mynewun* too of the eastern group has been partially explored by an Assistant Engineer who was detached from Hotha to survey the Sawuddy route via Mynewun to Bhamo.

Myntee, Mynela and Sanda lie within one valley range, Hotha and Latha occupy a second, Sayfan and Mynewun occupy a third, Mynechai, Mynechon and Mynemaw a fourth.

268. Each of these ranges or valleys lies more or less in a north easterly and south westerly direction in straight parallel courses. On their north eastern extremity they merge into the higher ranges which are continued in a southerly direction into the Cambodian and Malayan Peninsulas. On their west they are lost in the irregular groupings which constitute the so called Kakhyen Hills, so that the northern Shan States instead of being, as was once supposed, a wide expanse of open country leading on to the plains or Table land of China are in reality mere strips of narrow valley caused by a gradual opening out of the several hill ranges as they tend in a northerly direction from the Kakhyen chaotic group on the one side, and are shut in or lost at the other extremity by the snowy ranges of central Yunan.

269. The whole of these Shan and Kakhyen ranges of hills which comprise the 10 Northern Shan States lie within the basin of the Irrawaddy, and act as watersheds to one or more of the several tributaries which feed that river at this portion of its middle course. But on reaching the higher ranges on their north east extremity the valley of the Irrawaddy is defined and we seem to have reached the watershed of the Salween or at all events of some other river basin.

The general and physical geography of these hitherto unexplored regions is full of lively interest to every enquirer

---

* ch- pronounced as Greek X.

in the field of science, and it is tantalizing perhaps that our exploration has been necessarily limited to a comparatively small extent of unexplored territory. But the knowledge gained is not without interest and will eventually aid the solution of much geographical uncertainty.

270. The Shan State of Mynela pays an annual subsidy of 5,000 baskets of Paddy to the Panthay Government at Momein. The officials complain and think this an unreasonable assessment, not so much on account of its amount as because it is equivalent to what used to be paid to the Chinese Government, before the desolation caused by Mahomedan invasion. But complaint is unreasonable. Mynela as a State or Principality is divided into five districts each of which includes some 20 villages ; each village contains on an average 50 houses. The incidence of Imperial Taxation does not, at this rate, exceed one basket of paddy to each house or one and six pence per house per annum. This does not include other assessments which are levied for the maintenance of the Saubwa and his officers. The Saubwa is assisted in his Government by four Councillors or Ministers, to whom certain villages are assigned as Revenue, and subjected to a moderate assessment which is specially fixed by the Saubwa himself. Each village too supports a *Tamon* or Headman of its own selection, who acts as a subordinate Magistrate in chastising misdemeanors and the settlement of petty civil disputes.

There are no other state exactions, and the people enjoy a wonderful immunity from taxation as compared with the inhabitants of the adjoining countries or with their own Shan communities subject to Burma.

271. No direct means exist for arriving at an exact estimate of the population of the Shan States, but a pretty close approximation may be gained by observation and enquiry in the States visited, and the estimate arrived at by these means may be extended even to those States with which, perhaps, we had not the advantage of becoming personally cognizant. My own observation leads me to believe that the State or Principality of Mynela may be accepted as a very fair criterion of the extent and capabilities of the nine remaining Shan States. According to the computation given above of the number of houses contained in each village and allowing

an average of five persons to each house, the population of the Mynela State alone would amount to 25,000, and that of the ten States, at the same computation, to two hundred and fifty thousand, which may be generally assumed, as an approximate estimate only, to be within, rather than in excess of, actual fact.

272. This does not include the various Hill Tribes who occupy the several ranges which divide the States into separate valley compartments. The division in some instances has been so effectual as to have produced palpable variations in dress amongst the same race, and more than mere idiomatic or dialectic variations in language between closely adjoining States.

273. But ethnologically speaking, all Shans are alike. The type is well marked by facial characteristics which distinguish Shans from the several cognate races in the midst of whom they have their existence.

The Mongolian predominates, but the broad nose and thick lips of the veritable Burman are softened down into comparative symmetry, without altogether assuming the sharper and better defined facial outline of the Yunan Chinese.

It would be easy to look upon Shans as a cross between these two extremes, were it not that the distinctive nature of the Shan language is evidence of a distinct tribal origin, which is allowed to retain certain physical distinctions of race, owing to the geographical peculiarities and condition of the country it has so long occupied.

274. The dress too of the Shans is another indication of their distinctive nationality. The dark blue jackets and short loose trowsers of the men is somewhat Chinese in origin, and a very large percentage of the better classes of the males of *Sanda* and *Mynela* have assumed the Chinese pigtail and use Chinese chop-sticks. But Shan women dress after a fashion of their own which differs in every particular (if we except a portion of the Mynetha Shans of the Hotha valley) from anything akin to either Burma or China.

275. The Puggery or head dress is a long blue cotton scarf with embroidered ends, which is wound round the head so as to ascend in gradually increasing circles until it has assumed the shape and proportions (comparatively of course)

of an inverted pyramid. The jacket is made of white or light blue cloth or satin, and falls loosely to the hips without any pretension to cut or shape. But the collar is stand-up and close fitting *à la millitaire*, and both collar and sleeves are slashed and lined with red cloth.

The nether garment is a loose skirt, about a yard in diameter, which is brought together in front and tucked in at the waist. This skirt is made of plain dark cotton cloth, but the better classes attach a showy embroidery of gold or satin patchwork (or mosaic), a foot in depth, round the lower edge, which gives the garment a dressy appearance. Over this skirt as well as over the jacket a very richly embroidered shawl is drawn round the hips from behind and fastened in at the waist in front. It is an ugly appendage altogether and is only therefore worn in full dress! Fanciful gaiters of variegated cloth and embroidery fit closely to the legs from the ankle to the knee, and silver ornaments in profusion, head tiaras, earings, necklets, necklaces, bracelets, chatelains and various pendents without end, complete the costume.

276. The dress is a trying one no doubt, and the only wonder is how any woman can possibly look well in it. Shan women must be exceptions. There is something graceful in the dress and in the women, when the eye has familiarized itself to local peculiarities but I confess it takes time and a long separation from European civilization to convert a Shan woman with a hideously apportioned attire into a veritable beauty of feminine or seductive degree of desirability.

277. Letters were received from Momein on the 21st May, and on the same date my Chinese Interpreter Moung Shwè Yah, who had so disgracefully deserted the expedition at Ponlyne, suddenly presented himself with a number of Panthay Officers and a large military escort which had been sent by the Governor of Nantin to meet and conduct us on our route viâ Mauphoo.

278. Moung Shwè Yah entered into a few particulars relating to his desertion at Ponlyne, and was fertile in excuses which were not only intended to absolve him personally from all blame but to prove, with consummate plausibility, that he had been a faithful adherent to our cause throughout, and that his timely arrival at Momein had afforded the means of coun-

teracting evil and producing a friendly reaction in our favor. It is only necessary to record, in refutation of these plausible mis-statements, that Moung Shwè Yah did not attempt the journey to Momein after his sudden exodus from Ponlyne, until news had reached Bhamo of the favorable issue of my letters to the Panthay Governor, and of the generous advances which the latter had proffered in the furtherance of our enterprise.

Had these advances not been made it is more than evident that Moung Shwè Yah would never have left Burmese territory at all, and, judging of his conduct from first to last, I am bound to state that his private journey to Momein, without any intimation to me of his intentions, and after the news had been spread abroad of Panthay good-will and co-operation in our enterprise, was undertaken with the object of counteracting what had been favorable rather than of adding fresh facilities to our proposed advance.

279. But Moung Shwè Yah was too late. Shrewd and cunning by nature, it is no libel to say that his conscience allowed him at times to indulge largely in deceit and duplicity. The following may be assumed to be a very possible explanation and solution of his conduct and motives.

On reaching Momein he evidently found a state of affairs which had outreached his influences and promised a more certain remuneration to himself if *we* succeeded than if he continued an ineffectual endeavor to carry out the policy of his master the King. He had thus been accidentally converted into an indirect help, and it is due to him to say that during my stay at Momein he so far attached himself to our cause as to become (partly by necessity perhaps) my chief medium of communication with the Governor of Momein.

280. The three Panthay officers who accompanied the escort from Nantin called upon us in due form, and announced their arrival at our residence by sending in cards, or three separate sheets of colored paper, with their names and titles printed in Chinese. They are well dressed handsome looking men, and the Arab or Musselman type of countenance and features is unmistakably pronounced, in spite of a decided Chinese admixture.

Our conversation was friendly and unreserved, but it was rather perplexing to discover that our new friends were under an impression for some time that we were their brethren in creed as well as by race. It became necessary, in all our first interviews with Panthay officials, to provide against misconception of this kind, but the explanation was always made and received in good humour, and did not in any way interfere with the friendship of our intercourse.

The fact that the Jemadar and thirty of the Police Escort, as well as a large percentage of our private followers, were true believers in the creed of Mahomed, was an introduction in itself which went far towards conciliating Panthay prejudices and paving a way to confidential communications.

281. All was in readiness for an early start, and the Mynela officials having shuffled out of their responsibility by consigning us to the protection of a Panthay escort, our departure was no longer delayed and we left Mynela on the morning of the 23rd. A march of two miles brought us to the right bank of the Tahaw, and here the Panthay advance guard called a halt and announced that a strong party of dacoits were ahead and intended to dispute the entrance to the Mauphoo defile.

282. The Hotha Saubwa joined us during the halt with a large caravan of mules, and his information coincided with that received by the Panthay officers as to the fact that our route had been waylaid by a hostile assemblage of unfriendly dacoits. I use the word *unfriendly* because it is not unusual for travellers and residents of villages within the haunts of Chinese freebooters to compound with *local* brigands and purchase immunity from attack or plunder.

283. This sudden announcement of an intended attack was thoroughly embarrassing, and became almost ridiculous under Moung Shwè Yah's drunken exhortation to " go on " and fight the blackguards—who was afraid?" It was difficult to know whether his treacherous tendencies might not have been at work to lead us into an ambuscade, but he seemed in earnest, and to judge by appearances, we had no reason to apprehend really formidable opposition.

284. The route we were to follow had been traversed the day previous by our Panthay escort, and no report of an

intended attack had come to the notice of the Mynela authorities. On the contrary, they had given their consent to my proceeding and guaranteed safe conduct as far as Mauphoo.

Besides, to have turned our backs on an uncertainty without any positive assurance of real danger, would have ruined our prestige, and have prejudiced the chances of further progress.

To have remained and encamped where we then were must have argued weakness, and, if it was true that a resolute enemy was any where in our vicinity, would have inspired them with confidence and invited the attack which I was bound if possible to avoid.

285. Under these circumstances an advance was inevitable, but it was not until I had drawn up the Police in line and fired a very respectable volley to try their muskets (they had been loaded several days), that the Panthay officers evinced any sign of zealous excitement. They *now* exclaimed that with fifty muskets like ours, which would all "*go off*", they were ready at any time to "*whop creation*," or rather perform in their idea an equally arduous feat, and march to Pekin!

286. It was arranged that the Panthays should send out feelers, and in order to carry out this duty the more effectually I attached five Musselmen of our party to proceed in advance and take with them their muskets whose going off powers had already excited the valour and admiration of our Panthay escort. Captain Bowers was eager to head this party, but cheerfully submitted to my desire of avoiding what I conceived to be unnecessary exposure. Nothing would have tended more to compromise the future prospects of the expedition than the complications arising out of conflict with an enemy. It was necessary therefore to guard as much as possible against unnecessary risks, and court danger only when it became an indispensable aid to progress and safety.

287. We proceeded in this order some two or three miles and arrived at the duty Station of *Kanfan*, where a halt was called by the Hotha Saubwa. The Panthay guard had proceeded in advance, and after a short halt we were informed that they had reach the foot of the Mauphoo hills without encountering an enemy.

288. The valley had now narrowed very considerably, and as we approached its North Eastern extremity the only outlet was a narrow gorge or defile through which the Tahaw rushed with the force and velocity of a mountain torrent. The sides of the gorge were formed, for the most part, of bare precipitous rock, more or less scarped, which rose at intervals to a height of several hundred feet. No road-way would have been practicable through the gorge itself, and it become necessary therefore to ascend a portion of the Western range parallel with the gorge, for a distance of seven or eight miles, until a descent is made into the Nantin valley.

289. The far famed fort or stronghold of Mauphoo is situated on this high land, about half way between the ascent from the Sanda valley on the one side and the descent to the Nantin valley on the other side. Its appearance as we approached was singularly picturesque, not only by reason of natural scenery and position, but because a strong Panthay force which garrisoned the town had thought proper to embellish its battlements with numerous gay banners, and to present in their own persons a gaudy variety of costume and equipment.

290. Mauphoo itself is insignificant both as a town and fortification, but its position had been well chosen as a safe and convenient place of retreat and rendezvous, on account of natural defences and general inaccessibility. The Panthays for some years past had either tolerated or submitted to the presence at Mauphoo of an enemy who intercepted their communication with Burma and disputed with them the sovereignty of the Northern Shan States. It is now evident that this submission originated in a fear of offending against Burman scruples by direct interference with one who was known to be the secret Agent of the Burmese Government. It was not therefore until my letters had reached Momein, and the Governor had been led to believe that we were supported and countenaced by the Burmese Government, that the Governor undertook the work of reducing Mauphoo and of opening out communication with ourselves at Ponsee. He argued rightly, that either Mauphoo must cease to be a Chinese garrison, or the British Expedition must fail in gaining access to the Chinese frontier.

291. *Tah-sa-kon* took the field in person against Mauphoo with a force of 5,000 men. The besiegers contented themselves for several days by a close investment of both Mauphoo and Mawsoon, the only inhabited portions of the Mauphoo Hills. Every approach was strictly watched, and the assault only took place after a large portion of the besieged had either been reduced into capitulation, or had fallen in unsuccessful attempts to force a way through the Panthay cordon. More than 300 of Lees-hee-ta-hee's followers were killed during the investment, and although this number may be somewhat in excess of reality, still the putrefying remains of corpses even at the time of our arrival, made the vicinity of the town as well as its inner defences, an abomination of corrupt exhalations which revealed the truths of indiscriminate slaughter. Panthay revenge had satisfied itself to repletion on a hated band of Chinese marauders.

292. The march from Mauphoo to the Nantin valley will ever associate itself in our recollections with the gratifying marks of honorable greeting with which the Panthays bid us welcome to their hospitable possessions. Strong guards had been stationed at appointed intervals along the route, and the nature of the country was such as to enable them to be seen in the distance in all the gaiety with which full sunshine, variegated costumes, long silver lances, painted matchlocks and large national flags of multiform design and coloring, could possibly invest them. As we approached, the guards severally beat gongs, fired muskets, waved flags, and otherwise evinced, in their own fashion, a species of salutation which would have done honor to the resources and civilization of any state in Asia.

293. The descent into the Nantin valley brought us again to the bank of the Tahaw river, at a point where it enters the long narrow gorge above mentioned, through which it has worn for itself a way into the Sanda valley.

How superbly quiet and picturesque the view which is disclosed during the descent from the Mauphoo heights? At our feet lies the Tahaw, now a smooth quiet stream flowing between deep precipitous banks of alternate rock and vegetation, and spanned by a veritable iron suspension bridge, the first of a series, which assures us that we have passed the confines of the celestial Empire. Six miles in advance(though apparently at our feet) may be descried the towns of Mynetee and Nantin, the former Shan and the latter Chinese, though at present under the rule of a Panthay Governor. In the distance, the the valley stretches away into space, with a dark back ground of lofty mountains which trend northerly far into Yunan.

294. The average width of the valley did not exceed three miles, and the well defined terraces or gradations of terraces at corresponding heights on either side were evidences of a lacustrine period during which a gradual outlet was being forced through the Mauphoo gorge. The lake itself had silted up and formed the present rich alluvial expanse of plain and valley. There is reason to believe that the other Shan valleys we have thus far visited owe much of their present formation to a lacustrine origin, and that their unusual fertility and elevation is due as much to former sedimentary lake deposits as to a continual accession of productive matter which is being incessantly superadded by periodical flood, as well as by the descent of debris from the adjoining slopes towards their several valley centres.

295. The iron suspension bridge, at the foot of the descent from the Mauphoo hills into the Nantin valley, is used only during the rainy season, when the route from Mauphoo to Nantin lies along the high ground on the left bank of the river. On the present occasion we kept the right bank, and crossed the *Tahaw* at a ford opposite to the town of Mynetee. But on the return journey in July, the river was unfordable throughout its whole course and the "Iron-Bridge-Route" became a necessity.

296. The bridge itself is about 80 feet in length with a roadway 6 feet in breadth, which is formed by a number of parallel chains, which are stretched across the river from bank to bank and rigidly clenched behind strong stone embankments. The chains are made of red iron an inch in diameter, which is worked into single links a foot in length and about four inches in width. Joists or crossbeams overlay the chains, and the whole is covered with a flooring of earth and gravel so as to form a practical roadway. The approaches to the bridge on either bank are covered in, and form guard houses or resting places for travellers, and a Chinese ornamented

roofing gives a picturesque finish to the buildings and told of our advent to Chinese localities.

297. The present Shan town of Myneteo is distant at least a mile from Nantin, of which it may originally have been considered a suburb. It is the Head Quarters of the Shan Saubwa of the Myntee State, and although the town itself is inhabited by a Shan population, a new outline of appearances is everywhere visible, and we feel and know that we have passed Shan limits and are in a new country and under a new Government.

The line of demarcation is more strictly defined at Nantin itself, to all intents a Chinese walled city, in which the buildings, the pagodas, the bazars and the inhabitants are at once divested of all Shan associations. But it is a town of desolation and poverty; one half has become a ruin and the other half is occupied by a Chinese population of squalid aspect, who exhibit, as Chinamen, a manifest absence of ordinary thrift and national vitality.

298. We reached Nantin as it was getting dusk, and were conducted to the ruins of a Chinese Temple, which had been used as his Head Quarters by the Governor of Momein during the recent expedition against the Mauphoo stronghold. Very shortly after our arrival the Panthay Governor paid us a visit, accompanied by a Panthay military officer of high rank (a nephew of the Governor of Momein) and the Panthay Cazee or Magistrate of Nantin, a man of unmistakable Mahomedan bearing, and with perfectly orthodox beard and raiment. The visit was repeated on the following day, and the Governor was now accompanied by the famous Chinese Robber Chief *Thongwetshein*, who came in after the capture of Mauphoo and transferred his allegiance to the Panthay cause.

299. *Thongwetshein* evidenced in his outward exterior an impressive realization of a living Brigand. A man does not rise to power in these parts, even as a Robber Chief, unless possessed of a mental superiority which lifts him above the level of his followers. *Thongwetshein* had achieved this superiority and was the "Brigand" to perfection in his courteous bearing and off-hand civilities. But the tone of his voice was deep and sepulchral, and he gave vent to opinions

in a voluminous roll, which added to their effect and commanded the respect of attentive listeners. The transfer of his allegiance to Panthay rule is an event of importance which was indirectly influenced by our own expedition. It is reasonable therefore to conclude that a still more vigorous and determinate effort to promote intercourse and open out the old Trade Routes will be the surest and most effectual means of resettling the country, by securing the submission of other Chiefs against whom whole armies would be inoperative and assist rather than diminish the causes of disturbance.

300. I returned the Governor's visit the following day (25th May), and our reception, though purely ceremonial, was courteous to a degree and intensely gratifying. The Shan *Haws* (Palaces) already described, have evidently been built after a Chinese model. The Government house at Nantin represented a continued succession of quadrangular courtyards, flanked by lateral buildings, and connected with each other by a series of roofed archways, so arranged as to be exactly opposite, and present in line an imposing perspective.

301. A salute was fired as we reached the Palace, and, as a mark of special honor, the centre gates of the several archways were thrown open for our use. (The same custom prevails in Burma; only a King or a Prince of the Royal family is allowed admittance into the inner enclosure of a Palace through the large central gateway. All other persons enter by a small side wicket.)

The Hall of audience is a building which occupies the place of the penultimate archway, at the further extremity of the third courtyard. It was open in front but well furnished in Chinese style with chairs, tables, elegant wood carving and a variety of well colored Chinese paintings.

302. The Governor was dressed in a blue satin embroidered robe which reached to his feet, and possessed a peculiarity of cut which coincided, he told us, with the dress of Chinese Governors under a former Dynasty. This peculiarity consisted in a sort of clerical or rather quakerish stand up collar without roll or ornament; in other respects the grand robe had no cut at all, though full of a particular merit which might make it a cherished possession to those who delight in gaudy dressing gowns.

303. There had been a slight hitch in our relations with the Governor on account of my refusal to accede to his request of opening to view the contents of our packing cases. Having once explained that the cases contained either stores for our use or presents for his superiors, I looked upon the request to display their contents as an impertinent interference, which not only argued ill feeling and distrust, but was at variance with the spirit of cordial greeting which had welcomed our arrival within Panthay territory. The matter was not pressed, but I was given to understand that my refusal to comply with the Governor's wishes might entail delay or necessitate our detention until a report was made and instructions received from the Governor of Momein.

304. It was not until our friendly interview with the Governor at his own residence that I ascertained the real cause of his anxiety to learn the contents of our packages. Amongst the many injurious reports which preceded our arrival at Nantin was one which invested us with supernatural means of offensive action; some of our boxes were said to contain magical materials which could subdue whole cities and bring their inhabitants into complete subjection. Other cases were filled with living dragons which might be utilized at command into an irresistible weapon of offence against enemies.

305. Absurd in effect as these reports appeared, it was almost impossible to treat them with ridicule, or ignore the mischiefs they were intended to generate. I was now convinced that the original desire to inspect our boxes had neither been urged in malice nor dictated by curiosity. My stubborn nature forsook me in a moment and I was prepared I said to open to view any number of cases which appeared to the Governor either doubtful or suspicious. But common sense had taken the place of ignorant credulity, and no further allusion was made to our caged Dragons or to the boxed up infernal machines which were to have been the means of desolating whole Provinces, and subduing all men into compulsory allegiance.

306. The report, which attributed to us the possession of magic has been satisfactorily traced to a Burman origin. The Kakhyen chief Ponlyne was heard to excuse himself to the Governor of Bhamo for not having caused our destruction

by saying that Burmese had themselves informed him that we were veritable demons, and that some of our cases contained a peculiar fire with which we could at any moment destroy our enemies and burn up their possessions. He was deterred himself from open hostility by the certainty of provoking this irresistible power and overwhelming himself and his family in ruin.

Thus reports, conceived in a spirit of opposition, were happily converted into a positive protection, and acted in some respects as a wholesome check to the very evils which they were specially designed to create and make offensive.

307. The march from Nantin to Momein was full of interest. The configuration of the valley had somewhat changed, and the Eastern main range no longer continued to be a single continuous ridge such as that which had characterized its direction along the line of the Sanda valley. As apart from the main range there now appeared to be a ramification of irregular semi-detached spurs, all tending in a northerly direction and yet so closely allied to each other as to form a connected series of undulations, or in other words, a broad expanse of uneven table land high above the level of the circum-adjacent valleys.

308. The ascent to this table land is commenced half way between Nantin and Momein, and as soon as the high ground is reached it slopes away again by a gradual series of descents as far as the city of Momein, which is itself situated within the fork of two valleys, that on the West being a sinuous prolongation of the Nantin valley on the one side, whilst on the East another small valley has been formed between the Momein midvalley-ridges above-mentioned and the main eastern range (Deebay), which has again entered an appearance and is now the principal watershed between the Tahaw and Shwèlee affluents of the Irrawaddy.

309. The volcanic origin of the Momein plateau as well as of the whole surrounding region is very manifestly indicated by more than the usual signs of igneous activity and reproduction.

On one of the ridges which flank the plateau on its western side are a series of very remarkable hot springs, the largest of which at the time we visited it, did not exceed four feet in diameter, but its exposed surface was in a perpetual state of bubbling ferment, and violent jets of steam were projected from it, as well as from a number of smaller springs and cavernous fissures by which the larger spring was partially surrounded.

The deep dull sound, which was audible for a considerable distance from the springs, spoke of subterranean caverns at no great depth below the surface, and produced a sensation of distrust in the intervening crust, which seemed ready at any moment to fall in and carry all away with it into a boiling ocean below.

310. Dr. Anderson has brought away a quantity of the water for chemical analysis, and we shall learn in time its mineral ingredients. It is satisfactory for the present to know that this spring, in particular, has been rendered famous throughout the surrounding country for its curative properties, and the afflicted from all parts come and bathe in its waters, or utilize its vapours as a palliative to their several complaints. The temperature of the water is rather above the boiling point, and is highly serviceable to tourists in this respect for nearly all culinary purposes. But bathing is only practicable after the water has been carried away in a small rivulet to a considerable distance from the springs themselves, and has been cooled down by evaporation or mingled itself with cold water streams from other sources. The collective rivulets combine to make a small stream of tepid water which is borne away into the valley and soon loses itself in the waters of the Tahaw.

311. Another of the indications of volcanic origin is the existence of an extinct crater which occupies in fact a large portion of the Momein plateau, and presents a most interesting feature in the Physical geography of this particular region. So extensive is the space which formed the old aperture, and so indistinct at first sight to an inexperienced eye the indications which give special definition to this form of volcanic structure, that I think I should have passed the crater unheeded, had not Dr. Anderson pointed out its well defined splintery outline, as well as masses of rugged scorious black rocks everywhere strewn over a surface bared of all vegetation.

312. But I must go back to the hot springs. It was during the time we had halted to make an examination of their principal peculiarities, that a cruel and cowardly attack was made on our Panthay escort, which had proceeded in advance in charge of the mule caravan with our baggage. A portion of this escort had journeyed almost the day before on its way from Momein to Nantin; and so remote was the idea or anticipation of danger, that the Panthay officers of the escort, who belonged to the Nantin Garrison, were accompanied by their wives, or rather female relatives, who rode in front with the advance guard.

313. It was a novel and pleasing sight, in the absence of more genial female companionship, to see Panthay ladies in full Chinese costume riding at the head of our already singular and picturesque cavalcade. I noticed them when we made a start from Nantin and they were then apparently full of lively anticipations, and looked upon the journey to Momein in our company as an enjoyable diversion in the dull monotony of their every day-existence. The next time I saw them they were loudly bewailing the unfortunate slaughter of two of their nearest and dearest relatives.

314. The Panthay escort, having proceeded about three miles beyond the hot springs, had just rounded one of the many small lateral spurs which abut into the valley from the Eastern main ridges, when shot were fired from a concealed position above the road and two Panthay officers, who were some distance in advance of their own party, fell wounded. The dacoits, seeing that they were unsupported, rushed out from their place of concealment and hacked the officers to pieces with their swords. From all accounts it does not appear that the Panthay escort in the rear made any timely effort to save these officers or avenge their death. On the contrary, I believe that the suddenness of the attack caused a panic and that a fatal lapse of time was allowed to occur before the chief officer of the escort (a nephew of the Governor of Momein) was able to rally his men and make head against the dacoits.

315. It was during this interval that several of our own leading mules fell into the hands of the attacking party and were looted of their loads. A sick Panthay soldier too, who was being carried on a litter, had been deserted by his bearers and was barbarously murdered.

316. All this time the members of the expedition had been very diligently enjoying a halt at the Hot springs, with the full approval of the Hotha Saubwa who accompanied the the party as guide and adviser, and of the Panthay officers who were intended to act as our safeguard and escort. No warning was given of danger such as that which had called for caution on the march to *Mauphoo*. On the contrary, it was assumed as a certainty, that all due precaution had been taken against surprise and attack.

317. When we arrived at the scene of dacoity the sight was any thing but cheeful or encouraging. The bodies of the murdered officers had already been lashed to long bamboos; and were ready to be carried back to *Nantin*. Broken boxes lay in the way and in some instances their contents had been more or less pillaged. Unfortunately our personal baggage being light happened to be in advance and suffered most. Dr. Anderson's loss was a serious one—one of his tin packing cases had been opened and partially looted. Another which contained books, papers and instruments was apparently intact. The arrangements made for bringing it on with us miscarried and the box and its contents were never heard of afterwards. A few other articles might have been saved had we possessed the means of transport, but two mules had been carried away (or carried themselves away bodily) and the remainder had gone on to some distance or were otherwise unavailable.

318. We had still twelve miles of road to get over, and the Panthay Officers were excited and spoke of the likelihood of another attack which they rather deprecated in so cramped and indefensible a position. We pushed on therefore a mile or two to the foot of a steep ascent which led on to the high uneven table land stretching towards Momein. Here most of our baggage mules were halted, and I fell in again with the Hotha Saubwa who appeared faint-hearted in the extreme, and gave a very discouraging view of what was in store for us within the next six miles of our onward journey.

319. He now disclosed to me over biscuits and Brandy Pawnee, that, according to his information, the two Chinese Robber Chiefs Leogwanfan and Lees-hee-ta-hee had joined their forces, and that the present attack had been expressly

planned at Bhamo, with the full determination of preventing our arrival at Momein. Lees-hee-ta-hee was under a distinct promise, he said, to the Burmese officials at Bhamo to interrupt our progress, and had gone so far as to even guarantee our destruction.

320. I did not quarrel with the Saubwa outright, but I called him to account for former reticence as well as for having assented to our halt at the hot springs, when he must have been well aware that we thereby subjected ourselves to imminent peril.

321. But the Saubwa was intent on the dangers a-head and had no desire for retrospect as regarded the past. The attack which had just been made on our baggage was trifling, he said, in extent to what would be attempted as soon as we continued the march. Hitherto the Saubwa had shewn himself to be intelligent and obliging. But his doubts or his fears on the present occasion made him anything but an agreeable companion and forced him into the uncourteous admission that he had acted imprudently in having joined our party, and thereby incurred a risk which would have been avoided had he proceeded alone. His misgivings however were of no avail and I was glad to know that he could not retreat. Go on we must at all risks, and with the certain prospect (according to his account) of armed opposition.

322. Disposition was accordingly made, and a few scouts were sent a head as an advance guard to act as feelers. The interval of excitement was of short duration, for we had not proceeded more than a mile from our last halting place, before the advance guard reported that it had fallen in with a strong Panthay patrol from Momein, which had been sent by the Governor that day as an honorary addition to our military escort.

The route was clear and hopefully practicable. The scene had shifted from one of anticipated conflict to the more interesting prospect of visiting for the first time a frontier city of the Chinese Empire, and of feeling that a way was disclosed to the successful attainment of our expeditionary projects.

323. The approach to Momein is very grand and very beautiful. We had been descending for sometime the eastern side of the high ridges which I have already described as

intersecting to some extent the main valley of the Tahaw. The road after passing down a long series of grassy undulations, led round the southern slope of a tumulus shaped Hill, a thousand feet in height, crowned on its summit by a high Chinese Tower Pagoda. It is at this point that the city of Momein is suddenly brought into view in a hollow basin, enclosed on all sides by hills of every shape and altitude, which slope down apparently to its very walls.

324. In reality they are at some distance and the intervening valley spaces are either under cultivation or mark the remains of large Chinese Towns, now for the most part in ruins and deserted. Beyond the city, from our present point of view, the Tahaw and Momein valleys have formed a junction, and a narrow plain extends for about five miles in a northerly direction along the banks of the Tahaw, until limited in the distance by the gradual convergence of the lateral hill ranges. On the extreme North the horizon was bounded by a dark rugged outline of black mountains, with an apparent North and South direction which form, as far as it is allowed to deduce facts from observation and enquiry, a portion of the main central Himalayan chain, which is continued far South into Burma and the Malayan Peninsula.

325. But the most effective and heart stirring scene of the whole, as it then appeared to me, (with senses by this time somewhat deadened to the grandeur and attractions of mountain scenery) was that which presented itself in the foreground half way between our position at the foot of Pagoda hill and the southern face of the city wall. The Governor had thought fit to come out in full state to welcome us to Momein, and his guards and retinue formed a temporary encampment which was intended to be impressive and to display with effect the power and resources of the Mahomedan Government.

326. The encampment was marked by a long line of flags of never ending variety, shape and colouring. On coming within sight of them I halted for a few moments to make preparation for meeting so formidable an array of our expectant friends. We were a motley and mottled group of adventurers. A march of twenty three miles over dusty hills and across muddy ravines did not add to personal appearances or

to that dignity of demeanour which would be anxiously looked for in the pioneers of trade or the representatives of Western civilization. A dozen of the most respectable looking or least dirty of the escort were sent in advance to herald the way, headed by the Police Jemadar carrying my Burmese gold sword. The members of the expedition followed under the canopy of two large golden umbrellas, which were opened to their widest extent and carried by Burmans in green livery. The remainder of the escort brought up the rear, and our seedy accompaniments and general equipment was in striking contrast with the gay appurtenances and soldierly bearing of the Governor's body guard.

327. As we drew near guns were fired, gongs beaten, and bands of music struck up a selection of their own, which had the merit of being soft and harmonious as compared with the clanging harshness of Chinese performances.

I was altogether unprepared for a ceremonial reception on so formal a scale; for although the reports which reached us from Momein were calculated to produce a very favorable impression of the Governor's individual greatness, still it seemed unlikely that a state which for years past had been known to be a centre of riot and disturbance should have had it in its power to assume at a moment's notice the festive semblance of a holiday ovation.

328. The number of large standards, by a rough computation, exceeded two hundred; the staffs being in most instances covered with plain silver plating. The standard bearers were dressed in what may be said, on the "Lucus a non lucendo" principle, to have been uniform. There was a manifest diversity in the cut and the colouring of their several vestments; but the head-dress in every case was unique and striking. It consisted of a succession of large variegated rosettes which rose up from both ears to a point over the forehead, where they were terminated or rather continued by the long tail feathers of a new species of Pheasant of extraordinary beauty.

329. The standard bearers were ranged in line on either side of the road, and in front of them Panthay officers of all grades had deployed, so as to form a line through which it was intended that our procession should pass. Our appearance as we filed past this martial assemblage must have been as novel

and remarkable to the Panthays, by reason of its unaffected simplicity, as their gorgeous display seemed inconsistent and out of order on account of its comparative extent and unmeaning magnificence.

330. But the reception was flattering and courteous to excess, and as such produced feelings of special gratification in those who had come as strangers to an unknown Government, and after three months of obstruction and annoyance suddenly found themselves amongst powerful friends and raised to the position of well favoured guests.

Tah-sa-kon,* the Governor, had stationed himself at the extreme end of the lane or line of standard bearers and troops. His position was marked by three large red silk umbrellas with deep fringes of gold lace. Carpets had been spread and chairs arranged in line, with gaudy red cushions and rich silk drapery. The Governor was dressed in full Mandarin costume,† with a few Panthay modifications, and came forward to meet us as we advanced. We shook hands in a style which was Musselman on his part but English on ours. Very little was said or done beyond mutual recognition and greetings, and we moved on in the direction of the city followed by the Governor and his gorgeous attendants.

331. It happened to be market day, and the suburbs we passed through were thronged with vendors of petty wares, who were allowed in true Chinese fashion to erect temporary stalls in the midst of the thoroughfares; all was Chinese, houses, shops, people and language. We were conducted to a spacious temple outside the city at its South-west angle and in close contiguity with the Governor's residence, which, though inside the walls, was at all times within the reach of instant communication by means of a guard permanently located on the city walls immediately above our residence. The temple was built on the palatial or Government house plan, with a succession of quadrangular court-yards leading into each other, and flanked on either side by ranges of significant out buildings.

332. But we have now fairly got to Momein, and it is time perhaps to pause and make some apology for the extra-

---

* *Tah-sa-kon.*—The Government title of office.
† He afterwards presented me with the dress he wore on this occasion.

ordinary dimensions to which this narrative has already attained. It would have been a comparatively easy task to have generalized only on the events related, instead of recording them at length in descriptive detail, but I have conscientiously adopted the more laborious of the two courses with the double object of securing a base for my own observations, and of shewing how far those observations may have been correctly deduced. Whilst therefore I propose to continue the Report in its present form, I shall strive to avoid digression, and limit myself to matter which strictly pertains to the objects of the Expedition or tends to illustrate its action and interests.

333. Our life at Momein, and the manner in which the business of the Expedition was conducted at that city will be best described by extracts from my Diary.

28TH MAY, 1868.

Visited the Governor for the first time in an official form, accompanied by Dr. Anderson and Captain Bowers. Government House is a succession of quadrangular court yards leading into each other in the usual Chinese style already described (vide Plan and drawings). Our arrival was announced by a salute of three guns and a clanging of gongs and cymbals followed by the softer strains of flute and clarionet.

Tah-sa-kon was in full robes in the central Hall of audience, and came forward to receive us, shaking hands and motioning us to chairs at the "*West end*" of the apartment. The presents we brought with us were carried by twenty men (Musselmen) of the Police escort in undress, and laid on tables which ran down the centre of the audience hall. The presents looked well and were a passport in themselves to the good graces of the Governor and his attendant officials. They consisted of carpets, velvet pile table covers, double barrel guns, telscopes, binoculars, broad cloth, pistols, and a choice assortment of nicknac minutiæ of no great value in themselves, but in special favor and demand at Momein.

I open the conversation by assuring the Governor of the real obligations we were under to him for having so generously co-operated in the work which had brought a British expedition into Yunan. Without his active assistance, I said, in having provided the means of transit and personally superintended the removal of obstacles to our progress through the Shan States, it would have been out of my power to have reached Momein or to have even left Ponsee with possession of my baggage.

Tah-sa-kon replied by saying that it had rejoiced him from the first to learn that a British Mission had been sent from British territory with the object of entering into commercial relationship with his Government. He had himself entered into the enterprise with a will, and his first effort had been to despatch a force to Mauphoo and disperse the Chinese Brigands who held its passes into the Shan States. He had proceeded himself on the Mauphoo expedition, and after its successful accomplishment had collected the several cheifs of the Shan States at Nantin, and made arrangements for our advance, as well as for the future settlement and control of Customs Duty leviable on merchandize passing through the Shan States &c.,

I next spoke of my desire to proceed beyond Momein and confer with the Panthay Government at Talee. Tah-sa-kon informed me that we had arrived at a very inopportune period for prosecuting our journey further into Yunan. At the present time two separate forces, he said, were actively engaged in scouring the country between Momein and Yoonchan. For several months past there had been no free communication between these two places. Other routes to Talee were equally impracticable, unless we were prepared to encounter opposition and fight our way onward. It was far from his wish he said to stand in my way. He would even provide us with an armed escort if I finally determined upon an advance in opposition to his strong remonstrances and advice. The Panthay king at Talee had been informed of our intentions and had expressed satisfaction and a desire to second our efforts. At the same time he (Tah-sa-kon) felt certain that an advance beyond Momein was in our case both unsafe and impracticable. If hastily undertaken at the present time, without a prudent regard to time and circumstances, it might lead, he thought, to possible disaster, and destroy rather than assist in the eventualities for good which the expedition was designed to bring about.

I thank the Governor for the kindness and consideration of his remarks, and frankly assure him that, great as our desire was to penetrate further into Yunan, I was not prepared to neglect his advice or even act without his approval. I would therefore confidently leave the matter in his hands and await circumstances and further deliberation.

Tah-sa-kon.—"This is well—remain here a few days and "judge for yourself. Everything shall be done to further the "objects of your Expedition. One of your main objects is to "resuscitate Trade between Burma and China. I have al-"ready bound over the chiefs in the Shan States to aid the "enterprise. I will summon them again to Momein before "you leave."

To this I replied that I thought a congress of the several chiefs at Momein during my stay was highly desirable.

Tah-sa-kon assented, and wound up by exhorting me to be under no apprehension of apathy on his part or on the part of the Government at Talee. "A Trade route shall be opened "vià Bhamo. English merchants who arrive at Bhamo next "season will find carriage and safe escort to Momein; but "there is plenty of time to arrange all this before you leave. "I must at once report the news of your arrival to Talee and "shall forward on at the same time the presents you have "brought me.

"They will be very acceptable to the Panthay King &c."

I next referred to the death of the two Officers who were killed whilst on escort duty with our baggege between Nantin and Momein, and expressed our sympathy and concern in a loss which had been specially incurred in advancing our interests.

Tahsakon admitted that *he too* felt exceedingly the loss of these officers, as they were both brave men and had done good service.

They had died, he said, in the performance of their duty, and we were not to concern ourselves about them further.

The fact was not to be disguised, I said, that two Panthay Officers had met their death by giving assistance to a British Expedition; and I begged to assure the Governor that it would be my duty to report the circumstance to my Government, and make suitable provision for the families of those who had died in our service.

The reference to and remarks on this subject were apparently well timed. Tahsakon seemed personally gratified, and a murmur of approval add satisfaction made itself felt in the general assembly.

The conversation was continued for some time on various topics of interest, whilst Panthay attendants presented us with continuous courses of Tea, dried fruits, sugar candy and Chinese confectionary in profuse variety.

Several Panthay officers were present, amongst whom two were introduced to us as belonging to the Governor's council and consulted by him on all matters relating to the Government of the Province.

Another salute was fired as we left and more beating of gongs. The interview had been a success. Shortly after reaching our temple residence the Hotha Saubwa called and said he had been specially sent by *Tah-sa-kon*, with an invitation to all the members of the Expedition to dine with him on the following day. We were told that the Governor had been very favorably impressed by our visit and fully believed in the sincerity of our objects.

Moung Shwè Yah too, who had acted as Chinese interpreter, came in later in the afternoon with similar friendly messages. The Governor was delighted. The presents we had given him were a source of general admiration. *

They would be sent with a despatch to Talee. Other messengers also came from Government House with an abundant supply of Chinese confectionary, and fine white granulated honey. We were especially warned whilst eating the latter to avoid onions in our food, as an admixture of the two in the human system was universally followed, it was said, by fatal results.

29TH MAY, 1868.

The Governor has sent this morning to say that he intends returning our ceremonial visit to-day. The Officials and people about us are all smiles. This is merely a re-

---

* This must have been chaff, I fancy, as regards some of the articles, for instance, Edward Jones & Co's. 40 Rupee double barrel guns !

flection in them of the good will borne towards us by their Chief. Several Chinese merchants of the town have called upon us, and appear to be earnest in desiring an end to the present unsatisfactory state of affairs in Yunan. They liken the trade conditions of the Province to a stagnant lake, which has neither an outlet for its accumulations, nor an inlet for fresh supplies. In the mean time its stores of wealth deteriorate by time, waste and evaporation. The simile, as coming from them, is significant, and shews that they have rightly comprehended the evils which attach themselves to a country even temporarily cut off from its natural and legitimate trade communications.

The Governor called in state at about mid-day. He was dressed in full Mandarin Robes, and his followers wore gay uniforms and carried gold swords, silver spears, and the other insignia of a Governor's office. Presents were also brought as follows :—

1 Bullock,
2 Sheep,
Trays of fruits and confectionery
40,000 Cash.

I would have gladly rejected the cash, but my objections though courteously offered were summarily overruled. The money was distributed amongst our escort and followers, and proved very acceptable at a time when expedition funds were only available for actual necessaries. Each man received cash to the value of about one Rupee.

The visit being purely one of ceremony was soon over, but the Governor hinted on leaving that for the future he would call upon us without form, and begged that we also would treat him without reserve and make our visits to Government house as often as we felt inclined.

The Musselmen of our escort are in great favor with the Panthays. Both affect to be drawn towards each other by the inspiration of a common belief. The Panthays are evidently proud of the recognition which the Mahomedanism of Yunan receives at the hands of unadulterated believers from Hindoostan.

The Police Jemadar is a true 'Syed,' and is constantly summoned to officiate as Moollah in the Panthay Musjid. The

Panthays 'pump' him, under a belief that he will disclose the existence of any sinister designs connected with the expedition, but he remains staunch. The only dangerous man of our party in this respect, is, to my idea, our Native Doctor. He hates us, I believe, with all the fervour and some of the malice of his race and creed. Luckily he is simple and idiotic and his enmity if put into speech is not likely to be impressive.

30TH MAY 1868.

The Thermometer during the past few days has ranged between 53 and 70; not a high average for a hot weather month.

My compensated Aneroid Barometer shews the height of Momein to be seven thousand feet above sea level. We have risen by a succession of lofty terraces from the time we left the valley of the Irrawaddy. Momein itself, by native report, is the highest habited portion of the uneven table land which divides Western Yunan from the Shan States and Burma.

In the language spoken at Momein a traveller from any given direction journeying towards Momein is said to "*go up*" or "*ascend*", and in the same way on leaving the city he is said to "*descend.*" It is more than probable that this idea is fallacious and takes its rise in a natural misconception of comparative altitudes. We shall find I think on futher research that the plateau extends, with a varying increase in altitude, throughout the greater portion of Yunan Province.

The Governor visited us this morning in a quiet way. He is in plain clothes and has only half a dozen attendants with him.

We amuse and interest him by firing off our Revolvers and exhibiting a small Galvanic Battery with other scientific instruments.

In talking about the attack made on our baggage between *Nantin* and *Momein*, and the hostile demonstration on the march from Manwyne to Sanda, Tah-sa-kon remarked that he considered our misfortune in this respect to be due to the exaggerated reports that had reached Momein and Talee, and had excited even the cupidity of other adventurous communities, who were supposed to be more scrupulous in their dealings than ordinary Dacoits. He was prepared himself to hear the worst accounts of our party had we attempted an advance beyond the Kakhyen Hills without due precaution, or until the necessary preparation had been made for safe conduct.

Another great source of danger, as apart from our supposed wealth, lay, he said, in the evil reports which had been circulated by Burmese Agents, and which caused those who would otherwise have been friends to hold aloof and regard us with suspicion.

It was on that account that he had determined upon taking the field in person and securing Mauphoo. Severe fighting had taken place on both sides but success had attended his efforts in opening to us a road as far as his capital.

I could only acknowledge this confession of active co-operation in our cause as a sincere proof of friendship, which would be appreciated and duly acknowledged by every Government then interested in prosecuting commercial enterprise with South Western China.

Tah-sa-kon affirmed with much earnestness that not only himself but that the Panthay Government at Talee was eager in its desire to enter into commercial relations with Burma, and through Burma with Rangoon and the Pegu seaboard. The subject was one of vital importance to the whole of Yunan, and frequent references had already been made to the King of Burma to co-operate with the Panthay Government in the resuscitation of trade viâ Bhamo.

But the Burmese Government was lukewarm, and no steps were ever taken to further the renewal of direct trade communications, although the necessities of their situation forced the Yunanese population into an arduous and expensive alternative of reaching Mandalay with a limited caravan once a year rather than be excluded altogether from the most valuable of their trade resources. The news of our present expedition had been the more welcome to them because it seemed to afford evidence that the Burmese Government had co-operated with us, and assented to the re-opening of direct communication between Bhamo and Momein. It was this idea which had roused him (Tah-sa-kon) to action and justified the expulsion of Lees-hee-ta-hee from Mauphoo. A commencement had been made by the British Government and it would be zealously advanced by all the assistance they (the Panthays) could give, as well as by the despatch of a Government Mission from Talee to Rangoon. This could all be arranged hereafter. He (Tah-sa-kon) had come this morning to take us to an entertainment specially prepared for us at his own residence.

We accordingly adjourned to Government House, and the rest of the day was devoted to festivity and amusement. On our first ceremonial visit the Governor gave me a seat on his left in the body of the room in which he received us. On the present occasion we were asked, as a mark of special attention, to sit with him on a raised Dais at the further or most honorable extremity of the audience apartment.

The feast was sumptuous and interminable, but purely Chinese to the tea and even shamshoo. Tah-sa-kon did not drink himself but he was polite enough to disregard all Musselman restraints when hospitality was called for towards foreign guests.

An interesting feature in the entertainment was the presence of the Dowager Saubwa of *Mynetee*, who happened to be on a friendly visit at Momein. She was attended by a number of well dressed *Shan* ladies, who laughed and chatted in good humour and with true *Shan* good breeding. I took the opportunity of speaking to the Governor in her presence about the Shan States generally and their natural capabilities as a source of trade and revenue &c. I complimented him on the foresight and intelligence with which he had hitherto allowed the Shans to govern themselves, instead of imposing on them Chiefs and Governors of an alien race with whom there was no community of feelings or interest, and drew a comparison between the Shan States of Yunan and the more Southern States dependent on the Burmese Government. In the former case the Shans under the rule of their own hereditary Saubwas enjoyed comparative peace and prosperity. In Burma the hereditary rulers had either been summarily deposed or placed under the governance of Burmese officials. The consequence was that the States were subject to chronic disturbance, and industry had yielded to indolence and poverty &c, &c.

During the afternoon we adjourned to the Theatre, and were entertained for some time by a tragedy in which Kings,

Queens, Princes and Princeses took prominent parts. The dresses of the actors were gorgeous and genuine. The music soft and monotonous, with no deafening clatter of cymbals or brass drums, which usually ruin the interest of all Chinese performances.

After the Theatricals Tah-sa-kon led us through his private apartments to a garden in the rear, which was very tastefully laid out with dwarfed flowering and fruit trees in great variety. I noticed amongst them Peach, Plum, Fir, Box, Apple and Orange. The trees were generally from two to four feet in height and in most instances the dwarfing process had been carried out by tying knots in the stem whilst yet a sapling or contorting it into horizontal spiral twists so as to stunt the natural growth and diminish the height.

The Zenana occupied a range of pretty neat buildings on two sides of the garden. Our Burmese Assistant Surveyor has appropropriately noted them in his plan as *Lady's Chambers*.

The walls of Tah-sa-kon's private apartments were covered with Chinese paintings or hung with old armour. I also noticed an English Alarum-clock with a gaudy gilt face. The bed was an honest four-poster, draped with blue silk damask curtains which were looped up into festoons with silver chains. The dressing room contained several suits of military uniform, amongst which the Rosette and Pheasant-tail Head-dresses of Panthay standard bearers were most conspicuous &c.

31st May 1868.

Long conversations with Chinese merchants. The conclusion they have come to is that a resuscitation of the old trade route between Yunan and Burma will alone be effective in restoring order and tranquillity to the Province. If old routes and old sources of trade were available villagers, they say, would gradually gain confidence and thousands who now depend for a subsistence on predatory pursuits would find employment as labourers, agriculturists' servants, or petty traders.

During the day six noted Dacoits have been apprehended, tried, sentenced, and executed. All public executions have a brutalizing tendency no doubt, but the Panthay method of carrying out a sentence of death is kind and humane as compared with the cruel savagery of Burman practices. In the latter case the condemned criminals are taken in procession to the burial ground and kept in suspense for hours, whilst a crowd of drunken executioners dance before them with naked swords and intentionally add to the terrors of death by a hideous rehearsal of execution ceremonials; more than once the death dance is stopped and the executioners rush forward with swords uplifted as if to strike, but when half delivered the stroke is stayed as if by an after thought, and the blade (I speak as an eye witness) is quietly stropped on the victim's neck. But the end is not yet. The dance is continued and the condemned wretch with feelings at length deadened even to death, has passed through a hundred agonizing existences ere real dissolution comes as a reprieve to end the term of earthly torment. With the Panthays punishment is probably not less deterrent in its nature though marked by a hasty inpetousity in the mode of its infliction. In carrying out a sentence of death a military guard escorts the prisoners to the place of execution. There is no delay, no confession, no formalities beyond the firing of a musket as a signal to the executioners. A proper position having been taken up, each prisoner, still standing, is made to project his head a little and on doing so the fatal blow is dealt from behind. In nearly every instance one stroke suffices to sever the head from the body. Another musket shot announces the conclusion of the proceedings and the military guard returns to garrison.

The Panthays are no respectors of race in awarding death penalties. In the present case the victims were four Chinamen, one Shan, and one Panthay.

They were all taken red handed in crime, and justly punished on account of their offences.

Their bodies exhibited no marks of mutilation or torture. This too formed another contrast to a Burmese execution, when in most cases the criminal has been so barbarously subjected to a refinement of cruel appliances, to aid in extorting a confession of his crimes, that, maimed and unable to walk, he is thrown into a cart and borne in agony to the scene of his suffering.

2ND JUNE, 1868.

We have been to another entertainment at Government House. On the present occasion the corps dramatique seemed to think that a discrete admixture of becoming levity would better accord with our dissolute(?) tastes than the stern amount of tragic display which had greeted us on a first introduction to Momein theatricals.

Herewith my impressions of two performances which we witnessed—Tagedy and Burlesque.

No. 1.—(Tragedy).

Two famous robber chiefs, who had formerly lived at rivalry amongst themselves and at enmity with the Government, were induced to join their forces and aid the State against a foreign invader. One of them (Red Face) rose to high command and worked himself into royal favor to an extent which secured him the hand of a fair Princess ; but, unfortunately for his peace of mind, he possessed a political mother who had interested herself in state intrigues, hated the Princess, and favoured the cause of a rebellious pretender.

Red Face (against his will be it said) is bound in duty and by an elaborate exhibition of filial devotion, to join a conspiracy against his Father-in-law, and to this end it became necessary that there should be a complete severance between himself and the Princess. This is embarrassing, for husband and wife are supremely attached, and the manner in which it is arranged that the severance shall be effected, viz : by the death of the Princess at the hands of her husband, is a crisis too crude and sensational perhaps for even a Chinese stage.

But all agree that the Princess must die, and the husband is urged by filial affection and the commands of his mother to act the part of his wife's executioner. There is to be no plotting or other underhand contrivance, all is to be done with gentlemanly deliberation. The husband breaks to his wife the difficulties of the situation and obtains her consent to die at his hands! There is some real good acting at the last interview between husband and wife, in which love and duty are made to clash with an effective display of seeming emotion.

The wife is tractable and wonderfully accommodating.

With a generous fortitude, so true to the stage, she draws her husband's sword from its scabbard and saves him the pain of becoming her murderer by plunging it deep into her own bosom. The husband gazes, is overcome with grief and gives vent to loud howls; but somehow or other he suddenly recovers himself, cuts off the head of his deceased wife and bears it to his mother as an evidence of obedience to maternal commands.

The incomprehensible portion of the whole (unless we interpret it by that contradictory element in the Chinese character which makes their civilization a mystery to science) is that the political mother takes up the bleeding head of her victim, and joins the husband in what is intended to represent a genuine wail of lamentation and woe. The whole of the dramatis personæ now appear on the stage and the play is abruptly terminated by a beat to arms and a general rush of all parties to join new scenes of political discord.

No. 2.—(COMEDY).

The principal characters in this piece are a very old blasé King, a young and beautiful Queen, and a handsome Prince.

The trio proceed on a hunting excursion with a numerous retinue of Royal attendants and much scenic state pomp. The handsome Prince is a prodigy of valour, and his successful encounters with tigers and other wild beasts of the forest make him deservedly famous, and particularly excite the admiration of the Queen.

It soon becomes evident that her attentions to the Prince are more than Queenly, and subside occasionally into passionate flirtations.

The Prince is backward and exhibits less valour in love than war. The interest of the performance centres at this time (as between King and Queen) in the imbecile efforts of the former to conceal his jealousy and restrain her passion. All the old man's utterances and actions are cleverly designed to excite ridicule and expose the vices which grow up out of a matrimonial connectionship between youth and old age. In the mean time the queen is fertile in resources and has so far overcome the King's jealousy as to obtain his consent to her accompanying the Prince alone on one of his *Shikar* adventures. The most is made of this sportive opportunity, and on their return to head quarters the lovers present themselves before the king to try and blind his suspicions by a frank admission of each other's good qualities. But the wary old king refuses to be taken in and exclaims with a genuine sarcasm of fun which tells wonderfully on the audience, "Yes, this is all very nice for *you two* to be so pleased with "each other, but its precious poor fun for *me* I can tell you." The lovers are subsequently surprised by the old King in the ardent enjoyment of a vigorous flirtation. For a time he looks on in silence, until overcome at last by a feeling of his wrongs, he rushes into prominence and there is a stage denouement! Gongs are beaten, cymbals clashed. The play is over and we profess to have been abundantly amused by so faithful a caricature of royal domesticity.

Tah-sa-kon informed me to-day that he had despatched letters to Talee to inform the Government of his having advised us not to proceed further into Yunan during the present unsettled state of the country. Since our arrival, he said, he had received intelligence of several encounters between a portion of the Momein contingent and a Chinese force under the celebrated General Tahboukgyee and *Wansengyan* at Lonlyne on the direct route between Momein and Yoonchan.

Seeing that I was disappointed and that our hopes tended in the direction of Talee the Governor was courteous not to offend by open opposition to our plans, but his repeated mention of difficulties were simply dissuasive and intended to point out that an advance beyond Momein would be met by armed opposition and subject the expedition to more than mere ordinary risks. He will not admit that it is not in his power to send an escort with us of sufficient strength to ensure safe conduct, but his argument is that no escort he could send would be exempt from attack, and that such attack would extend to ourselves and place our party in extreme jeopardy &c. &c.

I again assured the Governor that I had no intention of quitting Momein without his express approval.

Having already experienced substantial proofs of Panthay sincerity we felt that his present advice was tendered out of no desire to frustrate our wishes or to nullify the objects of successful exploration, but was necessitated by a just regard to consequences and a hearty desire to guard against the certainties of conflict &c. &c.

It is market day to-day and the Governor sent a small guard with us to visit the bazar.

Markets occur at Momein as well as in the principal towns of the Shan States every fifth day, and the crowd is so great on these occasions and the curiosity to see and to surround Europeans when they present themselves so irresistible that without an accompaniment of men in authority who can command a right of way progress would (for us at least) have been altogether impossible.

At Momein the bazar is held in a broad street leading in a straight line from the Southern gate of the City.

The permanent shops on either side are supplemented by a line (sometimes a double line) of temporary stalls, at which a thriving trade is done in Chinese comestibles and small wares of every kind.

Rice, sweatmeats, cakes, cotton cloths, native yarns of every hue, gilt and colored papers, salt, tea, tobacco, jaggery, sugar-candy, drugs, jewellery, serpentine, amber, books, fans, chopsticks, looking glasses, pipes, shoes, gold embroidered skull caps, indian ink, opium lamps, walnuts, plums, apples, peaches, celery, potatoes, pork, mutton, beef &c. &c., with livestock consisting of bullocks, sheep, buffaloes and pigs formed a few of the articles exposed for sale on a market day at Momien. One street or quarter was devoted to the manufacture of copper utensils, another to jade stone sculpture, a third to ready made clothing, a fourth to bakers, carpenters, painters, and wood carvers &c. &c., but with the exception of the bustle and crowd on market days, the ordinary every day appearance of Momein manifests an absence of thrift or settled industry.

Visited a Chinese warehouse at the end of the Eastern suburb in which were stored a large number of bales of cotton belonging to the Hotha Saubwa. A Chinese merchant, to whom the warehouse belonged, invited us inside and was particularly attentive and hospitable. He told me that he had traded on a large scale with Burma before the Panthay outbreak. At that time Momein was a large flourishing city and the villages around centres of population and industry. Years of anarchy and disturbance had not only destroyed its trade but converted a country teeming with life and prosperity into a wretched scene of desolation and poverty. The old man, who had drawn a more unfavorable picture of affairs than affairs themselves warranted, was led by degrees to admit that there was still "corn in Egypt" and that any effort which could be made to resuscitate trade and give security to communication by a practicable route between Yunan and Burma would tend to a return of industry and production and restore the Province to its former prosperity.

I spoke to him of the short sighted Policy of his countrymen in Burma who were under a delusion that success to *us* meant ruin to *them*. They had deceived themselves into the belief that if our expedition proved instrumental in opening out the old Trade Route viâ Bhamo their interests would suffer by being brought into competition with English enterprise and English merchants. On the contrary I had expressed to them my opinion that the present object of their anxieties would turn out to be to them a source of advancement; for English Merchants would in the first place be under the necessity of selecting native Agents from amongst themselves (the Chinamen), and entrusting their consignments to middlemen who would thus be more advantageously employed in large undertakings and derive a greater emolument thereby than if engaged as at present in the miserable contrivances of a precarious subsistence.

The old man smiled a smile of significance, and said he was aware of all the troubles which had been thrown in our way in opening a route between Bhamo and Momein. He sympathized in our undertaking, and felt that now was the time to make an effort to save this country from the still greater calamities which threatened it unless some special power or providence interfered to stay a foreshadowed ruin. Left to itself the country must lapse from bad to worse and finally be left without either Government or subjects.

The old Chinaman promised to see me again and give me his ideas as to the most feasible plan of regenerating trade between Burma and Yunan.

3RD JUNE 1866.

The waterfall on the Tahaw at Momein, is worthy of notice. The whole water of the river falls perpendicularly a hundred feet at one drop or without a single interruption. It then rushes along in a succession of rapids until it reaches the level of the Nantin valley. The river, that is to say its water surface, at this season does not exceed a hundred feet in breadth and the discharge of water is not very great, but the crag over which the waterfall descends has been boldly scarped into the usual crescent form and presents on every side a luxurient growth of ferns, docks and bramble. Nothing can be more strikingly picturesque or beautiful in landscape scenery than the waterfall and its accompaniments as seen from a Southerly position on a level with the fall. In the immediate foreground is the river, spanned at a short distance above the fall by a Chinese double arched stone bridge with characteristic roofed approaches and stone parapet. The turreted walls of Momein are seen in prominent relief above temples and suburb, and the back ground is filled in by lofty hill ranges which commence immediately behind the city and are continued in successive variety till lost in distance. Oh! for a camera and a 12 × 10 plate with all its belongings.

After visiting the water fall we commenced the ascent of Pagoda Hill and passed through fields of potato and celery. The potato would appear to be an indigenous species, for it is difficult to conceive its introduction into Yunan or the Kakhyen hills (where it grows abundantly) from a European stock. The tubers are generally round and covered with an outer pellicle which is invariably pink.

The entire slope of the hill forms one vast burial ground, covered to the extent of fifty acres at least with substantial tombs or sepulchres of stone, of oblong tumulus form, from four to eight feet in height and about six or eight feet in length. The front or head of the tomb is arched and contains one or more Gothic niches which have the appearance of being mere portals to the sepulchre, and are closed with marble slabs bearing an in memoriam inscription to the deceased. Some of the sepulchres are twinlike in design and proclaim themselves to be family vaults in which husband and wife or parent and child have found a final resting place. At the same time there is a general resemblance in the architectural construction of all these tombs as tombs, although a poorer class of tumuli are met with which consist of simple mounds of earth or loose stones, much like our own graves in shape but raised at one end into an arched hollow niche or opening, which is invariably blocked up by a rough unhewn boulder, and is singularly suggestive of Jewish sepulture of the New Testament period.

Of them it may literally be said that a stone has been rolled to the mouth of the Sepulchre!

On all sides there is a profuse growth of brambles which produce blackberries, as well as varieties of red and yellow raspberries. The wild rose too, is in bloom everywhere and in these parts the flower is double with an abundance of petals. The seed when ripe is picked and sold abundantly in the Bazaars as a fruit.

4TH JUNE 1868.

The Governor has called again to day and is particularly kind and sociable in his manner. He refers to the presents which have been sent on to Talee and says that a suitable return will be made to the English Government. In the mean time he is anxious to present us with some slight memento of his friendship and asks us to name our particular fancies. I particularly begged that the Governor would not trouble himself with the consideration of making any return for the presents which we had brought to Momein. They were, as he well knew, trifling both in extent and value, although it was a source of gratification to us to know that the scarcity of most of the articles at Momein had enhanced their acceptability. The English Government did not expect any return and would be amply satisfied with the knowledge that the expedition had been well received by the Panthay Government and had enjoyed the support and friendship of the Chief of Momein.

Tah-sa-kon felt sure that the Government at Talee would insist on making a return for the presents it had received. The matter had already been discussed before my own arrival and it was generally determined that a deputation should proceed to Rangoon and carry presents to the British Government.

The Governor now unfastened a small gold dagger which hung suspended by a gold chain from his waist and handed it to me, saying that I was to keep and wear it as a memento of his friendship. At the same time he took off a jade-stone and four gold guard rings which he was wearing, and insisted on placing them all (5 rings) on the third finger of my left hand in exactly the same sequence as regarded the position of the Rings as he had been accustomed to observe in wearing them himself. I felt infinite pleasure in the acceptance of these gifts, not on account of their intrinsic value but because they were given with a chivalry of manner and purpose which, coming from a man of Tah-sa-kon's eminence and in the presence too of several of his Chief Officers, was a convincing mark, not only of real personal esteem, but of honorable and consummate attention.

The Governor remained to breakfast, after which he walked out with us through the city and paid visits at the houses of some of his Chief Officers. We are in high favor everywhere.

5TH JUNE, 1868.

The Dowager Saubwagadaw of *Mynetee* has called to-day and is accompanied by a very picturesque and attractive suite of Shan ladies who are wonderfully well behaved, but at the same time sufficiently easy and communicative in manner to make them very agreeable though rather distant companions. Even the ugly pyramidal turban is not unbecoming when set off by faces of delicate softness and pleasing if not beautiful delineation.

The old lady apologizes for the scantiness of her presents but invites us on our return from Momein to stay a few days with her at the Head Quarters of her Saubwaship at *Mynetee*.

I gave her a few suitable presents and then distributed needles, thread, scissors and small looking glasses amongs her maiden attendants, which took amazingly and won their affection. But we are on our good behaviour, any unduer levity would be a shock to the high state of morality which Shan ladies of an interesting age attain to instinctively in their domestic relations with the other sex. They nevertheless unbend to us very considerably under the effects of scissors, and afford proofs that as a race they are free from prejudice and can readily consort with foreign civilization.

Another long conversation with the head Chinese Merchants.

6TH, JUNE 1868.

Private interview with Tah-sa-kon at his own residence. Having full reliance on the Governor's friendship towards us my object was to try and obtain from him personally an expression of his opinion on the state of Yunan, with reference more especially to the political character and stability of the Panthay Government.

Hitherto our knowledge of the Province had been confined to rumours of incessant hostility between the Panthays and Chinese.

Panthays were declared to be rebels although they had established themselves as a Government for 14 years.

How far was that Government recognized by the Government at Pekin?

Was the present contest kept up by the mutual desire of the contending parties or was its continuance due to the want of mediation and proper understanding?

Were the Panthays eager to achieve fresh conquests, or would they be content to settle down and give good Government to the possessions they had already acquired?

We were interested I said in these questions, because the disturbed state of *Yunan* had effected British possessions and British trade in *Burma*. The British Government was represented by an Ambassador at the Court of *Pekin;* could his influence be utilized in any way to bring about a reconcilation of interests between the Imperial Government at *Pekin* and the Mahomedan Government at Talee?

These were the questions which I was enabled in my private conversations with the Governor to put to him in a way which was not only not thought obtrusive but which secured an expression of opinion that my anxiety to learn the true state of their affairs did not evince any traces of sinister design or of a wish to oppose Mahomedan advancement in a Province which belonged to them by right of conquest.

Tah-sa-kon said he was glad that I had introduced the subject. There was no doubt in his own mind that both the Chinese and Panthay Governments were tired of disputing the possession of Yunan. There were faults on both sides but the Panthays no longer manifested or supported an aggressive policy against China. The blame (if it was one) of keeping up the contest rested with the Governor of Yunan*(city), who, instead of making any serious attempt to recover lost territory, sent parties of marauders to harass and molest Panthay possessions. This led to retaliation and fresh conflict in which the Panthays were compelled in self defence to act on the offensive and to extend their territory without any definite design either of conquest or aggression. He would communicate all I had said to Head Quarters at Talee and inform me of results. In the event of my having left Momein before replies were received, he would write to me in full and for this purpose begged that I would make over to him a private seal which he would impress on his letters to assure me they were genuine. In like manner he promised to give me his own official seal to be used in my communications with him as a check upon fraud &c. &c. &c.

At a late hour the same evening my Chinese interpreter came towards me almost stealthily, and made known in an undertone that a very important visitor was outside and wished to speak to me.

Explanation followed and I discovered that the visitor or visitors turned out to be a deputation from the celebrated Chinese robber chief *Leoqwanfan* who professed an anxiety to make our friendship and provide us with an escort on our further travels.

A pony had been sent for my acceptance as a preliminary to further friendly recognition. My duty was clear though the position generally could not fail to be a little embarrasing. Politically we were guests of the Panthay Governor of Momein without any evidence of having espoused his cause or the cause of the Mahomedan Government in Yunan. At the

---
* called also *Mynseer*.

same time the British Government were bound to China by a treaty of friendship and commerce. But in the interests of trade and under a very laudable desire of ascertaining the cause, and providing a remedy against, a perpetual cessation of commercial relations between *Yunan* and *Burma*, the members of the expedition were of necessity led in their exploration to avail themselves of the assistance and hospitality of the Government which was in open conflict with their avowed Treaty friends the Chinese. That Government, though raised out of rebellion, had established itself as a Government for more than twelve years, in a Province which had originally belonged to China; so that the appellation of *Rebels* could no longer be consistently applied to it by Governments, however much such a term may have been jealously insisted upon by the Chinese Imperial Government at Pekin. To all intents and purposes we were neutrals, and in a civilized state the realities of our position would have at once been understood and recognised. But the niceties of European international law cannot be expected to influence the actions or feelings of native combatants in a frontier Province of the Chinese Empire.

The point of neutrality was therefore one which, though it might have been urged in sincerity, would have created suspicion and might have proved dangerous, if relied on as a means of securing the hospitality or seeking the aid alternately of either of the contending parties.

On these grounds I refused to receive the Chinese Deputation or to accept the presents sent me, whilst under the lawful protection of the Governor of *Momein*. I was glad, I said, to hear that the Chinese General Leoqwanfan was well disposed towards us, as we had come into *Yunan* with the earnest desire of securing the friendship of all parties, however adverse amongst themselves, and of aiding if possible in the adjustment of their disputes. It was on this account in particular that I was now debarred from adopting a secret or underhand course of action, which would belie my neutral character and compromise all honest efforts for good. At the same time, I said, I was quite willing to treat and confer with *Leoqwanfan* or the members of his deputation, provided I could do so openly and with the knowledge and consent of the Government at Momein.

The next day (I am now anticipating and abridging my diary) I was informed that the Governor had been made aware of the arrival of Leoqwanfan's deputation at Momein, and did not oppose it or apprehend its members because he believed that Leoqwanfan had taken advantage of the opportunity afforded by our arrival, to enter into a negociation and give in his adhesion to the Panthay Government.

This was what actually did take place. Leoqwanfan at this time put himself into correspondence wito the Governor of Momein, and a document was drawn up and agreed to in which Leoqwanfan stipulated for the privilege of establishing a duty station at a place called *Shatgan*, guaranteeing in return that Panthay possessions in *Yunan* should not be molested either by himself or by any of the force then under his command.

This may be received as a proof, perhaps, that Leoqwanfan did not in reality hold a commission under the Chinese Government, otherwise it is inconceivable that he should have stipulated for the posssession of a single duty station under the Panthay Government of Momein. Or, taking the converse of the question, if, as certain parties hold, Leoqwanfan *was* commissioned by the Chinese Government, his negotiations with the Governor of Momein for employment at *Shagan* may be assumed to imply that the Imperial Government of China had recognized another power in Yunan, and was ready to treat with it as an established Government.

But to continue the words of my diary of *7th June*:— "Our mission to Yunan, unpretending as it has been and void of those outward semblances of splendour or power which are an essential qualification in the composition of every Political Mission (we are not political bye the bye) to an Eastern Court, has nevertheless already tended in no small degree to effect the pacification of a large portion of the old Trade Route between Burma and China.

1. *Thoung-wet-shein*, a Chinese brigand chief of great power and note, has been defeated and captured at his stronghold of *Mauton*, on the Route between *Nantin* and *Momein*. He has now transferred his allegiance to the Panthay Government, and was one of the hosts who entertained us at Nantin.

2. Lees-hee-ta-hee has been driven from Mauphoo and is now a fugitive.

3. Leoqwanfan, the most powerful of the seven Robber chiefs of the old Trade Route, has volunteered his submission to the Panthay Government, and entered into a guarantee that he will not disturb Panthay possessions in any portion of Yunan Province.

Thus no chief of note is left to obstruct the Roads South and West of Momein. I do not mean by this that the country has been suddenly reduced to order, or that Dacoities and disturbances may not occur under the happiest conditions of society or Government, but accidents of this kind have been reduced, I consider, from certainties to contingencies, which must gradually succumb to ordinary efforts.

It is not too much say to that the present Expedition, in thus indirectly ridding the country of three of its most emicial hiand dreaded freebooters, has performed a work which is China-ial importance in estimatiing the value of present at-
,ts, and affording a reliable incentive to still further
.orts.

9TH JUNE 1868.

The Governor has visited us again to-day; I hint complainingly at our protracted stay and the compunctions we feel at trespassing so long on his generous hospitality.

Tah-sa-kon will not hear of our departure, and gives me to understand that the matter of hospitality is *his* affair, and that he will give us an opportunity of repaying it when the Mission from Talee visits Rangoon. He is aware that our life at Momein is not a very cheerful one, but it distresses him, nevertheless, to think that we are in such a hurry to leave. Are we so soon tired of his friendship.? He begs we will try and make ourselves at home for a few days longer. If it is our wish to visit any part of the country adjacent to Momein, he will send an armed escort to guide and protect us from all harm.

The real cause of the Governor's wish to delay our departure from Momein, is that he expects replies from Talee to his letters announcing our arrival at Momein. The Governor too is busy making up suits of clothing as presents to our police escort and followers, and his tailors are evidently not fast workmen. It is further alleged that the Governor feels a little proud and elated at the idea of having a British Expedition at his head quarters, and our presence lends a sort of prestige and security to his Governorship. All these causes operate more or less to cause our detention. Provisions are cheap, and our average expenditure or cost to the Governor does not probably exceed 30 Rupees per diem. The great drawback to ourselves is that we are ill supplied with cash, and although I have enough to pay our way back to Bhamo, there is nothing to spare in indulgences or in the purchase of much that would be interesting on our return.

To attempt to raise the wind here by a loan, or by drafts on Mandalay would be lowering to our position, and we therefore find it prudent to husband our Rupees as well as our dignity &c, &c.

15TH JUNE 1868.

It has rained most persistently since the 4th in The down pour at any one time has never been great, there is a continued misty drizzle which damps everything and is suggestive mentally and physically of an existence in clouds.

A walk on the city ramparts is however practicable at all seasons. The wall* is a work of prodigious labour. Many of the granite slabs with which it is faced are four feet in length and one foot in depth. The turrets are built of burnt blue bricks, which are so hard and perfect in construction that the wear and tear of three centuries has not availed to roughen their surface or blunt their keen sharp edge. There are no bastions, but small towers rise at intervals on the ramparts, within the wall instead of projecting from it, and the gateways are surmounted by large handsome buildings which are used as guard houses.

After attempting with no great success to probe my Interpreter and his Panthay companions into an intelligible relation of Momein Chronicles, I was led by degrees, whilst facing its battlements and musing on the past, to attempt a speculative flight into the haze of the future. We are now in the clouds and may indulge in a reverie.

---

* For dimensions and particulars vide Plan.

Seven thousand feet above sea level; an elevated expanse of table land diversified by lofty hills and rich fertile valleys, with the climate and produce of temperate regions!

The annexation of Upper Burma (if such an event ever takes place) would necessitate a readjustment of our North Eastern frontier. The Salween river under any circumstances would still form a natural boundary to our possessions Eastward, as far North at least as the latitude of Momein, when it is crossed by an iron bridge on the high road between *Momein* and *Yoonchan*. This boundary line would include Momein itself, a position of unquestionable importance in strategic requirements. Commanding as it does the principal approaches to China from Burma, and standing at the head of the Northern Shan States, the possession of Momein would not only secure the comparative independence of those States under a British Protectorate, but prove also the sole commercial high-way for all trade and commerce passing between China and the head waters of the Irrawaddy.

The Shans will have attained to the summit of their hopes in acknowledging British protection, and being secured thereby from all apprehension of foreign aggression.

The Kakhyen Hills will lay within British Territory, and the several hill tribes, no longer goaded into enmity and resentment by the wanton exercise of cruelty and misrule, will freely settle down into tranquillity and become a source of wealth and productiveness to themselves and to their rulers.

Immediate relief will have been granted to distressed millions who crowd the southern provinces of China and will gladly emigrate into the sparsely populated and inviting plains of upper and lower Burma.

From Peshawur to Momein the upper limb of the quadrilateral will then be complete, and Rangoon the Metropolis of a Presidency, develope itself in a decade into one of the richest and most favored ports in Asia.

This is a reverie, "Dulce est desipere in loco." The dream may serve at a future time as a nucleus for something more serious than mere meditative speculation!

18th June 1869.

The Shan Saubwa of Keeinkhan is here on a visit. His Saubwaship lays some five days journey South East of Yoonchan between the Salween and Cambodia rivers. This is his own definition of geography, the vagueness of which is hardly relieved by the further fact that the well known entrepôt of Kyaing-yoon-gyee is described as being twenty days journey south of Keeinkhan.

Keeinkhan itself is subject to the Panthay Government, and the Saubwa's definition of localities serves in some respects to shew the extent of Panthay conquests, which we thus find to extended themselves to the Southernmost limits of Yunan.

The Saubwa of Keeinkhan has heard nothing of the French exploring party from Saigon, but there is a report at *Momein* that seven Europeans have been seen *measuring roads and cities* on the eastern frontier of Yunan, some ten days journey east of Talee. This looks as if the French party has been making its way direct to Yunan (City) and avoiding Panthay possessions altogether.

There is a further report in circulation to the effect that the Panthays have made themselves masters of several of the towns to the eastward of Yunan (City). Tah-sa-kon confirms this report, and says that he believes that Yunan is at present in the possession of the Panthays. This is the Report, but he will not rely upon it without official confirmation. The capture of Yunan will not have the effect of removing the Panthay capital from Talee, which is said to contain a strong citadel within the City and is otherwise more favorably situated as regards supplies and the requirements of a military position than any other City within the province.

I have been fortunate enough to procure separate histories of *Yunan*, *Talee* and *Momein*; those of *Yunan* and *Talee* are illustrated with maps, and plans of the principal Cities and their neighbourhood. Each history is contained in ten printed volumes, and it will be a work of interest and labor to get them translated and reduced to an intelligible proportion. They may possibly throw some light on the alleged facts as stated at Momein that Talee was at no remote period a separate Kingdom, peopled by an extinct race whose language and customs bore no affinity to any of the Chinese races now extant in Yunan.

It was with great difficulty I procured copies of these histories; the parties who supplied them acted with a certain amount of secresy, and cautioned me to conceal their possession as long as I remained within Chinese limits. The instinct of conservatism was strong enough in this instance even at Momein (and under Panthay rule), to deprecate and view as a crime the diffusion of Political statistics to the people of a Foreign Government.

19TH JUNE 1868.

The Governor has sent his nephew with several officers and an armed escort to join us in a day's ramble into the interior. A guard had become a necessity owing to the unsettled state of the country and the numbers of half starved vagabonds who have been forced into brigandage as the only means left them of securing subsistence. The chances of an adventure with any of these lurchers is always imminent, and can only be avoided by a due regard to offensive and defensive preparations.

Our party mustered something like 35 men of all arms (swords, spears, and muskets), and taking a Southerly direction from the city we soon came in sight of the town of *Yaylaw*, which stretched out for a mile and a half along the base of the Deebay or Eastern range of the Momein valley. Proceeding Westerly we skirted Pagoda hill and arrived at the old town of *Shwědway*, so called on account of its vicinity to to a small current of water which was utilized as a source of power in supplying force to a mechanical contrivance for pounding paddy. Water-wheels of various construction are frequently met with on all the streams in the vicinity of Momein. The town is almost deserted, but the remains of masonry buildings and substantial stone terraces or causeways are proofs of former wealth and comparative prosperity.

We next visited a range of very interesting Chinese temples, which had been built into the side of an old quarry or ravine, partially excavated and scarped so as to allow the buildings to rise rather obliquely one above the other by a gradation of terraces. The images and interior decorations had escaped destruction and were apparently in all their pristine exaggeration. A centrepiece of statuary in pure white marble represented a life size image of the Goddess of conception. The face may have been a little out of proportion to suit Chinese tastes, but a perfect acquaintanceship with true art was manifested in the natural folds of the drapery, which had been chisled into form with all the flowing elegance of reality. The Goddess holds forward in prominent relief a naked male babe of wonderful parts and exceeding virility. Religion has been thus prostituted perhaps to a rather fanciful mode of administering relief to human short comings. There must be something comforting, however, in the belief which causes thousands of women, who, being disappointed in the object of their legitimate amours, seek if happily to find an imaginary remedy for mortal infirmities.

Opposite to Shwèdway on the Northern slope of an adjacent hill is the large Chinese Town of *Hawshoenshan*, which contains about 2000 houses and is the rallying point to which a certain number of fugitives have resorted from the desolated villages of *Shangnan, Tahinshan* &c. &c. Our guide pointed out an open grassy plain on the southern outskirts of the town, which only a few months before, he said, had been strewn with the dead bodies of Chinese insurgents. The people of *Hawshoenshan* had temporarily thrown off their allegiance to the Panthays and joined the ranks of the Chinese General *Leogwanfan*. They were attacked and defeated by a Panthay force, and the plain we were then riding over was at once their battlefield and graveyard. The slaughter which took place was cruel and excessive, but proportioned only to the system of retaliatory warfare, or to a struggle for independence on the one side, and extermination on the other. We return to our quarters before sunset, as pleased as it was possible to be with an excursion which passed off without accident and failed even to bring us into conflict with Momein brigands.

22ND JUNE 1868.

Masa Tahzyungyee, the chief military officer at Momein but subordinate to the Governor (who is both Governor and Commander in chief), has called to invite us to an entertainment specially prepared for us at his own residence. It would be difficult in any society to pick out a man of more polished habits or cultivated taste in his domestic arrangements than this soldier of fortune in the Panthay army.

The feast at his house commenced with a dessert of plums, peaches, sugar candy and sweat Toddy. Next several courses of roast, boiled and curried meats, with rice and vegetables, wine, shamshoo &c.

Tahzyungyee joined us at the final course, and a large jug of hot grog was brought to the front and set down before him. He filled a large goblet and handed it to me. One mouthful sufficed to take away my breath and leave an aftertaste of alchohol and pork-fat. The goblet was passed round several times. Tahzyungyee joining us in turn taking his liquor like a man and a Musselman. I was glad to see that he was less of a Wahabee in this respect than many of his confrères in Chinese Mahomedanism. At the same time he is a man of note in the Panthay Government, and acted as General in Chief of the Panthay force which made an irruption some five years ago into the Northern Shan States and brought them under Panthay rule.

His household arrangements are elegant and in good taste. The reception hall was hung with Chinese paintings. The panelling of the walls and ceiling, the window frames and some of the beams of the roof, and wall plates were beautifully carved, so as to represent landscape scenes, with trees, bridges and even running water. This apartment led into a garden which was intended to be perfection of its kind and was evidently nurtured with special care, but with the negative merit of stunting rather than of promoting growth. The walled enclosure was painted with Chinese frescoes of exaggerated design. Lofty crimson hollyhawks in full bloom grew in line at the garden-entrance. The whole of the trees within this line had been artificially dwarfed into a comparative diminutiveness which made them mere marvels of nature and of man's ingenuity.

Tahzyungyee is young and his antecedents and intelligence point him out as a man who is still destined to take a leading part in the future Mahomedan Government in Yunan.

This friendship for us over the punch-bowl had reached a climax when it led to an admission that he considered us so nearly allied to himself in race and social position, that he would be proud of adopting us into his family and bestowing upon us his daughters in marriage.

This probably was the extreme of Panthay courtesy and good breeding, and represented a figurative style of speech which meant nothing. It was a critical moment, however, for any amongst our party who might have objected to being hurried nolens volens into a matrimonial engagement. The difficulty was soon at an end: instead of wives we were each presented with Jade-stone-rings and white camelias.

Moung Shwè Yah, my interpreter, told me in a whisper that our jovial host was a man of amorous propensities and that it was his practice to drink every evening at bed time a decoction of Samber's horn mellowed down with honey and spirits, a medicine in great esteem in China on account of its invigorating and stimulant properties.

It struck me this might be the stimulant we were then imbibing, though nothing was said as to the additional item of pork fat, but when afterwards I mentioned my suspicions to Anderson he assured me that he had taken a sly look into the jug and amongst the sediment had discovered certain debris which bore unmistakable resemblance to pieces of hog-skin with the bristles still adhering to it.

But the evil effects of Sambers-horn and the debauchery to which it is said to give rise was disclosed bye and bye in the fact that two of Tahzyungyee's wives and three other females in the family were declared to be barren. Anderson was called upon professionally to prescribe. The inconsiderate males believed that an English physician possessed remedies which acted as a charm against barrenness or imbecility, without requiring that the patients male or female should themselves be subjected to professional examination. This we said was absurd. The women must shew. After some little hesitation two of the supposed sterile females were persuaded into making their appearance at a screened doorway. Both were fine healthy looking women, but one in particular was strikingly well made and a living development of all that seemed requisite to falsify the idea of conjugal disqualification.

It would have been a mockery to subject either women to enquiry or treatment. Anderson as much as said so and asked for the husbands.

This was awkward. The ladies retired and for some little time we were made to feel that a doubt had been thrown upon the practical efficacy of English medical science.

It was satisfactory however to find after some little delay that Anderson's suspicious had been rightly conceived and were duly appreciated.

Shortly before we left, a miserable looking individual of the Genus Homo was presented to us, in the last stage of imbecility, and a direct request made for medicine to cure in the male an affliction which had been already ascribed with palpable obliquity to the innocent female. *This* man was the husband of "living developement" above referred to, and I would not have given him a place in my diary were it not that, apart from the illustration afforded of the practical working of Samber-horn-mixture on the Panthay constitution, a light is thrown on the alleged sterility of Chinese ladies, which practically absolves them from a suspicion of infirmities, but leaves the cause of false accusation as confusing and inexplicable a mystery as ever.

24TH JUNE 1868.

A Chinese festival is being celebrated to-day in honor of Ceres, or some other divinity which presides over agriculture and the fructification of trees and plants. The offerings at the several shrines consist wholly of fruits or flowers. Food is distributed to the poor and trees are planted in the sure and steadfast hope that they will live and multiply. Chinese Theology or Mythology is a mystery. The temple we inhabit is sacred to the memory of ten learned Doctors of Medicine, who have been deified in virtue of their proficiency in the healing art. The idea seems to be that they either transmit their powers to those in the trade who seek their assistance, or that virtue passes out of them in their deified state, and is efficacious in healing the afflicted who resort to their shrine in contrite spirit *and with an abundance of offerings.!*

Chinese Priests in these parts appear to be mere temple scavengers, and take the place of Phyah Gyoons (slaves of the temple) at Budhist shrines in Burma. They have a small dwelling within the precincts of the temple, clear away accumulations of dirt, renew the incense pots and lead lives of piety and celibacy. Beyond this they do not seem to preside at religious ceremonies or take any part in expounding the scriptures. These remarks are limited perhaps in their application to Momein only, or to those portions of Yunan where Mahomedan influences have been at work in demolishing idols and degrading the Priesthood of an "infidel" worship.

It is evident that in the struggle which has been carried on for supremacy in *Yunan* there has been a decided tendency to indulge religious antipathies by a wanton desecration of places of public worship. On visiting the Panthay Musjid at this place a few days ago, I found it established in an ordinary Chinese building, with no pretentions whatever to Mahomedan architecture or decoration. On expressing surprise I was told that formerly Momein contained a magnificent Mosque, built in orthodox style and fitted up with all suitable appurtenances and ornament. It had been burnt down in revenge by a Chinese rabble, at the outbreak of the Mahomedan rising in Yunan.

The Panthays have retaliated without reserve by carrying destruction into every Chinese temple within their power. In this respect the war is one of religious extermination, and Panthay instincts are singularly intolerant, in spite of an affiliation with China which is said to extend over one thousand years.

By dint of repeated enquiry I have been enabled to procure a few short extracts from a manuscript in Chinese, which professes to account for the origin of Mahomedanism in China. The record is very meagre and has suffered no doubt by translation into Burmese, but it is confirmatory in a great measure of the contents of a paper read by General Fytche at a meeting of the Asiatic Society in December 1867. (I have translated it into English and placed it amongst the appendices.)

26TH JUNE 1868.

Tahzyungyee has called to say that he is about to start at the head of two thousand men against a large Chinese force which threatens the Panthay town of Kayto, about 30 miles in a North Westerly direction from Momein. He is afraid that we may have left before his return and has therefore come to say "*Good bye*", I have given him a double barrel rifle and we may calculate on life long friendship.

30TH JUNE 1868.

The Governor has been very unwell for some few days past, but I have had a long private interview with him to-day at which he disclosed information of much interest and importance relating to the present state of affairs in Yunan.

In the first place, letters have been received from Talee in which the Panthay King professes to have been well pleased with the news of our arrival at Momein, and had promised to forward presents in return for those which we had made to the Governor and which had duly arrived at Talee.

He had concluded against the adviseability of continuing our present exploration into Yunan, but gave us notice through the Governor of his intention to despatch a Mission to Rangoon, and apprise us moreover by letter of the earliest season when the state of the country would allow a British Expedition to reach Talee in safety to itself, and with credit to his Government.

Tah-sa-kon further informs me that authentic intelligence has arrived of the capture of Yunan and of its present occupation by a Panthay force.

The official letter giving details of the capture was brought and read in my presence, and proclamations in large type have been posted up upon the city walls as an official announcement of Panthay successes.

30TH JUNE, 1868.

A remaning item of intelligence relates to the French exploring party from Saigon. Tah-sa-kon states that the party came into collision with certain hostile tribes in the vicinity of *Kyaing-yoon-gyee* and suffered severe losses. Some of their number are said to have perished. The remnant arrived in wretched plight at a place called *Thela,* where they were well received and supplied with food and clothing. At that time they were in a state of complete prostration and absolute want.

The Governor regarded this information as correct and reliable in all its details. It had come to him direct, he said, from a Panthay relative who resided at *Thela*, and who had purchased some of the arms and other property which had belonged to the French party previous to the disaster.

It seemed to me extremely probable that the French party may have met with serious difficulties somewhere, as more than a year had elapsed since it was last heard of on the North Eastern confines of Burma, in the *Kyaingtoung* Saubwaship, which closely adjoins *Kyaing-Yoon-gyee*. I was loth however to give full credence to the Governor's information and gladly persuaded myself that it may have been based on exaggerations.

More startling information as regards our own Expedition is conveyed in the fact that a Burmese private Mission with presents from the King of Burma has been despatched from Mandalay direct via *Thinee* to *Yunan*, and it is at present at a place called *Sheedin*, on the high road between *Yoonchan* and Talee.

I never felt myself in a more critical and awkward position than when Tah-sa-kon informed me of this mission, and asked how it was that it had been despatched without my knowledge. Letters he said had reached him from the party at *Sheedin*, but the presents which were being conveyed on 20 mules, and consisted principally of raw cotton, could not be forwarded on account of the unsafe state of the roads between *Sheedin* and *Momein*.

My awkwardness arose out of the false position which I must have appeared to hold in the estimation of the Governor, who had been hitherto made to believe that the British Expedition had set out on its travels under the express patronage of the King of Burma.

In spite of the opposition of Burmese officials and although I knew that much of this opposition had been practically disclosed to the Governor himself, it had nevertheless been my Policy to avow that the King of Burma was still our friend, and that the difficulties we had been made to encounter originated with petty officials who were thereby serving their own private interests as opposed to the interests of the State and Government.

It was impossible any longer to continue this belief in what had now resolved itself into a palpable illusion. It became painfully evident, as soon as *my* turn came for making enquiries and seeking explanation, that the Burmese letters from *Sheedin* had put the Governor into possession of information which he would not disclose, and which, for a time at least, gave him the whiphand of me (so to speak), and produced on my part an awkward amount of reserve and confusion.

But Tah-sa-kon was too much of a gentleman to take advantage of his position, or to evince by any outward manifestation that his confidence or friendship had been in any way affected.

Still a thousand Viss of Cotton coming in so insidious and insinuating a form from a monarch so powerful as the King of Burma was a sore temptation to any Governor, and I could hardly repress either anger or humiliation at the idea that the design of the present had been studiously contrived in seeming antagonism to the British expedition.

I was further reduced to the very unpleasant and dishonorable position (in *appearances* only, be it remembered), of a political impostor, who had already defied the Burmese Government and thrust himself forward at all risks to sow dissension and plan the future conquest of Yunan.

Had Tah-sa-kon not been a man of sound sense and ready discernment, and provided also our expedition had been in any degree offensive to the Panthay Government, the secret mission from Mandalay might have proved still more embarrassing, and placed us individually in a position of extreme degradation and positive danger.

Our departure homewards from Momein is said now to be dependent on a break in the weather. At present rivers and rivulets are filled to over flowing, and are more or less impassable.

The Governor reports fresh disturbances on the Kakhyen Hills, and the Hotha Saubwa, instead of waiting to escort us on the return march to Bhamo, has proceeded in haste to his own domains to guard against an extension of disturbances in the direction of Hotha.

This is in reality only another pretext for our detention at Momein. Tah-sa-kon wants time to complete certain articles of dress which his tailors are hard at work in making up for our party. He is also in expectation of further advices from Talee regarding us, and desires that the work of the mission, as far as he is concerned, shall be made as complete as possible, before he agrees to our final departure.

6TH JULY 1868.

Tahzyungyee, who left this on 28th ultimo with a force of 2000 men, has come upon the Chinese rebels at *Kayto*. Momien is in a state of greedy excitement to day to learn the particulars of the late encounter. One thing is certain, the Panthays have succeeded in securing 300 ears; that is to say 300 of the enemy have bitten the dust and their left ears have been sliced off and sent in to head quarters as proof of the number killed. Bare despatches are not believed in, nevertheless they have been received this morning from Tahzyungyee and read aloud in public at Government house. The General admits that his loss even amounted to 40 in killed alone. This proves that there has been hard fighting.

Tah-sa-kon has sent to tell me that he has received further despatches from Talee. Presents have been forwarded for us from that place, but are detained at *Sheedin*, a large town half way between Momien and Talee.

The Burmese Mission from Mandalay is also at the same place and can neither advance or recede. It is not known whether the mission is to go on to Talee, but Tah-sa-kon says that they will not be allowed to advance beyond *Sheedin* until they have first visited Momien. This latter alternative is out of the question for some time to come on account of the disturbed state of the roads.

As an instance of the present insecurity, Tah-sa-kon mentions that out of three messengers who carried his dispatches from Sheedin, two were way-laid and killed. The third escaped and has arrived in safety at Momein but with a portion only of the Talee dispatches.

Hardly the sort of country for exploration in its present state, by a peaceable body of European travellers!

Had the Panthay Government really borne us ill will or desired our discomfiture, nothing was easier for it than to have committed the expedition to a further prosecution of its travels and thus have secured its certain destruction. On the contrary its policy towards us from first to last has been dictated by a friendly regard for present interests, and a prudent desire to provide against contingencies which might destroy in their results all hope of profitable relations with the British Government.

7TH JULY 1868.

Tah-sa-kon has called to say that letters have been dispatched by him to the Chiefs of *Nantia, Mynela, Sonda* and *Hotha* to make preparations for our return journey to Bhamo. He promises to send a Panthay armed escort of 300 men with us as far as *Mynela*. If the presents from Talee now at Sheedin do not arrive before our departure, they shall be forwarded with the Panthay Embassy which will proceed to Rangoon at the commencement of the next cool season.

Tah-sa-kon says that six or eight months at least must have elapsed since the disaster which befel the French exploring party in the Southern districts of Yunan. He maintains, in spite of our incredulity, that some of the party were killed and that their arms, baggage and equipage of every kind were abandoned.

I say that he has given too ready credence to exaggerated reports, but he only smiles and affirms more doggedly than ever that his information is correct in all material respects. I probe him as far as I am able as to names of places and dates, but in these matters he is at a loss, and his ideas of Geography are vague and illimitable. I do not dare to press matters further or commit what would seem to be a breach of courtesy, by discrediting statements which the Governor is so earnest in affirming to be true, and to be based on sound and reliable information.

Tah-sa-kon makes mention of another party of two hundred foreigners, called by him *Lawmike*, who he says were sent by the Chinese Government to assist in making war against the Panthays. The party was under the leadership of a foreigner who had been honoured by the Chinese Emperor with the Title of *Mike-Tah-See-Dun*, the first syllable being his own name, and the latter three his Chinese title. The party is said to have come from the direction of *Canton*, and to have been actually engaged against the Panthays in the vicinity of *Yunan*. The report is that they were defeated and nearly all killed.

Who can these rowdies be ? Tah-sa-kon says they are neither French nor English. This is said out of courtesy to us, for it is hardly conceivable in his present state of enlightenment that he should be able to draw a distinction between European races. He believes in the extermination of the party, and I am fain to admit that it has been deservedly punished for gratuitous interference with Panthay possessions.

The Governor has sent to invite me to a final conference to-morrow. After the conference we are to partake of a farewell dinner. I am warned to be in readiness to move any day after tomorrow. No exact time will be fixed. The object is to get us off quickly and give no opportunity to dacoits or other evilly disposed parties to conspire for mischief or waylay our route.

Stone celts are procurable in almost any quantity at Momein. They vary in size but are of uniform shape. The Chinese regard them with the same veneration as Burmans, and believe that thay have been hurled from the sky in their present shape as thunderbolts. To support this idea they say that the celts are frequently found embedded in the trunks of trees, where, under no other supposition, could they possibly have gained admittance. They are believed to possess medical and curative properties, and are brought into use as charms, and dipped into medicines under the belief that virtue has thereby passed out of them and duly communicated itself to the thing to be administered. Officers and soldiers proceeding on active service, if fortunate enough to possess celts, carry them on their persons, and are comforted by a feeling of perfect immunity from personal mishaps. In the event of a protracted labour women are are said to derive immediate relief from the presence of one of these *sky productions*. Pain ceases and the labour proceeds to a close with ease and certainty.

Bronze or copper celts are more uncommon, but we met with them at Manwyne and Hotha in the Shan States, on the return journey from Momein. The shape of those I saw were uniform but very peculiar. They are all provided with sockets so as to be easily adjusted to handles. One that I purchased at Manwyne for 25 Rupees (200 Rupees was the first price asked), was said to have been found in a paddy field, not far from the town and not much below the surface. So precious are they and so notorious does a man become by being a possessor, that I was frequently told at different intervals of our journey, of a certain Kakhyen Saubwa in some remote part of the hills, who was a fortunate owner, and who, if I ever met him, might be induced to sell on the receipt of suitable consideration. Copper celts are neatly encased by their owners in small bags and held by a guard chain which is suspended from the neck. But whether of stone or copper it argues a taste of barbarism, and amounts almost to sacrilege, to place a celt on the ground or in any position which, in Burman Ethics, betokens inferiority. The more reverently they are cared for the more powerful becomes their efficacy as an omen of success and good fortune in every human or inhuman adventure.

The conference with the Governor to-day has been very satisfactory. His Chief officers were present and a very fair settlement arrived at on points affecting the question of re-opening the old caravan trade between *Yunan* and *Burma*.

Tah-sa-kon is not quite satisfied as to the means which may or may not be at hand of transporting goods between Bhamo and Rangoon and vice versa. He is afraid that the provisions of our treaty with *Burma*, which directs that goods from China passing through Upper Burma to Pegu shall pay only a one per cent ad valorem duty in *Burma*, will cause ill feeling and continued opposition on the part of the Burmese Government: personally he is delighted at the prospect of avoiding Transit and Customs Duties on goods passing through Burma, but he is apprehensive of difficulties with the Burmese Government.

I assure him on these points, by stating that abundant means of carriage were at all times available on the Irrawaddy and that we had proved the navigability of the river above Mandalay, by having ourselves performed the journey in a large steamer provided by His Majesty the King of Burma.

In the matter of Transit and Customs Duty, I informed the Governor that he would see in the copies of our treaties with Burma which I had given him, that the articles of the treaty relating to duties were equally binding on both Governments, and had been specially conceived in a mutual endeavour to promote the welfare of their subjects and secure advantageous commercial relations with the Chinese frontier. The difficulties which the Governor had very naturally deemed possible as likely to arise out of indirect opposition on the part of the Burmese Government, would, if they existed, be amply met by the appointment, under our late Treaty with Burma, of British agents at *Bhamo* and *Menhla*, whose exclusive duty it would be to watch over the interests of Trade and guard against any infringement of Treaty stipulations.

The Governor informs me that he is determined to make the experiment this next cold season of despatching his caravans to Bhamo instead of to Mandalay direct, via Thinee. He has already reported his intention of doing so to the Talee Government and been given to understand in reply, that the Talee caravans will also receive orders to proceed to Bhamo provided it can be ascertained that there is sufficient inducement, or rather, that their goods can be sold, and that a sufficiency of raw cotton is procurable at Bhamo to load their return mules to *Yunan*. If these points are settled, there is nothing, the Governor says, to prevent the caravans accomplishing the Bhamo trip twice and even three times during a season, and within the period at present occupied by one trip to Mandalay.

I was in a position to assure the Governor that the necessary arrangements could be made at Bhamo during the forth-coming season, to supply the whole of the *Yunan* caravans with raw cotton, but I advised him to make the experiment with his *Momien* caravans and to be under no indefinite apprehension of failure. The Governor promised to send his caravans with the Mission which the King of Talee had proposed to send to Rangoon. The object of this mission he said, would be to enter into commercial relations with our Government, and obtain correct perceptions relating to the feasibility of trading direct with Rangoon instead of with Mandalay. Means of carriage, freight, charges by boat or steamers, general advantages &c., &c.

I did all I could to impress these objects on the mind of the Governor, and to encourage the experimental trip which was to be made to Bhamo. All the advice which my position and experience justified me in offering, amounted in fact to an urgent appeal in favor of the overland trade viâ Bhamo with China. In becoming the advocate of so noble an enterprise, I found myself in the happy circumstances of one who was appealing to a willing and sympathizing people, whose interests were specially bound up with our own, and who are as keenly alive to the benefits of promoting trade with Burma as we are eager to form a commercial relationship with South Western China.

The experimental trip to Bhamo and the Panthay mission to Rangoon had been adopted as the readiest and most certain means of brushing away past prejudices, and of gaining a personal insight into certain altered conditions in favor of commerce, which had arisen out of the British occupation of Pegu and our commercial treaties with the Burmese Government.

The Governor next called one of his secretaries, who brought and gave me a letter which I was asked to deliver to the English Governor at Rangoon. The letter was read out publicly and its contents translated. All was most favorable as evidence of our expeditionary success, and of the desire on the part of the Panthay Government to second any efforts we might make to establish commercial intercourse between Burma and Yunan.

I noticed, however, that no mention had been made of Transit or Customs Duties leviable on goods within Panthay possessions. Tah-sa-kon replied by saying that it did not appear to him either *courteous* or customary to allude to such matters in his first friendly letter to the Governor of Rangoon. He had no objection to furnish me separately with the list of duties payable at Momein or within Panthay territory, but at the same time he said that in the present unsettled state of affairs any such list was unnecessary and could not be deemed final or satisfactory as regarded the trade of *Yunan*.

There was nothing to be got by pressing matters, and I allowed the Governor to conclude our conversation on this subject with the following promising but off—hand remarks. "After all, what use are Tariff lists, are we not "brothers? my wish is to reduce the rates to the lowest pos-

"sible limit or even to abolish them altogether, if by doing
"so I can entice commerce to this route; I will be guided
"by your advice at all times on this and other subjects.

As a winding up to our conference the Governor presented me with two seals to be used in my correspondence with him after my return to Mandalay. I also gave him two large gold seals. One engraved with a coat of arms cut into white cornelian. The other represents an owl seated upon an hour glass eleborately engraved on a large Topaz. It was fortunate that these seals were in my possession at the time, as they well answered the purpose to which I have designed them, and are appreciated by the Governor. The seals I received in exchange are seals of Office, as peculiarly belonging to Tah-sa-kon in his capacity of Governor of Momein. It is believed that this interchange of seals, besides being intended as a special mark of confidence and esteem, will give an impress of reality to our correspondence, and secure us mutually against fraud and imposition.

10TH JULY 1868.

The whole day has been devoted to ceremonial visits and leave taking. We proceeded to Government House at mid-day to say goodbye; and the Governor almost immediately afterwards returned our visit with a full suite of his retainers, and a quantity of useful presents which he begged us to accept ourselves and to distribute amongst our escort and followers. It was expressly stated that the presents were not to be considered as in any way a return for those which had been given to him on our first arrival at Momein. Suitable return presents would be forwarded with the mission to Rangoon from Talee during the next cold season. In the meantime, the Governor wished us to accept a few articles as coming from himself, and which would be found of use during our return journey to Bhamo. The bulk of the presents consisted of

        80   Cotton jackets
        80   Chinese sun or rain hats
        80   Pieces of waterproof oiled paper.

Of the above, one each was to be distributed to each of

the Police escort and our native servants. The European members of the Expedition were each presented with.

- 1 Piece of flowered silk
- 1 Silk jacket
- 1 Amber rosary or necklace
- 1 Straw sun hat
- 1 Pair Chinese boots

In addition to the above, the Governor presented me personally with his own full dress mandarin suit, which consisted of a full flowing robe of blue satin covered with silk and gold embroidery. An official head dress with ornaments.

- 1 Pair black silk boots.
- 1 Gold and jade stone chatelaine.
- 4 Panthay spears with long silver-plated handles.

The Jemadar commanding the Police escort and his wife (a Burmese lady who accompanied him to Momein) were also each presented with a silk jacket and straw hat.

We could not fail to mark the kindness of disposition which led Tah-sa-kon to provide our escort and followers with means which were expressly intended to conduce to their personal comfort on the march to Bhamo. The rains had set in with violence and the waterproof oiled paper and rain-hats had become a positive necessity, which I could not conveniently have procured myself without the Governor's kind interference.

Tah-sa-kon next handed me a Chinese document of very formidable proportions, which was opened out and read aloud by his chief secretary.

The document was several feet in length and purported to be a transcript of the proclamation which had been posted upon the city wall as a public announcement of Panthay success at *Yunan*. Apart from its literary details, which are at present a mystery to us, the prodigious size of the document would make it a literary curiosity in any museum in the world.

Next came the promised letter addressed to myself on the subject of Customs Duty leviable within Panthay Territory. The only duty stations mentioned between the Burmese frontier and *Momein* are those situated at *Manphoo* and *Nantin*. On my noticing the deficiency as regarded the Shan States, the Governor remarked that those States had always been a mere dependency and had no special right to levy customs duty on Government account. This matter had already been explained to the Shan Chiefs, and definitely settled by communications which had been forwarded to them since the date of my arrival at *Momein*.

In reply I said that it appeared to me impolitic to make any arbitrary distinction (in the case of the Shan Chiefs) which limited their hereditary right to levy transit duty on goods passing through their respective Principalities.

I was arguing I said against our own interests perhaps in advocating the cause of the Shan Saubwas, and the Governor would be able to judge thereby of the sincerity of my suggestions. Tah-sa-kon was amused and hinted to me that the Shans knew very well how to take care of themselves. There were certain fees and perquisites attached to a Saubwaship which were very trifling and would not be interfered with. He did not think it advisable to formally recognize the right of each Saubwa to levy Custom's Duty at will within his own state. A precedent might thereby be established which would militate against his present idea of reducing customs duty to a limit which would encourage rather than act as a burden on trade.

For the same reason also he was not inclined to fix any definite Duty Rates for Momein. The time had not come for so much nicety in the collections. He was himself his own collector at Momein, and his desire was if possible in the matter of reductions to exceed even my own wishes. For instance if I mentioned a 1 per cent Duty his own inclination would lead him to be content with one half of that sum or eight annas!

I could not help believing in the sincerity of his intentins, for Tah-sa-kon had proved himself in his dealings with us from fist to last to be a man of large minded views and generous impulses.

I was obliged, however, to tell him that our mutual friendly regard for each other was not a sufficient guarantee to merchants in British Territory who would not consent to embark in trading adventures with *Yunan* without some definite guide by which to calculate their chances of profit or loss, as dependent on the amount of transit or Customs duty leviable beyond British Territory.

After a long conversation on this subject (the details of which are too tedious for record), the Governor gave me his verbal assurance that in no instance would the aggregate amount of duty taken at any or all of the duty stations between the Shan States and Talee exceed (as he expressed it) 10 Rupees on goods valued at 250 Rupees, or in other words a four per cent ad valorem rate.

I saw the necessity of being contented with this assurance. It would have been impolitic, at the very outset of our dealings with a new people and Government (having in contemplation the revival of an extinct trade in their country), to have insisted on a more definite or binding arrangement. The object in doing so, without being appreciated, was open to misapprehension and might have given rise to adverse suspicions. Besides the customs duty being the perquisite of Panthay Governors the matter was one which affected Tahsa-kon's private purse, and their reduction could not have been more persistently urged than they were without the fear of unnecessary offence.

Such persistency moreover would have been immature, I consider, as regards the present state of our national relations. We therefore parted under a mutual exhortation to cherish the recollection of present friendship and above all things to bear in mind that nothing would more directly tend to tranquillize *Yunan* and restore it with other neighbouring Provinces to their former prosperity than a steady adherence to the means now offered of resuscitating the old caravan trade viâ Bhamo, and of thereby extending that trade by the only direct natural outlet of the Irrawaddy to the rich commercial seaboard of Pegu and British Burma.

334. We have said goodbye to the Governor and are on the eve of departure from *Momien*. It is time therefore to make further apologies for the unwieldy character of the present Report. The copious reference to my Diary and the supplementary notices and observations which are every where

called for have led to digressions of a lengthy and sometimes a tedious character. They will rightly be regarded as an undue infringement of all the ordinary rules of official correspondence. To me the task of recording our experiences in their present form has been one in which I have seemed to live over again the toils and pleasures of a moderate adventure. Much of interest remains to be told. The return journey to Momien was not accomplished without an accumulatation of incident and observation which would preserve its interest in almost any form; but time, ill health and the more legitimate duties of my present office are all in active opposition to the continuance of the narrative in its present proportions. I am therefore compelled, somewhat reluctantly, to hurry over the return journey from Momien, and shall allow myself a limited margin only for remarks on special points in which my opinion is called for as leader of the Expedition.

335. When I found, after a protracted residence at Momein, that there was no prospective chance, within a reasonable period, of my being able to proceed further into Yunan without the certainty of encountering armed opposition and involving the Government in troublesome complications which it was my duty to avoid, I was compelled under a variety of pressing considerations to think of a return homewards, and preparations having accordingly been made we left Momein on 13th July and commenced the journey to Bhamo.

336. In my several conversations with the Governor as to the choice of a Route to *Bhamo* I had always taken care to let it be understood that my earnest desire was to return by a different route to that by which we had reached *Momein*. The Governor in his willingess to serve me feigned a compliance with my wishes, but with a certain hesitation of manner which at the time was a little mysterious. I afterwards discovered that the hesitation was due to a very reasonable supposition that the other route which I proposed to explore might be made to lead direct to *Yoonchan* and ignore the existence of *Momein* altogether.

337. I combated this idea so far as to cause arrangements to be entered into by which the Hotha Saubwa was directed to meet me at *Nantin* and escort us thence viâ *Shamalon*

and the *Hotha* valley to *Hotha*, from which place it would remain at my discretion either to pursue the *Sawuddy* or Southern route across the *Kakhyen* hills to *Bhamo*, or follow the direct central route which had hitherto been universally used by successive Burmese and Chinese Embassies in their political intercourse between Bhamo and China.

338. The Hotha Saubwa failed in his arrangement to meet me at *Nantin*, and I pushed on to Mynela in the hope of catching him there. Here, as well as at *Sanda* and *Manwyne*, the officials were openly opposed to my leaving the *Sanda* for the *Hotha* valley. Their opposition was natural enough, for the Shans, judging by what they had heard of our success at Momein, had actually realized the fact of a revived trade between *Bhamo* and *Momein*, and were reasonably averse to the idea of encouraging any proposal by which that trade would be so diverted as to exclude them from all immediate participation in its many advantages.

339. I upbraided them gently for the apparent selfishness of their motives as opposed to measures which were intended for the public good; but I could not help feeling at the same time that the reluctance to assist me at the cost of excluding themselves from a prominent position on the newly proposed trade route, afforded the strongest presumptive evidence of the success which the expedition had already secured for itself throughout an important section of the Northern Shan States.

340. A South West Moonsoon and continuous rain aided the Shans in their hospitable endeavours to retain us as their guests, and prolong our stay at their several chief towns. It was not until my arrival at *Manwyne* that the *Hotha* Saubwa was induced to remember his engagements and concert measures for crossing the hill range which separates the *Sanda* and *Hotha* valleys.

341. The alleged difficulties of this route were two-fold. The direct route leading from *Nantin* into the *Hotha* valley would necessarily cross the *Shamalon* range which was then known to be infested by parties of *Lees-hee-ta-hee's* freebooters, who, having been driven from *Mauphoo*, had taken shelter in another hill fortress. Thus far at least I was willing to admit that the objections to the direct *Nantin* route were in themselves reasonable and probably correct. But on reaching

Mynela and *Sanda*, from both of which places a practicable road was available between the *Hotha* and *Sanda* valleys (without passing *Shamulon*), it was at once apparent that the further objections raised for limiting our travels to the *Sanda* valley were based upon no more positive foundation than the simple though very laudable desire (as it may have seemed to them) of securing a permanent commercial highway through their own States, to the exclusion of any other more available line of country which our exploration might have disclosed.

342. In crossing from either *Mynela* or *Sanda* to the base of the range which divided the *Sanda* and *Hotha* valleys it was necessary to pass through a portion of the *Mynela* district (already alluded to) which owed allegiance to no particular Chief and had existed for some years past in a barbarous state of outlawry and misrule. It was affirmed with some shew of truth that the demonstration which had been made against us on the march between *Manwyne* and *Sanda* on 15th May had been planned and carried out by the lawless inhabitants of this disaffected district, and it was through a portion of this same district that our present route must of necessity pass in crossing the range between *Sanda* and *Hotha*.

343. I will not attempt to describe in detail the laborious conferences with Shan officials, the protocolling between *Sanda* and *Mynela*, and the various points d'apui which had to be maintained or conceded before a practicable breach was made in the formidable cordon by which our too-loving Shan friends of the *Sanda* valley had designed to make us exclusively their own.

344. They succeeded in forcing upon us the *Sanda* valley as far as *Manwyne*; but this resulted, I consider, in a positive advantage; for whereas there was no particular object to be gained by proceeding direct from *Nantin* to *Hotha* the prolonged stay amongst our friends at the chief towns of *Mynela*, *Sanda* and *Manwyne* did much to familiarize us with the people, and afford them convincing testimony of the sincerity of our intentions.

345. The final arrangement by which a passage through the *Mynela* disturbed district became in any wise practicable was due to our having won over to our cause two Shan officials

who had each acquired a moderate degree of notoriety as friends of disorder rather than as peaceable subjects of their respective Saubwas. Both men have already been mentioned, one was the *Poogen* or head man of *Monhleo*, who had resisted our advance whilst at *Ponsee* and proclaimed himself to be in open antagonism to all who claimed alliance with the *Panthay* Government.

346. The other was *Kingen*, a Tamon of *Mynela*, and one of the deputies on the part of the *Mynela* chief who was sent to meet us at *Ponsee* in May and afford escort from thence to the Shan States. It was not until after his duty had been performed on that occasion that I subsequently found cause to suspect that the hostile demonstration of the 15th May was in great measure due to his secret influences. Both men were possessed of authority in the disturbed portion of the *Mynela* district, and it was very evident that all the authority of the Mynela and Sanda Chiefs must have proved ineffectual in opening a way between Sanda and Hotha, unless I succeeded in subsidizing those who were powerful only in their association with outlaws.

347. It may be one of the anomalies of the present Shan Government that these said outlaws were allowed, in the presence of their legitimate Shan Chiefs, to guarantee us safe conduct through a State in which its lawful rulers were impotent and unrecognized. It is stranger still that the same chiefs, instead of asserting their rights and branding the outlaws, should have acknowledged their power and urged me to accept the proffered guarantee. As in *Yunan* so in the Shan States; brigands belonged to a recognized order; and legalized rule had dwindled into outlawry—might was right. There was no other line of interdependance between Kakhyens and Burmese; Burmese and Shans; Shans and Kakhyens; Chinese and Shans; Panthays and Chinese; Shans and Panthays; or the numerous other changes which might be rung on this high toned mass of incongruous materials.

348. But there was order in chaos—outlaws and States were equally tractable. *Monhleo* and *Kingen* were staunch in their adherence and zealously worked in the cause of our Mission. I paid then abundantly; metallic passes were frequent and effectual. Their services were recorded by me at their

special request in separate written certificates which they instinctively prized as their chief reward. Certificates were also asked for by the Shan Deputies of *Sanda* who accompanied us on the return journey as far as *Manwyne*. I was specially requested to stamp them with my seal, and give the documents an impress of validity which would secure the notice of future travellers and pave the way to further good offices. I parted from outlaws and deputies alike under a deep sense of gratitude for faithful service and a steady adherence to the cause of our Mission.

349. Amongst the events which marked our homeward journey I must pause for a moment to mention the arrival of Mr. Robert Gordon, who had been despatched to take the place of Captain J. M. Williams as engineer to the Expedition.

350. Some ten days previous to Mr. Gordon's arrival a Burmese armed party of one hundred men had reached *Mynela* with 5,000 Rupees, being a portion of the 10,000 forwarded from Rangoon for our use by the Chief Commissioner of British Burma. The Burmese officer[*] in command of this party was afraid, according to his own account, to move beyond *Mynela*, and had failed even to send on any communication by which news of his advent would have reached me at Momien. He happened to be the same official who headed the Burmese miners at Ponsee and who had at that time conducted himself towards us as a baneful, obstructive, and dangerous oppositionist. He was now abject and submissive, and crouchingly entreated me not to bear resentment towards him for past offences but to consider him my slave and and trust henceforth his aid and fidelity.

351. It had become a part of the Burmese programme that the Sayay-dau-gyee should make amendment for past shortcomings by proffering aid when no longer required, and exacting an acknowledgment of Burmese obligations. It was with grief therefore he learned I could do without him; but his disappointment was complete when I ordered him to leave and signified my intention of exploring new routes between the Shan States and Burma. The tables were turned and the Sayay-dau-gyee knew it. *We* were masters of the position and despised and dreaded a Burmese

---

[*] Goung Byon Sayay daugyee.

connectionship. The Sayay-dau-gyee was obliged to leave, but I afterwards heard that he lingered at Manwyne in the hope we might still abandon our plans and return in his train as rescued dependents.

352. Mr. Gordon's arrival has been a matter of unquestionable importance in supplying the desideratum of a professional opinion on a greater portion of the Route which the expedition has traversed. As compared with *our* trials and disappointments, his journey from Mandalay was signalized by facilities of significant good omen. Not only was he favoured by the *active* support of the Burmese Government, but profited to the full by our policy of conciliation. The Shans received him with open arms and his welcome everywhere was signal and triumphant. This is fortunate, for Mr. Gordon in his zealous resolve to join the expedition at all risks and under a misconception no doubt of probable consequences, had conceived the idea of *fighting his way* across the *Kakhyen* hills, and of rising superior to all opposition. All chances of conflict had been happily averted; and Burmese officials under altered circumstances vied with each other to be as complacent and yielding as they had formerly proved themselves inimical and obstructive.

353. There was further cause for congratulation in the fact, that the advance of a hundred and fifty armed Burmese to *Mynela* as bearers of supplies to the British expedition would work its effect on Panthay comprehensions and add a link to our own significance. But the crowning boon was the receipt of Rupees. I could now indulge in comparative munificence and provide the means of adding to our collections. In Shropshire, as elsewhere perhaps, "money makes the mare to go" but in the Shan States and amongst Kakhyens its effect is electrical and outstrips the measure of mere horse rapidity. But it is time to push on.

354. We left Manwyne at 10 A. M. on 10th August and the first few hours were passed in dubious efforts to cross the Tahpen. The baggage had already been packed on mule panniers and sent down the river in canoes to a point where the river communicated with a creek on the opposite bank. The object of sending the baggage by this creek was, that it could be transported to a desired point without being subjected to

the necessity of passing through a morass on the bank of the river opposite to Manwyne.

355. This morass was originally paddy land which had lately acquired a large residuum of alluvial soil from recent and continuous river inundations. The overflow had subsided a short time only before our arrival, and one or two days of sunshine had caked the mud sufficiently to give it the appearance of smooth sticky clay bared of all vegetation, and cracked up into a network of fissures which were the more awkward on account of the treacherous inconsistency of the immediate subsoil. Nevertheless we worked our way onwards for a considerable distance without extraordinary effort or exertion until apparently a point of greatest depression had been reached and the next hundred yards of our journey was ludicrously suggestive of a whole expedition hopelessly bogged?

356. My pony was leading and floundered head-foremost. I disengaged myself in time only to get my legs into the clay instead of my head and shoulders—others were less fortunate—long-legs were an advantage—Captain Bowers was obliged to pay down Rupees and submit to be dragged out of each fresh lodgement to which a move of position inevitably consigned him. By 2 P. M. we were well across and fairly extricated from our clayey attachments.

357. The road at starting led up an abrupt lateral spur which, to the height of a thousand feet or more, abounded in boulders and outcroppings of pure white marble, similar in all respects to that which occurs in the same range and at the same elevation in the vicinity of the *Ponsee* silver mines. Time being a consideration we pushed on without a halt until we had climbed 3,200 feet in four hours and had reached a point before night fall from which the Hotha valley was revealed in all the beauty of serene twilight. The longing desire which had so long possessed us to see and to know the physical character of the country beyond the Eastern range of the Sanda valley was at length gratified by the disclosure of another valley similar in general features to the Sanda valley, and flanked by a well defined continuous ridge which lay parallel to the range we had then been crossing.

358. The ascent from the Sanda side had been steep and abrupt; we were now descending the counter-slope into

the Hotha valley, and looked down on what, within a few hundred feet of the base of the range, appeared in the distance to be a billowy accumulation of grassy knolls, caused by the gradual projection into the valley of multitudinous spurs and their intersecting ravines and water courses. The valley itself, never perhaps more than from three to four miles broad (measured from the base of the flanking ranges), stretched away in a straight line for twenty miles and was numerously studded everywhere with villages and plantations.

359. Darkness intervened long before we had reached the level of the valley, and as one of the inconveniences and mishaps arising therefrom, a small party with which I had become detached lost its way, and arrived at 9 P. M. at a Shan village several miles out of the direct route, and where the presence of a European was as novel and unexpected as if we had suddenly tumbled (as in fact we almost had done) out of the clouds. The ride after night fall down rugged descents in close proximity to occasional precipitous ridges which, fortunately for our peace of mind, were partly shrouded in darkness, was anything but pleasurable when allied to the fact that we had lost our way too irretrievably to hope for relief at least till the morrow.

360. Anderson was with me and we formed a select party, which consisted of the Manhleo Poogen, my Shan interpreter, three Burmese Policemen carrying Tah-sa-kon's silver spears, and two lascars with my guns and ammunition. We reached a monastery the Phoongyees of which in affording us bare shelter were mutely apathetic as to other necessities. Food and bedding were out of the question. It was divinely suggested however that an apple tree grew by the way heavy with fruit which we were welcome to if any of our party could be persuaded into first going in search of the tree and then climbing up it in total darkness.

361. We had evidently fallen upon inhospitable quarters. A Burman Phoongyee would have done the good Samaritan at all costs of usage or convenience, but the Shan Divine was a little less tractable, so we lay down on the wooden floor as we were, and would soon have forgotten temporary cares in sleep had not the Priest and his collegiates chosen this particular time for Buddhist vespers which they

screached out for an hour in most irreverent discord. The hour was an age. The Priests and their sanctity were a hidious nightmare, more inimical to sleep than the hard floor or the clothes in which we lay still clammy and caked with clay incrustations.

362. One of the incidents of this prayer meeting roused me from stupor to a sense of reality. The well known voice of my Shan interpreter appeared to mingle with the prayers of the Phoongyees, and turning half unwillingly in the direction of the voices I noticed that the interpreter held out a silver coin and was bargaining lustily for a measure of rice. The chief Phoongyee got up, took the money, supplied the rice, and returned to his devotions.

363. Such arrant unorthodoxy in a Priest of Buddh can only be appreciated by those who claim an acquaintance with Burmese Buddhism.

Shan Phoongyees are evidently beings who disregard mere forms which place a barrier between themselves and the world, and would limit their utility to mental abstraction and religious imbecility.

364. Their night's devotion or my interpreter's coin had given a stimulus to priestly charity, for the Phoongyees relented about midnight and supplied mats and Phoongyee cloths as a protection against cold. There was no inducement however to indulge in a morning's snooze and we were up and on the move at daylight.

365. What a lovely valley! what thrift and care is exhibited in the nice definition of garden and paddy land and economical means of drainage and irrigation. A substantial roadway leads mid valley over grassy slopes, past carved stone fountains and Buddhist shrines, across neat stone bridges and shining rivulets, through orchards of apple trees and groves of chesnut, solitary firs and clumps of bamboo, and brings us too soon to our Hotha terminus.

366. On reaching the Saubwa's 'Haw' or Palace we were received with a salute of guns and by the Saubwa himself in full official robes, who conducted us inside and claimed us as his guests. The life at Hotha from 10th to 27th August was full of novelty. Living en famille as we did with the

Chief and his household, many precious opportunities were afforded of acquiring a correct practical knowledge of Shan domesticity and national characteristics.

367 With the exception of the Saubwas palace there is nothing in the appearance or condition of Hotha as a town to distinguish it from any of the other numerous towns or villages of the entire valley. This valley includes two Saubwaships known respectively as *Hotha* and *Latha*, but collectively designated '*Mynetha*', an appellation which has also been extended to its inhabitants to distinguish them from other divisions of the great Shan family.

368 The dress language and general physique of Mynetha Shans proclaim them to be distinct in tribal origin from their neighbours in the adjoining Shan States. The women wear short trousers and an apron (very masonic) with a broad stiff-embroidered belt, which is passed round the waist and gives support and configuration to the back and loins. The jacket is ornamented before and behind by masses of silver plate embossments. Instead of the inverted pyramidal shaped puggery worn by Shan women of the Sanda valley, the ladies of Mynetha plat their hair, twist it into a horizontal chignon at the crown of the head, and hold the whole together with a circlet of flat silver-headed hair-pins which are arranged so as to form a head ornament singularly unique and fancifully attractive.

The tout-ensemble of both men and women, including dress and general physiognomy, has a decided Chinese tendency, which is little in accord with the Shan orginalities of *Manwyne* and *Sanda*.

369 As regards language, there is a marked affinity between that spoken by the *Mynetha* Shans and the Leesaw hill tribes who occupy portions of these hill ranges and extend far away beyond Momein into central Yunan. I have already remarked that the Leesaw language bears a striking resemblance to Burmese, and it is difficult at present to account for this triple connectionship in language between races which, though perhaps ethnologically allied, have been separated for many centuries from contact or intercourse. The *Leesaws* are nearly allied to Chinese, and on this account I am content to particularize them as *Chinese Kakhyens* although the Kak-

hyens look upon them as a slave race and will not admit to even a tribal relationship. The singular resemblance in the language of these three distinct races is no mere coincidence, and may be accepted as an interesting base for philological enquiry.

370. But I must go back to the Expedition. The principal point for determination at Hotha was the selection of a route across the Kakhyen Hills between Hotha and Bhamo. My original wish and intention was to have proceeded from Hotha across the range which separates it from the Shan State of *Mynewun* (in Burmese *Mowon*) and to have pursued the route from thence to Sawuddy a small town on the Irrawaddy, twelve miles south of *Bhamo*. But on arrival at Hotha I was induced by a multiplicity of considerations to decide upon a practical exploration of the direct central or Embassy route, which from time immemorial had constituted the grand highway between China and Burma and was the route par excellence which Burmese and Chinese Embassies had invariably traversed when deputed by their respective Governments to the capitals of either country.

371. This route had however been practically closed for more than five years owing to the murder of seven unoffending Kakhyens by a drunken Burmese official of Bhamo. The principal Chiefs through whose districts the road passes, having applied in vain for justice and redress, entered into a compact to avenge their wrongs by forswearing all communication with Bhamo and combining in a plan of reprisals on Burmese villages.

372. Notwithstanding these temporary drawbacks the Hotha Saubwa favored the idea of re-opening this route under pleas and considerations both reasonable and advantageous. He affirmed that the journey between Bhamo and Momein was shortened by two days as compared with the Northern route via Ponlyne, and by five days as compared with the line known as the Southern or *Sawuddy* route. He further urged that he was on intimate and friendly relations with all the *Kakhyen* chiefs who held the route between *Hotha* and *Bhamo*, and guaranteed his influence over these chiefs, as sufficient, under the protection which would be afforded by the residence of a British Agent at *Bhamo*, to put an end to present feuds and restore through the medium of our interference a renewal of friendship between Kakhyens and Burmese.

373. The immediate objection to the *Sawuddy* route as regarded ourselves was that doubts were disclosed at Hotha affecting the unfriendly disposition of the Mynewun Saubwa who had succumbed, it was said, to Burmese influences, and was generally averse to European intercourse.

374. My Shan and Kakhyen interpreter Moung Mo (himself formerly a Burmese official,) suggested rather significantly as a reason for avoiding the *Sawuddy* route that the Burmese Authorities had been led to speculate upon our return viâ *Mynewun*, and might therefore interest themselves in raising difficulties or placing indirect obstacles to our progress by influencing the Kakhyen chiefs who held the passes leading to *Sawuddy*. It was not without mature deliberation, on these and other material points affecting the welfare and eventualities of the Expedition that I finally determined to proceed by the direct central route from *Hotha* to *Bhamo* and detach an Assistant Surveyor of the party, to make a flying survey of the Southern route leading viâ *Mynewun* to *Sawuddy*.

375. But before we leave Hotha, I may be excused for dwelling on a few incidents of interest illustrative of a residence in the *Mynetha* valley, and of our unrestrained intercourse with its friendly inhabitants.

376. I have already spoken of the *Mynetha* Shans, as distinguished by dress, language and general characteristics from the people of the neighbouring Shan States. My impression is that these distinctions are traceable to local causes or circumstances of position, and to a more general infusion of a Chinese element than is ordinarily met with amongst the average inhabitants of the northern Shan States. The chief of Hotha is a Chinaman by descent, and positively affirms that more than a half of his Mynetha subjects were originally Chinese who, by long contact with Shan associations, have lost much of their originality and degenerated at length into a Shan race.

377. The Mynetha valley is elevated 1800 feet above the valley of Sanda, and enjoys on this account a climate which has enriched it with the varied productions of a temperate zone; Apple, Pear, Chestnut and Peach trees, have taken the place of bamboo and mangoe. The hedge rows abound

in bramble and roses. Here and there is an occasional fir, and the hill sides are forests of chestnut and bauhinia.

378. The Shans themselves affirm that *Mynetha* exceeds in elevation all the valleys by which it is surrounded, and that a considerable descent is made on leaving Hotha to proceed to either *Sanda, Mynela, Mynetee Mynewun* or *Mynemaw*. This assertion as regards its elevation (that is to say the level of the Mynetha valley proper) holds good I was assured by the Saubwa (no mean authority in such matters), in its application to a system of valleys similar in general direction to that of *Sanda* and *Mynela*, and which are continued in almost endless succession (in the Saubwa's words) as far as *Quantong* (Canton), by which he probably refers to the nearest seaboard of Cambodia or Cochin China.

379. During our stay at Hotha, we accompanied the Saubwa at his own invitation on a Picnicing expedition to his country seat at *Saykow* (ancient Hotha), very charmingly situated on a slight eminence at the North Western extremity of the *Mynetha* valley. The ride through the valley was a source of gratification in unfolding exceptional beauties of scenery and landscape, and affording evidence of the economy and care which Shans bestow on agriculture and irrigation. It is at once apparent in this valley, as well as in the other states we have visited, that the whole population is purely agricultural. The land is held in hereditary allotments, and is the property of peasant proprietors who live on its produce.

380. The strongest possible inducement is thus given to industrious activity, and the result is improved production and universal abundance. The land not immediately under cultivation, is retained for grazing purposes and consists generally of undulating slopes, which are covered with a green velvety sward and intersected occasionally by an abrupt ravine or sparking rivulet as it finds its way from neighbouring heights to join the central stream of the valley.

381. The roads are excellent in their way in supplying the wants of the population, which are limited as regards carriage to mules and pack bullocks. In most places liable to inundation they are raised and paved with stone slabs laid on horizontally and fitted to each other with great nicety. The bridges are of stone, and built, after the Chinese model, of one

or more high circular or hemispherical arches, flanked at either extremity by Zayats or rest houses.

372. The direct road to Nantin from Hotha (a continuation of the old Embassy route from Bhamo), leads out of the Hotha valley at a point where the hill ranges converge, and shut in the valley at its North East extremity. The ascent from the valley to this pass is so gradual as to be almost imperceptable, and as the height of the Hotha valley is on a level (or nearly so) with the elevation of *Nantin* I am lead to believe, from a general view of the configuration of the country as well as from the information of the Hotha Chief, that the intervening distance between *Hotha* and *Nantin* is free from any serious physical obstruction, such as that caused by the *Mauphoo* range on the direct high way between *Mynela* and *Nantin*.

Another road leads from old *Hotha* into the Sanda valley in the direction of *Mynela*, through a gorge of very diminished elevation as compared with our mountain experiences between *Manwyne* and *Hotha*.

383. The Saubwa's country-seat at *Say-kow* consists of a series of buildings which lead into each other by a line of consecutive court yards and small garden enclosures. The house in which the Saubwa and his family reside is a wooden structure of Chinese design, and is specially interesting on account of the eleborate carvings and ornamentation which is every where displayed in prominent elegance.

484. The Saubwa accompanied us a short distance from the town for the purpose of visiting a very interesting group of Chinese Temples which had lately undergone extensive repairs and reornamentation. The Temples are Buddhistic, after a Chinese misconception (sic mihi videtur) of orthodox Buddhism. The principal range is occupied by a colossal figure of the "Thugea men" or King of angels, who is enshrined in a huge casement of wood carving of the most chaste design, and with graduated proportions which give grace and symmetry to what must otherwise have resembled an exaggerated side-board.

Gaudama and two other Buddhs have a building to themselves below, and are encompassed by a multitudinous group of life-size designs which represent the embryo God in the several existences which preceded an emergence into perfect Buddh.

The greater portion of an adjoining Temple is appropriated to *Quah-Gnein*, whom I have already mentioned as the Goddess of conception and Physician in ordinary to all women afflicted with barrenness. Here also as elsewhere she is represented nursing a naked babe with an inordinate development of male organization.

485. The Saubwa entertained us sumptuously at his country quarters; dinner was served in really good style, and with a profusion which takes a novice by surprise. One of the objects of these entertainments is to leave no available portion of a dining table without its appropriate burden. Dishes are drawn up in lines and squares so as to occupy the whole centre space of the table, and allow only a small outer margin for the convenience of guests. We drank shamshoo out of tumblers and finished off with a dessert of unripe Pears eaten with salt.

386. The eclipse of 18th August occurred during our stay at *Hotha* and was seen to perfection, but in the latitude we were in (25 N), there was of course no approach to totality. The first contact took place at about 9-45 A. M. and the last at 12-30 P. M. Not more than two thirds of the Sun appeared to be covered during the time of greatest obscuration, and though the quality of the light was sensibly affected, I could not perceive any appreciable diminution of its power. This fact was so evident that the Shans and Burmese who watched the eclipse with us, regretted that its existence would not be noticed by their fellow country men of the neighbouring towns and villages. They were not aware that I had already foretold the eclipse at *Mynela*, *Sanda* and *Manwyne*, and that the Chiefs and Phoongyees would eagerly seek to verify my prediction.

387. At Hotha itself the excitement was intense. The Saubwa with his usual intelligence was apparently impressed with our explanation of the causes which gave rise to an eclipse. He endeavoured to explain these causes himself to the superstitious crowds who flocked around him. Nevertheless we were specially requested to fire off our guns and aid in a general noisy demonstration which was intended to

avert calamities and more especially to terrify a leviathan frog (if there is such an animal), which, according to Shan belief, devours the Sun by degrees and requires intimidation to make him disgorge.

388. If the contact commences from the right limb of the Sun, Shans view the Phenomenon as a sign of approaching Famine. Contact from the left signifies plenty and prosperity.

In the present instance the contact was from above and opportunity was afforded of allaying anxieties. Personally we had reason to be thankful that the eclipse was only partial, and that on that account it failed to attract general notice Otherwise the prognostication of evil thereby implied would have been associated in the minds of the superstitious with our own advent, and have been prejudicial to ourselves individually and affected the interests of future exploration.

389. My conversation with the Hotha Saubwa on various subjects more or less connected with the prospects of re-opening the old Embassy route between *Bhamo* and *Yunan* not only proclaim him a man of shrewd intelligence, but testify also to the personal interest which he has taken in the present expedition. He is by no means disinterested, and looks forward to trade as a channel of emolument to himself and of wealth to his countrymen. He promises himself to be the chief trader on this route, and guarantees to dispose of all the produce that arrives at Bhamo. But at the same time he feels that the conflict in *Yunan* between Chinese and Mahomedans must operate, as long as it lasts, in preventing a corresponding export of produce from *Yunan* itself and the adjoining Provinces. There would be a difficulty in this respect in procuring return produce in exchange for foreign goods imported from Bhamo. Neither he nor Chinese traders from *Yunan* would have it in their power to pay advances for goods. Purchases would be made on credit for payment by an equivalent in Chinese produce within a given period. The introduction of a system of credits of this kind would tend, he believed, to renovate trade on a scale hitherto unknown, whereas the present mode of cash payments or immediate barter had the effect of reducing it to very circumscribed limits,

390. When I asked the Saubwa how he would ensure himself and others against accidents or contingencies, at all times imminent on account of the disturbed state of the country and the existence of an almost recognized system of theft and brigandage, he replied by assuring me that he was not likely to purchase goods unless with the certainty of safe transport to their intended destination.

It was as easy he said by proper arrangements to come to terms with dacoits and brigands as with recognized Chiefs and legitimate Governments.

391. This confirmed the impression I had already formed of the Saubwa's capacity for making things pleasant with all parties, under all conditions of time, place and circumstance.

At present I know that he openly maintains a separate understanding with the dacoit leader Lees-hee-ta-hee and the more renowned brigand Chief Leogwanfan. Nevertheless he is the acknowledged friend of the Governor of Momein and pays tribute to the Panthay Government. Amongst his own people he preserves a dignity suited to his position, and is deservedly respected within his little Kingdom at Hotha. Numbers of Kakhyen Chiefs too with whom he communicated treated him as their superior and obeyed all his orders.

392. As regards ourselves it is not too much to say that he esteems us as friends, and his intelligence combined with the little experience which our society has afforded, has taught him that Western civilization is a model of superiority which entitles it to the reverent imitation of all Shan creation.

It is this belief in British superiority which has allied the Saubwa to our cause and is destined further, in connection with his own private interests, to place him in a prominent position as a pioneer in the reconstruction of a vast trade between Burma, the Shan States and South Western China.

393. On one occasion the Saubwa sat down to table and dined with us by invitation with all the familiarity and good breeding of a polished Shan gentleman. He tasted freely of all that was offered to him, and exhibited only one peculiarity viz: a vigorous pull at his pipe between courses. This he explained had been a life-long practice, and caused tobacco at meal times to be as essential a portion of his dinner accompaniments as any other consumable production.

394. After dinner his conversation took an unusually sentimental turn. He was labouring under a presentiment of impending calamity. Either the Shans would fight amongst themselves (as was their wont sometimes in the Mynela District), or the Chinese or Panthays, as alternately victorious, would come down with a swoop and lay the country under ruinous contributions. The late destructive inundations and land slips were ominous of still further disturbances, and some change of vast import for good or evil was assuredly on the cards and must inevitably be fulfilled.

395. I quite agreed with the Saubwa in believing in his presentiment of coming change, and reminded him that an event was now in progress which affected his country with more serious interest than the ordinary consequences of landslips or invasion.

The present expedition was intended to produce a revolution in fact and ideas, which would rouse the Shans to a sense of their interests and combine all races for mutual good. This was the change which was being effected, I said, in spite of landslips or other portentous phenomina which had raised misgivings in the Saubwa's mind. The Chief laughed and courteously succumbed, but he proved himself still sceptical by saying that if disturbances arose which threatened the Shan States he would flee for a home, not to Burma, but to the secure borders of British Territory.

396. It was during the interval of our stay at Hotha that I was enabled to collect confirmatory evidence of sinister designs on the part of the Burmese Government, by which our plans were opposed and our existence imperilled.

Kingen (the Tamon of Mynela), who has already been spoken of as a Prince of outlaws but a man of wonderful resources under proper management, made known to me certain of his experiences which related to the time when the expedition was first spoken of as likely to enter the Shan States from *Bhamo*. He swears that at that time he read letters in the Shan language, forwarded from Bhamo, in which the people of the States were called upon as they valued their country to oppose the British Mission and to refuse it admittance into the Shan States. He also held conversation with Burmese Shan emissaries, from Bhamo who brought these letters, and sedulously strove to create false impressions of evil, and incite the masses to suspect and hate us.

397. But Shans, according to *Kingen*, are shrewd and argued as follows:—

"If the English are so dangerous as they are represented "to be, why did the Burmese allow them a passage through "their country? Having permitted the expedition to pass "their frontier, why do they now ask us to be the medium of "its destruction? There is something wrong and unreason-"able in this. We will wait and judge for ourselves."

398. The Hotha Saubwa too, in referring to the subject of Burmese opposition spoke on one occasion as follows:—

"Whilst you were still at Bhamo and before the Mis-"sion entered the Kakhyen hills, Burmese emissaries had "arrived in the Shan States and created a feeling of hosti-"lity to your advance.

"This *must* have resulted in disaster had you attempted "to enter the States before you did. Indeed, you could not "have done so without fighting, and your small party would "soon have been overpowered. My belief is that the Chi-"nese at Bhamo bribed the officials there to spread these re-"ports, because they feared that an influx of British Mer-"chants into Bhamo would interfere with their monopolies. "I have always believed in the sincerity of your intentions, "and am prepared to live and die in the good cause which "has brought you to this country."

399. On another occasion he told me that the messengers who were first sent to hire mules for our party in the Shan States (the Expedition had not then started from Bhamo) advised the Shans to send their mules without any regard to hire, and to feel secure as regarded payment by a proposal to seize and appropriate our baggage. It was never intended they said that we should cross the hills, but, having proceeded a certain distance only, means would be improvised for our discomfiture and property and baggage would be quietly appropiated by our fortunate carriers.

Mule proprietors were soon attracted by so pleasant a mode of becoming enriched and the necessary complement of animals was at once collected.

The above fact, as related by the Hotha Saubwa, throws considerable light upon the conduct of our mule men at Ponsee and their sudden and abrupt departure without notice, permission, or even a demand for mule hire.

400. I asked the Saubwa whether he could further account for this peculiarity in their behaviour.

Saubwa.—"Of course I can. You knew nothing about "the arrangements under which they had agreed to render "services and were unable therefore to divine the cause of "their departure without a demand for legitimate wages.

"Their intention in leaving you was simply to secure "their mules and then join the Kakhyens in a simultaneous "attack on your position and baggage."

Political Agent.—But no attack was made. What saved us?

Saubwa.—"Your own good fates, or rather a supernat-"ural power against evil with which you are endowed as the "result of good deeds in former existences! All other aid "would have been unavailing. Some unseen power interfered "to confound the designs of your enemies. When I first "heard of your troubles I had determined upon setting out my-"self to your assistance, but was prevented by learning that the "Burmese Officials of Bhamo were conspiring to injure you. "I was fearful of offending against Burman Policy, and did "not wish to be mixed up in their treacherous designs."

401. The above conversation has been copied from my rough notes in the exact words in which it took place. The Saubwa's idea of our supernatural power to avert calamity is not very flattering, as it sets a side the supposition that tact and endurance were brought into requisition as an aid to the unseen Agencies which the Saubwa believes effected our deliverance.

402. I have good reason to suspect that the Saubwa was himself at Bhamo at the very time that the conspiracy was hatched to ruin us at *Ponsee*. He eventually joined us at *Mynela*, after Burman intrigue had been successfully combated and every Shan State had agreed, under Panthay pressure, to contribute its mite towards our march to Momien. The fear of offending the Burmese Government by awarding us favors was no longer individually paramount, after a general combi-

nation had been entered into by all the States to side with and assist the British Expedition.

On this account the Saubwa of Hotha was encouraged to befriend us to the end, and to make us his guests for a lengthened period at his Hotha head quarters.

403. One of the causes which countributed to this prolonged stay in the Hotha valley was that preparations had to be made there for crossing the Kakhyen hills by the central Embassy route to Bhamo.

The route having been virtually closed to general traffic for several years past, it was necessary to summon the several Chiefs, and confer with them on the plan proposed by the Hotha Saubwa for allaying existing feuds between Kakhyens and Burmese, and obtaining consent in the present instance to our making use of it in returning to Bhamo.

404. The first Kakhyen Saubwa who answered the summons was the Chief of *Nambouk*. He arrived with a strong party of well armed followers, most of whom rode ponies and were more civilized in appearance than the ordinary Kakhyens we had met with at *Ponsee*.

As soon as the Chief saw me, he rushed forward eagerly and greeted me as his friend. We had met before once only at Bhamo where the Chief had received a few presents for which he even now seemed grateful. He had set out, he said, the very moment news reached him of our arrival at Hotha, and it was his intention, had he not been informed by the Saubwa of our intended visit, to have left several days earlier with a view of meeting us at *Sanda* or *Mynela*, and of persuading us to follow the Embassy route in preference to that which passed through *Ponsee*.

405. He expatiated at length on its many advantages, guaranteed the friendly aid of all Saubwas en route, and volunteered a sufficient supply of mule carriage to take us the whole way from *Hotha* to *Bhamo*.

406. I could not help noticing during my conversation with this Chief, the striking difference between a Kakhyen when left to his own natural impulses, and the same being when subjected to the advice and sinister influences of domineering Burmese. The Kakhyens have learned to judge of us by our actions, and their verdict is in favor of truth and

fair dealing. Here, at least on the Shan border, they can act independently of Burmese counsels, and know by intuition that it is to their advantage to render us honest services. The two months residence at *Ponsee* has established for us a reputation throughout Kakhyen land which cannot fail to be serviceable, for a generation at least, to all white faces which stand in need of Kakhyen assistance.

407. I must pass on to the time of our departure from *Hotha*, which took place on the 27th August. All the Chief Saubwas who occupied territory through which the central Embassy route passed had previously made their appearance (in person or by deputy) at Hotha, where a general meeting was held on 22nd August, and formal arrangements entered into for the survey of that route from *Hotha* to *Bhamo*.

408. The Saubwas themselves from the first expressed very general satisfaction at the determination arrived at to proceed and survey the central route.

The route they say has been untraversed for years, and that the rainy season was not a favorable one for coming to decision upon its particular merits. Nevertheless they believed in its practicability, and guaranteed to supply carriage and afford safe conduct so soon as we were prepared to start from Hotha.

409. I have already mentioned that in electing myself to return by the Embassy route to Bhamo I had made provision for a flying survey of the Southern route viâ Sawuddy, by detaching an Assistant surveyor (Moung Thazanoo) to proceed from Hotha to Mynewun for that especial purpose.

This survey involved both risk and responsibility, owing to the supposed opposition of the *Mynewun* Shans, and the absence of all means of communicating direct with the Kakhyen Chiefs whose consent was necessary to a free passage between Mynewun and Sawuddy. It was essential therefore that the surveyor should proceed somewhat in disguise and attract as little notice as possible by travelling almost alone, and with only such instruments as were indispensible to enable him to judge altitudes and direction, and prepare a rough sketch Map of the country he might pass through.

The object was not so much to obtain a complete survey of the route, as to gain some idea of its physical conditions (as observable by a practiced surveyor), and compare them with information already acquired from other sources.

410. Moung Thazanoo being a Burman, was easily transformed (in appearance) into a Shan, and set out from Hotha on 18th August, accompanied only by two followers; one a Shan guide who spoke the Kakhyen language (and recommended by the Hotha Saubwa as a man intimately acquainted with the principal Chiefs on the Sawuddy route), and the other a Shan and Kakhyen Interpreter of my own, who could now be spared from amongst our followers.

411. My instructions to the surveyor were, that if he found the Chiefs en route inclined to favor the project of establishing a general trade route viâ *Sawuddy* to *Bhamo*, he might disclose the true nature of his undertaking and assure them with reference to my own survey of the central or Embassy route that our object was to ascertain the most practicable route between Bhamo and the Shan States, and that the final selection of that route would depend in great measure, on our present means of survey and exploration. If favorably inclined towards us the Chiefs would of course find it to their advantage to assist those means, and Moung Thazanoo's work be simplified by a comparative absence of risk and difficulty.

412. The surveyor fully answered to the good opinion I had already had occasion to form of his diligence and ability. He not only managed to find favor at *Mynewun* but the Kakhyen Chiefs with whom he held intercourse rendered all the assistance in their power, and expressed a strong desire that British Merchants would select their route as the one best suited for the transport of merchandize between Burma the Shan States and South Western China.

413. On crossing the Eastern range of hills which separates the Hotha valley from the Shan States of *Mynewun*, the surveyor found another valley similar in extent and general direction to those of *Hotha*, *Sanda* and *Mynela*, bounded on the East by another parallel range, and drained by a mid-valley stream which found its way in a Southerly direction to the *Shwè Lee* river, one of the great affluents of the Irrawaddy.

414. The surveyor's report of this route is a very satisfactory confirmation of all that has been urged in its favor by information obtainable at *Bhamo* and elsewhere. The road is reported throughout to be a broad beaten track, passing for the most part over undulating country with gradual ascents and descents, and free from those rugged declivities which are occasionally met with on both the Northern and Central routes. I append *Moung Thazanoo*'s report in the vernacular, with a translation and sketch map. Other particulars will doubtless be reported by Mr. Gordon, who joined us at *Mynela* and was in charge of the engineer's department from thence to *Bhamo*.

415. Our own departure from *Hotha* took place on the 27th August. The *Hotha* Saubwa accompanied us as far as the boundary between the *Hotha* and *Latha* States, and then said 'goodbye'. The parting with his family was earnest and affectionate. Many were the wishes and prayers that our affairs might prosper and lead us back in haste to *Hotha*. Two grown up daughters of the Chief were amiable handsome girls, full of fun and innocently eager to learn our peculiarities. I am not sure that in our communications with them we ever exceeded the bounds of decorum, but this did not prevent them from indulging in what may have been a *Shan* modification of prudery, and constantly reminding us that we were to regard them as *sisters* and never venture upon passages of love. It was not quite clear from their own behaviour, at what point Shan young ladies draw the line between platonic affection and brotherly familiarity. Judged by their own standard of moral excellence some of our actions (hand shaking in particular) were open to misconstruction, and many of their own secret contrivances for facilitating communication and familiarity with ourselves would hardly have passed "muster" as mere sisterly affection, in a well ordered state of Belgravian society. But this is another digression which would hardly be pardonable unless it afforded a glimpse of *Shan* Society, and instanced the freedom with which English gentlemen have been admitted to 'sororize' with ladies of high rank in the family circle of a friendly Shan Chief.

416. The route from Hotha lay in a South Westerly direction, along the right bank of the *Namsa*, a small tributary

which drains the Hotha valley and finds its way into the *Tahpen* a little south of Ponsee. We cross the *Namsa* by a wooden bridge opposite to *Letha* the chief town of another State of that name, within the *Hotha* or *Mynetha* valley

417. It was my wish and intention to have visited the Saubwa of this State, and to have remained a day or two within his territory. But a family feud existed between the chiefs of the two states of *Hotha* and *Latha*, and it was moreover made to appear that the chief of the latter place, besides being old, imbecile and superstitious, was possessed of an idea that our advent into his house or town presaged evil to himself personally, and would be followed by injury or death to some of his family. In so little esteem was the *Latha* chief held that his neighbour of *Hotha* professed on many occasions to ignore his official existence, and assumed the exercise of jurisdiction and authority in disputes which arose within the confines of *Latha*. With the exception of this idiosyncrasy relating to the supposed evils which he believed would arise out of a personal interview, the *Latha* Saubwa was neither unfriendly in disposition or seriously opposed to our passage through his State.

418. The *Hotha* Saubwa had from the first been averse to my visiting *Latha*, and seemed to regard my desire of doing so as a personal matter which concerned himself. I was therefore constrained for prudential reasons to avoid *Latha* and give its imbecile proprietor as wide a berth as our route admitted.

I took care however, on the day we passed through the *Latha* district, to send the Saubwa a suitable present which was well received and satisfactorily acknowledged. A return present was brought by my messengers, who were directly instructed by the Saubwa in person to inform me that as far as he was himself concerned he would have been glad to meet me and receive our party with becoming hospitality, but some of his people had listened to stories which made us out to be sorcerers or magicians, and dangerous alike as friends or enemies. He had deferred in this instance to the scruples of his people and respectfully urged us to leave his coasts. He nevertheless begged me to be assured that on our return (whenever that happy event might take place) we should be well received, and that in the mean time he would do all that was required of him to restore confidence and teach his people the value of our friendship.

419. This message was intended to be both complimentary and reassuring, but it did not alter or falsify realities. It was the Saubwa himself, as opposed to his people, who had given way to fear and distrust, and who deprecated our visit out of superstitious misgivings which boded injury to himself and direful ills to all his household. I afterwards learned that he had been infected with the poisonous emanations which were foully issued from a Burman source at a time when all other means of indirect opposition had failed to restrain us to Burmese territory.

420. After crossing the *Namsa* at a long wooden bridge oppsite to *Latha* the road begins to ascend gradually and leads through a gorge into a lateral valley, and from thence over spurs with intervening valleys (valleys within a valley), the principal mountain ranges still maintaining their general parallelism, until we are fairly within that bewildering cluster of elevations hitherto vaguely described as the "*Kakhyen Hills.*"

421. We halted at Nambouk at 5 p. m., after a march of 14 miles performed in five hours. The Saubwa received us with a salute of 3 guns and had prepared a shed for our accommodation. He thought it due to his hospitality and to our own sense of of propriety and convenience that we should remain in his village for at least three days, and thus afford an opportunity to Kakhyens far and near who had already been favorably prepossessed towards us by report of our fame at Ponsee, to come in with presents and offerings and receive in return the usual tokens of our friendly regard.

We contrived however, after an extraordinary expenditure of arduous pleading and a varied distribution of substantial inducements, to waive a portion of his affectionate restrictions, and got off from *Nambouk* at midday on the 29th (August).

422. The 28th was passed in all the misery of making settlements with turbulent mule proprietors, who pressed forward certain hopeless claims for payment or extra-payment with all the violence and obstinacy of their race.

The real dfficulty in these cases is to find out what the recusants actually require. A too ready acquiescence with their imaginary demands (which I was inclined at times to admit without controversy on the principal of any thing for a quiet life), is a fatal error which adds tenfold to the distraction and worry which it was my anxiety to avert. *Their* object is to get a traveller fairly into their power and then enforce a compliance with their demands. But they are mere bullies at heart, and succumb at once as soon as they find themselves properly confronted. The rule is to proffer all that is due in justice but reject all claims which are pressed with bluster.

423. The temporary unpleasantness of these inevitable outbursts was more than compensated for by the manifest good feeling of the Kakhyen population. Their houses were our houses. We shared the accommodation of a Kakhyen homestead without inconvenience to its proprietors or annoyance to ourselves. Our presence caused no observable change in their domestic arrangements: pigs, buffaloes, and ponies herded in our apartments. The men smoked opium. Women sung songs, nursed their children, pounded paddy or weaved cloth whilst we eat, dressed, slept, took notes and made love, with all the zest of kindred companionship.

424. We did not succeed in getting away from *Nambouk* until after midday on the 29th. The road or rather mountain pathway was bad and overgrown from long disuse. Halted before dusk at the village of *Ashan* distance about eight miles from *Nambouk*. *Ashan* and *Nambouk* are on much the same level, and neither place is more than three hundred feet above the level of the *Hotha* valley. The road, which at present is made to pass over elevated spurs which rise at least 1,000 feet above these villages, might with ease be reduced to a uniform level.

425. The direct Embassy Central route after leaving *Ashan* passes viâ *Kangouk* to *Hoton* which is only one good day's march from *Ashan*. But some of the most influential of the chiefs under whose conduct we were proceeding would not be comforted unless we made a very considerable detour which would enable them to introduce us to portions of the hills over which they exercised special sovereignty. We were thus constrained to make three marches instead of one, and

to halt successively at *Monwye* and *Loaylon* before we were allowed to reach *Hoton*.

426. From *Ashan* the road dips down at once a thousand feet again to the bed of the *Namkhon*, a mountain torrent which empties itself into the *Tahpen* opposite to *Ponsee*. From this a steep ascent leads up eight hundred feet to the village of *Lasee*, and we dip once more to our Monwye encampment. It rained incessantly throughout the day, and the road on most of the inclines had been converted into slides down which men and ponies glided at times with ludicrous rapidity.

427. *Loaylon* had been determined upon as our halting place after *Ashan*, but the Saubwa of *Monwye*, who had acted as our Guide during the day's march, was led in his zeal to enveigle us to *Monwye*, instead of following the direct road to *Loaylon*. In this he deceived his own confrères most of whom had gone on with our baggage to the village of *Loaylon* and there awaited us. The Chiefs expressed disgust and annoyance, but in our case they had no room for displeasure, for the offending Saubwa had prepared accommodation and was profuse in that careful ministration to our creature comforts which induced good humour and healed the sore of temporary misarrangement.

428. We started from *Monwye* in the midst of pelting rain on the 31st of August, and descended a long steep declivity to the *Mynekha* stream, which forms a natural boundary between two divisions of the Kakhyen hills occupied by separate families of the Kakhyen race under the tribal denomination of *Kowlee* and *Lăkhon*. Both races possessed characteristic distinctions which are said to be very marked and determinable as amongst themselves, but to casual observers *Kowlees* and *Lăkhons* assimilate in dress, language and religion, so as to be apparently identical.

429. The *Kowlee* chiefs had assembled at *Loaylon* (called *Mynekha*) to receive us, and were determined to vie with the *Lăkhons* in their outward manifestations of hospitality and kindness. We were bound under certain conditions of Kakhyen etiquette to change horses or rather mules and porters at *Loaylon*, although I had tried hard to book ourselves through from *Hotha* to *Bhamo*. The direct object of the

change was that each section of the Kakhyen people through whose territory we passed might have the advantage of supplying carriage and of profiting in other indirect ways by our temporary presence amongst them.

430. A halt for one day was necessary at *Loaylon*, and the time was not unprofitably or unpleasantly spent in friendly intercourse with the chiefs and in special communications with the *Muthin* Saubwa, a man of rare excellence and intelligence, though only a hill chieftain in the wilds of *Kakhyenland*. He and the *Loaylon* Saubwa are sons of the old *Muthin* chief, who during his lifetime was acknowledged to be the richest and most powerful of all the hill chiefs bordering on Burma.

He too was the chief who had headed a confederacy to avenge the Burman murder of seven of their race by closing the Embassy route, and instituting retaliatory measures against Burmese villages. His son was now present to wipe out existing feuds and open out his country again to its former usefulness.

431. The present *Muthin* Saubwa spoke Burmese with ease and even fluency, and his ideas and principles, as deducible from general conversation, marked in him a higher degree of civilization than that which is compatible with the ordinary supposed state of a semi-barbarous hill race.

"Every hill in the country" he said," rejoices at the news "of your intention to renew the old trade with China. The "project was one which enlisted at once the sympathies and "interests of all Kakhyens and held forth to them the prospect "of wealth and happiness."

432. In presenting us with fowls, eggs, beer, shamshoo and a young bullock for slaughter, he apologized for short comings, and begged that I would remember that he was not at the time within the limits of his own Saubwaship. He is disappointed that we are in a hurry to return to *Bhamo* as he had calculated on detaining us at *Muthin* for a few days and giving us a true impression of Kakhyen hospitality.

433. This never ending desire to procrastinate is an unfortunate failing in the welcome afforded us by every Kakhyen Chief. It was of no avail to plead that the season was unfavour-

able, that some of our party were not in good health, that the incessant rain might induce general sickness, that we were badly off for clothes and provisions, and that our long sojourn for nine months in a strange land had made us intent on a speedy return to our homes and country.

The only plan by which I succeeded in finding a way to the fulfilment of our wishes was by a direct appeal to Kakhyen future interests, and by honestly pointing out that any needless excess of time occupied by me in pursuing the journey between *Hotha* and *Bhamo* would be viewed by our Government as an argument against the practicability of the *Embassy Route*, and afford cause for its rejection in favor of a highway which was more easily traversed or less obstructed by the *courtesies* of Chieftains.

434. This had its good effects in expediting our departure from *Loaylon* on the 2nd September, but it did not save me from a mountainous detour of 15 miles viâ *Loaylyne* and *Muthin* to *Hoton*, instead of a comparatively easy march of six miles by the direct route viâ *Sakhay*. But the digression was not without its reward. The reception at *Muthin* was not only honourable in itself but satisfactory as instancing the advanced state of Kakhyen civilization, and the eager desire of the people to welcome the prospect of renewed foreign intercourse. A salute of 3 guns announced our arrival, and the beating of gongs and cymbals was continued from the time we entered the village until we were fairly housed within the Saubwa's enclosure.

435. The village of *Muthin* is situated at a considerably higher elevation than any Kakhyen villlage we have as yet passed, being more then 5000 feet above sea level, whereas it has all along been observable that Kakhyens limit themselves or rather their villages to heights which do not generally exceed three thousand feet.

436. The Chief's house is a Kakhyen Palace, and occupies the highest point of an undulating table land on which the village is situated. It is approached by a broad flight of stone steps which lead to an arched gateway and walled enclosure of Chinese design. The house itself is a wooden structure, built on the elongated single ridge principle peculiar to Kakhyens. It is palatial in size, finish, and ornamentation, as compared

with the residencies of ordinary Kakhyen Saubwas. The ornamentation is confined to an abundance of wood carving which is every where prominently in view on the posts, wall plates, crossbeams and door frames.

437. We sat down in a lofty shed adjoining the house, drank Kakhyen beer, and were introduced to the Chief's family. Crowds of women and children had assembled within and without the enclosure, many of them fine interesting specimens of their race, and comely to a degree despite their matted locks and once-a-year ablutions.

There were other special attractions of a less delusive nature which would have induced us to loiter at *Muthin* and enjoy the hospitalities of its intelligent Chief, but the day being already far spent it was necessary to push on so as to reach our halting place at *Hoton* before sunset.

438. The descent from the Kakhyen hills by the Central or Embassy route to the Bhamo plain, (or rather to the belt of land which lies between the base of the hills and the left bank of the Irrawaddy), commenced at *Muthin*, which, as before remarked, is more than five thousand feet above sea level.

Hoton is an important Kakhyen Saubwaship, about two miles from *Muthin*. Within these two miles we have descended a thousand feet, and can now gaze over a magnificent expanse of plain, bounded on the North by the Mogoung Hills, on the West by the lofty ranges which divide *Burma* from *Arakan* on the South, the view is lost at an illimitable distance in haze and horizon. The course of the Irrawaddy, swollen now by rain and flood to a breadth computable in miles, is seen threading its way through mid-plain with a slender line of silvery brightness. The view would at any time be enchanting, but under present circumstances our followers, native and Burmese, strained forward to the plain as to a land of promise and spoke out their joy in bounds of excitement.

439. But we are still at *Hoton*, and had we been allowed to reach it direct from *Ashan* viâ *Kangouk* and *Sakhiy* instead of passing through *Monwye*, *Loaylon*, *Loaylyne*, and *Muthin* we should have performed *one* comparatively easy-day's journey instead of three toilsome marches which were imposed upon us as the penalty of friendship and because we were fit subjects for a disply of Kakhyen hospitality. *Hoton* is a place

of importance on the Central or Embassy route, being the first Kakhyen village of any size which is reached on ascending the hills from the *Bhamo* plain. The direct dry weather route, leads from *Hoton* viâ *Momouk* to *Bhamo*, but the plain through which it passes is more or less flooded during the rains, and I found it necessary on this account to descend immediately to the valley of the Tahpen and proceed by boat from thence to *Bhamo*.

440. After spending the night in the Chief's house at *Hoton* we were prepared to leave the next morning, but "l'homme propose" and the Kakhyen Deities which ruled at *Hoton* were as disposed as ever to favour postponements. The old Saubwa of *Hoton*, almost in his dotage, with his two wives and descendants of more than one generation, put in an appearance in their best attire, and presented me with the usual quantity of fowls, vegetables, cooked rice and beer. They were followed by the Saubwas of *Kadaw* and *Sikhiy* with their families, the men wearing old black satin jackets of ancestral date and the women clad in neat Kakhyen costume, but with a profusion of silver ornaments which proclaimed their *Shan* predilections.

441. The young Saubwa of *Kadaw*, who died of small pox during our stay at *Momein*, was the son of the old *Kadaw* Chief who was now our visitor. The old man took his leave with every token of friendship, and under an assurance on my part that, on reaching *Bhamo*, I would consult with the Kakhyen Chiefs who had promised to accompany me and do what was considered just and expedient in making some amends for his family losses.

But another member of the family, a brother of the deceased chief, was not as easy to deal with. He not only became turbulent and obstructive but insolently demanded immediate compensation.

442. I had become by this time sufficiently familiarized with Kakhyen incentives to thought and action to know that this blustering impudence was the simple result of my own indiscretion. I had foolishly allowed myself in a moment of weakness to make allusion to the young Chief's death and start the idea of pecuniary consideration. It was a well known fact that the young Saubwa had died a natural death, and that

though he had followed me to *Momein*, the action was a gratuitous one on his part and carried out against my wishes. It could not be said then that the death had taken place in our service, much less that it was in any way ascribable to our evil influences. But leaving a broad margin for Kakhyen influences and the superstitious element which would be infused into their mode of reasoning I deemed it prudent, out of regard to our future interests, to deal liberally in the matter and leave no cause for misconception.

443. But the blustering brother in assuming the offensive had enlisted the sympathies of a few of our mule-men, and whilst preparations were being made for our intended start I was distressed to find that baggage animals were not forthcoming and that our final departure was made to depend on an immediate compliance with the brother's demands. We were thus once more in a Kakhyen dilemma which called to mind the experiences of Ponsee.

444. The natural inclination of Kakhyens, more especially if they happen to be mule-proprietors, is to wrangle and create a savage discussion on every occasion which yields a chance of successful extortion. Chiefs are not above a jolly good quarrel with their subjects, and abuse is given and taken with a wonderful amount of outward demonstration but little or no resulting action. Either party works itself up into a fury of wrath which promises death and extermination as the most insignificant of its denunciations. Old scores are jealously registered, to be paid with interest by succeeding generations, but present punishment or immediate penalties form no part of the Kakhyen Criminal Code. A furious quarrel of an hour's duration ends as it commenced, in nothing save smoke. This was the case on the present occasion. All I had to do was to expostulate with the Chiefs kindly but firmly, and having secured a strong party feeling on our side to look on with indifference and let the disputants fight or rather wrangle it out.

445. We got off about mid-day and commenced at once a descent to the plains. The road led through the village of *Mantai*, where the Kakhyen Saubwa urged us to enter his house and accept the hospitality of himself and his family. He received us with a salute of Guns and we were made to

sit down and drink homebrewed beer which was poured out for us by a very demonstrative woman (his wife) and two lusty good looking girls his daughters.

446. This was the third time during the march from Hotha that we had been received with salutes of honor on entering the head quarters of a Kakhyen Saubwa. The fact is full of promising significance. It teaches us, I think, that a people who love Rupees, drink beer, and fire salutes in honor of European travellers, are neither dead to enterprise nor dangerously opposed to friendly intercourse.

447. We are principally indebted to Burmese Policy, or the conservative tendencies of its imaginative Government, for a fearful picture of Kakhyen *Bogeeism*. The picture is now pronounced a daub without form, colour, or truth. It was hideous only in its unseen blackness, exposed to light it has vanished in nothingness. This state of Burmese conservatism is the more apparent from the fact that the Kakhyens bordering immediately on *Burma*, derive all their civilization from *China*, and in a very large number of instances speak the Chinese language fluently whilst utterly at a loss to understand or to express themselves in Burmese.

448. The distance from Hoton to the level of the plain, where we halted on the the left bank of the *Nanthabet* river, is twelve miles, and the difference of elevation between the two places more than four thousand feet. The heavy rain of the past few days, the wetting mist, the steep declivities and slippery pathway along which we were hurried with slithering rapidity, all conduced to make us believe that we had fairly been washed out of Kakhyen localities.

449. The *Nanthabet* river was a broad deep stream, full to the banks and alarmingly rapid in it its current. The only means of effecting a passage was by a raft made fast to a rope of platted bamboos. Both rope and raft were imperfect, and our baggage being in rear we were obliged to halt and pass an abstemious night sub jove frigido supplemented by a rustic canopy of bamboo jungle. Luckily it did not rain during the night, but the morning which promised fair changed suddenly to foul and rain fell in torrents. We were drenched in a moment. All hands laboured for full two hours during heavy rain in the construction of a serviceable raft. Captain Bower's

superintended, and it required not only considerable personal exertion but all the professional ability which he was known to possess to join and plat split bamboos so as to improvise a hawser two hundred feet long which would bear a strain in any portion of its length of several tons.

450. By 10 A. M. we were all across. Burmese officials appeared by degrees, and actually *apologized for having kept us waiting!* Their astonishment at seeing us in the flesh after an eight months absence and a profound belief in the certainty of our annihilation had confused their ideas and made them view us for some time either as a charmed species of humanity or as veritable apparitions.

451. But the sun had come out. We were now on the plains—care was behind—success ahead—and welcome everywhere. "All nature smiled" with a radiance which inspired a love for even Burmese enemies. At 12 we had reached the *Tahpen* and found rafts and boats ready to transport us to the village of *Sit-gna*, where temporary accommodation had been prepared and our wants supplied in plenteous abundance.

452. The broad glassy *Tahpen*, gliding peacefully between banks of plenteousness, was a pleasing novelty as contrasted with the noisy rush of foaming torrents which had charmed to satiety. The rafts on which we had crossed from *Namphoung* to *Sit-gna* were nicely furnished with chairs, curtains, and carpets. A band of Burmese musicians was also in attendance, but their performances were abandoned in favor of two large Chinese gongs which had come overland with us from Celestial regions, and were triumphantly beaten by our followers into a clang which drowned all meaner sounds of Burmese harmony.

453. The rafts were towed by war boats, and we glided across to Sit-gna *in state*. How great the contrast between now and then! *Now* when difficulties had been surmounted, assistance no longer needed, and even neglect and insult a matter alike of contempt and indifference, the Burmese officials not only treat us as superiors in the prudish forms of colloquial address, but provide gratuitously when no longer required a profusion of supplies, which money and remonstrance were powerless to procure in an ill-starred season of comparative adversity.

454. We left *Sit-gua* on the 5th September in the rafts and boats which had been provided at *Nampkoung*, and dropped down the river towards *Bhamo* in an ecstacy of calm but triumphant satisfaction. And in this ecstacy we reach *Bhamo* and close the narrative of a journey, which, however bare in material incident, is big with signs of future promise and marks an era in our commercial destiny.

455. My narrative is at an end, and although I believe that what has already been stated is abundantly comprehensive when read as a whole to admit of clear and practical deductions, it may not be inconsistent with the obligations I am under as leader of the party to conclude this report by expressing a few of my own opinions and convictions on points which call for special elucidation.

456. In the first place then I may remark that two questions of vital importance had worked themselves up into prominent notice on our return to Bhamo. Reference may accordingly be more conveniently made to them here than in any previous portion of my narrative.

The first of these questions relates to the adoption of means for facilitating transit across the Kakhyen Hills, and of securing, as one of the permanent results of our enterprise, the friendship and good will of the Kakhyen hill races.

457. The second has reference to the establishment of a British Agency at Bhamo, and both questions appeared to me at the time to be so immediately urgent as to require special report as contained in my letters No. 193 and 194 of 25th September 1868 to the address of the Chief Commissioner British Burma and Agent to his Excellency the Viceroy and Governor General of India. These letters contain, in a condensed form, all that it is of interest or utility to make known, in connecting the subjects they relate to with the present report or with the plan and purposes of the recent expedition. I deem it advisable therefore, for the sake of preserving uniformity and sequence, to enter the letters in extenso in the body of the report, rather than submit them as correlative matter only, in an over crowded appendix.

No. 193.—From Captain E. B. SLADEN, Political Agent, Mandalay; to Colonel ALBERT FYTCHE, Chief Commissioner British Burma, and Agent to His Excellency the Viceroy and Governor-General, dated Mandalay, the 25th September 1868.

As one of the necessities arising out of the late expedition from *Bhamo* to *South Western China*, I do myself the honor of bringing to your notice that the establishment of a British Agency at *Bhamo* deserves very prominent and immediate consideration.

2. My experiences of the last few months lead me more than ever to believe that the Burmese Government will still require considerable pressure before it will voluntarily facilitate trade relations between *Burma* and *China*. All its feelings and antipathies are and always have been opposed to our free intercourse with foreign States through Upper Burma, and it is not too much to say that its energies will steadily be applied to the adoption of indirect means whereby to prevent and discourage foreign trade by the overland route now open through *Bhamo*.

3. If my suspicions as to the insincerity of the Burmese Government in this respect have any real foundation it may rightly be assumed that the indirect means above referred to can be more readily and effectually applied at *Bhamo* than at any other place. *There* it will be a simple matter for the Government to use its influence in a variety of ways by which to undo and reduce to a profitless minimum most of the advantages which the exploration party has so far secured.

4. It is with a view to counterbalance and counteract if possible these sinister influences that I now advocate the immediate appointment of a British Agent, whose duty it will be to reside at *Bhamo* under the late treaty and watch over the interests of inland trade. For let it be understood that although the tendencies of the Burmese Government are opposed, in my belief, to the extension of trade viâ *Bhamo*, it nevertheless professes to be actuated by different motives altogether, and would wish us to believe that it is as eager for overland trade and intercourse with foreign countries as we are ourselves.

It is on this account that the appointment of a British Agent at *Bhamo* is likely to have a beneficial influence in checking certain preventive measures, whereby the Burmese Government would otherwise have it in its power to obstruct and retard the revival of overland trade with China.

5. But apart from Burmese considerations altogether the British Agent at Bhamo becomes a necessity, not only as a guarantee of protection to traders from British territory, but as a means of encouragement and protection also to traders from beyond the Burmese frontier, many of whom have confessed to me that under no other security or consideration will it be possible for them to avail themselves permanently of the overland trade Route between *Bhamo* and *Yunan*.

6. The Governor of Momein, as well as all the *Shan* and *Kakhyen* Chiefs with whom I have conversed on this subject, were unanimous in their desire to have a British official permanently established at *Bhamo*, and received my announcement that such an appointment was likely soon to become a reality with expressions of unfeigned satisfaction.

7. I may mention that the (31) thirty one Kakhyen Chiefs who accompanied me lately from their hills to Bhamo, and there took an oath of fidelity to protect and give safe conduct at all times to traders of all denominations by the old Embassy route across their hills, begged me very earnestly to reside myself at *Bhamo*, or at all events to remain there until another official might arrive and take up the appointment of British Agent.

8. I am sorry to say that this request was made in consequence of the bad feeling which at present exists between *Kakhyens* and *Burmese*, and which leads the Kakhyens to assume with reason that Burmese officials under their present Governor at *Bhamo* are much inclined at the present time to despise and keep them at a greater social distance than ever. But this is a matter which it is my intention to submit to you in a separate communication. I merely refer to it here as another reason for our availing ourselves, as soon as possible, of some of the privileges provided for in our late Treaty with Burma.

9. A remaining point for consideration is the pay which the Agent should receive, and in this respect I attach more

than usual importance to the position which his salary and accompaniments will enable the Agent to assume and keep up at Bhamo. It will be necessary moreover to sanction the expenditure of sufficient funds wherewith to build a good and substantial residence, which should not be inferior in any respect to that occupied by the Governor himself. I am inclined to be particular on these otherwise trivial points because we cannot blind ourselves to the fact that *Shans*, *Kakhyens*, *Chinese*, and *Panthays* will judge of us by first impressions, and will estimate our official Agent at Bhamo, amongst other qualifying considerations, by his ability to maintain appearances, and possibly also, by the length of his purse.

No. 194.—From Captain E. B. SLADEN, Political Agent Mandalay; to Colonel ALBERT FYTCHE, Chief Commissioner British Burma, and Agent to His Excellency the Viceroy and Governor-General, dated Mandalay the 25th September 1868.

I do myself the honor of informing you that on my return to Bhamo with the expedition party which I was appointed to lead into South Western China I was accompanied by thirty one Kakhyen Chiefs and nearly two hundred followers, who had availed themselves of my escort and protection to enter Bhamo and conclude arrangements for free transit and safe conduct to all trade and traders, by the grand Central or Embassy route which I had just traversed from the Shan State of *Hotha* to *Namphoung* on the *Tahpen River*.

2. The Burmese officials at *Bhamo*, I am sorry to say, viewed my familiarity with *Kakhyens* and *their* ready acquiescence in my wishes with jealous distrust, which provoked the contempt and ridicule of even the *Kakhyens* themselves.

3. I had for sometime past had in consideration the question of an annual subsidy to be paid to *Kakhyen* Saubwas, as a means of making them our friends and of securing a safe and ready means of transit across their hills. The idea of a subsidy originated of course with the assumption or belief that by no other practicable means would it have been possible to enlist the sympathies of these hill people, or cause them to regard our presence in the capacity of traders as a source of advantage and prosperity to themselves. Having satisfied myself however by ample experience that Kakhyens are more eager and interested in the re-opening of a trade route through

their hills than we are ourselves, and that their ready co-operation may be freely relied on in any attempt we may make either to open out old routes or construct new ones, I have been advisedly led to avoid the inconvenience and complications which a subsidy might have given rise to, and hold to the fact that fair dealing and kind and straightforward treatment on our part is all that is required to secure the friendship of these people and ready access to Kakhyen land for all the essential purposes of a through-route between *Bhamo* and South Western China.

4. Whilst however the opportunity presented itself it was of importance to secure certain benefits which seemed to arise out of the friendship already contracted with the several Chiefs who had accompanied me to *Bhamo*. These benefits would be obtained by a partial adoption of the Kakhyen's natural custom, by which it is usual with them on similar occasions to bind themselves over to a particular purpose by an oath of fidelity sworn to and strengthened by all the savage solemnities of a religious ceremony. Such an oath, whilst it professed to secure for us the sworn friendship and fidelity of all who participated in it, and gave to traders and travellers free access to the *Kakhyen* hills (or to such portions of them as are included in the oath), would not, on the other hand, bind us over to reciprocal action of any sort, or give the Kakhyens any claim on us beyond the very laudable one of drawing commercial enterprise to their particular localities and inducing us to favor routes of which they were the sole acknowledged proprietors.

5. The Kakhyens entered into this proposed measure for strengthening and perpetuating our mutual friendship with a willingness which was the more astonishing in as much as it was carried out in defiance of a certain amount of jealous opposition on the part of the Burmese officials at *Bhamo*. In the first place Kakhyens were first informed that they could not be allowed to perform any of their religious ceremonies within the precincts of *Bhamo*. Ingress to the town or to my own residence was as difficult and troublesome as the obstructive ingenuity of Bhamo guards at the several gateways could make it. Kakhyens were called upon to deliver up their swords on entering either of the approaches of the town. The

purchase or sale of various articles, such as bamboos and especially bullocks and buffaloes which were essential in the ceremonial to be performed, was secretly interdicted, so as to make it a matter of difficulty to procure them. Whilst preparations were being made for the ceremony the Chiefs were called away and privately instructed by certain Burmese officials that they were not at liberty to enter into any engagement with foreigners.

All this petty opposition was eventually overcome by my explanation to the Governor, in which I proved to him that I was not acting solely on the part of the British Government but that I was carrying out the orders of His Majesty the King of Burma, who had expressly desired me to act on *his* account and make use of *his* name wherever I might find it necessary, by so doing, to conciliate existing differences, or secure the interests of trade and of the expedition under my leadership.

6. The Governor replied to my imputation of opposition on his part, by saying that if I had met with difficulties *he* was not to blame, as his officials had acted without his knowledge. The Kakhyens, he informed me, were at liberty to perform any rites they pleased, and as to the difficulty of purchasing bullocks, it was explained away by the fact that Burmese objected to see their animals slaughtered in celebrating Kakhyen savage rites.

7. I was content to accept this explanation without for a moment believing that it had been given in good faith, and the Kakhyen ceremonies proceeded to completion with all the usual formalities. It may not be out of place to record a brief account of the ceremonial and form of oath taken on the occasion. For each buffaloe to be slaughtered a separate building is constructed, consisting of strong posts sunk into the ground with cross pieces to which the animal is tied previous to sacrifice. A separate altar is also prepared twenty feet in height, with a platform of Bamboos some four feet square on which the sacrifice is offered. *Kakhyen* deities of every degree and denomination are invited to attend and bear evidence to the rite about to be solemnized.

The invocation is repeated twice, once before the animal is slaughtered, and again previous to laying the meat offering on the altar. It is performed by a special office bearer whose prayerful intonation on the occasion is strangely musical, and suggestive of portions of our own cathedral service.

8. The animal to be slaughtered is firmly bound by its horns to the wooden construction before mentioned and then thrown on one side. The whole weight and strain of the body is on the neck which is partially twisted. There is not a moment's delay, a Kakhyen specially equipped for the service rushes forward holding a plantain leaf cup of sacred water in one hand and a naked sword in the other. The former is thrown over the sacrifice whilst the latter is brought down with frightful effect on the portion of the neck where the strain is greatest. The result is complete. The savagery of the whole scene is somewhat atoned for by an absence of torture or suffering, from which the animal is saved in its almost instantaneous dissolution.

The carcase is cut up without loss of time, and the portion of it to which the deities are known by Kakhyen experience to be partial are alone cooked and laid on the altar to be feasted on by the gods. This is the time, whilst the deities are being propitiated with the semblance of a good dinner, that they are called upon to witness the oath for which the whole ceremony has been contrived. A small quantity of the blood of the slaughtered animal has been caught and is now mixed in a large vessel with an abundant supply of raw native spirits. The whole is stirred up with the points of swords and spears which are dipped into the liquor ad libitum, and each chief as he comes up in the supposed presence of the attendant deities, takes his draft from the sacred bowl, swears his oath of fidelity in muttered prayers which imply the most fearful denunciations as a certain consequence of infidelity.

9. The dipping of the swords and spears in the liquor in which the oath is drank is said to be typical (as far as I could understand the interpretation given me), of the violent death which would of a certainty be incurred by a departure from engagements contained in the oath. In the present instance the Kakhyens were simply called upon to protect and afford safe conduct to traders and travellers who might cross their respective hill ranges on the route between *Bhamo* and the *Shan States*. The means for securing so important an object may

appear to us profane and irrational, but as a native religious rite they are natural enough to *Kakhyens*, and have a powerful and binding effect in keeping them to their engagements.

10. And as regards a certain profanity in the proceedings, there is unfortunately little or no distinction between the Kakhyen ceremonial and that which is of necessity enforced in the administration of oaths to natives in our own courts of justice whenever a Burman or more particularly a Chinaman takes his place in the witness box.

11. Altogether the oath of fidelity was sworn to by thirty one Kakhyen Chiefs who are principally located on the grand Central or Embassy route between Bhamo and the Shan State of *Hotha*. The immediate benefits to those who may wish to avail themselves of the route are certain. The more remote though not less important results will be found to arise out of the increased influence we are likely to obtain by the notoriety of our friendly engagement with the Kakhyens, and the extensive circulation which their report of our true and liberal treatment of themselves will acquire throughout all parts of the country which we are engaged in conciliating to our cause and enlisting in the interests of trade with South Western China.

12. It will be observed that the experiment of binding over Kakhyen Saubwas by a custom of their own to protect and support traders of every denomination who may desire safe conduct across their hills has been limited in the first instance to the Chiefs who occupy hill ranges between Bhamo and the *Hotha* valley by the old Central or "Embassy Route." I was afraid that the introduction of Chiefs or Saubwas from other routes might create a spirit of jealous rivalry which might have marred to some extent the full accomplishment and object of the binding ceremonial. It will become necessary however, in the event of a British Agent being appointed to reside at *Bhamo*, to extend this ceremonial to the chiefs of the *Ponlyne* (or Northern) and *Sawuddy* (or Southern) Routes. If summoned in a friendly way to *Bhamo*, and solicited to give us a friendly support in the cause of trade, *they too* will be induced, by the anticipation of securing for themselves or for their particular route a monopoly of trade

transit, to bind themselves by the customary obligation already subscribed to by their bretheren on the Central or Embassy Route.

458. The concluding paragraph of the above letter suggests the necessity of a few remarks relative to the determination of a practicable trade Route between Bhamo and the Shan States, or rather we may say, between *Bhamo* and *Momein*, for the particular route pursued across the Kakhyen Hills practically determines its further course through the *Shan States* into *Yunan*.

459. For the sake of distinction I have already denominated the three principal Kakhyen routes with which we have become more or less practically acquainted, as follows:—

1. The Northern or *Ponlyne* route.
2. The Central or *Embassy* route.
3. The Southern or *Sawuddy* route.

And I shall limit myself in what I have to say regarding them to a few general facts without any desire of intrenching upon Engineering details which rightly belong to a separate department.

460. In the first place I start with the assertion that the question as to which route is most practicable in an Engineering point of view is one which it would be immature to puzzle ourselves about for all present purposes, until we are prepared to entertain a definite scheme of road improvement or even railroad communication.

461. What I mean is that Trade to an almost unlimited extent is now possible by any of the present existing Routes without reference to their engineering capabilities, and that the determination of either of these Routes as a through-Route for general traffic must depend for some time to come on questions of policy and general expedience, rather than of special adaptability or Physical disqualification.

462. One of the main results of the recent expedition is that it has assured us of the good will and hearty co-operation of the several races bordering on Burma, in the furtherance

and construction of any great permanent work which we may be led to project within their respective territories.

463. It has been further conclusive in showing that the Kakhyen Hills form no real physical barrier to the construc- of good practicable roads, and that the character and configuration of their several ranges is such as to afford ground for belief that a railroad which would connect *Bhamo* with the chief centres of trade in South Western China is an Engineering project which may be reasonably entertained and successfully accomplished.

464. It is now a significant and important truth that 130 miles of road or railway on the most practicable line between *Bhamo* and *Momein* would effectually tap the resources of *Yunan* and put us into direct communication with the wealth and resources of South Western China. But until such a work has been specially projected or until fresh surveys have been instituted with a view to the final determination of a direct *through* route between *Bhamo* and *Momein* my opinion with reference to the general adaptability of any of the existing routes for all present purposes of commerce and communication is strongly in favor of the *Central* or *Embassy* route, which leads direct from Bhamo to Hotha and my suggestions are that we should lose no time in utilizing to the utmost the substantial advantages which have so far secured to us by our late friendly alliances with the several Kakhyen Chiefs who hold that route.

465. As soon as the British Agency has been established at *Bhamo* we shall be in a position to enter into further friendly relations with the Chiefs also of the Northern and Southern routes, and an active officer of Engineers having his head quarters at *Bhamo* will be able, in conjunction with the British Agent, to arrange during a single season for a system of practical surveys which would add to our knowledge of the country and aid in the determination of a highway *(road, tramway* or *railway)* which must eventually and at no great distance of time connect the Irrawaddy with *Yunan*, or *Bhamo* with *Momein*.

466. I consider it moreover to be a matter of Political expedience that the Agent at Bhamo or the Engineer with

whom he may be associated should have it in their power to incur a considerable outlay in repairing and otherwise improving each of the present existing Routes. The expenditure incurred would be amply repaid by strengthening our hold over the Kakhyen Races and securing to them the certainty of remuneration in return for labour.

467. Such an advantage can hardly be overrated, for whilst it provides us with willing labourers amongst races working it may be said under the incentive of self interest, it will shew these same races that our undertaking is in earnest and that we have seriously determined upon utilizing themselves and their country in the commercial openings which look towards China.

The more prospective benefits will develop themselves gradually in the means afforded for facilitating communication between *Burma* and the Shan States, and of stimulating and drawing to its natural channel a trade which, for several years past, has either altogether ceased or been influenced by a variety of causes into partial, and let me add, temporary disuse.

468. And here I find myself brought face to face with the duty of resolving one of the main questions which gave rise to the present expedition. The chief objects of the mission as laid down in para 3 of my letter of instructions No. 12 of 11th November 1867 are threefold:—

1. To investigate thoroughly the causes of the cessation of trade.

2. To discover the exact position of the *Kakhyens* and *Shans* and *Panthay* Government in *Yunan*.

3. To influence these several communities towards the re-establishment of trade.

A reference to what has already been recorded in the narrative portion of this Report must simplify very materially the work of coming to definite conclusions on the principal questions involved, as contained in the detailed instructions already quoted.

469. The cessation of trade between Burma and China, consequent upon the breaking out of the Musselman rebel-

lion in *Yunan*, is of course primarily ascribable to that rebellion and its destructive influences on the resources and commerce of those portions of the country from which the chief products of trade were principally derived.

470. That rebellion dates from the year 1855 but during the last five or six years, or since the comparative consolidation of Mohamedan rule within the Province of *Yunan*, the necessities consequent upon comparative issolation, and the fact that *Yunan* was more or less politically cut off by rebellion from trade communication with other Provinces of the Chinese Empire, compelled the *Panthays* to look towards *Burma* and to contemplate a resuscitation of that trade which for generations past had found a natural outlet on the Irrawady and established for itself an extensive mart at the Burmese frontier Town of *Bhamo*. But a peculiarity however is observable in the Panthay mode of reviving this trade, and there is some reason to believe that at the outset of their undertaking certain Political reasons may have conspired to restrict them to a long overland journey of two months (viâ *Theinnee*) from their capital at Talee to the capital of the Burmese Empire situated at Mandalay.

471. These reasons were necessarily cogent and unavoidable as long as the *Panthays* felt themselves insecure as a Government, and had failed to add the Northern Shan States bordering on Burma to the list of their conquests. During the interval however, whilst the *Panthay* Government was in a measure debarred from reaching the old established and comparatively proximate trade mart at *Bhamo*, the necessities of its position were of so urgent a nature that trade with *Burma* was profitable at any cost, and the conquerors of *Yunan* found it to their advantage to commit their caravans to an expensive land Route of two months duration to *Mandalay*, rather than submit to complete isolation from all trade intercourse with Burma.

472. But when the way to *Bhamo* had been to all intents opened by the conquest of the Northern Shan States in 1864, and friendly alliances had been entered into with the *Kakhyens*, so that no apparent barriers remained to prevent the recurrence of trade to its former natural and legitimate

outlet, it is a rather significant fact that the projectors of the *Yunan* Caravans should *still* have found themselves restricted to the long overland journey to *Mandalay*, instead of being guided by interest and expedience to strike the Irrawaddy at *Bhamo*, and reduce by one fourth their time and their expenditure.

473. The reply to this seeming inconsistency is to be looked for I conceive in the anomalous attitude of the Burmese Government. It may be casting a slur on our diplomatic acumen to volunteer a confession I am only now beginning to realize to perfection, that the full amount of stern opposition with which the Burmese Government has indirectly confronted us, in denying a highway through *Burma* to *China*.

474. I can also account to myself for the reality of a hint thrown out in a former paragraph of this Report, that the British occupation of Pegu has of late years been made to play more than a subsidiary part in Burmese policy, in causing a cessation of the old *Irrawaddy* trade with South Western China. What Burma has always dreaded in that occupation is that British interests would not be confined to British possessions, but that contingencies might arise which would give the foreigner the right of extending his influence to Upper Burma and to a point above and beyond the limits of the present Burmese Capital.

475. Such a contingency was always imminent as long as it could be made demonstrable in any way that *Bhamo* might again become the natural emporium of a direct overland trade between *Burma* and *China*. The same objection did not hold good provided *Mandalay* could be made the mart for that trade instead of *Bhamo*, for in that case the intrusive Foreigner would still be somewhat under control, and his operations for good or evil would not probably extend themselves in the same dangerous degree or direction as they seemed destined to do if allowed to ramify from an emporium on the extreme confines of the empire, and in direct contiguity with races which did not owe allegiance to His Majesty of Burma.

476. On this account the *Chinese* or *Panthay* caravans have been encouraged to come to *Mandalay* to the exclusion

of *Bhamo*, and I most unhesitatingly conclude, from careful observation and from experience gained during the late expedition to *Momein*, that the causes which have actuated the Burmese Government in its deliberate disencouragement of all communication with *China* via *Bhamo* have arisen in a great measure out of an instinctive and almost superstitious fear that the extenson of British influence beyond the Capital of Burma would prove fatal to Burmese supremacy and destroy the vaunted exclusiveness of the Burmese Government.

477. Other predisposing causes have not been wanting in inclining the king of Burma to hug this Political conservatism, and to enforce it to the detriment of his subjects and at an enormous loss to his own private and public exchequer.

One of these reasons is that he knows that the vast increase of commerce which would be created by a resuscitation of the *Bhamo* route would necessitate the presence of a fleet of English steamers on the *Irrawaddy* above or to the North of his Capital. His own avowed objection to such a contingency is that the steamer being English would come into collision with hostile influences, and that differences and complications would necessarily follow between the British Government and his own. The real cause for kingly apprehension and anxiety is that the advent of steamers above the Capital would afford to crowds of oppressed and disaffected subjects, the same opportunities of fleeing his country as those of which they have so largely availed themselves of late years, by means of steamer Traffic between the Capital and the British Frontier.

478. Another cause for Political anxiety may have been that since the curtailment of Burmese power and resources by the occupation of Pegu the opening of a direct and proximate means of ingress and egress *to* and from *China* might conduce to a dangerous influx of Panthay material, and threaten the dominions of *Burma* on her Northern frontier and at no great distance from her Royal Capital.

479. Compassed about then as the question was by all these obstructive elements of Political discord, it will naturally enough be asked how the Burmese Government was ever

persuaded into agreeing to our proposed survey of the Bhamo Route? or why the King of Burma encouraged our advances for such a survey by cordial approval, and with promises of hearty co-operation?

480. The apparent anomaly is now disclosed in all the bare-nakedness of truth and fact. Refusal would have argued a want of interest in what concerned the prosperity of his own and of our possessions. Compliance would only strengthen his own secret policy, by giving us the opportunity of practically demonstrating the utter inutility of our combined efforts to open wide the portals to China. In this latter belief he was of course supported by the conviction that, despite Royal assurances of co-operation and aid, indirect obstructions could be successfully applied in manifold variety to defeat expeditionary efforts and convert them into a furtherance of his own loved scheme of conservative retrogression.

481. The history of his failure is imperfectly recorded in the above narrative, and will be best noticed by a supreme disregard. At the same time *we* too have a policy to pursue in the interests of our subjects in Burma and of commerce everywhere, and the influence of that policy should be promptly exercised in removing the cobweb of Burmese obstruction by honest straightforward diplomacy if possible, but with a determination of purpose which, if it fails to secure our legitimate ends, will, at all events, afford a proof that we no longer submit to cajolery and bad faith or to nefarious designs against the lives of our Officers after they had been duped into dependence by false promises of aid and protection.

482. My report would be considered defective perhaps unless it specially touched upon the capabilities and resources of *Yunan* as a profitable centre for the extension of British trade viâ the *Irrawady* and *Bhamo*.

It would be equally defective I conceive were I to adopt the opposite extreme, and assume that the journey to *Momein* gave us any definite claim to speak with authority on the statistics of *Yunan*. My note book contains information which might be cooked-up into price currents and other statistical memoranda, more valuable as literary curiosities than as aids in investigating the commercial status of *Yunan* Province.

483. As an instance of this I may notice that in *Yunan* itself the real price of natural productions had become greatly enhanced by reason of continued disturbances and temporary scarcity. European importations, very rarely met with in the Bazaar, sold for amounts which varied from 300 to 500 per cent above English prices.

From this it will readily be perceived that lists prepared in conformity with prices at present ruling in *Yunan* would be dangerous as a guide in estimating the value of the *Yunan* trade. One large consignment of European goods to *Momein* or the first sensation of a return to tranquillity would swamp the *Momein* market, and make present price lists a mere parody upon the ordinary realities of supply and demand.

484. The productive capabilities of *Yunan* may be more confidently estimated.

Its mineral wealth and natural resources have already been widely proclaimed by speculative theorists, who have zealously urged the expediency of reaching them by a Chinese overland Route through Burma. Those who have read the able Report of Captain Bowers who has been associated with the present expedition as Mercantile representative, will see that his practical experiences are a valuable addition to our Commercial knowledge of *Yunan*, and bear out all preconceived ideas of its adaptability to the requirements of British trade.

485. My own opinion deduced from observation and such information as was obtainable at Momein is that the mineral wealth alone of *Yunan* entitles it to special notice as a country with which it is almost a crime that British possessions in *Burma* are not already allied by links of friendship and commercial intercourse.

I am not exceeding facts when I state that most of the products of *Yunan* which would find favor in a European market are at present procurable at *Momein* and its vicinity, at prices which vary from 50 to 100 per cent below English rates. That these prices have ruled for years past and that they are in excess even of the prices which obtain further within the interior of the Province may be reasonably infered from the fact that *Yunan* merchants find it a profitable speculation to convey their produce by an expensive overland journey of two months to *Mandalay*, to pay all transit dues thereon, including a 10 per cent Customs Duty in Burma, and finally to dispose of that produce at rates which leave a large margin for profit in the English markets. At the same time it is always necessary to bear in mind that a large or sudden demand, such as that which would inevitably follow a renewal of the old trade with *Burma*, might produce a sensible influence on present prices in *Yunan* and (for a certain season at least or during the prevalence of present disturbances or until our trading capacity is fairly understood) produce disappointment by a probable failure of Export supplies.

486. The present importance therefore of Commercial relations with *Yunan*, in its more immediate results on the trade of British Burma, must be estimated rather by its capacity to consume European manufactures than as a producer of material to a European market. On this subject however, in which I am approaching the intricacies of trade details, I can only speak suggestively and with a diffidence proportioned, I hope, to my own want of experience. I am nevertheless firmly convinced under all conditions of policy or circumstance in the practicability of a large and extensive trade through Burma with China, and without any wish to discourage the proposed attempt of reaching a point in *Yunan* by a direct line of communication from a Rangoon terminus I am bound to express an opinion founded upon the experiences of our late expedition and to declare that the *Irrawaddy* route viâ *Bhamo* to *Momein* is already an accomplished reality, and requires only the stimulus of ordinary encouragement to develope itself into a mine of incalculable wealth to our Eastern Possessions.

487. The task of aiding this development rests with us, and depends upon the extent to which we are inclined to urge and enforce a progressive policy on the notice of the Burmese Government. The disturbed state of *Yunan* itself may probably prove a more serious difficulty, and makes it premature to calculate upon the fulfilment of an established trade until a definite understanding has been come to between the *Panthay* and *Chinese* Governments. This was the opinion of Panthay officials at *Momein*, and it will be traced very clearly in the tenor of the letter which I have had the honor of conveying from the Governor of Momein to the address of the English ruler at *Rangoon*.

488. It will be seen however, in the account of our residence at Momein, that the Panthay Governor expressed himself very clearly, in favor of a proposition to terminate hostilities in *Yunan* by the influence and intervention of the British Government, acting through its Ambassador at the Court of *Pekin*.

The exigencies of our mercantile interests in British Burma and the great import to the Commercial world at large of this question of direct overland trade through Burma with China, afford ample justification for the exercise of even extraordinary political means for the attainment of a charitable as well as an eminently advantageous result.

489. There are numerous other points connected with this expedition which have either been inadvertently omitted in the present Report or which if touched upon at all may perhaps call for further special explanation.

I must plead the inexhaustibility of the subject, the ramifications to which each section of it leads, the urgency of time, and the undue limits to which my report has already extended, as a few of the excuses which necessitate the reservation of further details.

For the same cogent reasons I am bound to withhold much that might have been profitably said regarding the languages ethnology and customs of the several races who have fallen under observation during the progress of our journey to and from the city of *Momein*.

490. My concluding remarks must be strictly confined to a brief resumé of the more prominent results of the recent expedition.

1. The Panthay Government has approved of the proposal to revive overland Trade viâ Bhamo, and volunteered on its own part to despatch a friendly mission to *Rangoon* to institute general enquiries into the most practical means of carrying on direct trade with British *Burma*.

2. It has further promised that mule caravans from *Yunan* shall in future make *Bhamo* their terminus on the *Irrawaddy*, instead of *Mandalay*, provided assurances are given

that produce from *Yunan* can be profitably disposed of at *Bhamo*, and that return produce will be available there to meet all requirements.

3. The Governor of *Momein* has addressed a letter to the Chief Commissioner of British Burma, and afforded written testimony of the friendly regard with which the Panthay Government has viewed our desire to promote commercial intercourse with *Yunan*.

4. He has also given me a writing under seal, in which mention is made of certain Transit Duties on goods passing between Burma and *Momein*. But on the point of Duties generally the Governor convinced me that it would be premature at present to lay down definite rules for their collection. From personal observation I am enabled to state with some degree of certainty that 12 annas per mule load* will clear goods as far as Momein, and as regards their further transit into *Yunan* the Governor's assurances are that Duties on exports and imports between the Kakhyen Hills and Talee will in no case exceed an aggregate ad valorem rate of 4 per cent.

5. That portion of the Shan States which is principally involved and interested in the resuscitation of overland trade between *Burma* and *China* has been effectually explored, and chiefs and people who were found to have been influenced by Burman intrigue and misrepresentation into a state bordering on active opposition have been gradually converted, by a truthful recognition of facts as practically disclosed by our residence amongst them, into hearty supporters and undisguised friends.

6. All three routes by which the Kakhyen Hills are crossed from *Burma* in the direction of the Chinese Frontier have been more or less explored and surveyed, two of them by our whole party, and the third by a competent surveyor who was specially detached on that duty. The results of these surveys in conjunction with other modifying considerations of policy and convenience will eventually aid in the determination of a definite line of road between *Bhamo* and *Momein*.

---

*A mule is warranted to carry 50 viss. This weight is exacted in the case of cotton bales. But ordinary packages should not be made to exceed 75lb each; two to the load.

7. Thirty one Kakhyen Chiefs of the *Central* or *Embassy* route have been bound over by an oath of fidelity to protect trade, and afford at all time safe conduct across their hills. The Kakhyens too of the other routes have been won over to friendship, and eagerly crave for their own particular line a monopoly of transit, which I tried to convince them would in time be sufficiently extensive for profitable distribution amongst them all.

8. We have been practically assured that although the discontinuance of trade between Burma and South Western China is primarily ascribable to the breaking out of a *Mohamedan* rebellion in the province of *Yunan*, the causes of present commercial inactivity may be traced to the adverse influences of the Burmese Government, and the jealous opposition with which it strives to guard against the extension of our commercial ascendency beyond or in rear of the Burmese capital.

9. Finally I record with deliberation my firm conviction that the Burmese Government if in earnest (or any other Government by which it may be supplanted and holding the same Geographical position) has it in its power at the present time almost without effort and in spite of present *Yunan* disturbances to open an immediate trade via *Bhamo*, not only with *Yunan* itself but probably also under suitable arrangements with other of the outlying provinces of South Western China.

491. It only remains for me to notice the services of those Officers who have been associated with me on the recent expedition.

Captain J. M. Williams, the Engineer who was first appointed to accompany the expedition to South Western China severed his connectionship with it at Ponsee, under circumstances the responsibilities of which I have already shewn rest entirely with myself. I should be wanting however in my duty to Government were I not to record that Captain Williams was out of place in his position as Engineer Officer to the late expedition. I do not refer to his professional abilities, for they are acknowledged to be of a superior order as testified by years of service in Burma, but his affections and interests were alien to our enterprise. He was already committed both in opinion and action to favour the scheme of direct railway communication or rather of a direct railway-survey of the country between *Rangoon* and *Kiaing-Yoon-Gyee*. I would in no wise affirm that such action or opinions would wrongly influence Captain Williams' conduct when once he had accepted the Bhamo appointment, but I positively declare, as the result of observation, that Captain Williams was unconsciously biassed in favor of a hobby, and that however he may have struggled to suppress the tendency, his inclinations led him to magnify difficulties, and to prejudge our enterprise as barren in promise and wanting in all the essentials of success. His opinions were opposed to an advance from Bhamo, and though that advance was eventually effected under a harrassing array of adverse circumstances, discouraging alike to all our party and full of painful anxieties to myself, it did not diminish the weight of responsibility to find that the Engineer officer was influenced by interest, and condemned my act in leaving Bhamo as one in which I had erred in judgment and set at nought the tenor of my instructions.

492. Trivial too as the circumstances may appear, I may be allowed to note that Captain Williams' want of interest in the expedition was further instanced by his refusal to comply with my earnest solicitation that he would leave his Photographic apparatus in my charge. I guaranteed its cost out of my own private funds, and went so far as to recall to Captain Williams that it was in deference to him and to the fact also of his having provided himself with Photographic materials which were *perhaps* more perfect than my own, that I had consented to leave my own apparatus at Mandalay though thoroughly complete and packed for the journey.

493. Captain Williams' assigned reason for not complying with my wishes was that the *Rangoon* survey party would probably leave *Rangoon* in October or November, and that he would not be able to provide himself with new and suitable apparatus from England between the time of his return from *Ponsee* (in April), and the departure from *Rangoon* of the expedition party to survey the direct route to *Kyaing-Yoon-gyee* in October.

494. I may mention also that after Captain Williams' departure from *Ponsee*, and whilst he was still at *Bhamo*, I wrote at the solicitation of Captain Bowers and requested that

he would send me a Government pocket Chronometer which he had taken away with him (and which should properly have remained in my charge) and the telescope of one of his Government sextants, as Captain Bowers had lost his own and the possibility of taking correct observations during our further progress had thereby become both remote and uncertain. Captain Williams' reasons for refusing my requests may have been honestly conceived and were probably sound and forcible in themselves, but I feel bound to confess that it would have argued a truer interest in our concerns to have sent what he was asked for, and have left the onus or utility of my request to the experience of those with whom it originated.

495. I find it impossible to laud too highly the services of Doctor John Anderson curator of the Indian Museum who was associated with the Expedition as Medical Officer and Naturalist. The earnest and searching nature of his enquiries into all matters of scientific interest, his devotion to the objects of the Mission, the zealous and attentive care with which as a Medical officer in the treatment of disease he ingratiated himself into the good opinion of the several races with whom we came into contact and impressed them favourably with a sense of English science and English generosity and of the English Mission generally, are facts which were patent to all and deservedly invite the recognition of Government.

496. In one department of his duties, Dr. Anderson was called upon to select and purchase valuable specimens from amongst the products and manufactures of the countries visited whenever our funds admitted of such an expenditure. It was deemed to be a matter which affected the well being and interests of the expedition to pay well for specimens, and thereby add to the certainties of collection. By this means vendors were induced to part with their property, or Shan and Kakhyen collectors found it to their advantage to roam the forests and return with an occasional valuable addition to natural History or Botanical discovery.

I would earnestly recommend that all such expenditure should be borne by Government, and be adjusted as an item of expedition accounts.

497. Captain Bowers, Commercial Agent attached to the expedition, deserves special mention as an officer whose

varied experience and professional knowledge have been of special utility in an enterprise with which he has been happily associated. I feel a true pleasure in recalling the numerous instances of unselfish and disinterested zeal with which he applied himself in every emergency to the solution of difficulties, and the general furtherance of our expeditionary interests.

498. Mr. T. Stewart served with the expedition as Mercantile Representative appointed by the Rangoon Chamber of Commerce, up to the time of his departure from *Ponsee* at the end of April 1868. I am indebted to him for many personal kindnesses but more particularly for the readiness which he manifested at all times to sink private considerations and make them subservient to the interests of our enterprise.

499. Mr. Robert Gordon, who took the place of Captain Williams and joined the expedition at *Mynela* on the 16th July, has evinced throughout a laudable activity which well merits the notice of the Chief Commissioner and of his departmental superiors. Of his professional abilities it would ill become me to speak, but I may allude to an excess of professional zeal, which required rather restraint than extraneous impetus to excite it to full action.

500. This fact leads me (now that I conceive I have fulfilled a duty, imperfectly perhaps, to all my associates in the recent expedition) to record in addition to my thanks my earnest apologies for having on many occasions interfered with their professional utility, by contracting the sphere of successful enquiry. It resolved itself into a duty at times to curtail enquiry, and more specially to forbid the use of scientific instruments whenever I saw that our acts were suspected, and that reason and explanation were impotent in themselves to stifle prejudice or remove misconception.

501. No one who has not accompanied the expedition throughout, or who does not bear in mind the force of retarding influences, the conflict of interests, Burman intrigue, and, above all things, the natural suspicions which would attach themselves to our first contact with much that was discordant in race and religion, can form any idea of the necessities for extraordinary caution in the minutest of our investigations.

502. To allude to these particulars or to mark the instances in which an interdict was necessary would be to resume the narrative of our expedition experiences. I can only beg therefore that my own short comings and that the short comings of any other member of our party whose fund of information in his particular department may seem to fall short of ordinary expectation, be laid to the charge of expedition interests without casting a slur on individual inclinations.

I have the honor to be

Sir

Your most obedient Servant

EDWARD B. SLADEN, CAPTAIN.

Political Agent and Leader of the late expedition via Bhamo to South Western China.

REPORT ON THE TRADE ROUTE BETWEEN BHAMO AND THE CHINESE PROVINCE OF YUNAN.

1. It has long been known that there are three general directions along which traffic has passed from time immemorial between Bhamo and Momien and the country beyond. These directions are along the Sanda Valley, the Hotha Valley, and the Muangwan (Burmese Momien) Valley, the former being the most northerly the latter the southernmost.

2. The Valleys are breaks at a lower elevation in directions about N. E. & S. W. in the great Mountain chain which passes down the centre of Upper Burma. This itself is a continuation of the Himalayas, and rises near Bhamo to heights of 5 to 10,000 feet above the sea.

3. High ridges separate the valleys. They are generally steepest on their northern slopes. The beds of the Valley are at different elevations. Thus the Sanda Valley is about 2,000 feet above Bhamo, while the Hotha Valley is 3,800 feet, and the intervening ridge where we crossed it, is over 5,000 feet. The Muangwan Valley is about 2,500 feet high and the ridge between Muangwan and Hotha varies in height from 400 feet upwards above Hotha.

4. Several different routes reach into each of these Valleys from Bhamo. Their character is decided by the nature of the intervening country; and they depend for their existence on the Kakhyen inhabitants of the hills who have cut them and keep them open. They are used firstly as pathways to the Kakhyen Villages, and secondly as means of through traffic, the carriage of which is monopolised by the people of the Villages touching the route.

5. Before considering in detail the paths actually traversed by the party, some of the natural features and characteristics of the country may be studied with advantage. Thus it will be seen that the Sanda Valley is a portion of the Valley of the Taping River, a branch of which, the Tahow, flows from Momien to the Irrawaddie near Bhamo. Along this Taping Valley are plains at increasing elevations communicating by defiles or gorges along which the river flows in rapids, preventing boat communication. The Sanda Valley is one of these, and except at the Taping it is closed in on all sides by elevated ground.

6. The Hotha Valley is drained by the Nam-sa, a tributary of the Taping, into the defile of which it flows. The South-west end of this valley is closed by ridges at an elevation of over 4,500 feet above Bhamo. It as well as the Sanda Valley can be communicated with by roads along the defiles of the Taping or over the boundary ridges.

7. The Nam-wan, tributary of the Nam-mow, or Swaylee, which enters Burma much south of Bhamo, drains the Muangwan Valley. No use can be made of this river line in communicating with Bhamo, and all the routes cross the intervening high land, the ridge of which, according to the barometric observation recorded by the Surveyor, is between 3,2000 and 3,300 feet above Bhamo, or about 750 above the Muangwan Valley.

8. All the roads to Momien converge at the north east ends of these valleys before reaching Nantin, some 20 miles from Momien. The elevations to be overcome on the different routes between Bhamo and Nantin have much weight in comparing their natural advantages. Dr. Anderson supplied me with some boiling point observations taken by himself. At Nantin water boiled at 206° F giving a height of 3,668 feet above the sea; and by the barometer it is some 2,700 or 2,800 feet above Bhamo.

9. The Muangwan Valley is nearly at the same level as Nantin being only about 200 feet lower. It is approached from Bhamo and Sawuaddy by several roads, which present no difficulties in the plain lands of Burma. The ascent of most of these roads to the top of the ridge is described as gradual, with occasional steep places. The roads do not always take the most favorable line of country, being rather laid out with a view to afford easy approach to the Villages. The ridge is about 750 feet above the plain land of the Valley, but the descent is easy. Through the Valley little difficulty may be anticipated. Between Muangwan and Nantin there is hilly and rolling ground, which is described as not difficult, but concerning which we have no precise information. There are more routes than one; but that mostly generally used passes close to Sheemalong the stronghold of Lee-see-ha-tai, a man at present at enmity with the Panthays, and believed to be inimical to the opening of the trade.

10. The Hotha Valley is at an elevation of nearly 1,100 feet above Nantin, I tried to examine the ground between Hotha and Nantin, Dr. Anderson volunteering to go with me, but after full enquiry from the Hotha Sawbwa and others it was learned that the routes lay through Lee-see-ha-tai's villages; and under the circumstances it was thought unadvisable to go. We went, however, to the head of the Hotha Valley, and found the height of the dividing ridge to be 455 feet above Hotha. Beyond the ridge only spurs of hills could be seen, and from the account I received from travellers over the ground, I learned that there is a great deal of hilly and rolling ground to be passed over, and another small ridge to be crossed.

11. Between Hotha and Bhamo we followed a route known as the Ambassador's road. Starting from Hotha at noon on the 27th August we passed along a granite causeway made of slabs about 4 feet long, 12 or 14 inches wide and 4 to 6 inches thick. This causeway runs nearly to the north end of the valley. Granite bridges carried the road over the smaller streams. They were very fine specimens of masonry, the stone being exceedingly hard and well worked. The arches were always semicircular. The largest span was about 24 feet. The workmanship was always neat and good; and sometimes the design was tasteful, the parapet walls being panelled and finished off with small griffins. The stone where exposed was much weather beaten, and proved that they had stood for a long time.

12. The valley averages 3 or 4 Miles in width, the northern boundary hills coming down in gradual slopes which round off into gently undulating land. The plain land where the paddy cultivation is, is more to the south eastern side; the river Nam-sa flowing thro' the centre of it. We left the principal road before it entered the town of Latha where a Sawbwa having separate jurisdiction resides; and crossed the Namsa by a plank bridge on trestles about 135 feet long and 2 feet wide, keeping on the south west side of the river, which shortly after turned off and disappeared between some hills flowing into the Taping. The valley soon narrowed, and some undulating land which came out from the base of the southern ridge of hills assumed as we went south a bolder appearance standing out from the plain land below

in well defined hills. The road wound round some of these and shortly began to ascend the sides of a small valley the drainage of which flows north eastward into the Namsa. This valley is under the Namboke Kakhyen Sawbwa.

13. We arrived at Namboke village in the evening and were detained there for one day. It is about 3,700 feet above Bhamo and nearly 600 above Hotha. The next day the journey was to Ashan; one point of the road as shewn by the aneroid was about 4,650 feet above Nantin. This was the highest point on the whole road, which kept along a ridge running parallel to the Taping. We stopped at Ashan village at a height of 3,713 feet above Bhamo.

14. The hills in this part are all of metamorphic formation with here and there granite appearing. The rocks generally are of quartzose and micaceous schist. The surface and the ground for a considerable depth is formed of disintegrations of this, and is easily worked; occasionally boulders, some of immense size, crop out, or rest on the surface. This road, in common with all the hill road, is excavated in the hill side. I saw cuttings of various depths up to twenty feet. The width is generally from 6 to 10 feet but there had not been much traffic on the path we were on for some years, and it was a good deal over-grown with jungle. We had passed hitherto along high ground keeping close to the hill tops and ridge lines. There were a few difficult places met with in two days march, but none which could not easily be overcome in the construction of an ordinary road.

15. Leaving Ashan on the morning of the 30th August we descended steadily to the bed of a stream called the Nam-Khong, some 958 feet below Ashan, and 2,755 feet above Bhamo. This far we had come the regular route; but some Kakhyen Saubwas wished to take us through their villages, and we were compelled to go a round about way. Hotone is only one days journey from this by the proper road but we did not arrive there till the 2nd September. The intermediate places we visited, and the route we traversed, need not be considered here. We were taken over high hills by long marches, much of which might have been escaped. Hotone is 2,450 feet above Bhamo and about 300 below the place where we crossed the Nam-khong. The intervening ground is all

hilly but it is said to be much easier than the road we came. From Hotone the descent was regular and the road easy till we came near the Taping river, where the fall was very rapid, and difficult. It descended to the river bank and kept close to it for two miles when we stopped at the Namthabet stream, which runs rapidly. It is about 120 feet wide and had to be crossed on rafts. From the Namthabet we passed over irregular hilly and undulating ground for about 5 miles. The path way was not good, but the physical difficulties in the way of making a good road are not great.

16. I have brought into view the principal points of this route taking it out of its turn for the purpose of comparing them with those of the route we passed over leading through the Sanda valley. This valley communicates with Burma through the defile of the Taping, which flows over a bed strewn with immense boulders, and having a great fall. A large amount of water passes down, which is represented in the upper valley by a stream 1,000 to 1,500 feet wide, and a depth of six feet, flowing at the average rate of four miles per hour. This is in the defile a confused mass, yellow with silt, with white foam forming on its surface as it rushes against the boulders, and rises into the air in broken heaps and spray accompanied by a loud roaring noise. In parts, the rocks on either side come steeply down to it, but generally they recede gradually, confining its channel to a narrow course, which is not so tortuous as might have been expected.

17. Dry weather roads follow each bank. That on the left bank turns off into the Hotha valley thro' the the defile of the Namsa; but it is also continued, I was informed, to the Sanda valley. Several small streams, and two of over 100 feet, have to be crossed by this route. It must be in many respects similar to the one on the right bank, five or six miles of which we followed. It has to conform to the windings of the river and the shape of the hills. Where the hills rise steeply from the river a large amount of cutting is required for any breadth of road, but for a road not exceeding 12 feet in width the banks of the Taping river afford the best line, as all unnecessary ascents and descents are avoided; and it gradually rises from the level of the Burman plains to the level of the valley.

18. The road followed by the party from Bhamo through Ponsee passes over the plain land near the Taping river which it crosses. The river varies considerably in width but may average from 1,000 to 1,200 feet. It is not deep, nor rapid; its velocity in the hills being checked by the broken character of the bed; and the large amount of silt brought down is deposited, and the channel kept broad and shallow. On the right bank of the Taping the road follows the villages on its bank to Old Bhamo, when it turns off through See-het to the base of the hills, a few miles from where the river runs out. In dry weather the road is a fair one, but is even then only a cart track on the surface of the ground. No embanked paths mark it out. The few wooden bridges that exist are old or in bad repair. In the rains there is hardly a road at all, a way may be made along the berms of paddy fields, but in some parts I had to swim the ponies through 3 or 4 feet of water. The whole of this, however, can be easily remedied. An embankment, with bridges of wood or masonry over the streams, will provide a permanently good road in all seasons in any part of the plains. In Pegu a road 20 feet wide completely metalled and bridged averages 10,000 Rs. per mile. If this line was followed the Taping would require to be bridged. A wooden bridge on piles well driven into the bed of the streams, with trusses and longitudinal girders over 30 or 40 feet spans, and a flooring 12 feet wide, could be built for 20 Rs. per running foot. This of 1,000 feet in length would be 20,000 Rupees.

19. Leaving See-het the road lay through level ground for about ½ a mile to the base of the hills, up a small spur of which it ascended. The ascent was moderately steep, for the path went straight up the face of the spur, no attempt having been made to carry it up in zigzags. We first topped a small ridge about 400 feet above the plain, and then descended 100 or 150 feet to a small valley. After one or two undulations of this kind, the ascent was more easy and steady to Ponelyne, a Kakhyen village, some of the houses of which had been burned down by Kanloungs another tribe of Kakhyens, a short time before I arrived. So far there were no difficulties in the way which could not easily be overcome. The road, as excavated by the Kakhyens, was rough in parts and difficult to travel on account of a few steep ascents.

It had been excavated in places to a width of 6 feet, and depths of up to fourteen feet. But little advantage had been taken of the shape of the ground to lay it out in a scientific manner, as of course might be reasonably expected. The greatest height above the plain shewn by my aneroid barometer was only 1,800 feet. By a careful selection of the most suitable places, and by winding or zigzaging the road up the hill side at the first ascent a good mountain road might be made to Ponelyne, at small cost, and with easy gradients.

The hills are of metamorphic rock, much weathered and disintegrated near the surface. I could easily crumble it in my hand even in the deepest cuttings. Strata of quartz appeared running through it at different angles and in various directions.

These would offer little resistance to working, as they break up into small crystal blocks.

The greater portion of the road as far as Ponelyne could be taken through easily worked ground, and any hard portions met with could be removed by blasting. The distance from Bhamo to the base of the hills is 23 miles and to Ponelyne 30 miles.

20. After passing Ponelyne the road continued easy for a mile or so keeping to high ground. But it then commenced to descend; and, after crossing a small stream and re-ascending a short distance, it again descended to the Nampoung, a stream which runs from a direction east of north into the Taping, and divides the hills into two ridges running nearly north and south. It is this stream which makes the principal objection to this route, as we found that the road goes down to the mouth of it just where it joins the Taping, of necessity the lowest point. The descent at first easy, gradually becomes steeper and at length precipitous. The Kakhyens had done little to render the descent easy. The path certainly zigzaged a little but it was the least possible amount which could apparently be given. The soil was of much the same nature as before, and the path had been worn out deeper by the traffic and running water so that it was almost like a V shaped groove with from 9 to 12 inches of foot way at bottom.

The Strata of quartz and hard rock which occasionally peeped out were here well developed by the softer parts being worn away, and made the path hurtful and dangerous to both animals and men. The aneroid shews the bottom of the stream to be 550 feet above Bhamo or 1,260 feet below Ponelyne from which it is 3 miles distant.

The reason for the road taking the lowest point of the stream I found to be that it is only fordable at that place in the wet season. When I crossed, it was a roaring torrent which animals with loads could not stem. The stream is only about 100 feet wide, and 3 feet deep, and could easily be bridged.

21. The road continues along the bank of the Taping River for about 3 miles. It has been excavated from 6 to 10 feet in the sides of the hills, which are in places very steep on to the river. This part of the road does not vary much in elevation, but contours the hills neatly, and is a specimen of what the whole road might be made along the water's edge of the Taping. At the same time its weakness is seen for it necessarily winds a great deal; and its width could not be increased much except at great expense. A road 10 or 12 feet in width or perhaps more might be made here, and all along the river bank without much trouble or heavy expense.

22. Leaving the river bank the road re-ascends, and for steepness and difficulty, owing to the want of contouring and grading, the ascent is a counterpart of the descent to the Nampoung. After the first mile it is not so bad, but with a little variation it continues ascending to the top of a hill called Meteet Toung, then it descends about 500 feet into a well cultivated valley before ascending to its highest point about 2,900 feet above Bahmo. The road after another small descent and rise gradually descended to Ponsee village.

23. By taking the road from Ponelyne to a point considerably higher up the Nampoung, and throwing a light bridge over at a great elevation between prominent hills, a great portion of the objectionable descent and re-ascent could be avoided, and the road could be carried at much the same level from Ponelyne to Ponsee; or, if it were not intended to make a large road, the present one could be very much improved by proper laying out. A substantial bridge is at present much needed, as the traffic is sometimes stopped for days after very heavy showers. This might be made at mod-

erate cost. A careful search over the whole ground could alone determine what improvements might ultimately be made in this route either by a change of the line, or alterations to the present one.

24. From Ponsee the road, after passing over hilly ground for two or three miles, enters a small valley which is in continuation of the Sanda valley. It is shut out from the Taping by a small range of hills, but the drainage flows north east into it. The path is cut on the side of the ridge, and gradually reaches the level land on the bottom of the the valley, and passes from thence to the larger valley. The Sanda valley is, up to Muangla, about 27 miles in length, and the plain land varies from 4 to 8 miles in breadth. At the south end, the ground is slightly uneven, as there are two or three terraces scooped out by water action. Further north these terraces blend together and disappear, the ground sloping down from the base of the hills to the river's edge; the older bank being several feet above the surface of the water. The smaller valley is wholly occupied by Kakhyens; and the road is here regularly excavated; but when once this is left there are several paths, but no roads regularly made, or on which any trouble is expended. One path leads near the river, but it is not used in the rains. The one one I passed over keeps on a high shelf of unculturable land used principally for burying places. Several small streams were passed over from 6 to 30 feet in width; one, the Nam-Soung is about 60 feet wide, but fordable. None were bridged. It is a characteristic of all the streams in these parts to be very broad, and very shallow for the amount of water brought down. No difficulty would be experienced in building bridges, as granite and lime are abundant, and easily obtained.

25. The paths all lead to Manwyne, the first Shan town, which is under a Swabwa-ga-daw or female Swabwa. The population is mixed Shan and Chinese, and includes the principal traders with Burma of the valley, with gamblers and thieves over whom there seems little authority. It is, like all the Chinese Shan towns and villages, surrounded with a wall five or six feet high made of concrete bricks. These are the principal building materials used in the valley. They are made of a natural concrete of lime, sand and pebbles, sundried and having a yellowish white colour, which gives a

pleasant appearance to the villages. A foundation is always made for these bricks of granite rubble, which keeps the damp from rising. Both isolated walls and houses are covered with burned clay tiles, flat or round. There is a great scarcity of timber in the valley. All the hills have been stripped of everything which can burn, to near their tops, where Kakhyen villages are seen. The Kakhyens bring down firewood and occasionally sawn boards for sale. The distance the timber has to be brought and its cost prevent its use to a great extent for building. Manwyne has a few very narrow streets paved with irregular masses of granite, which are bad for walking, and worse for riding. It is crowded with pigs, which alone superintend the conservancy.

26. From Manwyne to Sanda there is no regular road, except in the immediate neighbourhood of one or two large villages. Here there are roads like English lanes 15 or 16 feet wide, with ditches on each side, flanked with trees and overhanging bamboos. The extent of these is too limited to be of any account in through communication. There are some small bridges on these lanes but they are quite unimportant. Sanda is out of the line of through traffic; the road passing a mile to the south of it. It is at the base of a rounded hill 1,400 feet high, the summit of which is scarped in a curious manner, as is a hill opposite it to the North. Tradition says these hills were the scene of a defeat by the Chinese of a Burman army, which had entrenched itself there. The town itself is a small place, though neat and well kept, with broad paved streets. It has no claim to rank as a *Foo*, as it is shewn in some maps, not being fortified, or walled except like the neighbouring villages. Its population I estimated to be about 3,500 people.

27. Close to it are some hot springs, and a limestone hill from whence the people of the valley derive the lime they use. Across the Taping to the south of Manwyne is a spur of the main ridge containing beautiful statuary marble of even texture, fine grain, and pure white colour. It does not appear to be worked except for inscription slabs in the heads of graves.

28. The road crosses the Nam-Sanda, a fordable stream 120 feet wide, which flows into the Taping. At the north side of this stream a spur runs out from the north ridge of the hills, extending to the river, almost meeting a corresponding

spur from the south side, and dividing the valley into two. It is about 260 feet above the level of the plain and as the ground has a moderate slope up to it no difficulty would be found in taking a good road over it. From hence to Muangla the path is somewhat better though apparently no regard has been paid to it as a thoroughfare. Part of it runs on the top of an embankment by the river side, built to keep out the water from the crops. The track was very bad in some places, the mules having to go through water deep enough to wet their loads. Near Muangla the main branch of the Taping was crossed by ferry boats the water being some 800 feet broad and not over 6 feet deep.

29. The town of Muangla is situated on the slope at the base of a ridge, which divides the valley of the Taping into two branches. The river leading to Nantin and Momien is known as the Tahow. The other branch which is the largest, is called the Moo-wan, the same name given to the main river in the Sanda valley by the Shans. The population of Muangla I estimated to be about 6,500, nearly twice that of Sanda. Both Muangla and Sanda were partially destroyed by the Panthays on their descent a few years back. Many of the houses are covered with thatch instead of tiles, and few have been rebuilt on the former scale.

30. The whole valley is divided into three Sawbwaships; Muangla, Sanda, and Manwyne; the latter being under Muangtee. The first is the largest having over 200 villages in it. Allowing an average of 60 houses to each village, and 5 persons to each house, there will be over 60,000 persons in the Muangla district. This is a moderate computation, as some of the villages were very large. Sanda is said to be about half as large and may contain 30,000 people. The Muanwyne district has only about 1,000 houses or 5,000 people. Allowing 10,000 for the town of Sanda and Muangla I estimate the whole Chinese and Shan population of the valley to be about 105,000. The plain portion of the valley in which the Shans reside is about 26 miles long, by an average of $4\frac{1}{2}$ wide, giving 117 square miles. This gives nearly 900 to the square mile which may seem a large proportion but the numbers are founded on enquiries from persons competent to give tolerably correct information; and are supported by personal observations. The population is one of

the densest I have seen. There is a large Kakhyen population on the slopes of the hills and in the valley at the south end, which I estimate ar 30,000 or 40,000.

Altogether, I think there are about 150,000 people in the whole valley, the watershed of which to the north extends a great distance.

31. There are few industrial operations carried on except to supply the people with clothing and household wants; and as almost every house supplies itself there is little interchange of these. Nothing is made for export. There is little money in the valley, Chinese brass cash being used and exchanged at 450 to 500 for the rupee. Gold is very scarce; all the ornaments being made of silver. The population is mostly agricultural; rice being the staple produce, some of which is sent to China, and some to Burma. Fruits and garden vegetables are produced for home consumption, but potatoes are exported to Burma and find their way to Mandalay. The neatness of the paddy cultivation presents a singular contrast to that of the Burmese. The gently sloping ground is terraced into broad level areas, bounded by earthen bunds, all of which are regularly shaped with the spade, and sodded on top with grass. The hill streams are dammed up on entering the plains; and portions of water led off in canals, and evenly distributed amongst the fields of those who have combined to make the canal. The paddy when about 15 inches high is transplanted by hand at equal distances in regular rows. Every available spot of ground is utilized. It is the importance which is attached to agriculture, and the little benefit hitherto received from the through traffic, which makes the Shans neglect the road where it passes through their valley.

32. It would be very easy to make an excellent road or a railway through this Sanda valley. The distance from Bhamo to the south end of the valley is by the road 51 miles and to the north end 90 miles. This interval of 39 miles might be shortened by straightening the line. There is a rise of about 250 feet in the length of the valley.

33. I did not go any further than Muangla, as the day of my arrival the party came in from Momien. The town is 19 miles from Nantin; and about 42 from Momien. I was informed that though the road was rough in some

parts, and irksome to travel, there were few physical difficulties to interfere with making a good one. The valley line of the Tahow is followed; a slight deviation being made at Maupoo Hill. The Nantin valley and the Momien valley are plains of increasing elevation connected with the Sanda valley by defiles. The boiling point of water at Momein was 201° F which gives that place an elevation of 5,808 feet ebove the sea, or 2,140 above Nantin, and 2,670 above Muangla. This last place is 90 miles from Bhamo; Nantin 109; and Momein 142. There is, therefore, a rise of 530 feet in 19 miles between Muangla and Nantin; and 2140 feet in 23 miles from Nantin to Momein.

This last is a significant fact, as it shows that there is an ascent of 93 feet per mile on the average or a gradient of 1 in 57. The Tahow valley however presents natural facilities for overcoming this ascent; and there is nothing I heard of to prevent a good railway being carried the whole way. Momien appears to be near the highest part of the range between the Irrawaddie and the Salween.

34. The line of road now described, passing through Ponelyne, Ponsee, and the Sanda valley, is worth detailed consideration; as it is considered by the people of that part of the country the best road existing at present. It has only been constructed of late years. The Chinese traders subscribed a large sum of money for the excavation of the track, which is nominally kept in order by the Kakhyen inhabitants of the hills, whose ground it passes through. These in a great measure monopolize the carriage of traffic, or take tolls upon goods passing. The principal advantages of it are 1st, the short distance, about 30 miles in the Kakhyen Hills; 2nd, the small amount of unnecessary elevation to be overcome in ascending to the Sanda valley and 3rd, the passing through the Sanda valley itself, whose dense and laborious population may be expected to take a large amount of any goods which may be brought by that route. The disadvantages of it are; 1st, the having to cross the Taping River in Burma, and recross it in the Sanda valley 2nd the descent of 1,200 feet to the Nampoung, and re-ascent to Ponsee.

35. There are other routes to the north, which reach the Sanda valley; but all have to pass over higher and broken ground meeting the same descent to the Nampoung, and

in the opinion of the people themselves, not equal to the Ponsee Route. They serve a good purpose, however, in competing with the best route, and preventing monopoly having injurious effects.

36. The Hotha Routes have the advantage of not requiring to cross the Taping River. In other respects everything is against them; and for the purpose of making a good road on scientific principles, they cannot compete for an instant with either the Ponesee or Muangla routes. The excess height of 2,000 feet to be passed over before reaching the Hotha valley; its own great elevation above Nantin; and the rolling ground which intervenes between Hotha and Nantin, with the re-ascent of 450 feet, remove the route by this valley from serious consideration in an engineering sense. The small population of the valley also which, according to the Hotha Sawbwa, is not over 40,000 people is against it. In a political sense they are not unimportant; as they are not unsuitable to the existing traffic by mules in small parties, and will serve to keep down the price of carriage by other routes. They have been closed for several years, owing to the stoppage and plunder of a Burman Embassy to China, 12 years ago; and for the same reason the Kakhyens are unfriendly to the Burmese, giving a demonstration of it in their assistance to us. It would be as unwise to rely upon this state of things continuing permanent, as a reason to counterbalance the physical difficulties of the route, as it would be to condemn the Ponsee route because of of the opposition met with by the main party when first going. When I went by the latter I was most favorably received by the people, who gave me the best places in their houses, and evinced their hospitality in various ways.

37. The Muangwan Routes remain to be compared with the Ponsee Route. These were formerly, when the traffic was great, the favorite routes; but since the opening of the Ponsee line, faulty as it is, they have been less used. The Muangwan valley is much larger than the Hotha valley; but not so large as the the Sanda one. The population is said to be as large as that of Muangla, some 60,000. There is no large town of Muangwan, the word *Muang* meaning district, and *Ving* town. The village where the Sawbwa resides is called by the name of the district. A fair compa-

rison cannot now be made between the Ponsee and the Muangwan routes, as sufficient is not known of the latter The ridge to be crossed before reaching that valley is about 750 feet above the plain land, to which a descent is again made. This is not a grave objection, if a gentle slope can be made to it. It is less objectionable than the descent to the Nampoung on the Ponsee line; and the plain land of the valley is nearly on a level with Nantin. The few data known from the accounts given compare favorably with the Ponsee route. But uncertainty exists as to the land passed over between the Muangwan valley and Nantin. It is known that there is hilly ground, but there is said to be no great difficulty. A fair comparison can only be made after actually travelling over and carefully examining both routes. The Taping river will not have to be crossed; but the Nam-Wan, which is comparitively small, will. On the whole, I am of opinion that a good road with easy gradients can be made without great expense through either the Sanda or Muangwan valley. No difficulties greater than are ordinarily met with in constructing hill roads exist in the Kakhyen hills; and there are some advantages in the dense population accustomed to making roads.

38. The country will compare favorably with the Arracan Mountains opposite Prome, over which a 12 foot road has been made to the sea. This is altogether 100 miles long, 90 of which are in the hills. The total height to be overcome is over 3,000 feet above the sea level; and the descent to Prome is nearly as great. The rocks are in part of the hardest material; trap, and argillaceous schist. The shape of the hills is very irregular; and several ascents and descents have to be made before crossing the ridge line. There is not a village near the road from the 24th to the 110th miles, and all the labour and food for the workmen had to be conveyed from the plains. This was opened for cart traffic within three years from its commencement, but was not properly finished throughout its length. Its cost, including wooden bridges in the plains, was between 8 and 9 lacs; or about 8,000 Rupees per mile. I have had the road under my charge for three years; and have had opportunities of studying the country, and the manner in which the natural difficulties have been overcome; and I can affirm that in the 30 or 40 miles

of hilly ground necessary to pass over to reach the Sanda Valley from the plains, there are no greater difficulties than are met with on the Prome and Tonghoop Road.

39. While in the plain land the cost of a road increases as its breadth, in hilly ground it varies as the square of its breadth. Thus if a 20 feet wide road cost 10,000 Rs. per mile in plain land; one 30 feet wide will cost Rs. 15,000 under similar circumstances. But where a 12 feet wide hill road costs 10,000 Rs. one 20 feet in width may be expected to cost 27,777 Rs. per mile. If a road were constructed from Bhamo to Momien, the abundance of skilled labour in every part of the country, with the scarcity up to the present time of money, ought to cause the work to be done at cheaper rates than in British Burma; where the scarcity of population, and the great exportation of produce combine to keep labour at a high price. On the line of road from Bhamo to Momien there would be about 20 miles of road in the Burman plains; 30 miles in the Kakhyen Hills, 30 miles in the plain land of the Sanda Valley; and 40 partly through plain, and partly through hilly ground between Muangla and Momien. Taking half of this as hill, and half as plain, there would be altogether 70 miles of plain land, and 50 miles of hilly land through which the road would pass. If it were 20 feet wide in the plain land its cost complete might be taken at 10,000 Rs. there and hilly hand 12 feet wide, gradients of 1 in 30, its cost completely bridged should not be over 10,000 Rupees per mile; or the road could be made for £1,000 per mile through out; or on a length of 120 miles £120,000. Taking these data the cost of the road on any proposed width may be approximated to.

40. With regard to the question of making a railway to Momien, modern engineering practice enables it to be stated as matter of course, that a railway can be laid down and worked under circumstances of greater difficulty than exist here. And whether the Sanda valley line be chosen, I believe the only real difficulty will be found in the ascent from the Burman plain, over the Kakhyen Hills, to the Shan valley. The greater part of the remainder of the route offers unusual facilities for constructing either a road or railway. The ascents from the Sanda to the Nantin Valley, and from that to the Momien, are comparatively trifling; and I have

no doubt that on the Muangwan line the rolling ground between Muangwan and Nantin can be easily overcome. In a comparison of the Sanda and Muangwan Routes, so far as crossing the Kakhyen Hills is concerned, I would give the preference to the latter; for here the problem is reduced to taking the line up a hill side of moderate slope over a ridge 3,200 feet high and then descending 750 feet to the valley, while in the other case, the Nampoung stream, though not offering much obstacle to a common road, would cause great difficulty to a railway. In either case only such difficulties are met as are ordinarily met with in hill railways and over come by ordinary means. A regular survey and levelling of a line carefully selected, after preliminary surveys, and examination of the surrounding country, would be necessary to give an approximation to the nature of the works required and the probable cost.

41. I have restricted the preceding remarks to general observations on the country, and the routes between Bhamo and Momien; as the personal observation of the party did not extend further. I have attached in an appendix some barometrical observations, supplied by Dr. Anderson, and reduced for heights by myself; with some of my own, and those of the Surveyor with my aneroid on the Muangwan route; with the boiling points supplied by Dr. Anderson.

42. This report would be very incomplete, however, and the instructions of the Chief Commissioner would be very inadequately followed, were it to close without further considering the through routes to develope the old trade and to intercept and divert to the Irrawaddy the present great traffic from Talifoo and Yungchang to Mandalay. I have conversed with and obtained information from traders who have been over the routes and country in that part. The routes as far as possible are shewn in the map sent in with the report. Although all available maps and records bearing on the subject were consulted to direct my enquiries, I have only admitted into my map the names of such places as the persons I conversed with had themselves visited; and the natural features I have shewn in the map, such as ridges of hills, valleys, plains and streams, I satisfied myself actually exist.

43. The names of places may not agree with other maps; but I have written them on the principle that where the name of a place is not established by general usage, or chosen for special reasons, the name given to it by the residents should as far as possible be adopted. Thus the names of the Kakhyen villages have been supplied to me by Kakhyens, the Palong by a Palong and the Shan places by Shans. Places which are called by the Burmese Maing-la, Main-tee and Mowun, are called by the Shans themselves Muangla, Muangtee, and Muangwan.

44. Momien, or Teng-ye-chow, is situated near the ridge line of the great chain of mountains. It was, as the termination "Chow" indicates, the chief town of a third class district under the Chinese; and is now, under the Panthays, the seat of a governor of rank and power inferior to that of the Governor of Yungchang-Foo, the chief city of a first class district. It is of political importance in being the centre of the frontier district, but its great elevation of nearly 6,000 feet above the sea, and the mountainous character of the country around, deprive it of importance as a centre of trade and traffic; and make it not a good termination to a route. Little of the present traffic stops at Momien, but most passes on to Yungchang. From Momien the road, shortly crossing the highest point, begins to descend to the valley of the main branch of the Shwèlee, there called the Long-chang by the Chinese. There is high and hilly land between this and the Salween River, but it is not represented as being very difficult to travel. What the actual descent is from Momien to the Salween is not known; but the bed of the Salween must be at a much higher elevation than that of the Irrawaddy at the same latitude, as it is known to be a succession of rapids throughout its course from British Burma. There is no such ground to pass over as the ascent to the Kakhyen Hills from Bhamo; and the whole country, when once those hills are passed, appears to be plateau land of different elevations, with intervening ridges of various heights. The Salween River itself is crossed by an iron suspension bridge, built by the Chinese. Between the Salween and Yungchang there is hilly land, near Possyow, where there is a fortified post of Panthays. The journey from Momien to Yungchang actually takes four days, and the distance may be 50 or 60 miles.

45. Yungchang is the great centre of trade; as through it passes almost all the traffic to Mandalay, some 30,000 mules yearly, and from it diverge many roads through the province of Yunan. It is situated in a densely populated district, and offers many advantages as the terminus of a road, or as the place from which trade might be opened to Bhamo. There are other through routes to Yungchang than that through Momien, one of which, passing through the Muangwan valley, goes past Palong villages and through the densely populated Chinese Shan states of Sehfan, Muangkwan, and Muang-kah; all of which are tributary to the Panthays. This line would not have to pass over such high ground as the line through Momien. It would pass over one moderate ridge between Muangwan and Sehfan, and then cross the Nam-mow. It will nearly touch the Shan state of Muang-mow; which is believed to be the largest of the Chinese Shan states, and is at present independent, paying tribute to none. The line follows the valley line of the Nam-mow through Sehfan and Muangkwan, and then crosses a ridge of hills at Louglin, a large town. From there it descends to the Muangkah district, on the Salween; where it joins the Mandalay routes. This line appears, from the structure of the country, to offer advantages over the Momien line; and I think should be carefully examined.

46. Although the distance traversed by the party terminates at Momien, and the journeys were too hurried to allow careful surveys to be made for the best line, the results are satisfactory in shewing the extent of the difficulties to be overcome on the one route; and in proving that these are not insuperable; and that they are of such a nature as not to oppose any serious obstacle, in an engineering sense, to the construction of a road or railway. And at the some time they prove, from the existence of the numerous routes which are kept up at a great expenditure of time and labour, that there is a great local traffic at present; which, by decreasing the cost of carriage by good roads &c., might be turned into a greater traffic of nations; and they prove this,—a fact which cannot have too much stress laid upon it—that this part of the country is one of the most densely populated in the world.

47. Much remains to be done in the way of surveying, before such a knowledge of the country is obtained to enable a reliable opinion to be given as to the best line of road; but a surveying partly, lightly equipped, and composed of selected men would in one or two seasons survey with sufficient accuracy all the known routes, and adjacent country, to determine this; and to give an estimate of the approximate cost of the works required. If, until this was done, it were thought advisable to develope the traffic—by assisting the Kakhyens and Shans who keep up the present known routes; by a competant person shewing them how they could improve them, by more attention to natural facilities, and by suitable presents of money to induce them to do the work—much good could be done. The Engineer doing this would familiarize the people to his presence, and could gradually extend his observations to the whole of the country included in his intended survey.

ROBERT GORDON
Engineer,
Bhamo, Route Survey.

Henzadah, 6th January, 1869.

APPENDIX.

Shewing height of places visited on Bhamo Route Survey reduced from barometrical observations.

In every case the observations have been reduced by the formula given by Rankine (Civil Engineer) where the heights of upper station above lower =

$$= 60{,}630 \left\{ \log H \log h - .000044 \, (T.\, t.) \right\}$$

H and h symbolising the height of the barometer and T and t Do. Do. attached thermometer

Bhamo has been chosen as the place to which the heights have been reduced.

TABLE I.

Observations supplied by Dr. Anderson from his aneroid barometer—Forward Journey.

Date.	Place.	Means of observation. Bar.	Means of observation. Ther.	No. of observations.	Height above Bhamo.	Remarks.
Feby. 1868.						
8th to 13th	*Bhamo	29.695	$58\frac{3}{4}°$	18	0	* The heights have been reduced in this table from this observation at Bhamo.
27th	Setkaw	29.556	$62\frac{1}{4}°$	11	132	
March						
3rd to 5th	Ponelyne	27.397	$61\frac{1}{4}°$	6	2,127	
7th to 12th	Ponsee	26.727	$56\frac{1}{4}°$	18	2,750	
May						
14th to 15th	Sanda	27.343	$66\frac{1}{2}°$	4	2,194	No observation supplied for Manwyne.
18th to 23rd	Muangla	27.266	$68°$	16	2,271	

TABLE II.

RETURN JOURNEY.

Observations taken by Dr. Anderson and myself conjointly.

Date.	Palace.	Mean of observation.		No. of observations.	Height above Bhamo.	Remarks.
		Bar.	Ther.			
August						
5th to 9th	Manwyne	27.148	70¼°	12	1,960	
14th to 17th	Hotha	25.447	65¼°	10	3,649	
27th to 29th	Namboke	25.415	63¼°	6	3,676	
29th	Top of ridge	24.510	70°	1	4,649	
29th to 30th	Ashan	25.383	64½°	3	3,713	
30th	Namkhong chioung	26.340	71°	1	2,755	
30th	Ridge of hill near Mungwye	25.050	72°	1	4,082	
31st	Mungwye	25.275	62°.5	2	3,819	
31st	Munkah chioung	25.840	64°	1	3,242	
September						
31st to 2nd	Lwè-long	25.619	64°	4	3,468	
2nd	Ridge of hill	25.000	68°	1	4,123	
„	Hotone	26.650	72°	1	2,450	
3rd	Namthabet chioung	29.128	75°	1	120	
9th to 11th	Bhamo	29.259	75°	10	0	The above heights have been reduced from this observation at Bhamo.

TABLE III.

Observations of Barometer recorded by Mr. Gordon during journey over the Kakhyen Hills with heights reduced to Bhamo.

FORWARD JOURNEY.

Date.	Place.	Means of observation. Bar.	Means of observation. Ther.	No. of observations.	Height above Bhamo.	Remarks.
July 1st	Bhamo	29.29	82°	4	0	
7th	Ponelyne	27.29	73°	1	1,814	I did not go up to the large village on the hill where former party encamped.
7th and 8th	Nampoung near Taping river	28.63	76½°	2	573	
8th	Ponsee rock	26.20	73°	1	2,900	
10th	Ponsee	26.375	71°	1	2,719	
11th	Phala	26.97	77¾°	3	2,150	
11th to 13th	Manwyne	27.227	77½°	7	1,900	
15th to 20th	Muangla	27.03	77½°	20	2,091	No stoppage made at Sanda on forward journey.

RETURN JOURNEY.

Date.	Place.	Bar.	Ther.	No. of obs.	Height above Bhamo.	Remarks.
21st to 27th	Sanda	27.11	77½°	19	2,012	At Sanda on return journey attached thermometer was broken. From this time the thermometer observation are assumed from Dr. Anderson's which marked about 5.0 less than mine.
August 4th to 9th	Manwyne	27.134	77¾°	21	1,989	

MANWYNE TO HOTHA.

Date.	Place.	Bar.	Ther.	No. of obs.	Height above Bhamo.	Remarks.
9th	Spur of hill in journey to Hotha.	25.24	75°	1	3,888	
9th	Ridge of do.	23.84	70°	2	5,377	
10th to 18th	Hotha	25.192	72°	39	3,920	From Hotha my aneroid was taken along the Muangwan Route to Sawuddy by the Surveyor.

HOTHA TO MUANGWAN & SAWUDDY.

Date.	Place.	Bar.	Ther.	No. of obs.	Height above Bhamo.	Remarks.
19th	Top of ridge	24.37	70°	1	4,798	
20th	Muangwan	26.56	70°	2	2,532	From Muangwan to Ponekan the rise is very gradual.
20th & 21st	Lomepa	26.605	68°	3	2,484	
21st & 22nd	Noung-eng	26.65	69°	3	2,441	
23rd	Ponekan	25.85	66°	3	3,235	
25th	On ridge 9 a.m.	26.70	70°	1	2,389	Here there is a great and sudden fall. The only difficult part met with.
	12 noon	28.30	77°	1	875	
	3 p.m.	29.13	78°	1	122	
September 9th to 11th	Bhamo	29.258	86°	10	0	

The mean of the first and last observation or bar: 29.274 and Ther: 84° is taken for calculating out the heights of all places.

TABLE IV

Boiling point observations supplied by Dr. Anderson and reduced by Mr Gordon : C. E.

Place of observation.	Reading of Thermometer.	Heights above Sea Level.	Remarks.
Manwyne	206°	3138'	
Sanda	206°	3138'	
Muangla	206°	3138'	These heights have been accurately reduced from the observations given; but these last are not sufficiently delicate to ensure great accuracy.
Nantiu	205°	3668'	
Momein	201°	5808'	
Hotha	203°	4734'	

N. B. The Formula used is taken from Rankine, Viz ; height $= 517 (212° - t) + t^2$. T being the temperature Farhenheit.

ROBERT GORDON,
Engineer,
Bhamo Route Servey.

APPENDIX.

From Captain SLADEN, to Colonel FYTCHE, dated Bhamo 22nd January 1868.

I arrived here last evening, after a most pleasant trip, which has been signalized by the absence of difficulties of every kind, in river navigation. The problem, as regards the practicability of the upper waters of the Irrawaddy for steamer navigation, has been satisfactorily and finally settled. There is no doubt whatever, that the river is better in this respect, between Mandalay and Bhamo than it is between Mandalay and our frontier. True, our steamer did not draw more than three feet of water, but with this draft, we never grounded, and though the vessel bumped now and then, on a sandbank, it was only to fall back again immediately, into comparatively deep water. Our Burman Capatin had a good eye for water, and the journey might have been completed in 5 instead of 8 days, had not the dense morning fog interfered with our starting hour, and made it often 10, instead of 6 a.m. We stayed too, occasionally, at places which promised an equivalent for delay either in scientific or sporting results.

The murder of the old Bhamo Woon has had rather a depressing effect in these parts. The Kakhyens are said to show a more decided spirit of independence than ever. Yesterday, whilst the steamer was at anchor off Shwègoo-myo, I went on shore with Williams and a small party of our followers; we passed through several small Burmese villages, all of which were fortified with interlaced split bamboos, as a protection against the attacks of murderous and kidnapping Kakhyens. The villagers were afraid to leave their fortifications, and cross the short distances (not a mile) which separated some of their villages, unless in armed parties of 5 men and upwards. It was with some difficulty that I managed to get a Burman to accompany and show us where we might possibly fall in with a Kakhyen encampment. It was moderately risky work, but we were too strong to fear attack and felt sure that the Kakhyens, if properly spoken to and unmolested by us, would not attempt harm. Some villages had been deserted by Burmese in fear of Kakhyen inroads: we passed them, and after a while, our cautious guide pointed to a hut in the distance, in which he said we should find what we wanted. He remained, and we went on. The house or hut was filled with Kakhyens; when first they saw our party, strong in numbers and arms, they made a sudden movement, which might have been construed, either into an attempt to spring upon, or away from, us. But immediately I spoke, they were quiet, and understood that we meant peace. There were a dozen or more Kakhyens in the house, with their Chief or Saubwa, who spoke Burmese. They spread mats in the most polite manner, and invited us into the house. Our followers advised caution, but we entered and sat down, when a pleasant and interesting conversation took place. I was called the Engleit mengyee, and treated with every respect. After a time I persuaded the whole party of Kakhyens with their Saubwa, to leave their house and accompany us on our way back to the steamer. But after proceeding some distance, they held a council, and then informed me, that press of business would not allow of their coming all the way to the steamer. They were of course afraid of putting themselves too much in the power of the Burmese authorities at Shwè Goo, though they had so far placed reliance in us, as to let us lead them through the centre of some of the villages, specially fortified against their ingress. We parted as good friends, and I relate the incident at length because it augurs well for success in our further dealings with this much belied race.

This morning two Tsit-kays of Bhamo have paid me a formal visit on board the steamer. I received them formally and our escort was drawn up on either side with shouldered arms. The written order which I caused to be forwarded from Mandalay to have mules in readiness here for our onward journey only reached the old Bhamo-won, at *Momeit*, a few days before his murder, and the sensation produced by the murder itself, and the absence of a Governor at Head Quarters to arrange matters, has resulted in a miscarriage of intentions. The consequence is, that everything in the way of procuring carriage has to be done now. One road through the Kakhyen Hills is closed on account of recent disturbances. This is the central Momouk road. But the Sawuddy route on the south and the Tahpen route on the north—are reported to be practicable. Still no traffic exists on either. The Shans and Burmese on either side do not openly attempt the passage, and the Kakhyens alone do a small trade in salt and Gnapee.

But I do not intend to take more than ordinary notice of these sensational reports, which originate more in funk than reality. I have caused letters to be written by the Tsit-kays to the Saubwas and Chiefs on the Tahpen route (the most direct one) and sent my own men with the Tsit-kays' people, to watch events and explain our advent. In six days if all goes well we are to be supplied with 200 mules and 100 Kakhyen coolies. In the meantime I have leisure to make arragements here, and prosecute useful enquiries. It is not improbable that I may take the steamer up to the 1st Defile above this and test the navigability of the river as far up as I can. This will be better than absolute idleness. The authorities are building us a 'Thandai' on shore. For the present we retain our quarters on board.

Bhamo is a ruin of former prosperity. The extinction of trade and intercourse with China has reduced it from wealth to downright insignificance and even poverty. Most of the formerly inhabited portion of the town is now deserted and overgrown with jungle. The old stockade is dilapidated and useless for all practical purposes of defence. The Chinese population thrives as Chinese seem to do every where, but I have as yet to ascertain their special mode or means of livelihood. Every variety of Indo-chinese race abounds—and there is abundant food for ethnologists and photographers. Our steamer is daily crowded with curious visitants of all these races, who come in anxious bewilderment to look at the large fire ship, which moves apparently of its own accord against all opposition. The steamer has done her work well, and Burmese Captain and Burmese crew are acknowledged by all of us to be superior on trial to native lascars in all save cleanliness. Tomorrow I go in state to return the Tsitkay's call. Before I left Mandalay the King gave me two gold umbrellas, by way of adding to my importance on the journey, and I intend to bring them into use at once.

In a few days there will be more to say of a reliable nature regarding our route inland towards China: now we can only speculate on results—but the present absence, so to speak, of direct impediments is suggestive of success, and no party was ever in greater earnest than we are.

From Captain SLADEN to Colonel FYTCHE, dated Bhamo 23rd January 1868.

There has been a delay in the despatch of the boat from this, and I am able to send a few additional items of information. This morning I repaid the Tsitkays' visit with all due ceremony, and was received most courteously and hospitably—all promises well so far but I cannot quite shut my eyes to the wild stories afloat, regarding the difficulties of our expedition. No Burman or Chinese inhabitant here believes that we shall succeed. The difficulty does not lie with the Kakhyens, but the Shan States and the Chinese frontier have become impassable, it is said, owing to the depredations of large gangs of dacoits and marauders of all kinds, who have been compelled, by a state of protracted civil war, to get a livelihood by any other than lawful means—so much for report. We shall know very little for certain on this subject until we get further on towards the Chinese frontier. But with reference to the Kakhyens and late disturbances at Momeit I am sorry to find that the Burmese authorities here have not acted in a way which is likely to ensure us a safe or hospitable reception when once we leave Bhamo. No Kakhyens are allowed to enter this town, and the sale of salt and gnapee to Kakhyens is absolutely forbidden. I have interfered to have these restrictions removed, but the authorities believe they have good reason for punishing the Kakhyens, and it will be difficult to make them desist from retaliatory measures on our account whilst the Kakhyens show a hostile front and continue their depredations on isolated Shan and Burmese villages. I may be able to do something with the new Governor of Bhamo on his arrival, though in many respects it will be more advantageous, I believe, to treat directly with the Kakhyen Chiefs, if possible without any Burman intervention whatever.

From Captain SLADEN to Colonel FYTCHE, dated Bhamo 27th January 1868.

We are likely to remain here a few days longer, I'm afraid. In reply to the Tsitkays' letters to the neighbouring Kakhyen Saubwas they sent to say that without the direct orders of the Bhamo-won they would not come in to Bhamo. The men I sent were successful after a time in getting the Saubwas to understand that it would be to their advantage to come in and talk to me without any reference to the Bhamo officials, and I am assured that the principal Kakhyen Chiefs who have charge of the route I intend taking (the Tahpen route) will most probably be here to pay me a visit tomorrow or the next day. The only immediate difficulty will consist in procuring carriage; but if this is not obtainable we must go without it or take only what we can get. The Chiefs will do nothing, they say, until they have seen and arranged with me independently of the Burmese authorities. The satisfactory portion of the whole is that these Chiefs, as far as I can at present ascertain, promise us safe conduct through Kakhyen land; and I feel pretty sure they will do all that is required by us if we manage them properly. The Bhamo-won has not as yet arrived, but I expect him daily. The delay here will be profitable in many respects. It enables us all to collect information of various kinds. The mercantile representatives have no faith, as yet, in the practicability of trade being carried on to any extent even though we penetrate China. Reports from the frontier of Yunan describe a state of chronic disorganization, and a chaotic confusion of conflicting interests which no *present* means can possibly cure. There seems now to be no doubt that the road between Momein and Tali is occupied alternately by Chinese and Panthay outposts in open hostility to each other. No one supposes that we shall ever succeed in passing these outposts. But more of this anon. A boat is just starting without much previous notice, so I will not add more now. They have built us a residence on shore, but we still retain the Steamer here, and live on board. I think it right to keep the steamer until the Bhamo won's arrival, or until the Kakhyen Chiefs present themselves and we come to final arrangements with them.

From Captain SLADEN to Colonel FYTCHE, dated Bhamo 31st January 1868.

The Kakhyen Saubwas made their appearance for the 1st time yesterday, only two have come in but one of them, the Ponlyne Chief, is supposed to be a host in himself. I have had a long public interview this morning at which all the officials in the place attended. The Kakhyen Saubwa was very reserved and for a long time every kind of opposition was offered to the several propositions I made regarding the journey across Kakhyen-land. First the excuse was that carriage could not be procured—or if procurable, each mule would cost Rs. 15 from Tahpen to Manwyne, the first Shan village on the other side of the Kakhyen Hills. Next the Chief said that he would only be answerable for us within his own particular district—would not supply us with anything en route &c. &c. It struck me that most of the opposition was forced or due in great measure, if not entirely, to the presence of Burmese officials, and the knowledge the Chief may have been brought up in, to the effect that the Burmese Government had ever been averse to British officers penetrating beyond Bhamo. I succeeded eventually, at a more private interview, in getting the Saubwa to say that he was glad to hear we intended crossing his territory; that he would supply men and carriage, which should take us safely all the way to Manwyne, and even build sheds for us at the several halting stations. So far so good, but we are entirely dependent on this Saubwa, and this produces a feeling of helplessness. A single false step and we should never get beyond this place. As it is I am obliged to be cautious in every thing I say or do; no one here wishes us to proceed. The officials look pitiously upon the members of the expedition, and say in their own way that we are tempting Providence. Chinese and Burmese residents feel certain that success is an impossibility. They would rather remain as they are at present, and keep any small pickings there may be at Bhamo to themselves than assist in keeping a road open for trade competition at all. They do not openly say so; on the contrary they tell us "We should be glad to see the old trade route open again—but we know that this is an immpossibility" &c. I will not say more about our difficulties. The great draw back is the feeling and knowledge that every thing is done to discourage rather than give zest to our enterprize. Our zeal I hope is none the less. I am determined to push on in spite of every thing short of actual or imminent danger. We are well supplied at present with the good things of life, most of which I say must be left behind, when once we make a start. This does not accord with the feelings of some of our party, who have only now began to find out that travelling through *Kakhyen* land implies also an abnegation of certain personal and creature comforts. I have written thus far in the hope of being able to dispatch letters to day.

From Captain SLADEN to Colonel FYTCHE, dated 2nd February 1868.

The King's steamer returns to *Mandalay* to-day. I kept her here a few days for our own convenience partly: and because I wished the *Kakhyen Saubwas* to have an opportunity of seeing for themselves that I have come up with the consent of the Burmese Government. All are now convinced that I posses authority at Head Quarters, however great the opposition may be on the part of petty officials here and at *Mandalay*. There has been a good deal of this petty obstructiveness to contend against. My interview with the *Kakhyen Saubwa*, yesterday, was very satisfactory. Every thing is arranged regarding transit and carriage between this and *Manwyne*, the first Shan town on the other side of *Kakhyen* land. Carriage is very expensive, each mule 12 Rs. and each cooly 6 Rs., but a good deal of hagling took place to secure any thing, even at these rates. I took the *Saubwa* into my own room and talked to him privately. He emerged, all at once, from a state of savage stupidity into one of reasonable intelligence. He confessed to me that his only fear in taking us across his hills is that he will thereby incur the enmity of the Chinese of this place, and the Chinese dacoits between *Manywne* and *Momein* with whom he is now on friendly terms. He also confessed that the Chinese here had written to him and told him not to come in to me. The opposition of the Chinese has its foundation at *Mandalay*. I hope to be able to trace the matter out satisfactorily bye and bye. One thing however is certain, viz: that the *Bhamo* Chinese have written to their dacoit friends on this side of *Momein*, to stop us. I hope to outwit them. We shall still be here another week I expect, as the *Saubwa* requires time to collect mules. The *Bhamo-won* has not as yet arrived, and the officials here are at loggerheads with each other. This makes them very useless to us. There is very little to be learned even here about the true state of the country beyond the *Kakhyen* Hills. All accounts represent it as chaotic and disturbed. The object is to persuade us against an advance.

From Captain SLADEN to Colonel FYTCHE, dated Bahmo 15th February 1868.

I had hoped ere this to have reported our departure from *Bhamo*, but it is of no avail now to ignore the fact that it was never the intention of the Burmese authorities, either here or at *Mandalay*, that we should commence our journey before the new Governor's arrival at this place.

The King hinted as much when he placed his steamer at my disposal, by saying that I was not to go quickly, but arrange so that the Governor, who would be unavoidably detained at *Mandalay* after my own departure, might catch me up by boat before the steamer's arrival at *Bhamo*.

It is not improbable that the authorities, King included, speculated upon the chances of a break down, and the compulsory return of the steamer to *Mandalay*, where provision would have to be made for a new start by boat. This would have occasioned a month's delay at the very least.

The new Governor left *Mandalay* on 25th January, and will not be here until 20th instant, if even then.

Had I fully comprehended the state of affairs here before I left *Mandalay*, I would have waited and brought up the Governor with me in the steamer.

The absence of a chief controlling power at a frontier station like this, gives rise to a disorganization which gradually permeates with evil effect, until the disturbing causes affect the lowest strata and conditions of Society.

A Burman subordinate, in the absence of his Chief, is afraid to assume power or authority. Orders are given with the certainty, (or intention perhaps,) that they will never be obeyed. Liability attaches itself to no one in particular. Add to this the probabilities of secret instructions, and the natural obstructiveness of Burmese officials at loggerheads amongst themselves, and my state of helplessness, as regards the avoidance of wearying delays, becomes painfully manifest.

By dint of urgent presure of a kind and conciliating form, the Kakhyen Chief of *Ponlyne* has been induced to accede to my requisition and collect mule carriage.

One hundred mules have been brought, I hear, from Shan towns beyond the *Kakhyen* Hills. A certain amount of delay in procuring them was unavoidable. The mules cannot or will not come here, so we go to them. They are collected at a village called *Hentha* on the *Tahpen* river, some 20 miles above *Bhamo*.

The officials are determined that the old arrangement of not allowing us to start until the Governor's arrival shall be strictly carried out. I am not sorry for this. As matters stand at the present time it is very desirable that I should see the Governor and confer with him in person.

The presence of a Burmese Governor at Bhamo exercises a decided influence over the Hill Tribes to the East, who affect however to be independent of his power in all save a mere nominal allegiance.

The confused and abnormal state of affairs, produced by the murder of the old Governor—the protracted absence of his successor in office—and the imbecile action of the present authorities in this province, are manifest aids to failure at the very outset of our undertaking which must be provided against before we can leave *Bhamo*.

The Governor's presence here, and the moral effect of his implied support, may act as a guarantee against the present prevalent idea that the Burmese Government has no connectionship or concern in the future of the present expedition. Not that the Burmese Government is powerful, or feared as a Government by either Kakhyens, Shans or Chinese; but it has in its power amongst the inhabitants of Burma Proper very many Shans and Chinese families, who are connected, more or less, with the dacoit leaders on the frontier, and are known to have advised their friends to oppose our progress and even loot us at discretion en route.

I have tried myself to conciliate the Chinese here in every way in my power. They profess friendship, but offer no encouragement to our undertaking.

The whole of the petty trade of *Bhamo* is monopolized by them, and their private interests in this respect, coupled with a fair share of obstructive advice which comes up from their *Mandalay* brethren who profit by the *Thinnee* route, and therefore deprecate the resuscitation of trade viâ *Bhamo*, makes them believe that if our expedition is successful a crowd of English capitalists will come into the field and cut them out in their present petty speculations.

It is fortunate in some respects that we have not been able to leave *Bhamo* in too great a hurry; otherwise under the present condition of affairs, we should certainly have got ourselves into inextricable difficulties. The instructions of Government, which so forcibly warn me to avoid all risk of collision with the tribes and people through whose country we are to pass, are too peremptory to be hastily got rid of or evaded by a too earnest desire to succeed, without finally clearing up, as far as possible, all apparent causes of doubt and difficulty.

Eager therefore as I personally must be to risk much, and endure more, in the successful accomplishment of a much desired object, I am by no means sure that those with whom I am associated on this expedition would feel any confidence in my leadership, if I neglected all available means of dispelling or counteracting a prevalent belief in the supposed certainty of our proceeding only to meet with armed opposition and disaster.

We have nothing to fear from the Chinese, Panthay, or Shan Governments, where there is a Government, but the danger of ruin to our enterprize exists in the resistance and avaricious greed of large bands of reckless and irresponsible dacoits who have sprung up out of the Chinese and Panthay disturbances, and who are and ever have been the real impediment and obstruction to trade with *China* viâ *Bhamo* since the period of those disturbances.

This obstruction is irrespective of other serious drawbacks more closely connected with those disturbances, but the nature and extent of the obstruction itself will not be understood until we get further into the country and are able to record our practical experiences on this and other matters which rest now on mere supposition.

But I have said enough for the present. I shall probably not have an opportunity of forwarding this until the Governor's arrival.

From Captain SLADEN, to Colonel FYTCHE, dated Bhamo 25th February 1868.

Every thing has been so uncertain that I have put off writing till the last moment. Even now there is only time to say that our baggage is being sent off and we make a start in earnest to-morrow morning.

The new Governor arrived on 20th instant, but did not land from his boat till 23rd. He has not proved himself our friend, and is downright obstructive in the matter of not allowing it to be openly seen that our expedition is favoured and supported by the Burmese Government. I cannot enter into explanation now on this subject.

The Kakhyen Chief *Ponlyne* has come in again and guarantees to conduct us safely as far as the Shan town *Manwyne*, but no further.

Manwyne is about 5 marches from this, there we must hire fresh carriage for the onward movement to *Momein*. Whether we succeed or not in this is still a matter of much uncertainty.

A few days ago I despatched a letter privately to the Chiefs at *Momein*,—told them the object of the expedition,—asked them not to believe false rumours,—forwarded copy of letter from Burmese Government to them, soliciting their assistance and co-operation, and finally inserted copies of our former and recent treaties with Burma. If the Chiefs wish us to come on to *Momein* I have asked them to send and meet us with an escort at *Manwyne*.

I cannot rely entirely on the success of this letter, but it is a '*diplomatic venture*' in the right direction. I hope to confound the politics and villainy of the Chinese petty traders here. *Panthay* assistance alone will enable us to defeat the opposition of Chinese dacoits who hold the roads, and are to some extent in the pay or under the influence of the Chinese merchants or petty dealers of *Bhamo*.

I am hard up for funds. Duncan sent nothing to pay the Police escort. We lose 30 per cent in exchanging our rupees for silver bullion. The mercantile representatives find themselves badly supplied and say they ought never to have accompanied the expedition. There are no immediate prospects, *according to their own account*, of a renewal of trade. They have learned that even if we succeed in getting to the Chinese frontier, the present obstacles to the renewal of the old trade route are insurmountable, at all events, for some years.

Williams is seedy, and down in the mouth. He does not believe in this route. It is not an easy matter to be very cheerful under these circumstances. We have a very exciting time before us.

This will be the last you will hear from me for some time.

APPENDIX A.
PROCLAMATION.

Tah-sa-kon, Governor of Momein, hereby publishes for general information, a proclamation issued by His Highness Tayenshine Commander in Chief of the Panthay army.

The enemy has been defeated in all the battles fought by Tayenshine; we have advanced without opposition, and established our Government throughout the country. The opposition offered to us may be compared to that of an egg in conflict with stone.

Some time ago several divisions of our army proceeded to attack and reduce the city of *Yunan*. General Mahtatseeyoon who was sent against the city of *Reemin* effected its capture. He afterwards with the connivance of Htinchinree of *Tsinshin*, Rankveinbon of *Khwenyah*, Kvanyindin and Ex General Yopeetah Kyankyin, alias Mah Chein Sin of *Whaikyan* (all of whom opened the gates of their respective cities received the General and united their forces with his) attacked and captured the cities of *Cheinkon* and *Anlee*. Their united forces then marched upon *Yunan* and overran the districts of *Hookoon, Tsanyinkikezay*, and the highlands of *Woonsho*, which are situated to the south of *Yunan*. They captured more than 50 stockades and killed 2,000 men.

Another division of the army under Lyotahtsakyein and Mahtahtsalin attacked and captured the Town of *Pyekyeekoon*, and subsequently entrenched itself in a position to the West of the city of *Yunan*, whence it issued and captured more than 60 Chinese villages and killed not less than 3,000 men.

A third division commanded by Generals Mahtasakhwin, Yantatseekein and Myeeta-tsee-shin, after capturing the town of *Hoomyin* fixed its Head Quarters in more than 20 stockades on the Northern outskirts of the city of Yunan; and after killing 2,000 men took possession of more than 40 villages in that quarter of the *Yunan* suburb.

Yunan is closely invested and we are confident of effecting its capture. The enemy has lost an innumerable number in killed including their leaders Ngyo-sho-yoh, Shah-tsoo-sho, Wayteohton, Kyintsan-mah, and Way-shay-kyeing. Such is the terror inspired by our presence that the city gates are closed and the enemy has lost heart and will not fight.

General Tahseekho who had marched by a different route, attacked all the villages from *Boomyin* to *Chankho*; more than 10 towns were captured, and not less than 2000 men killed. Mahsyanlin and Mahyinkyo of *Tsongmyeng* opened the gates of that city, and received our

General Tahtseekho, who has since marched and laid seige to *Yanlintapanchyonk* and *Neelyan*. Both cities must soon fall.

Another division under Generals Syneyanway, Tahtootoo and Mahtatseetoo marched from *Boomyin* by the *Tsintin* route and attacked *Reelampeh*, which with more than 10 other towns was taken and a large number of the enemy slain. The capture of about 10 other Towns has been delayed, as the country on all sides is inundated. The enemy to the number of 50,000 or 60,000 advanced from the city of *Tonyyoung chyoo*, and is now engaged in defending the city of *Tsintin* and the hills of *Khonetsan*.

Mah-htinshwin and Mahwaitchein of *Tsintin* have sent in their submission and have been honorably treated. Our forces, with the aid of the troops under Syneyanway and Tah-too-too, managed to open communication with each other by filling the surrounding low land under water, with firewood, branches, and hay, and which enabled them to commence operations against the enemy. Our troops effected the capture of more than 10 Towns, and killed not less than 3000 men. The inhabitants generally of the villages about *Khoonkyoon* have sent in their submission, and are now our subjects. The troops were subsequently collected at *Tsintin* and from thence they marched and a battle was fought at *Khonetsan* hill where the Chinese gave way, and were put to the rout. They were pursued and more than 4000 men perished. The inhabitants of *Tonechyoontsin* came out, tendered their submission and were spared.

The Generals Tahtseetoo and Tahtootoo next held a council of war, at which it was resolved that as the city of Yunan had not as yet been taken, it would be imprudent to enter it without due precaution. So Tahtootoo was left with his troops to garrison the city of *Tsintin*, whilst Tahtseetoo received orders to march and fight his way along the *Yanlintapan* valley. Mahsheetai, Mahkhwei, Mahhowk Yantsinkyee with about 10 of the Chief Officials of *Yunan* acknowledged themselves beaten, came out with presents and tendered submission. They were spared themselves, and their city thus saved from assault.

Tayenshine having reason to believe that the people of *Htinchinree* would forsake the religion of the country and become Mahomedans, admitted them as auxiliaries to the forces then besieging *Yunan*.

Rankyeinbon and Kyanyinlin were respectively honored with the titles of Tahtseelyaw and Tahtseekyee. Mahsyeetai, Mahshanlin, Mahyingyo, Mah-htinshwin, Mahwaitchyein, Mahtsayinkyee and Mahkhwei, were also honored with the titles of Tahsarankyins and Kyareetsarankyins.

More than 60,000 men from different parts have given in their submission. The news of our successes has been noised abroad and caused Kyinwoonkyoung of *Kwaikyo* to join our forces with contingents from the cities of *Shinree*, *Kyeingbon*, *Tsinchein* and *Nan-an*.

Kyinwoonkyoung has accordingly been honored with the title of Tahtootoo. A large body of fighting men from different parts of the country placed their services at our disposal, and with them their own provisions and equipments. Yunan is now like a 'fish out of water,' ready to be chopped up and put into the frying pan.

The enemy under General Seinyooyin has succeeded in raising troops at *Linan*, and laid seige to the towns of *Reemin* and *Boolin* which had fallen into the hands of our General Tayenshine. The enemy also despatched troops from *Whaichyoon* under Generals Yeinreekhaw and Panhtee Yein. They encamped about a mile distant from the town of *Tahyowk*. Our General in Chief Mahtatsceyoon ascertained that a strong force of the enemy had been sent for the express purpose of recapturing the towns of *Yetma*, *Wooto* and *Lawsee*, and despatched a force under Mahpyin-nan Tahtsarankyin to counteract this movement. The enemy was attacked routed, and lost 2,000 men. We also captured and destroyed more than 60 intrenchments. The troops engaged in beseiging *Boolen* were also attacked by Lyohawkyankyin and utterly routed. More than 40 towns were taken and destroyed, and upwards of 300 persons burnt to death.

Generals Mahtatsapyin and Yowhtatseeway marched with a force of 2,000 men from *Seizin* city by way of *Tahyowk* to the towns of *Wootee* and *Lawsee* and engaged the enemy under Ramreekhaw and Panhteerein. Several stockades were destroyed and not less than 3,000 men were killed.

We have not as yet retaken the towns of *Wootee* and *Lawsee*, but there is every probability of their early capture.

This proclamation is issued for general information to Generals, Officers, Soldiers, and the people of the country. The inhabitants of *Yunan* are in a state of alarm, our enemies have been defeated in every engagement. Their Gods even withhold assistance. We are destined to be victors.

But we must still watch and guard against evil. Do not be deceived; but regard what I say as the warning of Providence.

No return has as yet been published of the numbers killed in the engagements at Reemin, Lansee, Boolin, Yetmah, and Wootee.

I pity those who must still perish. All are hereby warned that death awaits them if they give ear to the words of our enemies.

Issued this 7th waxing of the month of Wahzoh 1230.

True translation,

EWD. SLADEN, CAPTAIN.

Political Agent, Mandalay.

APPENDIX B.

From Tahsakon, Governor of Momein, to the English Ruler.

Having been informed that the Political Agent Captain Sladen was expected to arrive at *Momein* viâ *Bhamo* with a party of upwards of (70) seventy followers, for the purpose of opening a gold and silver road, and of entering into commercial relations with our Government, orders were despatched to the officers of the several forts, outposts and halting places, along the road by which he would pass, to protect his party from injury, and to escort them as far as *Momein*, where they have been received with all honor.

We beg to acknowledge with grateful thanks, the receipt of the presents brought by Captain Sladen, and to inform you that it was our earnest desire that he should proceed on his journey, and personally deliver the presents to our sovereign at Talee. But we regret to state that the continuance of hostilities in Yunan has rendered it expedient to prohibit foreigners and traders from entering the country during present disturbances. At the same time we beg to intimate to the English Government, that it is our sincere wish to open out our country to trade, and to encourage commercial relations with other Governments, as soon as the country is sufficiently settled for that purpose.

We are moreover much gratified by the friendship which on the present occasion you have manifested towards us, and trust that it may endure for ever.

But as war is still being carried on throughout the country and along all the several roads by which Captain Sladen and his party would have to pass, we have deemed it right to caution him against being in too great a hurry to enter Yunan, and have been induced in our anxiety to protect him against all harm, to advise a return for the present, without continuing his journey beyond Momein. The object of Captain Sladen's expedition is directed to the revival of trade whereby a gold and silver road will be established between our respective countries. As such the expedition is entitled to, and has received, our warm support and commendation.

Our excellent sovereign has raised an army which consists of one hundred thousand fighting men commanded by officers who have been honored by the following titles.

Tah Tsee, *Tah-kyan-kyin*, *Tan Sankyin* and *Tah-Too-Too*. They have already captured and hold more than one hundred districts and towns within the Province of *Yunan*. We have also received under our Government, and given the title and rank of *Tah Tsee Lyaw* to *Sahyah*, *Yun-myo* and *Kyein Bon* of Thookhooyan and several other Independent Chiefs of different Chinese races. Thoogyee *Kyan-yei-lin* of Whaikyan has been raised to the rank and position of *Tah Tseekyee Chinree* of Tsinshin is styled *Tah-Tseehoo*. *Kyinwoonkyoung* of Kwai-chyo has the title of *Tahtootoo*.

Mamyoh Chein-Lin of Ree-hton. *Mamyoh See-yan-lin* and *Mamyoh Yinkyo* of Tsoan-myin *Mamyoh Waitchein* and *Htinshin* of Tsindin. *Mamyoh Shee Tei, Mamyoh Khwei, Mamyoh Howk*, and *Yan-myo Tsinkyee* who are all officials of the city of *Yunan* are conscious of our power, and have sent us presents. They further promise to assist us in accomplishing the conquest of the whole of *Yunan*: and have accordingly been rewarded with the titles of *Tahtsayankyin, Tahtsankyin, Tahtootoo, Kyareetsaran kyin, Sankyin* and *Tootoo.* Upwards of ten thousand of the principal inhabitants of the suburbs have also sent in their submission. The population generally of towns and districts throughout the country, has proffered help and seek to join us with arms and provisions. We have surrounded the city of *Yunan* and our troops have established a complete blockade. The city is without provisions, or hope of relief. The enemy has lost a million of men in the several battles which have been fought, in, and around *Yunan*, of prisoners too, we have captured more than a thousand Officers of all ranks. Our spoils in guns, muskets, swords, spears, and arrows are too infinite to admit of calculation.

Yunan is now in the position of an egg which may at any moment, be crushed to atoms by our forces. It is a well known fact that in every engagement victory has been with us.

Governors and Magistrates have been appointed in the several captured Towns and Districts. Forts have also been built and garrisons placed in them. We have further established outposts along the chief lines of communication, and at all halting places, within the interior of the Province. Notwithstanding these arrangements, we cannot guarantee protection to foreigners travelling through the country, at the present season. If injury befell them, our Government would be burdened with a heavy responsibility.

We therefore write to inform you, that in accordance with the esteem and friendship, in which we hold Captain Sladen, and his party, we have advised them to return from *Momein* without proceeding further into *Yunan*, and have signified our intention of accompanying the party on its return journey, with a suitable military escort.

With reference to what has been said on the subject of commercial relations, we beg again to assure you that as soon as the country is restored to tranquillity, it is our intention to despatch an Envoy with letters, to confirm and perpetuate our present friendly relations with your Government.

We wish you well (Salutation) and beg that you will take a friendly interest in our affairs.

(SD.) TAH-SA-KON, (with titles.)

Dated Momein the waning of Wahzoh 1230.

True Translation,

EWD. B. SLADEN, CAPTAIN.
Political Agent Mandalay

APPENDIX C.

From Panthay Governor of Nantin, to Captain Sladen, Political Agent.

Your letter of 10th Labyeegyaw reached this on the 11th and brought the intelligence of your arrival at Mynela.

I have sent a guard to escort you from Mauphoo, and have reported your arrival to Tah-sa-kon. He will send to escort you from Nantin.

Bring your Shan escort, as far as Mauphoo; our guards will meet you there.

(SD.) WANHOO,
of Sha race.

13th Labyeegyaw.

True translation.
EWD: B. SLADEN, CAPTAIN,
Political Agent.

APPENDIX D.

From Governor of Momein, to Captain Sladen, Political Agent.

The Panthays send greetings to their friends.

When Lanloo and other Kakhyens came to Momein, we conversed with them freely, and were extremely happy to learn that 300 Foreigners had arrived at Bhamo.

Being of the same belief as yourselves, we know your willingness to help and assist us. We are the descendants of three thousand men of the Lerroo country, who being unable to return to their native land, settled down in China; where we have been upwards of a thousand years. Some ten years ago, the Chinese Government became so intolerably oppressive, that by God's help Tahin-Shee, of the Too race, was commanded to separate the good from the wicked, and obtained possession of the Western Provinces of the Chinese Empire.

At present also we are carrying on war around Yunan. The whole country has sided with us, and we daily expect to capture that city. Already our rule at Momein has became so popular, that those who were formerly inimical, have gladly joined our cause and Government.

The Shan Chiefs have also voluntarily placed themselves under our protection and have been confirmed in their several states.

We have given peace to the Country and Merchants and people can now carry on their several avocations with ease and security.

With regard to your intention of visiting Momein, we wish to consult your pleasure and convenience. We have sent word of your intentions to Tahinshoo, our King, and will write also to the Shan Chiefs to help and assist you on your journey.

Fear nothing, but come by the '*Momonk*' route which leads direct to Momein. On your arrival all matters relating to trade and merchandize will be satisfactorily settled in accordance with your wishes.

We are of the same nation. Come without fear or anxiety of any sort.

(WRITER.)—Qualyen a friend of the Lee race.

9th Day of the Waxing of the Moon month of Nayong.

(True Translation.)

E. B. SLADEN, CAPTAIN,
Political Agent.

APPENDIX E.

From Tah-sa-kon, Governor of Momein to Captain Sladen, Political Agent.

In accordance with the affectionate esteem in which we regard each other, and our mutual desire to open out commercial relations between the two great Countries, I wish you to procure and forward price lists of Goods, as per enclosed Memorandum.

Orders have been issued to the several out posts and Guard Stations, to place no restrictions or impediments in the way of Trade.

The Duties leviable within our Territories, are as follows:—

At	*Mauphoo*	...	...	4 Annas.	
,,	*Chatout*	...	...	2 do.	per Mule.
,,	*Mawson*	...	...	2 do.	
,,	*Nantin*	...	...	4 do.	

At Momein itself this duty shall be reduced to a minimum rate.

It is my great love for you, which has caused me now to write, and impress you with a confidence and belief, that in the matter of Trade, it is our wish that both Countries, should be as one Country.

(Signed and Sealed.)

TAH-SA-KON,
Governor of Momein.

Dated Momein.

(True Translation.)

E. B. SLADEN, CAPTAIN,
Political Agent.

APPENDIX. F.

From Tah-sa-kon, Governor Momein, to Kakhyen Chiefs.

The Chiefs of Saray, Loayyen and Ponsee. As we are at present engaged in active operations with the Chinese Rebels at Mauphoo, we wish our English friends to stay where they are, and not advance beyond Ponsee until we have restored tranquility and cleared the way for them.

     (SD.) HOUNG SHAN. } *of Lee race.*
     (SD.) WHAW.

7th increase of the month of Kasong.
    True Translation.

      EWD: B. SLADEN, CAPTAIN
          Political Agent

APPENDIX. G.

From Tah-sa-kon, Governor of Momein, to the Kakhyen Chiefs.

The Chiefs of Saray, Loay yen and Kounglah are hereby informed that the intelligence conveyed in the letters brought by Way-young-tha-yan-chin is to the effect, that owing to the continued fighting at Mawson and Mauphoo, the roads are at present impassable. We are unable therefore to make suitable provision for our English friends.

The Kakhyen Chiefs will be good enough to request them, to stay where they are for the present, and wait for further advice as to the most convenient time for an advance to Momein.

      KWAILWIN, of the Lee race.

Kasong lazan 14th.
    True translation.
      EWD: B. SLADEN, CAPTAIN,
          Political Agent.

APPENDIX. H.

From the Governor of Momein, to the Chiefs of Manwyne.

This letter is sent to the Shan Chiefs of Manwyne, to inform them, that as the English are coming from Ponsee to Momein I wish all to aid and greet them with a hearty welcome.

I have also despatched Lanloo to Manwyne, with full instructions. Consult with him and escort the English to Momein, where on arrival you will be well rewarded.

1230 8th Labyeegyaw Kasong.

   Uinman of the Sha Caste, whose title is Tootoo.

    True Translation,

      EWD: B. SLADEN, CAPTAIN.
        Political Agent.

APPENDIX. I.

From Oolooquan or Quai Lwin, to Ponsee Lauton Saubwa.

Saubwa Lauton of Ponsee is informed that the Chiefs of Mynela and Sanda have undertaken to escort our English friends to Momein. A careful inventory should be taken of their property. Charges on account of mule hire will be paid on arrival.

      (SD.) KWAI LWIN,
        of Lee race.

10th increase.

    True Translation.

      EWD: B. SLADEN, CAPTAIN.
        Political Agent.

APPENDIX. J.

From Tahsakon Governor of Momein, to Shan Chief and Governor's Secretary Oolooqwan.

Has the Shan Chief Oolooqwan received my previous Messages?

Our English Friends wrote on the 14th Lazan to inform us, that they would arrive at Momein with upwards of 80 Mules.

The charges for Carriage supplied by the Kakhyen Chiefs, amount to 750. But as our English Friends have come from a great distance to open commercial relations Oolooqwan will please pay the 750 Rs. in advance.

All charges will be satisfactorily adjusted as soon as the Party arrives at Momein.

Qualnin (Scribe) 14th Lazan.

    True Translation

      EWD: B. SLADEN, CAPTAIN.
        Political Agent.

APPENDIX. K.

From Governor of Nantin, to the Kakhyen Chiefs.

Greeting to the three Kakhyen Chiefs, named Saray, Loay-yen, and Ponsee.

We write to inform you that our (English) friends have expressed a desire to meet us at Momein, and are now at Ponsee.

Our desire is that the Kakhyen Chiefs should receive them liberally. Our thanks will be specially due to you for this service.

We further request that the Kakhyen Chiefs will procure mules for our English friends, and escort them with their baggage safely into the Shan States. We will send to Mynela and pay you in full, on account of all Mule charges.

We wish the Kakhyen Chiefs also to come up as far as Momein. We intend to confer with them on matters relating to trade.

Tah-sa-kon will make you suitable presents. Letters forwarded by the Governors of Nantin.

Houng Shan of the Lee caste, whose title is Sayanchin and Shee Quam of the Mah caste, whose title is Sayan Chin, and Shee Quam of the Mah caste whose title is Tahyechan.

True translation.

EWD: B. SLADEN, CAPTAIN,
Political Agent.

APPENDIX. L.

Translation of a Chinese Document, which purports to account for the origin and establishment of Mahomedanism in China.

The Chief Queen of the Emperor *Tanwan*, adopted a child and called him *Anlaushan*. In time the child developed into a man of extraordinary comliness, and wonderful intellect.

The Queen was enamoured; and the adopted son became her Paramour.

Anlaushan soon rose to distinction. His abilities were of the highest order; and raised him at once to fame and influence. The Queenly passion was not disclosed; but suspicion had been sufficiently roused to make it prudent on the Queen's part to get rid of her lover; and defeat all signs of illicit intercourse.

Anlaushan was accordingly accused of being privy to a conspiracy to dethrone the Emperor. The influence of the Queen prevailed to obtain a conviction, and her favourite was banished from the Royal Capital.

But the injustice of his accusation and a sense of wrongs roused Anlaushan to action, and induced him to become in reality a leader of Rebellion. He lost no time in collecting a large force with which he was able to make head against the Government, and successfully encounter the troops of the Emperor. In time he had approached within a league of the Capital, and city and Palace, were alike threatened.

The Emperor *Tunwan* in this emergency adopted the suggestion of his vizier *Kanseree*, and despatched a mission to *Seeyoogwet*, and implored Foreign aid. A force of three thousand men was sent, under the command and guidance of three learned Teachers, who arrived in due time at *Tunwan's* capital. By their aid *Anlaushan* was defeated, and eventually captured.

The Rebellion was at an end, and the Foreign contingent left *China*, to return to its own country. Here however a difficulty arose. Their rulers refused them admittance, and alleged as a cause for doing so, that it was against the constitution of the country, to receive back men, who had come into contact with Pork-eating infidels. They had herded in fact with pigs and infidels, and could no longer be regarded as unpolluted subjects or as fit members of a society which held pork in Religious detestation.

They returned therefore to China, and became permanent sojourners in a Foreign land. They are the original stock from which Mahomedanism has sprung up in China, in various communities, and under several denominations &c., &c.

(True translation.)

EWD: B. SLADEN, CAPTAIN.

APPENDIX M.

List of Articles which the Governor of Momein has asked to purchase.

Musket, Percussion	Rs.	300
Pistols, Revolvers	,,	20
Double barrel Guns	,,	50
Caps, Musket	,,	30,000
Do. Gun	,,	20,000
Gunpowder	Viss	100
Saltpetre	do.	10
Broad Cloth black	Pieces.	5
Do. Green	do.	5
Do. Red	do.	10
Do. Yellow	do.	5
Do. White	do.	5
Do. Pink	do.	5
Strong Silk Alpacca Red	do.	10
Do. Blue	do.	20
Do. Black	do.	10
Gun Flints Stone	do.	30,000
Good Steel	Viss.	100

Judson's Dyes.

Red, Yellow, Black, Blue, Dark Red, bottles 20 of each color.

(True translation.)

EWD: B. SLADEN, CAPTAIN.
Political Agent.

APPENDIX. N

Names of the Chiefs or Saubwas who took the Oath of Fidelity at Bhamo on 12th September 1868.

#	Name		#	Name	
1	Muthin	(Chief of)	17	Ponsaw	(Chief of)
2	Mantai	,,	18	Loaysyne	,,
3	Loavlon	,,	19	Kădau Gyee	,,
4	Monkha	,,	20	Kyetyen	,,
5	Lauyen	,,	21	Namroung	,,
6	Yinson	,,	22	Lonza	,,
7	Săkhiy	,,	23	Pombya	,,
8	Hōtōn	,,	24	Maro-lonkram	,,
9	Ponwa	,,	25	Sinlon	,,
10	Lăsee	,,	26	Mynesoo	,,
11	Lamiypan	,,	27	Kounson	,,
12	Mynesen	,,	28	Pongatoung	,,
13	Kădau Kowra	,,	29	Sărauwa	,,
14	Kădau Manta	,,	30	Ma-onwa	,,
15	Pagwon	,,	31	Oungloung	,,
16	Myueton	,,			

EWD: B. SLADEN, Captain.
Political Agent.

APPENDIX O.

Instruction to Moung Tha Zanoo.

1. Note down distances from observation. Time of starting, and time of arrival—at each station.

2. Direction travelled by *Company*.

3. Altitude of Hills by *Aneroid*.

4. Make rough sketch of Route traversed—with names of principal villages, streams, &c.

5. Enquire about direct routes from Momein to Yoonchan.

E. B. SLADEN, Captain.

Hotha, Shan States, 17th Aug. 1868.

APPENDIX P.

Report of Assistant Surveyor Moung Thazanoo, on the Southern or Sawuddy Route across the Kakhyen Hills between Bhamo and Mowun.

I started from *Hotha* on the 18th August, and arrived at *Mynewun* on 19th where I put up in the Saubwa's house, and made all necessary enquiries.

The old Saubwa of the *Mynewun* Shan State was murdered some years ago by his younger Brother, who fled to the *Looylyne* Hills, and sought shelter amongst the Kakhyens. The Kakhyens were eventually induced to give him up to the Shans of *Mynewun*, by whom he was put to death as his brother's murderer. The *Mynewun* State is now governed by the old Saubwa's mother, during the minority of her grandson, who is about 15 years of age. The old grandmother is very powerful, and has great influence over her subjects.

It is arranged that the young Saubwa shall marry in two years time and assume the Government of the *Mynewun* Saubwaship.

There is a constant stream of trade viâ Mynewun (Burmese Mowon) merchants, mules, and pack bullocks are always passing. The Route is clear of all obstructions, and is wonderfully pleasant. A very large number of traders pass along the Route viâ *Sanhoung*, to the east of the *Mynewun* River. The Saubwa-gadaw, and all her Headmen and councillors, were of one mind, in saying that if English merchants and traders could be induced to adopt the *Sawuddy* Route to *Mynewun*, a guarantee would be given of safe conduct and protection against all annoyances.

The Kakyen Saubwa of *Bhayon* holds the Route from Synekha to *Kahyee* and charges one Rupee upon each mule, and eight annas for each pack bullock which passes through his territory.

This was the rate fixed of old by Chinese traders, and will be continued in the case of English traders. There will be no other restrictions of any sort. The Saubwa is agreed to this.

The next Saubwaship is that of Phongaw, which extends from *Kahyee* to *Tanza*. Saubwa is most willing that English Traders should make use of this route, and guarantees that there shall be no other restriction or annoyance beyond the customary charge of eight annas per mule—and four annas per pack bullock.

The whole Route from *Sawuddy* to *Mynewun* is smooth and even throughout. There are no difficulties of a nature to induce fatigue or wretchedness. The Route is yearly in constant use. Traders who pass along it, on reaching *Mynewun*, strike off from thence, and follow any given route according to their pleasure.

The highest portion of the Route lays in the *Phongan* Saubwaship. Looking down from the the Hills at this point on a clear day, the course of the *Irrawaddy* can be seen as far as *Bhamo*.

(Sd.) MOUNG THAZANOO,

Surveyor,

31st August, 1868.

(True translation.)

E. B. SLADEN, Captain,

Political Agent.

APPENDIX Q.

Memorandum of Villages from Hotha to Sawadee via Mowon.

From what state			To what state			Direction	Distance	Houses	Nations
Date	Time	Name of Village	Date	Time	Name of Village				
1868			1868						
18th August	5 p.m.	Ho-Tha	18th August	6 p.m.	La Kome	S. S. W.	About 2 h.	50	Myne-tha-Shan
19th	11 a.m.	La Khome	19th	6 p.m.	Man Htap	S. E.	7	30	Shan-Ta-roke
20th	1 p.m.	Man Htap	20th	5 p.m.	Lome Pa	S. E.	7	60	do
21st	10 a.m.	Lome Pa	21st	5 p.m.	Noung Eng	S. S. E.	8½	75	do
22nd	9 a.m.	Noung Eng	22nd	6 p.m.	Zayat	S. S. W.	15½	...	—
23rd	7 a.m.	Zayat	23rd	2 p.m.	Phone Kangyee	W. W. N.	12	90	Kakhyen
24th	9 a.m.	Phone Kangyee	24th	11 a.m.	Phone Kangalay	N. W.	4	12	do
25th	8 a.m.	Phone Kangalay	25th	1 p.m.	Man Chai	N. W.	7	25	Burmese Shan
26th	8 a.m.	Man Chai	26th	1 p.m.	Sawadee	W. W. N.	9	15	do
26th	2 p.m.	Sawadee	26th	5½ p.m.	Bhamo	N. N. E.	About 7 mile		

BHAMO,
31st August 1868.

MOUNG THAZANOO,
Surveyor.

APPENDIX R.

Approximate Heights of places visited by the Expedition.

		above sea level
Ponlyne		2,500
Ponsee		2,600
Manwyne } Sanda } Mynela }	General elevation of Sanda valley	3,200
Nantin		4,100
Momein		6,300
Hotha	including the Hotha valley	5,500
Nambouk		5,700
Ashan		5,700
Loaylon		5,400
Muthin		5,500
Hoton		4,500
Bhamo		600

EWD. B. SLADEN, CAPTAN.

Political Agent.

APPENDIX S.
TRANSLATION.

Statement made by Moung Moh, Kakhyen Interpreter, resident of Bhamo, on the 27th November 1868.

The Tseetkay, Chief Writer Nga Kan, Officials of Bhamo sent me and Nga Nyee Tsway with letters to the Pon Tsee Toung Tsa, Tsadoo and the Pwon Nein Toung Tsa Tsouk-ya—when we delivered the letter on our arrival to the Pwon Nein Toung Tsa, he asked Captain Sladen's writer to read it to him, and he finding that the contents of the letter were bad, took it to Captain Sladen and shewed it to him—the contents of the letter were that the two officials named were to allow Captain Sladen, the merchants and other gentlemen and all the followers of the party to go forward so that they may die and be no more seen but that no *return* was to be permitted, they were to be deserted and the two officials after leaving them, were to return to Bhamo. After this I returned to Bhamo and after 6 or 7 days again went with my cousin Moung No to Pwon Tsee Toung—on my arrival as the Engineer, and the mercantile gentleman were alarmed and wished to return home

Captain Sladen sent me as Interpreter with these two gentlemen. On arrival at Bhamo the Chief writer who was acting as Goung of the city said to me "We wrote to say that the English were to be allowed to proceed but that there was to be no return for them, how came you to bring these people back again"? After stopping two or three days at Bhamo I returned to Captain Sladen at Pwon Tsee Toung, and shortly after arrival there I received a letter from my wife begging me to return as she had been put in Gaol because I had brought two of the gentlemen back to Bhamo. I took this letter and shewed it to Captain Sladen, who said he would guarantee my wife's safety, and he wrote to the Governor of Bhamo telling him not to imprison or persecute my wife. I then proceeded with the expedition and when I finally returned to Bhamo I found that my wife had been imprisoned for two days and had had to pay ten (10) ticals of silver. The letters to the Pwon Tsee Toung Tsa and the Pwon Nein Toung Tsa said that the expedition was to be quietly deserted to die and perish either at Nan Boung Choung or at Pwon Tsee Toung.

(SD.) NGA MOH,

Kakhyen Interpreter.

Rangoon, 27th November, 1868.

(True translation.)

R. S. EDWARDS.

APPENDIX. T.

PROPER NAMES WHICH OCCUR IN THE REPORT, WITH GLOSSARY.

A.—ASHAN.—Kakhyen Village (Central Route.)
    AYEYBYNE.—My Burmese official title.

B.—BHAMO.—Burmese Frontier Town.

C.—CAZEE.—Panthay official.
    CHEOUNG-OKE.—Burmese official over villages on the Tahpon River.
    CHEOUNG-KAN.— Do. do. under Cheoung-oke.

D.—DEEBAY.—Chinese Town near Momein.

H.—HAW.—Shan Saubwa's Palace.
    HAWSHOENSHAN.—Chinese Town near Momein.
    HOTHA.—Shan State. Name of Chief town.
    HOTON.—Kakhyen Village (Central Route.)

K.—KAKHYEN.
    KADAW.—Kakhyen Village (Central Route.)
    KANFAN.—Shan Duty Station (between Mynela and Nantin.)
    KANGOUK.—Kakhyen Village (Central Route.)
    KARAHOKHA.—Chinese Bazar (between Manwyne and Sanda.

KAYTO.—Panthay Town (Momein Division.)
KEEINKHAN.—Shan Saubwaship (South of *Yoonchan*.)
KINGEN.—Mynela official and outlaw.
KOWLEE.—A trial denomination of Kakhyens.
KYAING-TOUNG.—Shan Saubwaship.   } Written according to their
KYAING YOON-GYEE.—Do.   Do.   } Burmese *Pronounciation*

L.—LEESHEETAHEE.—Robber Chief on Chinese Frontier.
LEOQWANFAN.—   Do.   Do.
LOAY-LYNE.—Kakhyen Saubwaship.
LAKHON.—Tribal denomination of Kakhyens.
LOAYYEN.—Kakhyen Village (Central Route.)
LOAYLON.—   Do.   Do.
LAWMIKE.—European rowdies defeated by Panthay in Yunan.
LAULOO.—Kakhyen Saubwa.
LEESAW.—A Hill Race (Chinese Kakhyens.)
LONLYNE.—Kakhyen Village.

M.—MAUWYNE.—Town in Shan States.
MEETWAY.—Kakhyen Priest.
MOMEIN.—Panthay Walled City.
MYNEKHA.—Kakhyen Village (Central Route.)
MYNELA.—Shan State (Chief Town of.)
MYNE-THA.—The name of the Valley which includes the Shan States of Hotha and Latha.
MYNE-TEE.—Shan Town.
MYNE-MAU.—Shan Saubwaship.
MYNEWAN.—Saubwaship.
MUTHIN.—Kakhyen Saubwaship.
MOMOUK.—Shan Town.
MAWSOON.—Deserted Fort near Mauphoo.
MASA TAHZYUNGYEE.—Title of Chief Panthay Military Officer at Momein.
MIKE-TAH-SEE-DUM.—Title of Leader of European rowdies defeated at Yunan.
MOUNG-SHOAY-YAIL.—Chinese Interpreter.
MOUNG-MO.—Shan and Kakhyen interpreter.
MOUNG-THAZANOO.—Assistant Surveyor.
MENHLA.—Burmese Duty Station.
MAU-PHOO.—Hill Fort.
MONWYE.—Kakhyen Village (Central Route.)
MANHLEO.—Shan Town.
MANTAI.—Kakhyen Saubwaship.

N.—NANTIN.—Chinese Town (Panthay.)
NAMMON.—Shan Town, near junction of Tahpen and Tahaw rivers.
NANLYAW.—Shan Burmese Village.
NAMBOUK.—Kakhyen Village (Central Route.)
NAMSA.—River Hotha Valley.
NAMKHON.—Mountain Torrent.

   NUKHANDAW.—Burmese official.
   NAMPHOUNG.—Burmese Village on the Tahpen.
   NYOUN-GEN.—Kakhyen Village (Northern Route.)

P.—PANTHAY.—Chinese Mahomedan.
   PHALOUNG.—A race of Shans.
   PONWA.—Kakhyen Village (Northern Route.)
   POOGEN.—Shan Magistrate.
   PONLYNE.—Kakhyen Village (Northern Route) Kakhyen Saubwa.
   PONSEE.— Do.   Do.   Do.
   PAW-MYNE.—Kakhyen Chief (under a Saubwa.)

S.—SANDA.—Shan State and Town.
   SITKAW.—Burmese Village od the Tahpen.
   SARAY.—Kakhyen Village and Saubwa (northern Route.)
   SEHEK.—Burmese Village.
   SAWUDDY.—Burmese Village.
   SAUBWA.—Title of Shan and Kakhyen Chiefs.
   SAUBWAGADAW.—Wife of a Saubwa.
   SIT-GNA.—Burmese Village on the *Tahpen*.
   SAKHIY.—Kakhyen Village (Central Route.)
   SHEE-DIN.—Panthay City.
   SHAMALON.—Hill Range (Nantin Shan States.)
   SAYKOW.—Ancient Hotha.
   SHA-TOO-DOO.—Panthay Military Title.
   SUDDAN.—Kakhyen Village (Northern Route.)
   SAYFAN.—Shan State.
   SHOAY-DWAY-Chinese Town near Momein.

T.—TAMON.—Shan Village Head-man.
   TAH-SA-KON.—Official title of present Governor of Momein.
   TALEE.—Panthay Capital.
   TAHPEN.—Affluent of Irrawaddy.
   TAHAW.— Do. Do. falls into the Tahpen near Mynela.
   TSITKAY.—Burmese official (under a Governor.)
   THON-GWET-SHEIN.—Name of Chinese Brigand Chief.
   THINEE.—Burmese Shan State.
   TAH-BOUK-GYEE.—Chinese General (name of a.)

W.—WANSEN-GYAN.—Name of a Chinese General.
   WACHEOON.—Kakhyen Village (Northern Route.)

Y.—YOONCHAN.—Chinese (Panthay) City.

                E. B. SLADEN,
                  Captain,
                 Political Agent.

No. 127 P-54 P S.—From COLONEL ALBERT FYTCHE, Chief Commissioner British Burma, and Agent to His Excellency the Viceroy, and Governor General of India, to SIR WILLIAM MUIR, K.C.S.I. Secretary to the Government of India, Foreign Department. Dated Rangoon, 21st June 1867.

Referring to letter No. 462 of the 12th May 1862, from the Secretary to the Government of India, Foreign Department, to the address of the Chief Commissioner, British Burma, I have the honour to state, that I find in the fourth paragraph the points to which the attention of the Chief Commissioner was directed, on the occasion of his projected visit in that year to Mandalay, for the purpose of negotiating a Treaty with the King of Burma; and to observe that, the second, third, and fourth points therein enumerated, have reference to the re-opening of the Caravan route from Western China by the Town of Bhamo, and the obtaining facilities for the residence of British Merchants at that Town, as well as their free passage by that route to Yunan; and to the free passage of Chinese from Yunan to British Territory, including Assam.

2. Certain of these objects were attained by the Treaty of November 1862. Thus by Article 7, British Merchants were allowed to settle and have lands for the erection of houses of business in any part of the Burmese Territory; and by Article 9, people from whatever country or nation, who may wish to proceed to the British Territory, the Burmese Ruler shall allow to pass without hindrance.

3. But the re-opening of the Caravan Route from Ava via Bhamo to Yunan, by a joint British and Burmese Mission to the Frontier, which was indicated in the second point of the fourth paragraph of the above letter, has not yet been accomplished—neither has it been possible for Merchants or their Agents to proceed by that route to China.

4. Should the Government decide that I should proceed to Mandalay for the purpose of negotiating a fresh Treaty with the Court of Ava, it may be worthy of consideration whether I should not be authorized to obtain, if

possible, permission for an Exploring party to attempt the passage of the above route.

5. If it be found feasible to conclude a Treaty with the King, as contained in the draft submitted to the Court by Colonel Phayre last year, then, by Article 5, the British Government will be entitled to place a British Officer at Bhamo, as a station at which taxes are collected: and I think it would be well to endeavour to gain the assent of the King to the resuscitation of the nearly extinct trade by that route.

6. This trade, although it has now almost ceased, amounted as late as the year 1855, to nearly half a million of pounds sterling; and is fully described at pages 147, 148 and 149 of Yule's Embassy to Ava. The route has the unusual advantage of having been used for centuries as a line of traffic; and that it should have retained its vitality so long, among all the disturbing influences of the flow and ebb of the Chinese and Burmese power, is a conclusive proof of the urgent necessity for the interchange of commodities between the respective countries; and is also a strong indication that, somehow or other, the line possesses *some practical advantages over other through routes.*

7. However, I may remark that I do not desire that the Exploration and re-opening of the Bhamo route, should be understood as intending to interfere with, or affect in any way, the prosecution of the present survey for a line of Railway from Rangoon to China, by the best practicable route. The views of those who support the latter measure, are to avoid the long valley line from Rangoon to Mandalay or Bhamo, and to seek a more direct line further to the Eastward. The Government have already surveyed one line of country from Rangoon to our North-Eastern Frontier, and it is in every way desirable that the survey be prosecuted until the Chinese Frontier be reached.

8. But the present proposition regarding the Bhamo route can in no way affect the direct Railway question. The immediate object of the party, if one be sent viâ Bhamo to China, would be to find out the different interests of the Khakyens, the Shan Chiefs, and the nearest authorities in Yunan—which have caused the cessation of trade—and to see

what measures could be adopted to reconcile these interests. The re-establishment of trade would manifestly be a gain to all parties, and a neutral authority would be best able to remove the obstacles which at present exist.

9. Could the route be re-opened simultaneously with the appointment of a British Official at Bhamo, the impetus given to our trade with Burma would be immediate. It is for this reason that the Mercantile Community in Rangoon feel so much interest in the question, while they continue to attach so much importance to the further distinct and separate scheme of Railway communication with China, by a more direct route;—a measure which, however vigorously prosecuted, will require a considerable period of time to elapse before completion.

10. The real difficulties of the party would be, probably, in the passage of the hills between Bhamo and the Shan Towns, a distance of about thirty-five miles; and the only Europeans who of late years have visited Bhamo, viz: Dr. Williams in 1863, and the Right Revd. Bishop Bigandet in 1865, were persuaded of the feasibility of the journey, and were both ready to attempt it.

11. A remaining difficulty is to obtain the assistance of the Court of Ava to the Mission, and it must be confessed that hitherto it has shown great distrust of any such expedition and has thrown every obstacle in the way of its fulfilment. It is possible, therefore, that from this cause it may be found impracticable to carry out the measure; but I think that we should not cease to bring before the King the continued desire of the British Government that the route should be opened, and endeavour to persuade him of the palpable advantages which would accrue to his Dominions by his co-operation.

12. I would propose that the Expedition be composed of three—one as head, the second an Engineer and the third a Medical Officer. Composed in this way the party would be able to report more fully on all subjects connected with the route. The first Officer would acquaint himself with the position of the several authorities with whom they might come in contact, and explain to them the objects of the Mission; the second could report on the features of the

country, and nature of the route: and the third on the products and articles of commerce.

13. They would require a Guard of Khakyens to guide them through the hills; but beyond this no permanent guard would probably be necessary, except their own armed followers.

14. It is difficult to decide whether the advance of the party should be restricted to the Shan Towns of Sanda, Moungtsan, Mowun or Moungmo: or whether they should be permitted to proceed to Momein, Yunchan, or even Talifoo: but I am inclined to think that the limit should be fixed at Momein, unless unusual facilities for, and inducements to their further progress should there present themselves.

15. The cost would probably be:—

Monthly pay of Leader	Rs.	1,200
,, Engineer	,,	1,000
,, Medical Officer	,,	1,000
	Rs.	3,200
For five months	Rs.	16,000
Fare of party to Bhamo	,,	1,000
Hire of Khakyens	,,	500
Presents for Shan Chiefs and Khakyens	,,	2,500
Contingencies	,,	3,500
	Rs.	23,500

or say a Total of Rs. 25,000.

16. I have not thought it necessary to enter so fully into the importance of the question of re-opening the Bhamo route as I should have done, had I not been aware that the subject had been already under the careful consideration of Government, as shewn by the communication I have referred to in the first paragraph of this letter.

17. If a party be sanctioned by Government, and if I can obtain the co-operation of the King of Burma, the expedition could not start before the latter end of October, or the beginning of November, that is to say the close of the rains. But I would solicit the orders of His Excellency the Viceroy as to whether I should introduce the subject with the Court of Ava, and whether—if circumstances be favourable—an Expedition

such as I have referred to would meet with His Excellency's sanction.

No. 105.—From the Secretary to the Government of India, Foreign Department, with the Governor General, to the Chief Commissioner, British Burma—No. 712, dated Simla, the 18th July 1867.

I have received and laid before His Excellency the Governor General in Council your letter, dated 21st ultimo, No, 127P.–54P.S., proposing the despatch of an expedition to explore the trade route between Ava and the Western Frontier of China *via* Bhamo.

2. His Excellency in Council doubts the expediency of this proposition, and would rather confine action at present to the enquiry already sanctioned and commenced for the discovery of the best route direct from Rangoon to the Frontier of China. It does not suit the convenience of the Government of India to furnish a second party of explorers.

3. You do not show how the trade *via* Bhamo, which in 1855 was estimated at half a million sterling, has now become extinct, or nearly so. This result must have been brought about by some strong causes, which an exploring party might ascertain, but could not remove. Probably these causes will be found to lie in the political state of the country and the insecurity of life and property.

4. Should the Government of India eventually determine to despatch you on a mission to Mandalay, there will be no objection to your speaking to the King on the subject of the old caravan route, and endeavoring to obtain all the information which may be available as to its present condition. But as matters now stand in Burma, His Excellency in Council cannot sanction more being done.

5. Indeed, His Excellency in Council can hardly conceive any step which under present circumstances would be more imprudent than for British Merchants to settle at Bhamo, or a British Official to be stationed there for any purpose.

From COLONEL ALBERT FYTCHE, Chief Commissioner British Burma and Agent to the Governor General, to SIR WILLIAM MUIR, K.C.S.I. Secretary to the Government of India, Foreign Department—Dated Rangoon, August 26th 1867.

I have the honour to acknowledge the receipt of your letter No. 712 of 18th July 1867, informing me that His Excellency the Viceroy and Governor General of India in Council does not think it expedient at present to sanction the despatch of a party to explore the trade route between Western China and Burma viâ Bhamo, as suggested in my letter No. $\frac{127\,P.}{54\,P.s.}$ dated 21st June last. With reference to the remark in the third Para: of your letter pointing out that the reason for the suspension of the trade via Bhamo (estimated in 1855 at half a million sterling) had not been given in my communication, I now beg to lay before you the causes which, it is believed, have led to the temporary extinction of this valuable line of commerce.

2. The Bhamo route, leaving the town of that name on the Irrawaddy, runs in a North Easterly direction to Talifoo, the present capital of Western Yunan, passing over the Khakyen hills, then through a narrow belt of Shan States, and so reaching the border towns of Yunan, viz: Momein, or Mainglon, whence by Yunchan (the centre of the trade in Western Yunan) it proceeds to Talifoo.

3. The trade which formerly flowed East and West by this line has been interrupted by the progress of the Mahomedan insurrection in Yunan. The rebel "Pansees" have their seat of Government at Talifoo, and for years past have been too much engaged against the Chinese authorities, to devote any attention to the trade with Burma. Meanwhile the Khakyens on the hills eastward of Bhamo have, in the disturbed state of the neighbouring powers, succeeded in establishing for themselves a position, they never before occupied. They hold the passes through the hills, and would now, probably, require to be paid before allowing caravans to cross.

4. Similarly the Shan States between the Khakyen hills and the Frontier Yunan towns are not able to show any activity in restoring the trade, which to them was most important. Originally subject to Burma, they came under Chinese rule about one hundred years ago, and on

the occasion of the Pansee outbreak, became involved in the conflict between the new Power and the Chinese Government; and are now divided between these authorities, tho' mostly subject to the Pansees.

5. It will be seen, therefore, that the Pansee Rebellion has been the cause of the cessation of the trade from Yunan to Bhamo, in as much as the disorganization of Yunan itself has for the time diverted the energies of the inhabitants to other more pressing events, and has enabled the occupiers of the route to throw new difficulties in the way of its future passage. Still there is not one of the different parties who would not gladly see the trade via Bhamo revive. It is of course useless for the Khakyens to hold trade routes through which no trade flows, and they are quite alive to this fact. They are anxious for the re-establishment of the old traffic, and state their readiness to give protection to future caravans. Thus in 1863 one of the Chiefs expressed himself to Dr. Williams, who visited Bhamo, in the following terms:

"I will make a road across my District, and will con-"duct any number of Merchants safely into China: no "other route shall be like it, and I don't care whether they "be English, Burmese, or Chinese. I want them through "my District, and will guarantee that nothing shall happen "to them."

6. The Shan Chiefs also would only too gladly see the old interchange of commodities renewed. They are an enterprizing race, and the present unsatisfactory position they occupy—disunited and preyed upon by both Chinese and Pansees—makes them anxious for any movement which would be likely to lead to a more satisfactory state of affairs and enable them to develope their natural industry.

7. The Pansees are apparently now so well established that they only require a specific inducement to make them again send their Caravans to Bhamo. They are not in immediate contact with the hills through which the passes lead, and are therefore deterred from attempting the passage while it is uncertain what difficulties may be experienced by them in its execution.

8. The circumstances appear to my mind, exactly those where the interposition of a neutral interest might have the best result, in solving the various obstacles at present existing:—in themselves not great, but still, from their nature, incapable of early solution by the parties affected. I feel sure that a British Mission would find the task by no means a difficult one, and that its influence would be readily yielded to by those whose interests, however dissimilar in other respects, unite in pointing to the re-estabment of trade.

9. The present time appears to me most opportune for undertaking such a measure. Previous to this, the uncertain condition of the Pansee Government would probably have prevented any definite action in the matter; but now that power is sufficiently established—as far as we may judge from our present knowledge of its affairs—to take up the question in a satisfactory way. To the King of Burma, also, it is increasingly important that he should neglect no opportunity of improving the trade of his Dominions, and thereby of augmenting his fast failing revenue. If he be at any time likely to give heed to propositions which have this object in view, the present I anticipate to be the occasion on which they could best be brought forward.

10. Of the importance of at some early period reaching Western China by means of our trade I cannot speak too strongly, and that the period should not be too far distant is of great urgency. It is for this reason that the proposition to re-open-traffic by the Bhamo route from Rangoon to China stands upon a different footing from that of the proposed direct Railway route from Rangoon to China: in fact the two schemes are so distinct that the progress of the one need not in any way influence the other. The object of the Bhamo route party would be to re-open a temporarily closed trade, by a line of country already known:—the object of the other Survey is, to discover a route by which a Railway may be constructed.

11. The country to be reached from Bhamo is the northern portion of Yunan and Sechuen—say above the 25th Parallel of North Latitude;—the points aimed at by the Railway survey lie between Kiang Hung and Maing Maing, or say from the 22° to 24° North Latitude, at least if forced to run

further north, the extreme length of the Railway will be a serious obstacle to its success. The result of the Bhamo Mission, if successful, would be felt at once in a large development of our trade:—the construction of the projected Railway would not probably be completed for many years.

12. It would be a mistake therefore to suppose that the measures being taken towards the construction of a railway by a direct route to Western China, supersede the necessity of endeavouring to re-open the Bhamo route. The objects of the two schemes are sufficiently distinct to require them to be judged of on their own merits, and in one important feature, rapidity of execution and realization of results, the Bhamo project possesses unusual claims.

13. In reviewing the Report of the China route survey for the past season (vide my letter No. 355—4-C. C. of 25th June 1867, to Secretary to Government Public Works Department) I have expressed my opinion that the survey should be continued until the Cambodia be reached, as the feasibility of the railway scheme can never be satisfactorily decided until a professional examination of the whole line has given all concerned the specific information necessary to the prosecution or abandonment of the line. But considering the undoubted importance of the early diversion of the Western China traffic towards a British outlet, I would on no account recommend that any measure towards that object be retarded on account of the more prospective, tho' possibly more extensive project, of reaching China by a railway from British Burma.

14. There are two considerations which show how desirable it is that the re-opening of the Bhamo route should be undertaken at an early date, and should possess the influence and prestige of a Government mission. The first is, that it will certainly be attempted by the mercantile community; and the second, that the French authorities at Saigon have already deputed an influential mission along the course of the Cambodia, who have succeeded in reaching a point so far to the north as to intersect our line of communication with southern Yunan.

15. I have said that in rapidity of execution and realization of results the re-opening of the Bhamo route claimed special attention, and so much are its feasibilities

believed in, and the advantages to be derived from it felt, by the mercantile community of Rangoon, that already a European gentleman has proceeded to Mandalay, with the intention of attempting the passage to China. He has under article four of the treaty of 1862, and rules attached to Act XII of 1864, declared a consignment of goods for export beyond the Burmese territory, and it is probably in view to test the provisions of Article VII of the same treaty.

16. For many good reasons, however, it would be preferable that the solution of the question should be undertaken by Government, rather than left to private enterprize. The difficulties to be encountered either political or physical, but mainly the former, are such as require a definite adjustment through the interposition of our Government, if we wish to avoid having the task forced upon us at a time when the circumstances will be much less favorable.

17. The French survey party which left Saigon more than a year ago (the statement in my letter No. 66 P. of 9th August that they had only been out five months was made by error) consists of five officers, with a European staff of twenty-five persons, and a guard of one hundred Annamite soldiers. They have probably ascended the Cambodia river visiting the different semi-independant Chiefs on the bank, until they reached Kiang-Hung; up to this point the Cambodia is navigable for small boats, altho' there are rapids in some places. I reported in my letter just quoted that information had reached me that the party had arrived at Mainglon, to the eastward of Bhamo, whence they had written to Mandalay; but I am now inclined to think that they more probably wrote from the places marked in Yule's map as Muang Lam and Muang-Lon—in Burmese Main-lon-gyee—and both on the road from Kiang-Hung to Theinnee.

18. The traffic on the lower portion of the Cambodia river is understood to have been considerable in earlier times; but since the destruction of Wint-Chian or Chandapooree by the Siamese in the beginning of this century the traffic has almost ceased. But under French protection and guidance, the re-establishment of the trade will probably be effected, and we may be certain it is being aimed at.

19. It must be remembered that in 1837, Captain (now Major General) McLeod, was deputed to Kiang-Hung from Maulmain, to endeavour to induce the Chinese traders from that great entrepôt to come onward through the Zimmay Shan states to Maulmain. The difficulties of this land route were too great, however, for the success of the enterprize. But if such a project appeared feasible to our Government how much more likely of execution is the French attempt (if the river be navigable) to bring the China trade down the Cambodia. The mission have devoted a year to the important duty of examining the country between Saigon and Kiang-Hung, and if they can there establish a line of traffic they will be richly rewarded.

20. I think it probable that from Kiang-Hung they have turned to the North West, or possibly due West, because the banks of the Cambodia above Kiang-Hung for some distance, are occupied by savage tribes who bar all passage through their country; but the intention of the party was to strike the Irrawaddy at Bhamo, and, as I reported in my previous letter, my information is to the effect that they were to the Eastward of Bhamo when they wrote to the Court of Ava.

―――o―――

D. O.

Rangoon, August 26th, 1867.

DEAR SIR WILLIAM MUIR,

I have written to you officially by this mail explaining shortly the causes which have led to the closing of the Bhamo route to China, and I am somewhat anxious that His Excellency the Viceroy would be pleased to reconsider the question of its re-establishment, I anticipate that on the conclusion of the new Treaty, vigorous efforts will be made by the Mercantile Community to develope the trade with Upper Burma, and through it with China, and I am aware that the Houses in Rangoon are now making arrangements for river steamers, suited not only for traffic to Mandalay but also to Bhamo. It is certainly their intention to press for an Agency at Bhamo. The Treaty of 1862 provides for Merchants residing there, and the new Treaty secures us the right of placing a British Officer at that point, in fact, as I understand it the provisions of Article 5 of

Colonel Phayre's Draft were expressly designed to meet this object: and I am persuaded that constant agitation will be kept up, until the step is adopted. I have mentioned in my Official letter that a European Gentleman has already passed a consignment of goods through the Custom House for export to China, under Article 4 of the Treaty of 1862 and has proceeded to Mandalay for the purpose of bringing the question to an issue. The Gentleman is Mr. Fowle who has long been resident in Burma, has a thorough knowledge of Burmese, and is known to the Court of Ava, and I have reason to believe that in this matter he is in reality acting under the influence, and with the support of the most important Houses of business in Rangoon. He will, I am led to believe, make a definite effort to go by the Bhamo route to China and doubtless has selected his particular time in anticipation of possible difficulties being thrown in his way in contravention of the existing Treaty, when he will make a formal reference to me at Mandalay and call for my support.

I need hardly say that the Mercantile Community here look to a large development of trade with Upper Burma from the opening of the Bhamo route, and there can be no doubt that they do not overrate the immense advantages which, in the future, will accrue from such a measure. The great thing is that it should be rightly started and I think that this can only be done by Government. I think I could so explain the advantages to the King that the objections hitherto shown to it may be overcome, and I am quite sure that were I authorized specifically to announce the intention of sending a British Mission, the King would agree at once.

I look with interest to the arrival of the French survey party at Mandalay, and the effect of their presence there. They are, I believe, in sufficient strength to mark their importance, five Officers and twenty-five European Subordinates, with one hundred Annamite Soldiers, and I understand that they maintain some considerable dignity in their style.

As they have spent some twelve months in the leisurely ascent of the Cambodia to Kiang-Hung there can be no reasonable doubt that they have been politically busy. The Native States on the lower portion of the Cambodia are partly tributary to China, and partly to Cochin China: but as you reach Kiang-Hung they are nominally under Burma. The French could no doubt quickly assume under their protection the lower Chiefs: but *the point* they must have in view is to enter into communication with the Shan State of Kiang-Hung. This stretches Eastward to China proper, and through it runs the main route of Chinese traffic westward to the Takau-Ferry, and into the true Burman Shan States. The position of the Town of Kiang-Hung itself in fact is such that it commands the line of trade from the Westward to China proper, and to the Southern portion of Yunan. If the French have succeeded, or hereafter succeed, in forestalling us there, they will have reason for congratulation.

A great deal depends on the capabilities of the Cambodia river for navigation. I believe that there are rapids in the course, which may require transhipment of goods, in the upper portion of its course between Saigon and Kiang-Hung to the Irrawaddy at whatever point it may be reached.

Their visit to the Court of Ava is doubtless to satisfy themselves of our position with the King of Burma, as well as his feelings and status towards the far Easterly Shan States, who are but nominally tributary to him.

It becomes important that the survey towards Kyang-Hung should be certainly persevered with this year, so that our party may show themselves, as it were, to the authorities there and so far counteract the effect of the French visit; and it is in my mind also very important that we should as soon as possible establish trade relations with Eastern China through Bhamo, and thus early divert as much traffic as we can by that route. It is a *long look forward* to the construction of a Railway to Kiang-Hung, or any neighbouring point to British Burma.

I anticipate that I cannot receive the answer from the King of Burma to my despatch about the Treaty before the 10th proximo; if it is favorable I propose to start for Mandalay on the 14th.

Yours faithfully,

ALBERT FYTCHE,

xiv

No. 912.—From Sir W. Muir, K.C.S.I. Foreign Secretary, India. To Colonel A. Fytche, Chief Commissioner, Burma. Dated Simla, 12th September 1866.

I have received and laid before the Right Honorable the Governor General in Council your letter No. 76 dated 26th August, in which you again urge the expediency of deputing a party to explore and open out the commercial route viâ Bhamo to Western China.

2. The cessation of the large trade which formerly took this route, is explained by the disturbed state in which the border districts were for some time involved. These obstacles are stated no longer to exist; and the Chiefs concerned are described as anxious for the re-establishment of the trade. But the arrangements necessary for setting the traffic in motion must, in your opinion, be made by ourselves.

3. Under these circumstances His Excellency in Council consents to the deputation of a party as proposed in your letter of 21st June,° at an aggregate cost of Rupees 23,500, which covers the cost for 5 months.

*Monthly pay of Leader	Rs.	1,200
Do. Engineer	,,	1,000
Do. Medical Officer	,,	1,000
	,,	3,200
For five months	,,	16,000
Fare of party to Bhamo	,,	1,000
Hire of Kahkyens	,,	500
Presents for Shan Chiefs and Khakyens	,,	2,500
Contingencies	,,	3,500
	Rs.	23,500

4. The party should be accompanied by a Havildar's guard of 10 or 12 men.

5. The Agents must be selected with great care. They must be persons of prudence and experience in the Burmese manners and language. If Captain Sladen could be spared for the conduct of the Expedition, and arrangements made for temporarily filling his place, it might be proper to entrust the expedition to his charge. Under any circumstances you will exercise every care and precaution in the selection of the Agents employed.

———o———

No. 12 M.—From Colonel Albert Fytche, Chief Commissioner British Burma, and Agent to the Viceroy and Governor General. To Captain Sladen, Political Agent to the Chief Commissioner at Mandalay. Dated Rangoon 11 November 1867.

I have the honour to communicate to you the following instructions regarding the object and course to be pursued by the exploring party proceeding under your command viâ Bhamo to Western China. The constitution and other details of the composition and pay of the party will be communicated to you in a separate letter.

2. I annex for your information copy of a letter* I addressed to the Foreign Secretary, in which the reasons which have led to the Expedition are given, and reference is made to the results expected from its prosecution. The trade which flowed from Yunan to Burma in 1855 is described by Yule (vide his Mission to Ava passim) as valued at half a million pounds sterling:—but you are aware that, since the rise of the Pansee Government in that locality, this trade has almost entirely ceased.

*No. 76 dated 26th August 1867.

3. The principal object of the Mission then is to investigate thoroughly the causes of the cessation of trade—to discover the exact political position occupied by the Khakyens, the Shans to the Eastward, and the Pansee Government in Yunan:—and to endeavour to influence these several communities towards the re-establishment of trade.

4. How far the Khakyens may have established a right over the several routes, is not clearly known: but it is probable that they virtually hold the Passes and would expect to be subsidized, if not as a continuance, at least on the occasion of Caravans crossing. It will be important that you should discover as far as possible whether any agreement could be made with them so as to ensure the safe passage of traders. This will depend somewhat on the constitution of these Clans or Tribes, and how far they act in concert or can be treated with separately; and to this point your investigations should be directed.

5. Regarding the Shan State to the Eastward of the Khakyen hills, there may be some delicacy in connection with the Court of Ava. The States were tributary to Burma, altho' it is believed they have not been so for the last one hundred years: but possibly if a Burmese Official accompany you, the question of the relationship may be raised. On this point your instructions are to avoid taking any share in any political discussion or in any way associating the British Government in any proposition which might possibly be made by the Burmese Government.

6. It is very desirable that the position of the Shan States as regards the Chinese on the one hand, and the Pansees on the other, should be ascertained: it is probable that they have entirely broken off the connection with the Burmese government; but the relation in which they stand to the Pansee authorities should be investigated.

7. The enquiries to be made regarding the exact position of the Pansee Government is however really the most important object of the expedition, at least there can be no doubt that no resuscitation of trade can take place except with their concurrence, as it is members of their body who, we may expect, will compose the trade Caravans: it is very important, therefore, that you should reach at least Yunchang, where it is believed a high official of that Government is stationed. The subject of the route to be taken by the Expedition will be adverted to hereafter; but here I may notice that, if found feasible, it would be an immense gain to reach Talifoo, which is supposed to be the centre of the Pansee Government. It is impossible now to estimate how far this may be possible, but it would appear probable that the Pansees are an organized Government, and that the advance may be made. From their visits in former years, (and a few in late years even,) they must be well aware of the position of the British in Lower Burma; and the enterprize which led them to stretch their trade to Bhamo, will enable them to appreciate the object of the mission.

8. It need hardly be said to you that the object of the mission is not political; it is purely in the interests of trade; and therefore you will be guarded in allowing them to suppose that we have any political aim; or that you are authorized to entertain any propositions of a nature other than commercial.

9. The condition of the Pansee Government, its constitution, resources, and position towards the Chinese Government, should be carefully enquired into.

10. It will of course be necessary to make yourself acquainted with any propositions which may be made to the Pansee Government by the Court of Ava, should an officer from that Court accompany you. It is believed that communications have been interchanged between the Go-

vernments; and it is important that, while holding aloof from any possibility of committing the British Government to any measures that may be proposed or adopted, you should inform yourself of the nature of the relations that they may wish to establish. It is advisable that you should use your influence with the Burmese official to prevent any agreement which might seem to hamper the direct trade between British Merchants and the Province of Yunan.

11. In contemplation of the future trade between the countries I think it advisable that you should especially direct your attention to the organization of *Fairs* at some fixed periods of the year, in localities which may seem suited to such a measure. On this point the concurrence of the Burmese Government must be obtained; and they would probably suggest Mandalay. It may be questioned, however, whether Bhamo is not a better site. It has the advantage of being within a more reasonable distance of Yunan, has the prestige of being on old Entrepôt, and will doubtless be reached by British Merchants from Mandalay more readily than Mandalay could be by Pansee traders from it. To this point I would therefore draw marked attention; as the experience gained in many quarters of the globe teaches us the immense advantages of these stated Fairs, where trade is not—from the influence of the seasons—continuous throughout the year but is restricted to certain periods.

12. The foregoing remarks apply to the points to which I would ask your attention as Political Officer in charge of the Mission. There are of course further general subjects which will deserve your personal observation, connected with the population, produce, ethnology, language, and customs of the people, but these I leave to your judgment and intelligence.

13. Associated with you as Engineer Officer will be Captain Williams, whose duty it will be to report on the features of the country and the state of the route. The survey which he is expected to take is intended to be sufficient to enable him to report generally on the physical conditions of the route, and how far these might be ameliorated. It will be, in addition, his object to make as full enquiries as possible regarding communications eastward from Yunan to China Proper, as well as regarding all through routes

to the westward, whether these lead Southwest from Yunan to Burma, or Northwest towards Assam. Any East and West routes from China to India which lie further to the north should be enquired for, and their nature ascertained.

14. A medical officer will also accompany the party, and it is hoped that he will be qualified to report on the Geology and Natural History of the several localities visited.

15. Regarding the route, I would observe that the starting point is Bhamo, and it is left to your judgment, after enquiry on the spot, to select the particular pass through the hills which it may seem most advisable to follow, bearing in mind that you should, if possible, reach Yunchan quickly, as there the most important points will be determined. Every effort should be made therefore to reach Yunchan: but whether it will be feasible, or if feasible, whether it will be prudent that you should go on to Talifoo, I am unable to say. It is however, I consider, important that you should—if circumstances will permit—reach Talifoo, especially if you ascertain that the seat of the Pansee Government is held there: you are therefore authorized to proceed to that point, if you have reasonable expectation that the safety of the party will not be endangered.

16. I need not caution you to be very careful to avoid coming into collision with any of the authorities on the route: or attempting to force a passage against hostile opposition. The aim being the future establishment of a route for traders it is manifest that the forcible advance of the exploring party would be more likely to increase any difficulties that exist, than to lead to their amelioration. Where opposition may be shown therefore to your advance, you must use your judgment and discretion in endeavouring to overcome the antagonism by other means than force.

17. There is one point which remains to be considered, and that is the route to be taken on your return. It is believed that a trade route runs direct from Talifoo Southwest to Theinnee, and also from the Shan Town of Maingmo, or Moungmo, Eastward of the Khakyen hills direct to the same point. From Theinnee to Mandalay it is known that a trade route exists. It might be advantageous that this route

also should be traversed, if circumstances connected with the passage of the Khakyen hills to Bhamo render it advisable to return by that route. I would therefore leave the choice of this route for your return to Mandalay to your discretion, with the distinct proviso, however, that the main object of the present expedition is not only—or not so much—the mere examination of the route viâ Bhamo to Yunan, but the adoption of measures, if any be found, to re-establish trade by that route. You will therefore please to bear in mind, that if your return by Bhamo will in any way facilitate this latter measure, it is expected that you will return by that route, in preference to the one I have now mentioned.

No. 14 M.—From Colonel ALBERT FYTCHE, Chief Commissioner British Burma, and Agent to the Viceroy and Governor-General—to Sir WILLIAM MUIR, K.C.S.I., Secretary to Government of India, Foreign Department—dated Rangoon, 11th November 1867.

Referring to your letter and telegram as per margin, and also to the previous correspondence regarding the despatch of an exploring party to Western China viâ Bhamo, I have the honor to report that during my stay at Mandalay I communicated to the Court of Ava the intention of His Excellency the Viceroy and Governor-General to despatch a party with the above object, and, through Captain Sladen, explained to His Majesty the great advantages that would in all probability ensue from the re-establishment of the extinct trade, which formerly flowed by that route into Burma. His Majesty seemed fully alive to the good results which would flow from such a measure, and on my personally addressing him on the subject, at once expressed his readiness to assist saying "I will send Sladen all the way to China:"—and in reply to a letter which I presented on the same subject, His Majesty issued a Royal Edict (copy attached) in which he directs all officials to assist in the progress of the party.

Letter No. 912 of 12th September. Telegram of 18th September.

2. His Majesty was anxious that Captain Sladen should head the Expedition, and at the same time observed that he did not think any officer would be required to take his place, as he would only be absent for a few months. I

have therefore (in accordance also with the 5th para: of the letter noted in the margin above) appointed Captain Sladen as the leader of the Expedition.

3. By a Telegram of 22nd October from the Secretary to the Government of India in the Public Works Department the services of Captain Williams were made available as the Engineer Officer of the Party, and I have consequently appointed him to that position, as eminently qualified for the duty. His salary if he had proceeded on the China Route survey this season was to have been Rs. 2,000 per mensem, and possibly as the Government Telegram placing his services at my disposal for this expedition specified no salary, it was intended that he should receive a similar amount; but in the absence of definite orders on the subject, and as the cost of the expedition will now exceed my original estimate, I have entered his salary at Rs. 1,500 only. I hope, however, that the Government will not allow Captain Williams to be a loser by the transfer.

4. By the telegram marginally noted in the first paragraph, I have been authorized to increase the Guard proposed in the 4th para. of your letter No. 912 of 12th September, and on this point I consulted Captain Sladen who considers that the Guard should consist of Police, one half Burman and one half Mahomedan, of the total strength of one Inspector, three Serjeants, and fifty Constables. A Guard of this strength is, therefore, being now prepared to accompany the Expedition.

5. The Medical Officer, it is hoped, will be Assistant Surgeon Cuteliffe, who was to have proceeded with the intended China Railway Survey, and who has been telegraphed to, to enquire whether he would wish to join this expedition, and if so, to apply to Government for permission, and to proceed to Rangoon forthwith.

6. These changes will somewhat affect the estimated cost of the party as sanctioned in the 3rd para. of your letter: I would now estimate the probable charge for the expedition as follows:—

Captain Sladen per mensem	....	....	Rs.	2,000
Captain Williams ,,	....	....	,,	1,500
Medical Officer ,,	....	....	,,	1,000
Police Inspector ,,	....	....	,,	120
3 Sergeants at Rs. 30 per mensem	....	....	,,	90
50 Constables at Rs. 15 ,,	....	....	,,	750

SURVEY ESTABLISHMENT.

One Surveyor per mensem	....	....	,,	120
8 Klashies at 15 ,,	....	....	,,	120
1 Tindal at 18 ,,	....	....	,,	18
				5,718
For five months	....	....	....	28,590
Fare of Party to Bhamo	....	....	....	2,000
Hire of Khakyens	....	....	....	500
Presents	....	....	....	4,500
Contingencies	....	....	....	6,000
			Total Rs.	41,590

In the above, however, there will a saving from the apparent cost of the party, no person being appointed in lieu of Captain Sladen, and if the Officer who succeeds Captain Williams only draws deputation allowance the saving will be the present pay of Captain Sladen and half the pay of Captain Williams, amounting together to Rs. 2000 per mensem, which for five months would be Rs. 10,000, reducing the real cost of the expedition to Rs. 31,590.

7. I beg to enclose copies of my letters of instructions to Captains Sladen and Williams which fully detail what I consider should be the object of the Expedition, and which, I trust, will meet with the approval of His Excellency the Viceroy and Governor General of India in Council.

TRANSLATION OF ROYAL EDICT.

Colonel Albert Fytche, Chief Commissioner of British Burma has represented to me that commerce is likely to be immensely increased and improved and the prosperity of both countries secured by opening out the old overland trade route between Bhamo and the Chinese frontier.

He further informs me that it is his intention to despatch an expeditionary party, whose duty it will be, under instructions received from the Government of India, to proceed overland from Bhamo as far as the Chinese Cities of Yunchang, and Talifoo in Yunan.

My co-operation and assistance is solicited in a work which is intended to increase trade and add to the material prosperity of both countries.

I therefore agree to assist this party as far as lays in my power; and will cause it to be well received at each of the places at which it may arrive en route.

All officials, Saubwas, Magistrates, and Tseekays within my Territories, are hereby ordered not to impede in any way but to further the progress of the English Party, by every means in their power.

>Given at our Royal Palace at Mandalay, the first day of the increasing moon Ta-shoung-hmon 1229 B. E.

No. 16 M.—From Colonel ALBERT FYTCHE, Chief Commissioner, British Burma, and Agent to His Excellency the Viceroy and Governor General, to the Engineer Officer, Bhamo Expedition, dated Rangoon, 12th November, 1867.

I have the honor to inform you that you have been appointed one of the exploring party organized to proceed viâ Bhamo to Yunan, under the leadership of Captain Sladen, Political Agent at Mandalay, who will be in charge of the Expedition.

2. The primary object of the Expedition is to enquire into the causes of the cessation of trade by the route in question, a trade which ten years ago amounted to half a million sterling yearly, and to report what measures may be deemed advisable to resuscitate this extinct Commerce.

3. At the same time it is considered important to have a report on the physical conditions of the route itself, and for this purpose you have been attached to the party.

4. Your object, therefore, will be to make a flying survey of the route actually traversed, and a report as to any measures that might improve the route as a dry weather track for Caravans; its possible adaptability for the

construction of a Railway may be kept in view but the progress of the Expedition should not be retarded on this account if the question require too minute an examination.

5. The survey is subsidiary to the main question viz: the resuscitation of the trade, and while Captain Sladen will be directed to give every facility for its satisfactory prosecution, it must in all instances rest with him how far that must yield to the more immediate object of the expedition.

6. Captain Sladen has been directed to reach Yunchang if possible, and if considered advisable to advance to Talifoo. From there several routes run, it is believed, southwest to Theinnee, and a discretionary authority is given to that Officer to return to Mandalay by one of these routes, if such a measure do not interfere with the solution of the question of the re-opening of the Bhamo route.

7. I would call your special attention to the importance of obtaining full information regarding the routes from Talifoo, Eastward to China Proper, as well as Westward to India. Careful enquiry, also, should be made regarding any East and West routes from China to India, to the North of Talifoo.

8. In addition to the purely professional Survey Report I trust that you will find it feasible to gather much information regarding the general features of the countries traversed, and the geography of these hitherto unexplored regions. Increased attention is being directed to the Headwaters of the Yantsekyang, of the Irrawaddy, and of the Brahmapooter, as well as to the general subject of through communication between India and China. Every effort therefore should be made to obtain any available details regarding these important questions.

———o———

No. 1150.—From Sir William Muir, K C.S.I., Foreign Secretary, India,—to the Chief Commissioner of British Burma,—dated Fort William, the 28th November 1867.

I have the honor to acknowledge the receipt of your letter, No. 14 M., dated the 11th instant, reporting that His

[xxiv]

Majesty the King of Burma has cordially assented to the proposed despatch of an exploring party to Western China, *via* Bhamo.

2. It appears from your letter that during your recent visit to Mandalay, you represented to His Majesty the advantages which would accrue to the Burmese and British territories from a revival of the trade between Burma and Western China, which is now quite extinct, but which ten years ago was estimated at half a million sterling per annum.

3. His Majesty has expressed his readiness to assist an exploring party to Western China as far as lay in his power, and issued a Royal Edict ordering that all officials within Burmese territory should do their utmost to further the progress of the English party.

4. I have now the honor to state that the Viceroy and Governor General in Council considers that the consent of His Majesty to the proposed expedition to Bhamo is very satisfactory, and a Khureeta is enclosed expressing the acknowledgments of the Government of India, which you are requested to instruct Captain Sladen to deliver to the King in a suitable manner.

5. With respect to the exploring party, the Governor-General approves of the instructions you have communicated to Captain Sladen, who is to lead the party, as well as of those to Captain J. M. Williams, who will accompany Captain Sladen for the purpose of making a flying survey of the route.

6. As regards the further progress of the route beyond Bhamo, His Excellency in Council observes that this point must be left entirely to the discretion of Captain Sladen. Should the party meet with facilities for its further advance, and Captain Sladen feel satisfied that it would run no risk of danger, he may go as far as he considers it desirable, up to the Chinese Frontier; but the Governor-General in Council doubts the expediency of a further progress towards the Pansee capital of Talifoo.

7. If Captain Sladen decides upon crossing the Khakyen Hills, he should only do so on the explicit understanding that the people have really consented to his advance

through their country. He should endeavour to arrive at some explicit arrangements with these tribes to permit the trade to pass through their territory; but he should enter into no engagements which would impose any obligations upon the British Government. The primary object to be kept in view throughout any negotiations with the Khakyens is to convince the people that a systematic arrangement on liberal terms, providing for the full security of all traders passing through their country, would encourage the commerce of neighbouring States, and prove a material benefit to themselves.

8. The Governor-General in Council is of opinion that it is desirable that all the information that can be procured of a useful character, referring either to the route to Bhamo, or to the country in its vicinity, or to the people and region beyond it, should be collected and placed upon record. In reference to the nature of the information which is more particularly required, His Excellency in Council would especially specify such details as related to the character and disposition of the people, and the facilities for carrying on trade. The question of whether it would be expedient hereafter to appoint a British Agent at Bhamo should also be carefully considered and fully reported upon. It would also be desirable to ascertain the views and wishes of the people of Bhamo with respect to this particular measure, as well as the probable security of a British Officer in so isolated a position, and the question of whether the appointment of a Native Agent would not, in the first instance, prove a more suitable arrangement.

9. Notwithstanding, however, the importance of collecting the information thus indicated, and of reviving the extinct commerce between Burmah and Western China, I am directed to observe that the Viceroy and Governor General in Council would prefer to see the expedition return without accomplishing the objects for which it has been undertaken, rather than learn that the safety of Captain Sladen and the party accompanying him had been in any degree compromised.

10. The pay and allowances of Captain Sladen and his party, as proposed by you, have been referred to the Financial Department for favorable consideration.

[xxvi]

No. 77.—From H. F. BLANFORD, Esq., Honorary Secretary Trustees, Indian Museum, to Colonel FYTCHE, Chief Commissioner, British Burma, dated Calcutta, 29th November, 1867.

I have the honor to inform you that the Trustees of the Indian Museum having carefully considered your application that Dr. J. Anderson be allowed five months leave to enable him to accompany the expedition to Yunan as surgeon and naturalist, in consideration of the great and unusual opportunities offered by this expedition for gaining acquaintance with the natural history of a country hitherto unexplored and almost unknown to European science, have resolved to accord the leave required.

They feel assured that ample provision will be made by you to enable Dr. Anderson to avail himself to the utmost of this rare opportunity, to collect and preserve specimens illustrative of the natural history of the regions to be traversed by the expedition; and they trust that you will consider the Indian Museum a fit repository for at least one complete series of the specimens that may be obtained by Dr. Anderson.

———o———

No. 1,005 A.—From Colonel ALBERT FYTCHE, Chief Commissioner, British Burma and Agent to the Viceroy and Governor General, to JOHN ANDERSON, Esq., M. D., Conservator Indian Museum, dated Calcutta, November 30th, 1867.

I have the honor to inform you that with the concurrence of the Trustees of the Indian Museum you have been appointed as Surgeon and Naturalist to the exploring party proceeding under the leadership of Captain Sladen, viâ Bhamo to Western China.

2. Full instructions regarding the route to be pursued and the constitution and other details of the composition of the party have been communicated to Captain Sladen: but I may mention that your chief duties will be to report on the Geology and Natural History of the several localities visited.

3. A passage has been taken for you and five followers by the British India Steam Vessel *Busheer* leaving Calcutta for Rangoon on 2nd proximo;—and on the 8th idem a Steamer will be starting for Mandalay from Rangoon, by which you should proceed and place yourself under the

orders of Captain Sladen, who will await your arrival at that place. Captain Williams Engineer Officer to the Expedition will proceed to Mandalay by the same opportunity, and on your arrival at Rangoon you should communicate with that Officer without delay.

4. Your pay during the time you are employed will Rs. 1,000 per mensem, and the period which it is supposed the Mission will take, will be about five months.

———o———

No. 189.—From Captain E. B. SLADEN, Political Agent to Chief Commissioner, British Burma—to Colonel ALBERT FYTCHE, Chief Commissioner of British Burma and Agent to the Governor-General—dated Mandalay, 11th January 1868.

I have the honor to report for your information, that the Officers named in the margin, who have been directed to accompany the Mission under my command (which is about to proceed over land viâ Bhamo, to the Chinese Frontier) arrived at this place, in the Steamer *Nerbudda*, on the 8th instant.

<small>Captain J. M. Williams,
Dr. Anderson,
Captain Bowers,
Mr. F. N. Burn,
Mr. Stewart.</small>

2. The party will leave this on board the King's Steamer, the *Yanan Sekia* en route to Bhamo, on the 13th instant.

3. As soon as I was in possession of reliable information of the Steamer *Nerbudda's* near approach to Mandalay, I applied to His Majesty the King of Burma, to have a Royal Steamer, which had already been promised for the conveyance of the party northwards, made over to my charge.

4. This was at once done; but a difficulty arose as to the immediate departure of the steamer: owing to the necessity the Government felt under of despatching in her a new Governor of Bhamo, in the room of the old incumbent, whose assassination by Shan and Kachyen Rebels at Momeit, was lately reported by me.

5. The new Governor of Bhamo only arrived at Mandalay from his last place of residence on the day that the Mission Party reached this in the *Nerbudda*. He had come in haste from a distant district, without any of his followers, and it was thought expedient by the Government to grant time to prepare for the Bhamo trip, as the

[xxviii]

Governor declared that without his own old followers, who had not reached Mandalay at the time, he would be helpless in a new district, and unable to give that assistance to the expeditionary party which they would stand in need of on arrival at Bhamo.

6. Though I strongly objected to delay under any circumstances I was obliged to allow that unavoidable grounds existed for compliance with the request made that the steamer in which we were to proceed should not start until the 15th instant.

7. The murder of the old Bhamo-won was an unforseen event, and it was only reasonable to expect that unless a new Governor was appointed and at his post by the time the party arrived at Bhamo, there would be certain difficulty in making provision for the further prosecution of the expedition inland towards the confines of China.

8. The detention of a few days though unfortunate and unavoidable in itself, has enabled me to carry out successfully the ratification of the new Treaty, the circumstances attending which will be duly reported on in a separate communication.

9. It has also allowed me the opportunity of presenting to His Majesty, with full state ceremony, the Khareeta from His Excellency the Viceroy and Governor General.

10. Your letters Nos. 1003 A and 1004 A containing the ratified Treaty and Khareeta, dated 28th November 1867, only reached me per Steamer *Nerbudda* on the 8th instant. I have been busily and constantly engaged at the Palace every day since, but will make every endeavour to leave this, as already stated, on the 13th instant.

No. 28.—From the Officiating Under Secretary to the Government of India,—to the Chief Commissioner of Burmah,—dated Fort William, the 10th January 1868.

With reference to the correspondence marginally noted,[a] regarding the despatch of an expedition to explore the caravan route between Ava and the Western Frontier of China viâ Bhamo, I am directed to forward for your information, copy of a despatch from Her Majesty's Secretary of State for India, No. 189 dated 23rd November last.

* From you dated 21st June 1867, No. 127 P.
To you dated 13th July 1867 No. 712.

No. 189.—From Sir Stafford H. Northcote,—to His Excellency the Right Hon'ble the Governor General of India in Council,—dated London, 23rd November 1867.

Para:—1. I learn from the Letter of your Excellency's Government in the Foreign Department, No. 138, of the 26th August 1867, that you have negatived Col. Fytche's proposal to explore the ancient caravan route from Ava to the Chinese frontier, viâ Bhamo, a route which, though now closed, probably owing to the disturbed state of the country, formerly commanded a trade valued at nearly half a million sterling annually, and, therefore, not unlikely to possess many natural advantages.

2. These it may be possible to utilize, though, in the present disturbed state of the country, it may be premature to take any immediate steps towards doing so.

3. But since your Despatch was written, the objection urged by you, that another exploring party is now carrying on its operations, no longer applies, its proceedings having been suspended at your suggestion, in accordance with my Despatch, No. 111 dated 31st October 1867, in the Public Works Department. And, as the exploration of these ancient caravan routes is, in the opinion of Her Majesty's Government, in itself desirable it would be advisable to take advantage of any favorable opportunities for the attainment of this object which may may present themselves, whether now, in consequence of Colonel Fytche's visit to Mandalay, or at a future period.

———o———

No. 207.—From Sir Stafford H. Northcote,—to His Excellency the Right Hon'ble the Governor General of India in Council,—dated London, 9th December 1867.

Para:—1. I have had under my consideration in Council the Letter of your Excellency's Government No. 158, in the Foreign Department, dated 15th October 1867, respecting the proposed exploration of the ancient caravan route from Burmah, viâ Bhamo into Western China.

2. The sentiments of Her Majesty's Government on this matter have already been communicated to you in my recent Despatch, No. 189, of the 23rd November 1867, and I have now only to express their satisfaction that you have, owing to the cessation of disturbance in the country to be

traversed, found it possible to acquiesce in the recommendation of the Chief Commissioner of British Burmah, and to sanction the Deputation of a party to "explore and open out" the route in question.

3. The Officer in charge of the party, as well as the Engineer and Medical Officers under his orders, will, of course, have been instructed to keep full and accurate journals of all noteworthy occurrences and phenomena, as well as of the character of the populations, and the natural products of the country, through which they may pass.

---o---

No. 101.—From Under Secretary to the Government of India,—to the Chief Commissioner British Burmah,—dated Fort William, Foreign Department, the 28th January 1868.

Copy forwarded to the Chief Commissioner British Burmah, with reference to the correspondence ending with this Office Telegram dated 18th September last, and his attention directed to para 3 of the despatch.

---o---

No. 24.—From Chief Commissioner British Burma and Agent to the Viceroy and Governor General, to the Secretary to Government of India, Foreign Department, dated Rangoon, February 1st. 1868.

I have the honor to report for the information of His Excellency the Viceroy and Governor General of India in Coucil, that Captain Williams and Dr. Anderson arrived at Mandalay on 8th ultimo, and the expedition started for Bhamo on the 13th following.

2. His Majesty the King of Burma made over his only available steamer, the *Yaynansekya*, to convey the party as far as Bhamo. His Majesty still continues to take great interest in the expedition and has done everything in his power to further its interests. The Irrawaddy river is at its lowest during the months of January and February, and it will be a point gained if the steamer gets up to Bhamo as it will be the first steamer that has ever proceeded so high up the river. Arrangements have been made for a speedy supply of boats in the event of the steamer grounding and being unable to proceed. A Panthay Chinaman of Yunan, who understands the Burmese language, and has frequently travelled by the Bhamo route,

has been made over by the King to the Mission, and the King has also furnished Captain Sladen with letters for delivery to the Panthay, Chinese, and Shan authorities.

3. A Caravan of 500 mules has lately arrived at Mandalay from Yunan by the Theinee route. The head of the Caravan, who has visited Captain Sladen, states that fighting is still going on between the Panthays and the Chinese troops in Eastern Yunan, and one of the principal causes of the Bhamo route being now discontinued was on account of Chinese guards being stationed in the Shan-Sheet-Pyay (the eight Shan States of which several are tributary to China) and that there would be a risk for Panthay Caravans passing through that part of the country at present: but it was supposed that this would not interfere with the English Mission.

---o---

No. 31-418.—From Chief Commissioner British Burma, and Agent to the Viceroy and Governor General, to the Secretary to the Government of India, Foreign Department, dated Rangoon, 12th February 1868.

I have the honor to report for the information of the Viceroy and Governor General in Council that Captain Sladen and party arrived at Bhamo on the 21st January, performing the journey from Mandalay in eight days. Captain Sladen reports that the river navigation between Mandalay and Bhamo is better for steamers than it is between Mandalay and our Frontier. The Kings steamer that conveyed the party drew three feet of water, never grounded once nor met with difficulties of any kind. The journey was performed in eight days, but might have been performed in five if it had not been for the dense morning fogs which prevented the steamer starting before 9 and 10 A. M. The party stayed occasionaly, too, for a short time at different places on the voyage.

2. The Mission would be delayed for a few days at Bhamo for carriage and that enquiries might be made regarding the route. Captain Sladen does not anticipate any difficulties in passing thro' the Kakhyen Hills; but has heard that he may meet with some obstructions when he gets to the borders of the Shan States between these hills and the frontier of Yunan, where the Panthays and Chinese appear to be still fighting and the latter occupy several of the Shan Towns.

[xxxii]

No. 225.—From Sir RICHARD TEMPLE, K.C.S.I., Officiating Secretary to the Government of India, Foreign Department,—to Colonel A. FYTCHE, Chief Commissioner of British Burmah, dated Fort William, the 29th, February 1868;

In reference to the correspondence marginally° noted regarding Captain Sladen's deputation to Bhamo, I am directed to enclose for your information and guidance copy of a letter addressed to H. B. M's. Envoy at Pekin: in reference to the possibility of the party extending its journey through Yunan towards Canton.

*From you, dated 11th Nov. 1867, No. 14 M.
To you, „ 28th do. No. 1150.
From you, „ 1st Febry. 1868, No. 24.
To you, „ 12th do. No. 31-428.

2. It will be in your recollection that in the first instance the Government of India was doubtful of the possibility of the party proceeding beyond Talifoo the Panthay capital of Yunan; but from information since received it seems possible that they might reach Canton from Bhamo by direct route and then return to Burmah round by Sea from Hong-Kong.

3. If Captain Sladen should find such an extension of the journey to be fairly practicable, he might exercise his discretion in attempting it: and in that case he should endeavour to communicate with H. M's. Envoy in China and with the Chinese authorities. But if he saw any danger or even serious difficulty, he should, of course, refrain from making such an attempt.

———o———

No. 224.—From Sir R. TEMPLE, K.C.S.I., Officiating Secretary to the Government of India, to His Excellency Sir RUTHERFORD ALCOCK, K.C.B., H. B. M's Envoy Extraordinary and Chief Superintendent of Trade in China, Dated Fort William, the 29th February, 1868.

I am directed by the Government of India to apprise you that a party of British Officers under the guidance of Captain Sladen, has been deputed to proceed up the valley of the Irrawaddy to Bhamo and thence to the frontier of Yunan. The object of this deputation is to enquire into the condition and prospects of the Trade between Burmah and China; to examine the routes on the Burmese frontier in the direction of the Chinese territories; and to make such suggestions as may be practicable for the promotion of commerce in the interests of the British Government in its territories on the eastern shores of the Bay of Bengal.

2. Copies of the instructions originally given to the party are hereto appended.

3. The party consisting of Captain Sladen, Captain Williams, Doctor Anderson and Messrs. Bowers and Stewart reached Bhamo on the 21st January last. A copy of the last account received of them is hereto appended. They hoped to penetrate to the Yunan frontier, but beyond that their course must be regulated by circumstances, and by the facilities or otherwise for prosecuting any journey in the Chinese territories. If any such extension of their travels were safe and prudent it would of course be desirable that they should proceed through Yunan to Canton and Hong Kong; and thence return to Burma round by sea. They should not however attempt this unless there be a reasonable probability of the trip being successfully and beneficially made. From information which has reached the Government of India through Mr. Parry of the Firm of Messrs. Burlay of Hong Kong, there seems to be a chance of the above route proving feasible for this party.

4. It is with a view to the last named contingency that I am directed by the Viceroy and Governor-General of India in Council to solicit your good offices and consideration. Perhaps you might see fit to bring the matter to the favorable notice of the Chinese authorities, with a view of assistance being furnished to the British party, or to information at all events being afforded to them, as to whether they should proceed or not. And His Excellency in Council entertains the hope that you will favor this Government with your opinion as to the advisability or otherwise of endeavoring to explore the commercial routes in that quarter, and to improve a trade which seems to have been, at one time, more flourishing than at present.

No. 258.—From Sir RICHARD TEMPLE, K. C. S. I., Secretary to the Government of India, to Colonel A. FYTCHE, Chief Commissioner of Burma, dated Fort William, the 13th March, 1868.

In continuation of my letter No. 225, of the 29th ultimo, regarding the extension of Captain Sladen's mission in the direction of Chinese territory: I am directed to transmit for your information copy of a despatch from H. M.'s Secretary of State, on the subject.

2. In advertence to para: 3rd of that despatch I am to again draw attention to what has been already enjoined in respect to circumspection and caution: and with respect to communicating with the Chinese authorities before attempting to enter their jurisdiction. Indeed, it is essential that Captain Sladen should come to a satisfactory understanding with them; and before advancing beyond the Burmese frontier. If possible, he should also endeavour to obtain intelligence from H. M.'s Envoy at Pekin, as to the advisability of proceeding in that direction.

No. 12.—From SIR STAFFORD H. NORTHCOTE,—to His Excellency the Right Hon'ble the Governor General of India in Council,—dated London, 8th February 1868.

Para:—1. I have received and considered in Council the letter of your Excellency's Government in the Foreign Department, No. 182, of the 9th December 1867, reporting the cordial assent of the King of Burmah to the despatch of the proposed expedition to explore the ancient caravan route viâ Bhamo, to the Chinese frontier.

2. The instructions contained in your Secretary's letter of the 28th November 1867, to the Chief Commissioner of Burmah, as to the objects and the conduct of the expedition, are rightly conceived in a spirit of caution, and I approve your having required the consent of the Kakhyen Chiefs as an indispensable preliminary to a passage through their territory being attempted.

3. The previous services of Captain Sladen justify me in believing that he will wisely exercise the discretion entrusted to him as to his advance up to the Chinese Frontier. Beyond that line it would, in your opinion, be inexpedient to advance. In this view of the matter Her Majesty's Government concur. It would be most indiscreet to enter Chinese territory without a more accurate knowledge of current events within it than we at present possess, and any such step on our part could not fail to give umbrage to the Court of Pekin, which claims to exercise, though it appears only imperfectly, jurisdiction over that part of the Province of Yunan on which the expedition would first set foot.

No. 72 of 1868.—From Colonel ALBERT FYTCHE, Chief Commissioner British Burma and Agent to the Viceroy and Governor-General—to Sir RICHARD TEMPLE, K.C.S.I., Secretary to the Government of India, Foreign Department, Fort William—dated Rangoon, April 14th, 1868.

In continuation of my letter No. 69-418 of 28th March, I have the honor to inform you that Captain Sladen and Party left Bhamo, as intimated in my letter, on 26th February, and since then no communication has been received from him, or from any of his party.

2. Under date the 24th March the Kulah-won* wrote from Mandalay, that the Governor of Bhamo had reported a stoppage of Captain Sladen's party in the Khakyen Hills five days march from Bhamo, at a place marked Pong-tein, East and a little North of Bhamo, on the road to Sanda, viâ Chee-thee, and Mawae, (vide Map of Trade Routes between Burma and Western China). The report stated that on account of the accidental burning of some Khakyen huts large compensation had been demanded from the party, which Captain Sladen apparently had declined to pay. The Kulah-won at the same time stated that His Majesty the King of Burma had sent orders to the Governor of Bhamo to give every assistance in adjusting the difficulty. From letters of a later date it would appear that the party had gone on, as under date of the 4th April the Kulah-won writes that the Expedition had passed thro' the Khakyen districts, and had reached the Shan States bordering on Yunan.

* Minister for Foreigners

3. There have been rumours of the party having been attacked in the Khakyen Hills and even of the death of some of the guard and of a European Official, but this appears to be only an exaggerated account of the original difficulty when the party was stopped. No report of this kind has been sent to me by the Burmese Government, and I feel assured that if such a circumstance had occurred it must be known to them, and, if known to them, would have been reported.

4. It appears that Captain Sladen was not making for Mowun, as reported in my former letters, but for Mawae, two marches South West of Sanda.

[xxxvi]

Service Message.—From Sir R. TEMPLE, Calcutta, to Chief Commissioner Rangoon, dated 15th April, 1868—Clear the Line.

Is the news true as given in *Rangoon Times*, of April 4th, that Sladen's party have been stopped by the Panthays on a pecuniary demand; if so, have you taken any steps? Perhaps it would be best to send instructions for their liberation on payment of amount demanded, on condition of their being safely escorted back to Burmese frontier. Telegraph what you propose to do: remember that conciliatory measures are essential.

From Chief Commissioner, British Burma, to Sir R. TEMPLE, Calcutta, dated Rangoon, 19th April, 1868—Clear the line.

Your telegram of fifteenth received to-day. The latest reliable information regarding Captain Sladen's party is that they have crossed the Kakhyen Hills, and reached the minor Shan States. See my letter number seventy-two of fourteenth instant.

No. 247C-26 C.—From ALEX. FRASER, Lieut.-Col., R. E., Secretary to the Chief Commissioner British Burma, Public Works Department, to ROBERT GORDON, Esquire, C. E., Executive Engineer, U. P. W. A. Roads, Prome, dated Rangoon, 30th May 1868.

Annexed is a copy of a telegraphic message despatched to you to-day. The Chief Commissioner and Agent to the Viceroy has been pleased to appoint you as Engineer Officer to the Expedition to Western China under Captain Sladen, vice Captain J. M. Williams, and I am directed to inform you that you are to carry out, when you join Captain Sladen, the instructions issued to Captain Williams, copy of which will be furnished to you by Captain Sladen. Your salary will be settled hereafter.

2. On your arrival at Mandalay, whither you will proceed in the most expeditious way possible, you will wait on Mr. Manook, the Kalahwoon, to whom the Chief Commissioner has written to request him to give you every assistance in his power in forwarding you on the track taken by Captain Sladen which you are desired to follow viâ Bhamo.

3. The Deputy Commissioner of Prome has been instructed to furnish you with such funds in advance as you may require and Mr. Manook has also been requested to meet your wants in this respect.

4. It is particularly desired that you should not burden yourself with unnecessary baggage, and it is thought that one small portmanteau and a couple of blankets woudl be enough, as the carriage is the great difficulty. You should take a sufficient amount of money to prevent your becoming any embarrassment to Captain Sladen. If you take Rs. 400 in addition to what you require to enable you to reach Bhamo, the Chief Commissioner is of opinion that with extreme economy while on the journey you will have sufficient funds to meet all necessary expenditure on your own account.

Service Telegram, No. 248 C-26 C.—From Colonel FRASER, Secretary to Chief Commissioner, to ROBERT GORDON, Esquire, Executive Engineer, Prome, dated Rangoon, 30th May, 1868.

The Chief Commissioner wishes you at once to join the expedition to Talifoo viâ Mandalay and Bhamo, and to place yourself under the orders of Captain Sladen.

Prepare accordingly for getting to Mandalay in the best and quickest way you can after receipt of instructions which will leave this to night by the King's dâk boat.

Make over your division temporarily to Mr. Dunn.

Telegraph Message No. 246 C-26 C.—From Secretary to Chief Commissioner, to Mr. Gordon, Dated Rangoon, 9th June, 1868.

You are to report your progress whenever you have opportunity *direct* to Chief Commissioner, till you join Captain Sladen.

Chief Commissioner wishes particularly to hear from Mandalay after you have seen the Kalahwoon.

No. 39-19—From Colonel ALBERT FYTCHE, Chief Commissioner British Burma, and Agent to the Viceroy and Governor General of India,—to the Secretary to the Government of India, Foreign Department,—dated Rangoon, 2nd June 1868.

I have the honor to forward for the information of His Excellency the Viceroy and Gonor General of India copies as per margin furnishing the latest accounts of the Expedition under Captain Sladen now engaged in traversing the route from Bhamo to Yunan.

Letter of 28th April from Captain Sladen.
Letter No. 1 of 4th May from Captain Williams Engineer to the Expedition with its accompaniments.
Letter No. 2 dated 13th May from the same Officer.

2. Captain Sladen's letter describes the events which have marked the progress of the party since they left Bhamo, and is most interesting and hopeful. It would appear that the Khakyen Chiefs who engaged to convoy the expedition to *Manwyne* (written *Manwae* on the Map) would take them only the length of *Pongsee* forty miles from Bhamo, which will be seen on the Map just westward of Manwae, eight miles. The grounds of nonfulfilment of their engagement were due to the action of the minor Shan Chiefs Manwyne, Sanda, and Manleo (probably the Maingla of the Map) South-East of Sanda. They were under the influence of a Chinese Marauder who had possession of Mopoo, which will be found on the route from Sanda to Momein.

3. Captain Sladen had, however, with much judgment opened up communication with Officers of the Panthay Government at Momein, and from them received every encouragement and support to persevere in his endeavours to reach them. They urged him not to fall back, and promised that they would clear the way.

4. This they did by attacking the Chinese Marauder at Mopoo and dispersing his band. They had promised to come on to Sanda and furnish Captain Sladen with an escort, and by a private letter of the 30th April he informs me that he had heard of their arrival at Sanda which is only five marches from Manwyne and he expected that they would in a few days come on to where he was with mules and an escort.

5. Captain Sladen describes the altered tone of the Khakyens and Shan Chiefs as soon as they became aware of his friendly relations with the Panthay Government, and also remarks on the satisfaction of the latter at the destruction of the Chinese Marauder's party.

6. It would seem from the whole circumstances connected with the advance of the party so far, that the Panthay Government is eager to assist the resuscitation of the trade by the old route, and that it is strong enough to occupy the road to the bottom of the Khakyen Hills on the Eastern side. With this apparently willing co-operation of the Panthays there seems good hope that the object of the expedition may eventually be fulfilled.

7. If Captain Sladen be successful in effecting a junction with the Panthay Officers there is every prospect of his being accorded a good reception and of his being invited to enter their territories with their full consent. I have every confidence that Captain Sladen will use these advantages with discretion.

8. The delay which has occurred is not to be regretted. It has no doubt enabled Captain Sladen to obtain considerable information regarding the Khakyens, who, holding the hills, must always form an important element in any scheme for re opening the route, and it has given them an opportunity of learning more fully the intentions of the expedition. But, more important still, the delay has insured (in all probability) Captain Sladen's advance with all the prestige of the direct support and encouragement of the Panthay Government, whose predominance has been manifested by their rapid occupation of the route up to the base of the Khakyen hills.

9. I am glad to record my opinion of the judgment and tact shown by Captain Sladen. He wisely chose to wait patiently for a favorable turn of affairs despite the disadvantages in some respects of the delay thereby necessitated. This and his success in engaging the interests of the Panthay Officials promise well for the future progress of the party.

10. Regarding Captain Williams, the Engineer Officer of the Expedition, having left the party, the circumstances are fully described in his letters appended hereto, and it will be seen from Captain Sladen's letter of 28th April, that he considered that it would have been almost impossible to have continued the expedition unless by a reduction in the strength of the party. He suggested to the members therefore that, in the interests of the Public Service, some of them should return, and with his approval Captain Williams and Mr. Stewart left the party. Referring to Captain Sladen's remark that he was not in a position to pass an order regarding Captain Williams' stay or departure, I may remark that Captain Williams was distinctly placed under the orders of Captain Sladen, and my instructions to that effect were conveyed to the latter Officer on the organization of the party.

11. It is to be regretted that the Engineer found it necessary to leave, as a professional opinion on the route which may hereafter be taken by the expedition is of the highest importance. In addition to this, one of the principal duties of the Engineer was to make a full enquiry regarding the through routes between China and India, which are believed to exist in the neighbourhood of, and to the northward of, Bhamo. Entering the Panthay Territories with the apparent goodwill of the Government, his enquiries might have been most successfully pushed. I thought it necessary therefore to detail an Engineer Officer to join the Expedition, and I have selected at the recommendation of the Chief Engineer, Mr. Gordon, C.E., Executive Engineer of the Upper Pegu and Arakan roads, an officer of well known active habits and great personal energy. Mr. Gordon was at Prome, and has been directed by telegraph to proceed as rapidly as possible to Bhamo and to follow the track of the expedition. I have addressed the Burmese Government and requested His Majesty to give every facility for Mr. Gordon's advance, and as he will be unhampered with baggage, I do not think that he will find any difficulty in crossing the hills.

12. It will be seen that Captain Sladen states that the reduction of the party was necessary on account of the requisite funds. When the party originally left British Territory, Captain Sladen was furnished with the sum of Rs. 5000, which he specified as being the amount he required, besides presents he had in the shape of goods to about the same amount. I have already informed Government that on hearing that his funds were running short, I sent up the sum of Rs. 10,000 and I am informed by Captain Williams that the money was forwarded under the protection of the Burmese Government when he was at Mandalay.

13. I have learned from the Kalah-won that His Majesty has expressed himself as being much dissatisfied with the conduct of his Officials at Bhamo who have thrown obstructions in the progress of the party, and has directed their removal.

From Captain E. B. SLADEN,—to Colonel ALBERT FYTCHE, Chief Commissioner British Burmah, and Agent to the Viceroy and Governor General of India,—dated Camp Ponsee, Kakhyen Mountains 28th April 1868.

At last there is an opportunity of writing, with the certainty that my letter will reach you. Captain Williams and Mr. Stewart leave tomorrow to return to Rangoon. I have been unexpectedly and unavoidably detained here, for an indefinite length of time: and the funds at my disposal have become so limited that it would have been almost impossible to have continued the expedition, unless by a sensible reduction in the strength of our party and a consequent decrease in the limit of my expenditure. Besides which the South West monsoon has set in in these parts, and surveying or exploration, in the general acceptation of those terms, has become comparatively impracticable.

My plan has been, to lay, in a circular letter, all the facts of the case before the Members of the Expedition, and to leave it to their good judgment to act in accordance with my suggestions in the interests of the public service.

It was of course understood that I had determined to stay out myself, as long as any hope remained of prosecuting the journey and reaching a suitable destination, either at *Momien*, or *Talifoo*. My chances, however, of making further progress or of having it in my power to remain here or elsewhere for a further indefinite period, were almost wholly dependent on a return of some of our party to British Territory, and a corresponding decrease in baggage and expenditure.

Williams and Stewart have been induced, at a great personal sacrifice to sever their connection with the expedition and return to Rangoon. I have arranged that Dr. Anderson shall remain with me; it would hardly have been deemed prudent, I imagine, to proceed alone without efficient medical aid.

Besides, Anderson is most anxious, on his own account, to continue with the expedition; and is very sanguine on the subject of enriching the Museum, and adding materially to scientific research, by visiting the *Terra incognita* which lays before us—almost at our feet. Captain Bowers has elected to stay with me; and will not return without special orders, which I do not feel myself in a position to issue. But you will be eager to know something of events since the date of my last letter. *Ponsee*, from which I date this letter, is only five Marches from *Bhamo*: our detention here since 6th March has arisen from causes the results of which could not be foreseen and over which there was no possibility of exercising control. *Manwyne*, the first Shan town at the foot of these hills, is distant from us only eight miles. My engagement with the Khakyen chiefs and Burmese officials at *Bhamo* was for carriage and safe conduct as far as *Manwyne* : but on the day after my arrival at this place the whole of our mule men detached their burdens from the mule paniers and deserted in a body with their animals. No persuasion short of force could have averted this misfortune. The men alleged, as a reason for the nonfulfilment of their engagement, that orders had been received from the several chiefs of the Shan States to the effect that death would be the penalty inflicted on them, if they persisted in affording our party the means of reaching Shan Territory.

This report, though true to a certain extent, was intensified and exaggerated by the Khakyen chiefs, who had leagued themselves with the Burmese officials for the purpose of obstructing our progress; and who had compromised themselves with the mule men, by misappropriating the greater portion of the advances made on account of mule hire. It was their object to get rid of the mule men at all risks and to detain us here indefinitely, for the purpose of enriching themselves at our expense by a system of a direct obstructiveness and extortion which would enable them to fulfil the wishes and commands of the Burmese officials and of the Chinese oppositionists at *Bhamo*.

A day or two after our arrival at this place a heavy claim was made by the Khakyen chiefs, as compensation on account of a village which was said to have been accidentally destroyed, by a jungle fire caused during one of our marches. The claim was perplexing, and required to be delicately entertained, not by the reason of its amount but because it had evidently been put forward as a feeler, a forerunner of further similar impositions. It had no sooner been satisfactorily adjusted, under the promise and consideration of an immediate supply of carriage wherewith to proceed to *Manwyne*, than the chiefs and people affirmed, with some semblance and evidence of truth, that a large party of Shans and Khakyengalays, numbering many hundreds, had assembled on the route we were to take, with the determination of actively resisting our contemplated advance.

Burmese and Chinese intrigue had prevailed for a time. I ascertained beyond all doubt, that not only had the most damning reports relative to the objects of the mission been openly circulated throughout the parts to which we were journeying, but that the Chinese Robber Chieftain *Lee-sa-ta-hee*, who held a fortified position at a place called *Mauphoo* on our direct route, had received letters from Chinese Brethren at *Bhamo* (under Burmese tuition) in which he was instructed and besought, for his own sake and their's, to oppose our progress by every means in his power, and to cut up our party to a man.

It was this villainous underhand procedure on the part of the Burmese Officials which first induced me, whilst at *Bhamo*, to try and outwit these intriguers, and to counteract error and evil, by what I have styled in a former communication, "a diplomatic venture" with the Panthay Chiefs at *Momein*.

Lee-sa-ta-hee, as long as he remained in power, exercised a direct influence over the Chief Saubwas of the Shan States which lie between this and Momein.

It was in consequence of the fear instilled by his large force of marauders, that the Shan Chiefs had been overawed into the necessity of opposing us, and withholding the necessary permission to enter their respective states. This was a complication which I hardly anticipated on leaving Mandalay, but which the experiences at *Bhamo* had in a measure prepared me for. How was it to be best met? Further lengthened delays became inevitable. I managed to despatch private messengers with suitable presents to the chiefs of *Manwyne*, *Sanda*, and *Manleo* or *Manhleo*, the latter by all accounts the most obstinate and unyielding of our opponents and a man of known influence and position.

My presents were returned in due time; and I was *politely* informed that their acceptance was against all rule until *all* the chiefs had become unanimous in according us their permission to proceed.

Notwithstanding this slight rebuff I continued to write and keep up a communication with the chiefs, in the hope of inspiring a certain amount of friendly confidence and of making all more or less acquainted with the objects of the expedition.

In the meantime my letters from *Bhamo* to the *Momein* Chiefs had reached their destination and were working out a very favorable diversion in our behalf. Satisfactory replies were received by me, a few days after my arrival at this place; and the effect produced on the Shan Saubwas and Khakyen Chiefs, by a knowledge that we were in friendly communication with the Panthay Government, was a wonderful aid in the maintenance of my position, in spite of difficulties created by the unceasing intrigue of Burmese officials.

The "Diplomatic venture" had been productive of results which exceeded my most sanguine expectations. The Momein Chiefs addressed friendly letters to the Shan Saubwas and to certain of the more influential Khakyen Chiefs, and all were exhorted to give us support and assistance, as soon as the time arrived for continuing our march.

I also continued to receive messages and letters of assurance and support from the Panthay Chiefs at Momein, and was informed of their intention to clear the way for my advance by sending a force against the Chinese Robber Chieftain at *Mauphoo*, and capturing his hold at that place. I was also advised to remain where I was, and by no means to despond or to relinquish the idea of prosecuting my march, until I received further advices from *Momein*. The Panthay Government even went so far as to guarantee all expenditure which the chiefs en route might be put to in providing me with carriage and other requisites for the journey.

This very opportune and friendly demonstration on the part of the Panthays gave me confidence and position. The wavering Saubwas became, by magic as it were, decided and well disposed; but active co-operation was withheld, because *Leo-sa-ta-hee* was still in existence, and it seemed doubtful whether the Panthay power would be able, after several previous attempts and failures, to dislodge him from his commanding position at *Mauphoo* and maintain its own supremacy.

It was not until the 19th instant that news reached me of the fall of *Mauphoo*, which took place four days before, of the flight of Leesatahee fled and of his robber bands being broken up and dispersed. *Mauphoo* and the parts around are now in the possession of the Panthay General *Tah-sa-kone*, who has written to inform me of his success, and asked me to advance as far as *Sanda*, to which place he has despatched an armed party to meet and escort me to *Momein*.

I have been trying for a long time past to get on from this to *Manwyne*; but the Chiefs here have *taken so kindly* to us, that they will not supply carriage or provide other means for an advance. My Diary is likely to be amusing and instructive, on this point, to future explorers in these parts.

It must be borne in mind that the delay here has been by no means unprofitable or without its special advantages in some respects, though a serious drawback in itself, on account of the advanced state of the season at which it has occurred.

It has allowed time for chiefs and people in the several states around to find out and judge for themselves by personal observation, and by the simple evidence afforded of our desire to open out the country to Foreign trade and resuscitate old sources of prosperity, whether our Mission would be injurious to their interests, or be likely to be of future benefit to their country.

Our unaffected and unpretending presence on the spot has done more to reassure men's minds than all the diplomacy in the world carried on at a distance. The Veni-Vidi-Vici principle was impracticable with the means at my disposal and in the presence of opposition of a kind which could only be met by straightforward action and a readiness to conciliate, or even to yield, in all matters which could be made to appear in the least degree objectionable to those with whom we were treating. My policy, expressed by words and by letters to the Chiefs who have visited me, has always been to the effect that my presence amongst them was dependent on their friendship; that opposition on their part, after they had been made acquainted with the true objects of the Mission, would cause my departure, and prove detrimental to their interests by leaving unfulfilled and incomplete the good work of reviving the old trade route through their country; and that I would only consent to advance under their protection, and with the firm assurance of their support and good will.

It will be understood that, under any circumstances, my advance beyond Ponsee, or at the furthest *Manwyne*, was effectually barred, so long as *Mauphoo* continued to be held by *Lee-sa-ta-hee* and his bands of Chinese robbers. His defeat did not take place until the 19th instant; and it is satisfactory to know that the means have been at hand of exterminating this villain, and confounding the machinations of Burman and Chinese vagabonds who had arranged and plotted our destruction, by means which have tended to our success and the ruin of their accomplices.

It was the petty intriguing correspondence with *Lee-sa-ta-hee*, which first induced me to address the authorities at Momein, and request counteraction and co-operation.

The chief obstruction in the way of trade by this route has thus been removed, as if by accident, by the active interference of the Mahomedan Government in Yunan.

This friendly co-operation of the Panthays, and the knowledge that they are eager for trade and intercourse with us, are the reasons which have principally influenced me in my determination to combat delays of every kind, in the hope of reaching *Momein*, and entering into friendly relations with the chiefs there. Of course these relations only refer to the means which will be at my disposal of enlightening the chiefs on certain facts connected with our position in British Burma,—our Treaties with the King of Upper Burma, and the probability of conducting a large trade with Rangoon, in spite of Burmese interference and opposition, however offered.

Were it not that I entertain a sanguine hope of effecting this grand object, as well as the still more important idea of tempting the Panthay Government to open out Yunan to Chinese traders from other Southwestern Provinces of China, I would almost decide (whilst taking into consideration the present advanced season of the year,) upon returning to British Territory, or resuming my appointment at Mandalay. But the prize at stake is of too infinite value to be sacrificed to the inconveniences or discomfort of exploring a new country in the face of a South West Monsoon, or the more trifling consideration of remaining on the field of operation for a couple or three months beyond the time originally computed as necessary to complete the whole work of the expedition.

I am in daily expectation of receiving a convoy of mules from the Shan States, which will enable me to leave Ponsee and reach Manwyne, from which place Momein may be reached in five days. If this carriage fails, it is my serious resolve to do away with baggage altogether and trust to the country for supplies of all kinds. By this means I shall reach *Momein*, and push my way to Talifoo, if I can do so safely, and without the fear of getting into difficulties with either Government. I shall also on my return endeavour to try another route over these Khakyen mountains, which I believe to be more feasible in every way than the one we have been committed to under Burman advice.

Nearly all my difficulties thus far owe their origin to the perverse opposition of Burmese officials. So obstinate have they been in their desire to add to my perplexities that they have contrived to put it out of my power to secure the services of a Khakyen interpreter. Numbers of applicants were anxious to accompany me, but all were significantly warned against giving us assistance in this, or in any other respect.

I left *Bhamo* under the understanding that two Head men of Shan villages, who spoke Khakyen, had been ordered to accompany me. Such an order was given in my presence with the sole view of misleading, and was afterwards countermanded without my knowledge as soon as it was known that I was dependent on it for an interpreter and had failed to procure one from other sources.

I have been openly assured on the authority of the Khakyen Chiefs themselves that the private instructions as directly issued to them through the petty officials at *Bhamo*, impressed them with the idea that our progress to the Shan States was to be impeded by active opposition, and, if necessary, the indiscriminate slaughter of all our party. I should be sorry to think that the King was in any way concerned in these base and treacherous designs; I feel sure however that the opposition we have had to contend against has originated and been contenanced at Mandalay, otherwise it would not have been carried out with such obstinate pertinacity, by those who have little real interest in the matter beyond a servile obedience to Royal orders.

We are nearly 4000 feet above the Sea-level and the Thermometer during the month, has ranged between 55° and 80°. The climate is perfection and the soil throughout the several Ranges of these mountains is abundantly fertile, Opium and Tobacco growing in profusion: Tea would be a certain success: all our European fruit trees are found in luxuriance in a wild state, and might be cultivated to any pitch of perfection. Anderson is hard at work in his researches, and his account of these fertile Regions is likely to attract the attention and interest of the speculative world at large.

No news from Mandalay since I left. They will be able to do without me there I hope for another two or three months.

I shall not have another opportunity of writing for some time perhaps, but do not be anxious as we are going amongst friends.

No. 39-36.—From Colonel ALBERT FYTCHE, Chief Commissioner, British Burma and Agent to Viceroy and Governor General, to the Secretary to the Government of India, Foreign Department, dated Rangoon, July 4th 1868.

I have the honor to forward a demi-official letter from Captain Sladen dated "Ponsee Khakyen Mountains 10th May 1868." It will be remembered that in his last communication (dated 28th April and forwarded with my letter No. 39-19 dated 2nd June ultimo) Captain Sladen was in anticipation of a Deputation visiting him for the purpose of escorting him to Momein. This Deputation has now, it will be seen from his present letter, reached him, and his communications with them seem to have been of the most satisfactory nature.

2. In suggesting the Expedition, I had the honor to point out to the Government of India, that I looked to the presence of a British Mission as likely to bring about some adjustment of the contending interests of the several Authorities on the route from Bhamo to Yunan; and this was based on the presumption, that an energetic and enterprizing people like the Shans, would gladly welcome a resuscitation of trade, and that the Panthays would also willingly join in a movement calculated to bring them into friendly relations with the Governing Authorities to the westward, where probably they would find the safest and shortest outlet for their produce.

3. Captain Sladen in his present letter looks to the most favorable realization of these anticipations. He describes the Shan Deputies as characterized by much intelligence, and states that they are fully alive to the importance of the success of our Expedition,—indeed they seem prepared and anxious to come to definite arrangements regarding the future.

4. All this is very encouraging as an introduction to the further and more important reception of the Expedition by the Panthay authorities. Captain Sladen looks confidently to an easy progress to Talifoo, and should this be accomplished, it may fairly be anticipated that the most valuable information will be gained of a large tract of country hitherto almost unknown, and of the political status of powers whose condition of late has undergone numerous changes.

5. Captain Sladen continues to show much tact and judgment in his conduct of the Expedition. From the tenor of his letter it is likely that the Shan and Panthay Authorities are prepared to accede to the Mission a political importance which was not contemplated in its despatch, but I have full confidence in Captain Sladen's discretion, in the somewhat novel and delicate position which may be accorded him.

From Captain E. B. SLADEN, to Colonel ALBERT FYTCHE, Chief Commissioner British Burma, and Agent to the Viceroy and Governor-General of India, dated Camp Ponsee, Khakyen Hills, 10th May 1868.

It is satisfactory, to be able to write again, so soon after my last, and to give a propitious account of our expeditiona-affairs. Within the last few days Deputies of a high order have reached me from each of the Chief Saubwas of the Shan States—all the principal cities are represented; and the object of the Deputation is to make known to me, officially, that the Chiefs of the Shan States have *combined* to award us a favourable reception, and to conduct the expedition to Momein in a friendly and becoming style.

Each of the states has contributed a quota of the necessary carriage; and thereby afforded testimony to an unanimity of feelings and interests, which have influenced the whole of them, in regarding the true objects of our mission to their country.

It is not flattering to our intelligence to find, that hitherto all have been blinded into the belief, that a sudden inroad, or a flying visit into the Shan States by our party was either politic or practicable, so long as one dissentient voice even could make itself heard in condemnation in the Councils of the collected Shan Chiefs. I am inclined now to laugh over my Diaries for the last two months, in which I have noted down the several futile and abortive attempts to procure carriage, wherewith to reach Manwyne.

The true cause of failure did not rest solely with the Khakyens, but can now be traced to indirect opposition on the part of certain Shan Chiefs, actuated no doubt by evil report and Burmese secret influences. They have at length succumbed to reason and truth, and there is no longer room for doubt, that the delay of the expedition at Ponsee has interfered providentially in its interests by preventing collision with any dissentient chiefs who might have chosen to place themselves in opposition to our advance. Had even the means of transport been available, no alternative remained, whilst estimating the position of affairs at *Manphoo*, as well as secret opposing interests in the Shan States, save that of awaiting Panthay successes at the one place, and trusting, as regarded the other, to the means in my power of bringing about a gradual inclination on the part of the Shan Saubwas to be unanimous in furthering our progress through their respective Territories.

The Deputies, now with me, are fine looking fellows who seem to us, after long contact and association with Khakyens, to have attained a higher state of intelligence and civilization than the general run of Shans, or even of Chinese gentlemen.

My conversations with them have been very interesting. They knew (by instinct I suppose) that I belonged to a large and powerful nation, but were in profound ignorance of British influence in Burma, or of our Treaty alliances with the golden foot.

They complain bitterly of the devastation and pillage to which their cities have been subjected of late years by the civil war in Yunan; and confess to a sense of the benefit of which this Expedition has already been productive in having caused the discomfiture and expulsion from *Mauphoo* of the Chinese Robber Chieftain Lee-sa-ta-hee and his hordes of marauding pillagers. They are quite aware that this Lee-sa-ta-hee has been driven out of the field, in consequence of communications which passed between myself and the Panthay Government at Momein. They express a hope that I will not leave the country until final arrangements are made for securing a perfect trade route between British Burma and South West China, with definite terms and conditions affecting the hire of carriage and the levying of customs or transit Duties. The Shan States alone, they say, are capable of producing 100,000 mules annually, for the purposes of carriage. I explained our Treaties with Burma, which provide for the transit of goods to and from China through Burmese Territory, as well as for the appointment of a British official at the frontier Custom House Station in Burma, to supervize and regulate the collection of Custom's Duty. Both provisions give confidence and satisfaction, but with reference to the length of my present stay in the Shan States I am obliged to inform the Deputies that my mission, *this year*, is one of exploration, and that it has been undertaken with the object of ascertaining with precision whether the Chiefs of the countries through which I pass, will agree to enter into friendly commercial relations, and guarantee protection and support to Traders and travellers of every degree from British and Burmese Territory. It is understood, nevertheless, that if the expedition is successful, and I am able to take away with me a guarantee of good faith and the expression of a hearty desire on the part of the several Chiefs to further trade and commercial intercourse between the two countries, it will be my duty to lay the whole subject before the British Government, and return with power to enter into any final compact or stipulation, which either or both parties may deem to be prudent or essential.

I am giving a mere outline of my conversation with these Shan Deputies. The Chiefs themselves have still to be met and consulted. But it is only fair and reasonable, in estimating the high position which the Deputies hold and the authority with which they seem to be invested, to put a favourable construction on the promises of future good which may be inferred or implied in their conversation and and expressed opinion.

We leave this to-morrow morning; and it is said that the chief Saubwa of Sanda, will meet us at a place called *Mungun*, with a large retinue of officers from Manwyne and the states generally. I hope to be at Momein in a week, and unless final and satisfactory arrangements can be immediately entered into there, it is my intention, if all is favorable, to push on to Tali, and obtain orders for a congress of chiefs at Momein, (to assemble on my return there from the capital) and discuss the preliminaries of a commercial alliance. Without being too sanguine, I think I may now predict a more favorable termination to the labors of the expedition than the wildest advocates of the scheme ever dreamed of, when the expedition was first organized.

The Bhamo route will, for some years to come, be made the high commercial road to Western China, in spite of Burma and Burmese officials who *must* succumb and withdraw all petty indirect opposition, when pressure is brought to bear from both sides (the Panthays forming one motive power), and the Resident at Mandalay is in a position to make his voice heard in the councils and administration of the country.

The rains which have set in in these parts have moderated, and will not barr our return, as the Khakyen Hills are traversible during the monsoons: and a few duckings will do us no harm.

Our stay in Khakyen-land is an event of importance in itself. It has enabled me to observe and estimate the people in their true native character. They too have taken a proper estimate of us; and I am looked up to as a Kingly benefactor. The Saubwa declared to-day that we had been the means of enriching his people, that all looked upon our departure with regret, and that we had left none but friends behind us in our track through his country.

Our little differences have tended to cement a friendship, which is not the less respected since it has become so palpable that we are favored by the Panthays (who rule the Shan States) and have been visited and treated as men in authority by the chiefs of those states. I only wish the Physique and personal appearance of my Police escort could be improved, and that the funds which I have in hand were more in accordance, as regards amount, with what will be required to sustain the position I hold, or find it necessary to assume.

The presents too are very paltry—Jones & Co.'s 40 Rupee guns are not likely to take with the haughty Panthay chief, Tah-sa-kone who was lavish in his presents, even to the Khakyen messengers whom I first despatched to him with letters. He dressed them up, in embroidered jackets slashed with velvet, and gave them gold embroidered caps and shoes, which converted them, to all appearance at least, into Chinese Mandarins of no mean order.

Of course I shall be able to excuse the absence of valuable presents on the plea that the expedition started in uncertainty and without any sure knowledge of the country it was going to or the kind of reception we might meet with at the hands of a new people and new rulers. It will be necessary moreover on this point to make reference to my possible return next season with a suitable embassy, and presents proportioned to the occasion, and to the power and friendly attitude of the chiefs and rulers to whom the embassy would be deputed.

At present I can learn nothing of a definite character regarding the internal state of Yunan and the Political relations in which the Panthay and Chinese Governments stand towards each other. Report on this subject must be deferred until I reach Momein.

The trip to Talifoo, if undertaken, will be directed towards a careful enquiry into the political state of Yunan; with a view to devising some means of effecting a limited adjustment even between the Panthay and Chinese Governments, by which the trade of Sechuen, or other S. W. Provinces of China, might be allowed to pass through Panthay possessions in Yunan without regard to the various political differences or considerations which affect the rival Governments in those parts.

P. S.—As I have not written officially it will be as well I think to treat this and my last as demi official.

Proceeding No. 39-61.—From Colonel ALBERT FYTCHE, Chief Commissioner British Burma, and Agent to His Excellency the Viceroy and Governor-General, to THE SECRETARY TO THE GOVERNMENT INDIA, Foreign Department, dated Rangoon, July 30th, 1868.

I have the honor to forward a copy of a letter dated 26th April addressed to the *North-China Daily News* by Mr. T. T. Cooper, who is endeavoring to traverse the through route from China viâ Thibet to India. This letter has been kindly forwarded to me by H. B. M. Consul at Shanghai under date the 16th June.

2. It will be seen that Mr. Cooper writes from a place named Tai-Tsiau-loo on the extreme Western Frontier of China, bordering on Thibet. He contemplates, should he fail in being able to pursue that route, to try and make his way to Tali and so to Bhamo and Mandalay.

3. From his present letter however it appears that he has met traders on the Yangsè-Kiang river who had been to Tali, and who intended returning, so that there would seem to be a traffic route still open between Western China proper and that portion of Yunan under the new Mahomedan Ruler, who has placed Custom Houses on his Eastern Frontier.

4. The information Mr. Cooper has obtained in these Western Chinese Provinces corroborates the importance I

have attached to the resuscitation of the trade by the Bhamo route. He states, "so sure as the Bhamo and Tali "Route is opened so sure will Burma take to herself the "trade of the Provinces of Yunan and Kwei-chow."

---o---

Mr. T. T. COOPER'S EXPEDITION.

The following letter from Mr. T. T. Cooper will doubtless prove of interest to our readers.

TAI-TSIAN-LOO,
Western Borders of China.
26th April, 1868.

TO THE EDITOR OF THE "NORTH-CHINA DAILY NEWS."

DEAR SIR,—Since writing you from the Village of Hi-yan-su, a troublesome and dangerous journey of 7 days brought us on the 9th instant, in company with the good Bishop of Tibet, Monsgr. Cheauvan, to this place. Our road for the first four days lay through a country similar to that about Hi-yan-su. On the morning of the fifth we arrived at Loo-din chow, a small town on the left bank of the Tai-tow-ho, a branch of the river Min at Kia-tung-foo, and navigable for small junks only 80 miles West of that place. This city is famous in China for its chain suspension bridge some 150 yards in span, built about 80 years ago. Crossing the river at this point we continued along its right bank, North for two days, the road winding along frightful precipices sometimes 500 feet above the river, the wall-like sides of the mountains forming gorges of terrible grandeur. At noon on our sixth day leaving the Tai-tow-ho, we entered what is called the Tai-tsian-loo gorge or Valley. This place, so I am told, is the most dangerous part of the grand route from Chen-tu to Lassa; to form an idea of it you must picture to yourself two mountains from 1,000 to 1,200 feet high, running parallel to each other, their sides perpendicular, and in many places, overhanging the mountain torrent rushing in white anger at the base, their summits capped with snow and a cloud of white mist throwing into this terrible gorge the gloom of twilight. The torrent (scarcely 30 yards wide,) as it leaps on its head-long course to the Tai-tow-ho, washes in many places, the narrow path running along its right bank with spray from numerous water falls, while huge boulders forced from their resting places high over head by the fierce hurricane which seems ever to sweep the bleak summits of these mountains, fill the gorge with the noise of a hundred thunders as they crash into the angry stream below—such is the Tai-tsian-loo gorge, at the head of which, 38 miles west of the Tai-tow-ho, lies this border town of Tai-tsian-loo.

The town Tai-tsian-loo divides the province of Sze-Chuen from the Mandzu country, which extends to Kyan-kha, (being so called in contra-distinction to Tibet proper, which commences only at Kyan-Kha, the tribes inhabiting this country generally speaking Tibetian, wearing the same costume, and believing in the same religion, and are subject to Tibet) and is of great importance as an exchange trading mart. Thither come Shan-si merchants with Tea, Glassbeads, and Tobacco, which they exchange with the Mandzus for Hartshorn, Gold, Musk (from Musk Deer) and Lynx, Fox, Wolf, and Leopard skins, and a variety of a commoner sort, such as Sheep, Deer and Yak, this is the principal trade of the place. It is also of importance as a Chinese Military Station containing nearly 1,000 soldiers.

As my next step onward will take me out of China into a country, the trade of which can never be of great importance to my commercial friends in Shanghai, I will take leave of them with a few words relative to foreign trade with Western China. Many merchants in Shanghai told me that the exploration of the Upper Yang-tze and Western China was of no importance to their trade and sceptically asked me to prove to the contrary. I could then only point to the enormous wealth of Sze-chuen, its gigantic trade with Hankow in Rhubarb, hemp, native Medicines, Sugar and Tobacco as Exports, and Cotton and piece Goods as Imports, all this was nothing new to them, and they looked upon my expedition as likely to result only in good Pheasant or Snipe shooting for myself. Even with the report of a meeting of the Royal Geographical Society extracted in your columns from the *Times* of the 6th June 1867, before them, and reading therein the importance which Sir A. Phayre attaches to the Burmah Trade with Yunan, they remained unconvinced. Many, however, warmly upheld my undertaking, and to these gentlemen I address the following remarks.

Chung-king the trade gorge of four Provinces, Sz-chuen, Yunnan, Kwei-choo, and Chen-si, depends upon Hankow for the supply of Foreign piece Goods which it annually sends into these four Provinces. The present Junk transport on the Yang-tze between these two places, besides being extremely disastrous to trade on account of the total loss of many Junks and their cargoes, is very expensive, and this added to the Mandarins' squeezes renders the price of foreign piece Goods after leaving Chentu so heavy, that they are unsaleable beyond the Yang-ling range of the Mountains near Chin-Chi-Chien, and this is the limit of Foreign trade with Western China, numerous small rivers forming the arteries through which trade flows from Chung-king into Kwei-chow, Eastern Yunnan and southern Chen-si. The present trade between Chung-king and Yunnan and Kwei-chow, is only temporary on account of the closure of the Bhamo and Tarli Route and as sure as this route is opened, so sure will Burmah take to herself the trade of these two provinces and if, as is probable, British merchants establish at Ava, then a rivalship for the trade of Western Sz-chuen between China and Burmah merchants seems almost certain, the result telling probably in favor of the latter, both in Export and Import. Trade by this route has flourished before without European enterprise and as soon as it is re-opened, the trade between Hankow and Chung-king will be lessened by one third. The Mahomedan Chief at Tarli has already established Custom houses on the Eastern border of his territory, and at Hi Yan-sú I met several merchants who had come from Tarli and intended to return there to trade in spite of their having to pay Imperial and Mahomedan duty. Perhaps these facts are important for the Shanghai Trade, if so then the China merchants have but one object to gain, to rival with equality the Burmah merchants and that is the opening of the upper Yangtzse, to Chung-king. The Chinese authorities might be glad to checkmate the Mahomedan chief by this means. If the King of Burmah abdicates in favor of British rule, that will place all India alongside of Western China and no official mis-management will cramp the energies and resources of the British merchant in Burmah. For steamers properly constructed and drawing not more than 6 feet of water, the navigation of the Yang-tze to Chung-king is possible. At the lowest winter level (Jan.1868) known for some years, there were 7 feet of water at the lowest rapids.

As to the route between Sudya and Likiang, this in Shanghai seemed to me practically useful for the Calcutta trade with China, but I am constrained to admit now, the fallacy of such a hope, and this admission is based upon the following remarks of Monsgr. Cheauvean, who resided for many years in the neighbourhood of Tar-li and Likiang. He tells me, "Likiang is a name only, the place whereof is marked by a few small houses near the foot of the Snowy mountains, which are impassable on account of perpetual snow and want of passes, while the Lao-tsan and Now-kiang rivers are fierce, unnavigable and unbridged; the country through which they flow being inhabited by savage tribes constantly at war with each other, and beyond this in Bing there is another obstacle in the Pat-koi range. Admitting for the sake of argument, that a practicable route could be found, the goods which Calcutta would send to China, Burma would send at a less cost. No! India has a brighter prospect in store for her trade with Tibet, and this must flow either through Nepaul to Lassa or Sudya to Bathang, the latter route however having to pass the Himalayas and a dreadfully hilly country to within a short distance of Bathang. At Lassa there are already over 3,000 Nepaulese trading in European goods, while to deal in the figurative the rivers of Bathing run with gold.

For the information of my sporting friends in Shanghai I may tell them that so far my bag consists of one wild goose shot near Hankow, my Journey to this place having been through a country destitute of sport.

Up to this time I have cherished the hope of being able to reach Sudya from Bathang, but important considerations force me to abandon the idea. Without instruments and funds I cannot and dare not penetrate the unknown country between these two places. With help of providence I will reach Lassa, where disposing of my mules and ponies I will foot it to Khatmandoo, hoping at some future time to accompany a proper expedition through this country.

Nothing can exceed the kindness of the Catholic Missionaries in China, especially Monsgr. Desflech, Bishop of Chung-king, and Monsgr. Cheauvean. To the latter I shall ever owe a deep debt of gratitude, while to the united help of the French and Italian Catholic Missionaries generally I am indebted for the pleasure of being at this moment on the Western Borders of China.

Personally, with the exception of a slight cold and profuse sweatings at night, I have nothing to complain of, or rather feel that it is no use complaining: otherwise I might fill pages with grumbling at martyrdom from vermin, bad housing, the pardonable tyranny of my Chinese Interpreter, and wretched food. With regard to the latter, the ghost of departed dinners *a la Russe* with old dry sherry and champagne trouble me no more, but occasionally in moments of thirst dim visions of Allsopp's best India Pale rise up before me, which are instantly dispelled by resort to the Celestial drink—Tea.

For the information of future travellers I should mention that beyond this place as far as Lassa, money is at a great discount, 2 or 3 needles and a little thread or a piece of red Chinese cloth often procuring what money cannot. Rupees pass for 32 tael cents, but the Mandzu people do not particularly care for them, and sycee is used at a great loss. I have laid in a stock of needles, thread, cloth and a kind of Turquoise stone much prized by Mandzus and brought hither from Shansi. These stones about the size of French beans, I purchased at $2\frac{1}{2}$ Taels per hundred. The idea of becoming a needle and thread hawker is novel and amusing.

I leave this on Wednesday the 29th inst., having been detained more than 20 days to procure mules, ponies and an interpreter. If I am stopped at Tsamdo by the Tibetans, I shall return to this place and make for Ava *via* Tarli and Bhamo, but I hope this is the last you will hear of me until I reach Nepaul.

Trusting that this will reach you in safety.

I am, Yours very truly,

T. T. COOPER.

No. 39-77.—From Colonel ALBERT FYTCHE, Chief Commissioner British Burma, to W. S SETON KARR, Esq. Secretary to the Government of India, Foreign Department, dated Rangoon, September 19th, 1868.

I have the honor to forward a copy of a demi-official letter received by me from Captain Sladen, dated Bhamo the 5th September, announcing the safe return of his party to that town, and giving many interesting details of his visit to Momein, the seat of an important Officer of the Panthay Government.

2. It will be unnecessary to remark at length on all that is described by Captain Sladen in this letter, as his Official Report will shortly be received, and the whole question of the trade route by Bhamo will require to be fully discussed—but I think I may even here notice one or two points of interest connected with the progress and results of the expedition. I am of opinion Captain Sladen was right in deciding not to go beyond Momein under the circumstances which he explains. The original purpose for which the expedition was started, was to discover the position held by the Kakhyens, Shans, and Panthays, and their disposition, or otherwise, to resuscitate the extinct trade which formerly existed through their Territories. This purpose has been fully carried out. It would doubtless have been interesting from some points of view had the party succeeded in reaching Talifoo, the Head Quarters of the Panthay Government, but it certainly appears that the Panthay Authorities whom Captain Sladen met at Momein, were of sufficient importance and position to render their views and opinions a safe criterion of the feeling of the Panthay Government in the matter. It is evident that on their part a strong desire exists for the resuscitation of the trade. The long residence of the party among the Kakhyens and in the Shan States has been productive of the best results. Apart from some local jealousies—caused by a wish to secure for themselves the advantages of having the route through their individual territories—it would seem that the Shan Chiefs are fully alive to the gain to them of the renewal of trade; while the Kakhyens seem to have realized the peaceable character of the Mission, and the profitable future they may secure, if the route be re-established. Even the physical difficulties of the route are

by no means great, and they can be materially modified whenever it may be considered advisable to do so, by local labor which is only too anxious to be employed.

3. The previous history of this line of commerce proves beyond doubt that there exists an important field for trade in these localities; and the knowledge acquired by the present Mission assures us that the parties most interested in this commerce are eager for its re-establishment. It remains solely with Government to decide whether or not it shall be re-established. If a determination be arrived at that there is here a scheme worthy of being carefully and persistently carried out, the result admits of no doubt. I feel certain that there depends on the decision of Government a question of the very highest Imperial importance. Our Seaborne trade with China is being actively competed for by America. It seems inevitable that sooner or later it will be diverted to the Pacific Coast of that Continent, and that New York will reap the "Exchange" on the commerce with China, which is now shared between India and England. Not content with the Pacific Railroad, which is being pushed on with unexampled energy, I observe that the American Goverment has officially recommended to the European States, the great enterprize of a ship canal to be constructed across the Isthmus of Darien.

4. I mention these considerations because I would not have the Government suppose that, in strongly advocating the continuance of our efforts to open this trade with Western China, I am solely influenced by a wish to advance the interests of this Province. The gain to British Burma in being a new highway to China would, doubtless, be very great, but it would be entirely subsidiary to the still greater gain of the Empire, in having that highway established. Time becomes an important element in a question like this, and if Government is to act with effect, it should doubtless act at once. I conceive that the good effects of the visit of Captain Sladen and his party should be promptly and vigorously followed up. I strongly support his recommendation that an officer be placed at Bhamo as soon as possible. He would be there to keep up the reality of our intentions, and to maintain communication with the Shan Chiefs, and the Panthay Government; and he would also

continue to influence the Kakhyens towards giving facilities for safe transit of goods. The intention of placing a British Official at Bhamo, has been kept in in view in all our treaties and communications with the Burmese Court, and it appears to me that the time has come for carrying it into effect. I should be glad to receive the views of Government on this subject. The officer would have to be carefully selected, and his proposed appointment to Bhamo communicated to the Burmese Government as soon as possible.

5. Captain Sladen mentions the fact of two Panthay officers having been shot, while escorting him to Momein, and suggests that a sum of money be presented to their families on the part of Government. I would recommend that I be authorized to give five hundred rupees to the relations of each of the officers, or one thousand rupees in all.

6. I propose to await the official report of the whole course of the Expedition before reviewing the various incidents which require notice; but as the specific work of the Mission is virtually ended, I take this opportunity of meanwhile recording my opinion, that the successful termination of the Expedition reflects very great credit on the energy and good judgment of Captain Sladen. He seems to me to have acted throughout with sound discretion: and he has shown much discrimination and tact in his intercourse with the various authorities with whom he has had to deal.

From Captain E. B. SLADEN,—to Colonel ALBERT FYTCHE, Chief Commissioner British Burmah, and Agent to the Viceroy and Governor General of India,—dated Bhamo, 5th September 1868.

You will be glad to hear of our return in triumph to Bhamo. All has been successful thus far; though some little disappointment will probably be felt at the fact of my having found it impracticable to extend our exploration beyond *Momein*.

Anxious and *eager* as we all were to push on to Tali, several weighty considerations combined to make a further advance into *Yunan* a matter which must have led to inevitable complication; in addition to the *certainty* of conflict with large bands of Chinese Dacoits, against whom the Governor of *Momein* confessed that with all the assistance he could give us, even to to the extent of providing an escort, it was out of his power to guarantee protection, or *ensure* us against hostile attack. The road was effectually closed in two places, between *Momein* and *Yunchan;* and a strong body of Chinese had taken up a position in the vicinity of *Sheedin*, an important town where the grand caravan route from Southern Yunan and *Mandalay*, viâ *Theebo* and *Thiennee* joins the highway between *Yunchan* and *Tali.* At the time we reached *Momein* a Panthay Force was actively engaged in an endeavour to open up the country in the direction of *Yunchan*. Large bands of Chinese Dacoits occupied positions in the vicinity of the direct route to Yunchan, and their leaders assumed to hold commissions as officers under the immediate orders of the Chinese Government. During our stay too at *Momein* an additional Force of 2,000 men was sent out to assist in the subjugation of various portions of the country in the immediate neighbourhood, which were still a prey to Chinese influences, and opposed therefore to Panthay interests and the tranquilization of *Yunan*.

The Governor of *Momein*, (a man who deservedly gained our respect and esteem, by several friendly acts which afforded proof of a sincere desire on his part to promote our interests personally, and to further the general objects of the expedition) strongly advised me not to advance in the direction of *Yunchan*. In giving this advice, he was not actuated by Political considerations, or a wish to preserve *Yunan* in jealous exclusiveness. He naturally enough anticipated evil results if I continued my journey at a time when the route to be taken was unfortunately more than usually impracticable. He asked me to await events and to allow time for communication with *Tali*, on the subject of our further advance through *Yunan*. If determined to proceed in opposition to his advice, he felt bound to provide me with a military escort: and it would be a matter of comparatively trifling concern to himself, he said, to hear that the escort had been engaged and suffered reverses; but if one of my own particular party fell in conflict with the Chinese, it appeared to him that complications might arise which would lead to further troubles and injure the hope we entertained of restoring tranquility and re-opening trade between Burma and the South Western provinces of China.

But in coming to a decision regarding the practicability or consequences of an advance with my party beyond *Momein*, it was necessary to bear in mind that evidence was not wanting which would lead to a well grounded supposition that some of the so called Chinese Bands with whom we must have come into conflict whilst under Panthay escort and protection, were indirectly connected with the Chinese imperial army; and that their leaders were supported and encouraged at Chinese Head Quarters in *Yunan* (city) to harrass and disturb Panthay possessions within the Province by every possible species of cruel and vicious hostility. To have held communication of any sort with members of the Chinese Government, whilst under Panthay protection, would not only have been in itself a matter of extreme difficulty but must have exposed the Expedition to an amount of suspicious distrust which would have interfered injuriously to ruin the fair prospect of making the Panthays true friends.

These and other cogent reasons will appear bye and bye, to shew that I should have been guilty of great disregard to the wishes of Government and to your own, had I exceeded my instructions in advancing beyond *Momein; especially so, after arriving at a belief that the several objects which the Expedition had in view could be as completely realized at Momein as at Tali.*

My inability however to make progress beyond *Momein*, without incurring a risk which would have compromised all the good which the Expedition was intended to bring about, is more than compensated for by the knowledge that in all other respects a fuller amount of success has attended our efforts for good than could ever have been reasonably expected when the idea was first formed of penetrating Western China by an Expedition which was to take its start from British Burma. But this is mere preface. I must take up the story of our progress from the date of my last communication dated at Ponsee, 11th May 1868. We left that place on the 12th May and reached *Momein* on the 26th of the same month. The advance through the Shan States was, in effect, an ovation. The population generally speaking of towns and villages, turned out in crowds, and on several occasions greeted us with unmistakeable signs of welcome as we passed through their several districts. It was necessary to remain a few days at each of the larger towns of *Manwyne*, *Sanda*, *Mynela*, and *Myne-tee;* and this detention will account for our not having reached *Momein* until the 26th May. The interval was well spent in friendly intercourse with the Saubwas and people; and in giving them a true insight into the objects and purposes of the Expedition. Of all the Shan chiefs the Saubwas of Sanda and Hotha particularly have been conspicuous for the friendly welcome awarded, and the marked hospitality with which they have entertained my whole party during the time passed in their respective states. On both occasions of our visit to Sanda, going and returning, the old Saubwa himself attended at our departure, and caused salutes of guns to be fired and his own trumpeters blowing *long* brass Horns to proceed in advance of our party through the town to its extreme limits; an honor which is only paid to the highest authority in the country. He further asked me to adopt a boy of 8 years of age, his Grandson and heir to the Saubwaship, whom, he begged, I would in future look upon as my own son. A Panthay military escort met me at Mynela, and escorted us from thence across the *Mauphoo* Range (always a dangerous locality) to *Nantin* or *Myne-tee*, where a still larger body of men arrived in time to conduct the Expedition into *Momein*. At Momein the Governor himself came out in right regal style to meet me half a mile from the city, and gave the Expedition a ceremonial reception, the interest and magnificence of which will not soon be forgotten by any of us. But I must reserve details for a further report. I have already said that our advance through the Shan States wore the semblance of an ovation. On one occasion however, whilst in the Sanda district, we experienced an imbecile attempt at opposition, made by a small party of Dacoits who fired three shots at us from the *Mynela* side of the *Tahpen* river, at the respectable or respectful distance of between 300 and 400 yards. I took no notice of them and they found it prudent to keep the river between themselves and my party. The defaulters in this instance are well known and their cause of grievance, in addition to the inducement held out of improving their worldly means at our expense, is described to have been brought about by offence taken at my refusal to proceed from Manwyne to Sanda by a route which led through their particular district.

The Mynela and Sanda Deputies, who met us at Ponsee, almost quarrelled over a question raised as to which particular route the Expedition was to honor, in its passage through their respective states.

Again, on the march from Nantin to Momein, the Panthay escort which went in advance, in charge of our baggage, was fired into by Dacoits, and the two leading men, both unfortunately officers of rank, were shot dead. The Dacoits looted two mules and a portion of their loads before the escort had time to engage and put them to flight. I and the rest of my party were at the time some three miles from the scene of action. So little idea was there of opposition or attack, that we had stayed to explore and examine some remarkable Hot Springs which are met with on the route between Nantin and Momein, and in which we were, very innocently and unconsciously, disporting our naked bodies at the time of the cowardly attack on the Panthay advance guard. The death of the two Panthay officers was of course a matter of much concern to us all; but especially so to the Governor of Momein, as both were men of note and had done good service in their time. They have left families, and having died, it may be almost said in *our* service, I am going to ask you to solicit Government to recompense each family by a donation of 500 or 1,000 rupees. The maxim " Bis dat, qui cito dat," will be appreciated in this instance and I hope no great length of time will be allowed to elapse before the recompence is made. The facts of this Dacoity have been greatly exaggerated; and I am only afraid that rumour will have converted them into a report of our utter ruin and discomfiture, before any true statement of events can possibly have reached *Bhamo* or *Mandalay*.

Nothing can have exceeded the friendly hospitality with which the Governor almost overwhelmed us, during the whole period of our stay at *Momein*. I was treated in all material respects with the honour due to a Mission from a

Foreign power. It would have been a vain attempt at hypocrisy to have ignored my political existence, or the political nature of the work I was engaged in.

A spacious temple with every accommodation had been prepared for us, outside the city, in close communication with the Governor's Residence; and rations, including necessaries of all kinds, were daily supplied in abundance to the whole party.

My first visit to the Governor was purely ceremonial, and we were received at Government House with salutes both on arrival and departure. The visit was returned in full state by the Governor and his suite, but after these first preliminaries had been got over, we came to a mutual understanding that our visits (which were frequent) should be made in simple friendly form; and ceremony was altogether dropped. The Governor occasionally asked us to dinner, and enlivened our stay with Chinese plays and other entertainments. But by far the most satisfactory portion of my several interviews had reference to the subject of the British Mission to *Yunan*, and to explained and received opinions, affecting the main objects for which the Mission had been undertaken. The work was comparatively an easy one, for I found the Governor and all his officials as eager and earnest as ourselves in their desire for trade and for friendly commercial relations with Foreign Governments. Perhaps the most delicate and difficult task I had to get through was that which related to our relations with the Court of Pekin. I never tried to disguise the fact that the British and Chinese Governments were on friendly terms, and were bound by Treaty stipulations in their intercourse with each other. I even went so far as to intimate that the friendly state of our relations with the Court of Pekin might be utilized to the extent of bringing about a reconciliation of contending interests in *Yunan*, provided I could assure myself, during my stay in the Province, that the Government at Tali and the Chinese Head Quarter Government, (wherever it might be in *Yunan*) could be made to agree as to the terms of a mediation. The excuse I made for bringing forward this proposition, was that present disturbances in Yunan affected the prosperity of British possessions in Burma; and our

Government would not be slow at the present time, in the interests of trade, to exert itself in any legitimate manner or direction which might be deemed advantageous to the several states or countries most concerned. My meaning was understood, and received with a sincere expression of friendly good feeling. The Governor promised to communicate with *Tali* on the express subject of my proposition, and to give me a distinct reply before my departure. But the subject was necessarily dropped in consequence of important events which were then being enacted in *Yunan*. Before we left Momein official intelligence had arrived of renewed hostilities between the *Chinese* and *Panthay* Governments which had resulted in the capture of *Yunan* (city) by the latter and the occupation of what may be called the whole of *Yunan* Province by the Panthay Government. I have a copy of the Government proclamation, a document several feet in length, which was posted up at *Momein*, as an official public announcement of Panthay successes in *Yunan* including the capture and possession of its chief city.

But it is time to return to our doings at *Momein*, where I remained for a month and a half in almost daily communication with the Governor and other Provincial Officers.

Tah-sâ-köne, a designation by which the Governor is officially known, is a tall handsome man generous and liberal minded to a degree. He has risen to power and command by the force of natural ability, added to a wonderful capacity for military adventure. It may literally and truly be said of him that he is riddled and scarred all over with a variety of wounds received in action. But to be brief, I may as well record at once the general results of my conferences at Momein: and I preface them by the remark that the *results* themselves could not in my opinion and belief have been more complete, with the limited powers I held, even though the conferences had been held at Tali itself. Tah-sâ-köne, the Governor of Momein, is generally spoken of as second only in the Government to the King of Tali: and his power to act *throughout Momein Province*, including the Shan States dependent on the Panthay Government, is absolute in all matters in which the expedition was interested either in discussing or bringing to a definite issue.

Results:—1. The Government at Tali has fully approved of the proposal to revive overland trade between Burma and South Western China viâ *Bhamo*. It has expressed a sincere wish to co-operate with and assist our efforts to accomplish so desirable an object: at *Momein* itself the resuscitation of this trade is already declared to be a certainty.

2. The Panthay Government has *volunteered* to send a Mission at the end of the present year from *Tali* and *Momein* to *Rangoon* with presents in return for those presented by me at *Momein*. The principal object of the Mission will be to institute a general enquiry into the feasibility of direct trade with *Rangoon* merchants, by the interchange of commodities at *Bhamo*, or other commercial mart. The mission will also be required to obtain information on all points connected with trade, and with the facilities, means, and cost of transit of goods, including duties, between *Bhamo* and *Rangoon*, and vice versâ.

3. The Government at *Tali* has given its consent to a proposition made by me to the Governor of *Momein*, to the effect that the mule caravans from *Yunan* for the ensuing season shall proceed direct to *Bhamo* instead of to Mandalay—provided it is assured in time, that *Yunan* produce can be disposed of at the former place, and that return produce will be available as desired.

(I could not myself undertake to give *assurances* on these points; because I recognized the difficulty, as regarded time, of supplying Raw Cotton *(at Bhamo,)* the article in principal demand by the *Yunan* caravans.

4. The Governor of Momein has given me a letter to be presented to the Chief Commissioner in which my arrival in Yunan is spoken of in congratulatory terms. He further congratulates himself for the part taken by him in having fought and cleared the way for us at *Mauphoo*, as well as in having provided the means of transit and protection through the Shan States. Reasons are assigned in the letter to account for my not having been conducted beyond *Momein*; and assurances are given that, a beginning having now been made in resuscitating overland trade between Burma and S. W. China, the Governor of

Momein is prepared to further our commercial enterprise by all means in his power which are likely to conduce to success.

5. The Governor has further given me a writing under seal, which relates to the collection of Transit duties on goods to and from *Momein*.

This document is of no practical importance, as it does not settle definitely the amount of duty to be taken in the Shan States, or at *Momein* itself. On the point of duties generally, the Governor convinced me that it would be premature at present to lay down definite rules. Having secured our friendship, he said, and considering *my* relationship to himself to be that of a Brother (I believe I am styled so in the official correspondence) he promises to be faithfully guided by my advice, in all matters relating to the imposition or abolition of duties, and the general improvement of trade. He does not admit that the Shan Saubwas have any right to impose duties at all, but I discouraged this cavalier fashion of dealing with Shan privileges, and insisted upon the adviseability of fixing definite rules, or rates of duty: it being an acknowledged fact, that Shan chiefs have always exercised the right of exacting transit dues on goods, though to a very trifling extent. From personal observation I may state with some degree of certainty that 12 annas per mule load will clear goods through the Shan States as far as Myne-tee; and as regards their further transit to and from Tali, Tah-sâ-köne gave me his word and assurance that Transit duty on exports and imports, between the Khakyen Hills and Tali, should in no case be allowed to exceed an ad valorem rate of 4 per cent.

6. That portion of the Shan States which is principally involved or interested in the re-opening of overland trade between Bhamo and China has been explored, and chiefs and people who were found to have been influenced by intrigue and misrepresentation into a state bordering on active opposition have been gradually converted by a truthful recognition of facts, as practically disclosed by our residence amongst them, into holding feelings of friendly encouragement and undisguised good will.

7. All three routes by which the *Kakhyen* Hills are crossed from *Bhamo*, have been explored and surveyed; two of them by myself and party, and the third by a competent surveyor whom I detached on special duty from *Hotha*, at the time when the expedition was about to set out from the same place to *Bhamo*, by the central or Ambassador's route. The result of these surveys in conjunction with other modifying considerations of policy and convenience, will eventually define and decide the most practicable line for a through trade route. In the mean time it may be generally stated, that the Kakhyen Chiefs on both routes have been won over to friendship; and eagerly crave for their own particular line a monopoly of transit, which I try and convince them will eventually be large enough for distribution amongst all.

Such is the beginning which has been made: and in arriving at even these results it will be acknowledged that, in the absence of all real political power, I have gone to the full length of my letter, without compromising Government, or binding it to any particular line of reciprocal action in return for advantages offered and obtained. I may have exhibited the bright side of the picture in recording results, but the picture itself has not been exaggerated or falsified by over coloring. What has been accomplished will serve primarily as a means of estimating the present disposition of the people and chiefs with whom I have held intercourse, and act as a guide to further political or commercial intercourse. Personally I cannot help feeling satisfaction at the fact that our endeavours to promote the good work for which the Expedition was undertaken, whatever their result may be in other respects, have been thus far concluded without a single important mishap; and that although conflicting interests of no mean order have been at times opposed to us with all the intensity which it was possible to superadd by the insidious designs of self interested intriguers, they have been successfully combated by a spirit of straightforward conciliation, which has given assurance to those who were inclined to waver, and raised up a genuine feeling of friendly regard for ourselves and sympathy in our undertaking which cannot fail to prove a secure base and groundwork for further exploration and commercial enterprise in all parts of the country to which the influences of our visit must eventually extend.

I commenced the return journey from Momein on the 13th July; but not until communication had been held with Tali, and the Head Quarters Government had signified its approval of my visit, and despatched a quantity of presents in return for those which I had given to the Governor of *Momein*. These presents only came as far as *Sheedin*, a large town half way between *Momein* and *Tali*, where they were necessarily detained, owing to the insecurity of the road to *Momein*. Six Burmese officials had also arrived at the same place by the *Theinnee* Route, direct from Mandalay, with letters and 50 bales of cotton as a present from the King of Burma to the Governor of *Momein*! Neither the Burmans, nor their cotton, nor our presents could come on to Momein, neither could we get them, but letters had reached the *Momein* Governor, stating the nature and object of the Burmese official visit. I rather gloried I must confess in the discomfiture of this Burmese secret mission, for it was by no means a pleasant idea, in the position I then held at *Momein*, to feel that Burman intrigue and opposition, which had so signally failed at *Bhamo* and *Ponsee*, might still be following us into *Yunan*, to create suspicion and distrust in Quarters where all had been brought into a state of mutual friendly reliance. The purport of the Burmese letter was not disclosed. Probably it contained nothing of importance; but had its contents been favourable I cannot conceive the existence of any sufficient reason for keeping them secret after I had expressed a wish to have them made known. As a further cause for suspecting that the letter and presents signified no good to our undertaking, it is only necessary to keep in view the anomalous character of a Burmese private embassy with presents to *Momein*, at a time when the British and Burmese Government were engaged in a *joint* undertaking to reopen trade with *Yunan*, by the despatch of a British expedition under Burmese patronage!

On the journey from *Momein* I heard at *Yyne-tee* of the arrival of a party of Burmans at *Sanda*, or *Myne-la*, who had been despatched, it was said, to escort us back to Burmese territory! This seemed a mystery: and it was only solved on my own arrival at *Myne-la*, by the receipt of your letters and the somewhat ghostly appearance of a European in those parts, in the person of Mr. Gordon.

The Burman party of 100 men had been at *Myne-la* some eight or ten days: and the Sayaydaugyee in charge had made no attempt to get on himself or to communicate with me at Momein. He was in too great a funk, I believe, to do anything.

Gordon intended coming on he says, had we not met him at *Myne-la*; but it is very fortunate that he did not do so without first giving notice of his intentions at Momein and receiving Panthay aid; otherwise nothing can have saved him from conflict, in which I do not think that Burmans would have distinguished themselves. It is further a subject of congratulation to us all that Gordon enjoyed the *real* support of the Burmese Government, as well as the full advantage of our conciliatory policy which had preceded him, and made friends of all on the route he was to take.

The money you sent, ~~Rs~~ 7,000 of which reached me at *Mynela*, has been of very essential service. It has enabled me to spend freely, and make presents in Rupees (which are more acceptable in these parts than any other kind of gift.) Had your letters and Rupees reached me at *Momein*, I might have been influenced to make a longer stay there, in the hope that something might have resulted out of the capture of Yunan city by the Panthays which would have afforded a means of my proceeding beyond *Momein*.

You seem to have been informed that the French exploring expedition from Saigon has succeeded in its object of penetrating China. The information I obtained on the same subject at *Momein*, on the authority of the Governor, tends, I am sorry to say, to a belief that the expedition terminated in disaster, somewhere in the vicinity of *Kiaing-Yung-Gyee*.

I pressed the Governor very closely as to the sources of his information; so much so that he quite laughed at my doubts when I suggested that the story of the disaster might be only partially true, or very greatly exaggerated.

The Governor assured me that his information was obtained from a Panthay relative who held some appointment not far from *Kiaing-Yung-Gyee*. The French party is said to have been treacherously led into difficulties and then attacked by Hill savages, who killed two or three of the party and looted the whole of the baggage. An account is given of a few who escaped and took refuge in a neighbouring village, where they arrived in a state of nudity and starvation. Muskets which belonged to the French party were seen in the possession of natives and some of them were afterwards bought by the Governor's relative: such is the story. I do not pretend to believe it myself though the Governor of *Momein*, my informant, vouched for its authenticity, even after I had warned him that the matter was a serious one, and begged that he would not mislead me or cause me to mislead others if the slightest doubt existed in his own mind as to the truth of what he related or the fate of the French party. I am inclined to think that the party may have simply met with a reverse which has been magnified into a disaster. Our hope is that *your* information is correct, and that the party has long ere this returned to *Saigon* crowned with success and covered with glory.

It only remains to say a few words about my return from *Momein* viâ *Hotha* and the old Embassy route across the *Khakyen* Hills to *Bhamo*. When I found after a protracted residence at *Momein*, that there was no prospective chance within reasonable limits of my being able to get on further into *Yunan* without encountering armed opposition, and involving the Government in troublesome complications which it was my bounden duty to avoid, I was compelled under a variety of pressing considerations to think of a return homewards, and made preparations accordingly. It had always been my intention, in case the expedition succeeded in reaching its destination, wherever that might be, to return if practicable by a separate route across the *Khakyen* Hills, to that taken on my journey to *Momein*. I several times conferred with the Governor of *Momein* on the subject, and he *apparently* seconded my wishes, though with an evident hesitation which could not at the time be well accounted for. I afterwards ascertained beyond doubt that the Governor was not personally inclined to favour other routes as apart from that which the Expedition had taken as far as *Momein*, because he laboured under an impression not without reason, that such other routes might lead direct into *Yunan* viâ *Yoonchan*, and ignore the existence of *Momein* altogether. I tried to combat this idea, and succeeded so far as to cause arrangements to be made so that on arrival myself at *Nantin* or *Myne-tee*, I should be met by the *Hotha* (Shan) Saubwa, and be escorted by him through the *Hotha* valley to *Mynewon*, (or as Burmans call it *Mowon*) and from thence proceed by the southernmost or *Sawaddy* route to *Bhamo*. This arrangement was not fully completed; the direct route from *Nantin* to *Hotha* viâ the *Shammaloon* Hill was reported unsafe: and some of Leesa-ta-hee's Dacoits held certain of the villages on the route. This may or may not have been true. At any rate had there been no other reasons on the part of the Momein Governor for wishing to confine me to the Sanda valley, I think I might have crossed direct from Nantin via Shammalon, into the Hotha route. The *Hotha* Saubwa failed in his agreement to meet me at *Nantin*; and I was obliged therefore after some little delay to push on to *Mynela* in the hope of catching him there. Here as well as at *Sanda* and *Manwyne* the officials were almost openly opposed to the very idea of my leaving the *Sanda* for the *Hotha* valley. Their opposition was natural enough; for the Shans, judging by my reception and success at *Momein*, had actually realized the fact of revived trade between Burma and South Western China, and were reasonably averse therefore to the idea of encouraging any arrangement by which that trade would be diverted to parts which would virtually exclude them from immediate participation in its advantages. I upbraided them gently for shortsightedness in opposing plans which were intended for general good; but could not help feeling at the same time an inward sense of satisfaction at the fact that their reluctance to assist me, by excluding themselves from occupying a prominent position on a direct trade route, afforded the strongest presumptive evidence of a certain degree of success which the Expedition had already secured for itself within the Shan states. I stayed several days at *Mynela* and *Sanda*. Heavy and continuous rain aided to prolong my stay at each place beyond average limits; and it was not until my arrival at *Mânwyne* that I was able to induce the *Hotha* Saubwa to join me and keep to his agreement of escorting the Mission to his Saubwaship at *Hotha*. After all there was but little reason to regret that I could not proceed from *Nantin* to *Hotha* direct without passing through *Mynela* and *Sanda*.

The prolonged stay at each of the places has done *much* to familiarize us with the people, and convince them of the sincerity of our intentions. They have shown the warmest sympathy with us throughout; and at each place our departure always seemed to be a cause of regret to the population generally, who would have detained us with pleasure amongst them for months had it been in their power to do so. The real object I had in view in wishing to return viâ Hotha has been accomplished: that is to say we have, to all intents and purposes, inspected the whole *Hotha* valley, and thoroughly *done* the *Khakyen* Hills: neither they (the Hills) nor the Khakyens themselves are any longer a bugbear to trade or a Bogy by which it has hitherto been the practice of Burmese Officials to terrorize and obstruct would be traders to China. The *Hotha* Saubwa received us in state with a salute at Hotha; and housed all the members of the Expedition in his own *Haw* or Palace with marked kindness and hospitality. His interests are of course bound up in securing a revived trade route through his own domains in the Hotha valley; but he would hardly dare to encourage such a route at the expense of offending his superiors or of opposing the wishes and interests of the Governor of *Momein*. Once at *Hotha* it became necessary to decide upon the most desirable route across the Khakyen Hills to Bhamo. My original intention was to have proceeded by what is known as the Southern or Sawaddy route: but after mature consideration at *Hotha* I determined finally on exploring the grand central (Embassy or Ambassador's) route myself; and sending an intelligent Burmese Surveyor who was made over to me by Captain Williams, when he left the expedition at Ponsee in April last, to proceed and report upon the *Sawaddy* route, viâ *Mowon*. Both surveys have been successfully made. I remained at Hotha until all the Khakyen Saubwas had been summoned there, and had not only formally assented to our proceeding across their respective Hills or districts, but had invited us to do so. The Khakyens themselves provided the necessary carriage and leaving *Hotha* on the 27th August we reached this place on the 5th instant. It rained in torrents throughout the journey. This and the fact of my having found it necessary now and then to leave the direct route for the purpose of visiting the abode of some remarkable Saubwa who desired the honor of a visit, will account for certain delays en-route. The three principal Khakyen Saubwas on this route received the Expedition at their several Head Quarters with cannon salutes and the beating of gongs in real Chinese. Imagine the civilization to which Khakyens have attained! and their desire to do right when unbiased by sinister influence and intrigue! · The Khakyens have faithfully adhered to their promises: and conducted the Expedition from *Hotha* to its destination without a single loss or mishap of any kind. They vied with each other in shewing us Khakyen hospitality. If two routes led to the same place, one Saubwa would almost quarrel with another for the honor of getting us to visit any particular village, or give any particular route the preference over others. Although our journey, as far as Khakyens were concerned, ended at *Nanphoung* on the *Tahpen* some 20 miles above this, several Saubwas with nearly a hundred followers have followed me into Bhamo on their own account, with the sole idea of influencing my decision and causing me to give preference to the old Embassy route across the Hills, and make it the sole commercial highway in the direction of China. It would be premature and out of order I find, to think of subsidizing Khakyen Saubwas at present on either of the available routes. The idea of a subsidy only originated with the false impression that Khakyen assistance was otherwise unattainable. All that Khakyens want is just treatment, a fair allowance of wages, and temperate management. With these inducements to serve, we may reasonably calculate on faithful services and free and unfettered transit for travellers and traders alike, through any portion of Khakyen land to which our influences may extend themselves. Khakyens exult in the idea of our employing them as hired labourers to construct a road across their Hills, or keep in repair existing routes. In this respect there will be no difficulty in the construction of any kind of road through the Hills. At present nothing more is required than a good mule track in the most direct line. I am no advocate for railways *at present* in these parts. When they do come it is satisfactory to know that physical difficulties as regards route and country do not exist to any great extent; and that Khakyens, Shans, and Panthays will give willing assistance and combine with effect for the furtherance of so extensive a work. For the present at least we shall have an open road into China, and it will be our duty to improve it as circumstances and conditions call for active interference; and as regards interference of any sort in the opening of a trade route towards China, I am led to the very important consideration of a British Agent at Bhamo, as provided for in our late Treaty with Burma. It is essential that this appointment should at once be created and filled. If possible the Agent should be a man well acquainted with Burmese character and policy; and able to combat any amount of indirect opposition and corrupt petty intrigue with which Burmese Officials will still for some time continue to surround every attempt to extend our influence in these parts, or on the overland highway towards *Yunan*. All Khakyen and Shan Saubwas, as well as the Governor of *Momein* to whom I mentioned the subject of an Agent, seemed to think that under no other circumstances would it be possible to resuscitate for any length of time the old overland trade between the two countries. I perfectly agree with them, and feel convinced that unless an Agent is at once appointed and enters upon his duties at Bhamo, many if not all off the benefits which the present expedition has so far secured will succumb to influences over which we shall be able to exercise little or no control. I will write officially on the subject bye and bye, but in the mean time my recommendation is that no time be lost in the selection of a *competent* British Agent to reside at Bhamo. Let him be a man of good common sense and conciliatory in manner but firm and inflexible in purpose. He should be well paid and provided with means and an establishment which would convince Shans and Khakyens of his importance, and show them that we were sincerely in earnest in stimulating trade in these parts at any cost.

The Burmese authorities have received me on my return here like a Prince. Boats and barges were in readiness at *Nanphoung* on the *Tahpen*, and necessaries provided in abundance for our whole party. The officials are servile and subservient now because they are conscious that they have been outwitted in former attempts to bring ruin on the Expedition, and know moreover that the evidences of their villainy are too patent and palpable to be evaded, unless by a shew of conciliatory kindness by which to compensate and atone for past offences. There is not much more to add. If I except myself I may say generally, that all the members of the Expedition have returned in good health and in high spirits; though exposed to months of continuous rain and climatic extremes of all sorts, there has been little or no sickness. A taxidermist in the employ of Dr. Anderson died at Momein of small pox: and one of the police escort died at *Ponlyne* on the first march into the Khakyen Hills from the effects of an over draught of water when heated. With these exceptions the expedition has returned as it started: and few of us are sorry to get *home* again, for after all there has been hard work at times, and our followers have cheerfully submitted to privations which under other circumstances would have entitled them to growl and grumble to some purpose. I am much indebted to all for hearty assistance and support on many trying occasions. A great deal has yet to be done and many drawbacks still exist, (such as those resulting from indirect opposition in Burma: the unsettled state of affairs in *Yunan*: and the high cost of mule carriage on the overland route,) which will require modification and adjustment, before any real commercial results are achieved, but a beginning has been made and our merchants at Home and abroad have reason to congratulate themselves that a road has been opened from Burma by which their goods can be forwarded overland to China. That such a road is open to commerce, and that goods will be so forwarded and bartered at remunerative rates for Chinese inland produce without undue risk or opposition, are facts the certainty of which is ready for realization, as soon as sufficient commercial enterprise is brought into the field under the fostering care and encouragement of able and interested Governments.

No. 194.—From Captain E. B. SLADEN, Political Agent,—to Colonel ALBERT FYTCHE, Chief Commissioner British Burma, and Agent to the Governor General,—Dated Mandalay, 25th September 1868.

I do myself the honour of informing you that on my return to Bhamo with the Exploration party which I was appointed to lead into South Western China, I was accompanied by thirty one Khakyen Chiefs and nearly two hundred followers, who had availed themselves of my escort and protection to enter Bhamo and conclude arrangements for free transit and safe conduct to all traders and travellers by the grand central or Embassy route, which I had just traversed, from the Shan State of *Hotha* to *Nanphoung* on the *Tahpen* River.

2. The Burmese officials at Bhamo, I am sorry to say, viewed my familiarity with Khakyens and their ready acquiescence in my wishes, with a species of jealous distrust which provoked the contempt and ridicule of even the Khakyens themselves.

3. I had for some time past had in consideration the question of an annual subsidy to be paid to Khakyen Saubwas, as a means of making them our friends and of securing a safe and ready means of transit across their Hills. The idea of a subsidy originated of course with the assumption, or belief, that by no other practicable means would it have been possible to enlist the sympathies of these Hill people or to cause them to regard our presence, in the capacity of traders, as a source of advantage and prosperity to themselves. Having satisfied myself however by ample experience that Khakyens are more eager and interested in the reopening of a trade route through their Hills than we are ourselves, and that their ready co-operation may be freely relied on in any attempt we may make, either to open out old routes or construct new ones, I have been advisedly led to avoid the inconveniences and complication which a subsidy might have given rise to, and hold to the facts that fair dealing and kind straight forward treat-

ment on our part, is all that is required to secure the friendship of these people and ready access to Khakyen land, for all the essential purposes of a through route between *Bhamo* and *S. Western China*.

4. Whilst, however, the opportunity presented itself, it was of importance to secure certain benefits, which seemed to rise out of the friendship already contracted with the several Chiefs who had accompanied me to Bhamo. These benefits would be obtained by a partial adoption of Khakyen national custom, by which it is usual with them, on similar occasions, to bind themselves over to a particular purpose by an oath of fidelity sworn to and strengthened by all the savage solemnities of a Religious ceremony. Such an oath, whilst it professed to secure for us the sworn friendship and fidelity of all who participated in it and gave to traders and travellers free access to the Khakyen Hills (or to such portion of them as are included in the oath,) would not, on the other hand, bind us over to reciprocal action of any sort, or give the Khakyens any claim on us beyond the very laudable one of drawing commercial enterprise to their particular localities, and inducing us to favor routes of which they were the sole acknowledged proprietors.

The Khakyens entered into this proposed measure for strengthening and perpetuating their friendship, with a willingness which was the more astonishing in as much as it was carried out in defiance of a certain amount of jealous opposition on the part of Burmese Officials at Bhamo. In the first place the Khakyens were informed that they could not be allowed to perform any of their Religious Ceremonies within the precincts of Bhamo. Ingress to the town, or to my own residence, was as difficult and troublesome as the obstructive ingenuity of Bhamo guards at the several gateways could make it. Khakyens were called upon to deliver up their swords and spears on entering either of the approaches to the Town. The purchase or sale of various articles, such as Bamboos and especially Bullocks and Baffaloes, which were essential in the performance of the Ceremony to be performed, was secretly interdicted, so as to make it a matter of difficulty to procure them. While preparations were being made for the Ceremony, the Chiefs were called away and privately instructed by certain Burmese Officials that they were not at liberty to enter into any engagement with foreigners.

5. All this petty opposition was eventually overcome by my explanations to the Governor, in which I proved to him that I was not acting solely on the part of the British Government but that I was carrying out the orders of His Majesty the King of Burma, who had expressly desired me to act on his account and make use of his name whenever I might find it necessary by so doing to conciliate existing differences or secure the interests of the trade and of the Expedition under my leadership.

6. The Governor replied to my imputation of opposition on his part by saying that if I had met with difficulties he was not to blame, as his officials had acted without his knowledge. The Kahkyens, he informed me, were at liberty to perform any rites they pleased; and as to the difficulty of purchasing Bullocks, it was explained away by the fact that Burmese objected to see their animals slaughtered in the celebration of Khakyen savage Rites.

7. I was content to accept this explanation without for a moment believing that it had been given in good faith; and the Khakyen ceremonies proceeded to completion with all the usual formalities.

8. It may not be out of place to record a brief account of the ceremonial and form of oath taken on the occasion. For each Buffaloe slaughtered a separate building is constructed, consisting of strong posts sunk into the ground, with cross pieces to which the animal is tied previous to sacrifice.

A separate Altar is also prepared 20 feet in height, with a platform of bamboos some four feet square, on which the sacrifice is offered. Khakyen Deities of every degree and denomination are invited to attend and bear evidence to the rite about to be solemnized or oath taken.

The invocation is repeated twice; once before slaughter, and again previous to laying the meat offering on the Altar. It is performed by a special office bearer, whose prayerful intonation is strangely musical and suggestive of portions of our own Cathedral service. The animal

[lxxxiii

to be slaughtered is firmly bound by its horn to the wooden construction before mentioned, and then thrown on one side. The whole weight and strain of the body is on the neck, which is partially twisted. There is not a moment's delay: a Khakyen, specially equipped for the service, holding a plantain leaf cup of sacred water in one hand, and a naked sword in the other, rushes forward. The water is thrown over the sacrifice, whilst the sharp edge of the sword is brought down with frightful effect on that portion of the neck where the strain is greatest: the result is complete. The savagery of the whole scene is somewhat atoned for by an absence of torture or suffering, from which the animal is saved in its almost instantneous death.

The carcase is cut up without loss of time, and the portion of it alone to which the Deities are known, by Kakhyen experience, to be partial are cooked and laid on the Altar, to be feasted on by the gods. This is the time, whilst the Deities are being propitiated with the semllance of a good dinner, that they are called upon to witness the oath to which the whole Ceremony leads up.

A small quantity of the blood of the slaughtered animal has been caught and is now mixed in a large vessel with an abundant supply of raw native spirits. The whole is stirred up with the points of swords and of spears, which are dipped into the liquor ad libitum; and each chief, as he comes up in the supposed presence of the attendant Deities and takes his draft from the secred bowl, swears his oath of fidelity in muttered prayers which imply the most fearful results as a certain consequence of infidelity.

9. The dipping of the spears and swords in the liquor in which the oath is drank is said to be typical (as far as I could understand the interpretation given me,) of the violent death which would of a certainty be incurred by a departure from the engagements contained in the oath.

10. In the present instance the Khakyens were simply called upon to protect and afford safe conduct to traders and travellers who might cross their respective Hill Ranges, on the route between Bhamo and the Shan States.

11. The means for securing so important an object may appear to us profane or irrational, but as a native Religious rite they are natural enough to Khakyens, and have a powerful and binding effect in keeping them to their engagements.

And as regards a certain profanity in the proceedings there is unfortunately little or no distinction between the Khakyen ceremonial and that which is of necessity enforced in the administration of oaths to natives in our own courts of justice, whenever Burman or more particularly a China man takes his place in the witness box.

12. Altogether the oath of fidelity was sworn to by 51 Khakyen Chiefs, who are principally located in the grand Central or Embassy route between Bhamo and the Shan State of Hotha. The immediate benefit to those who may wish to avail themselves of the route are certain. The more remote though not less important results will be found to arise out of the increased influence which the notoriety of our friendly engagements with Khakyens and the extensive circulation which their report of our true and liberal treatment of themselves will acquire for us throughout all parts of the country which we are engaged in conciliating to our cause and enlisting in the interest of trade with South Western China.

13. It will be observed that the experiment of binding over Khakyen Saubwas by a custom of their own to protect and support traders of every denomination who may desire safe conduct across their Hills has been limited, in the first instance, to the Chiefs who occupy Hill Ranges between Bhamo and the Hotha valley by the old central or Embassy route.

I was afraid that the introduction of Chiefs or Saubwas from other routes would create a spirit of jealous rivalry, which might have marred to some extent the full accomplishment and object of the binding ceremonial.

14. It will become necessary, however, in the event of a British Agent being appointed to reside at Bhamo, to extend the ceremonial to the Chiefs of the Ponlyne (or Northern) and Sawaddy (or Southern) Routes. If summoned in a friendly way to Bhamo and solicited to give us

friendly support in the cause of trade they too will be induced, by the anticipation of securing for themselves or for their particular route a monopoly of trade transit, to bind themselves by suitable and customary obligations such as those already subscribed to by their bretheren on the central Embassy route.

Names of Kahkyen Chiefs or Saubwas, who took the oath of fidelity, at Bhamo, on the 12th September 1868.

1.	Chief of	Muthin.	17.	Chief of	Ponsaw
2.	,,	Mantai	18.	,,	Loaysayne
3.	,,	Loay-lon	19.	,,	Kädau Gyee
4.	,,	Monkha	20.	,,	Kyetyen
5.	,,	Lauyen	21.	,,	Namroung
6.	,,	Tinson	22.	,,	Louza
7.	,,	Sakhiy	23.	,,	Pombya
8.	,,	Hoton	24.	,,	Märôlonkram
9.	,,	Pouwa	25.	,,	Sinlon
10.	,,	Lasee	26.	,,	Mynesoo
11.	,,	Lamiy-pan	27.	,,	Kounson
12.	,,	Myneson	28.	,,	Pongätoung
13.	,,	Kädu Kowra	29.	,,	Säraiwa
14.	,,	Kädan Manta			
15.	,,	Pägwon	30.	,,	Moanwa
16.	,,	Myneton	31.	,,	Oungloung.

———o———

No. 1177.—From W. S. SETON-KARR, Esquire, Secretary to the Government of India, to Colonel A. FYTCHE, Chief Commissioner of British Burma, dated Simla, the 13th October, 1868.

I have the honor to acknowledge the receipt of your letter, No. 39-77, dated 19th September last, and of its enclosure, intimating the safe return of Captain Sladen and his party to Bhamo.

2. His Excellency in Council will await the receipt of the official report which you promise. But two points are raised in the present communication concerning which the Viceroy and Governor General in Council considers it necessary to intimate his opinion at once, before the arrival of the fuller report.

1st. You propose to give Rs. 500 to the relations of each of the two Panthay officers who were killed whilst escorting the members of the Expedition to Momein.

2nd. You recommend the appointment of an Agent at Bhamo for the purpose of maintaining and improving commercial intercourse between British Burma and Western China.

3. His Excellency in Council sanctions the first proposal, and desires that no delay may occur in making the recompense now sanctioned for the families of the deceased Panthay officers. As regards the second of these two propositions, the Viceroy and Governor General in Council much doubts whether it would be prudent, under the existing state of affairs in Burma, to appoint an Englishman as Agent to the British Government at Bhamo.

4. From paragraph 4 of your letter His Excellency in Council apprehends that you contemplate the nomination of a British officer as Agent, and not of a native, and he observes, that not long ago you yourself pointed out, demi-officially, the present insecurity of the King's position and life, and showed that another revolution was not an improbable contingency. Under any circumstances, and even in peaceful times, the officer appointed to this charge, in an isolated position, ought to be a person possessed of a certain amount of ability, and of much tact and great powers of conciliation; while, in case of any internal commotion in Burma, his position, at a distance from aid or support, would expose him to very considerable risk. All these contingencies, I am to observe, demand careful consideration, and it will be for you to say, supposing they are not insurmountable, whether there is any English officer in British Burma whom, in the face of those difficulties, you could safely and conscientiously recommend for the post. The King of Ava must be consulted in this matter before any action is taken, and you must use all your endeavours to ascertain his real opinion on the subject of the appointment of such an Agent. It should be carefully explained to the King that by this proposal the Government of India only contemplate the revival and development of trade.

5. The information which His Excellency in Council has now received, through your letter and enclosures under acknowledgment, sufficiently proves the energy and tact with which Captain Sladen, in spite of many obstacles, has carried out the work assigned to him. The report of Captain Sladen has been perused with interest, and the results of the Expedition have been more successful than at one time there was reason to expect.

6. In replying to the present letter you should state what salary you would assign to the proposed Agent, and what establishment he would require.

———o———

No. 39-94.—From Colonel ALBERT FYTCHE, Chief Commissioner British Burma, Agent to His Excellency the Viceroy and Governor-General, to W. S. SETON KARR Esquire, Foreign Secretary to the Government of India, dated Rangoon, 30th October 1868.

I have the honor to acknowledge the receipt of your letter No. 1177 of the 13th October instant, sanctioning a recompense of five hundred rupees to each of the families of the two Panthay Officers, who were killed in escorting Captain Sladen: and conveying to me the remarks of His Excellency in Council on the proposition to place a British Agent at Bhamo.

2. I shall, as requested in your third paragraph, at once communicate with Captain Sladen regarding the early disbursement of the bonus sanctioned to the families of the Panthay Officers.

3. Regarding the establishment of a British Agent at Bhamo, you will observe that my letter suggesting the measure was dated 19th September, and I have since received a letter from Captain Sladen dated 25th September (copy of which is attached) urging the importance of the appointment in question. In a private letter of the same date Captain Sladen describes his first interview with the King after his return, which took place on the 24th idem. After some general conversation and congratulations on his return, His Majesty enquired of Captain Sladen:—

KING.—"Are you going back to Bhamo?"

POLITICAL AGENT.—"No—but I believe that a British Agent " will soon be appointed to reside there."

[lxxxviii]

KING.—"I will take care, whoever he is, that there "shall be a Governor with whom he will pull well and be "on friendly terms."

After these remarks no further allusion was made to business on that occasion, and I understand that in subsequent interviews with the King no remarks have been made by His Majesty regarding the Expedition.

4. I have carefully considered the observations of His Excellency in Council, contained in the concluding portion of the third and in the fourth paragraphs of your letter under reply. I do not conceal from myself that their must be some personal risk undertaken by the officer placed at Bhamo, in the event of internal disturbance in the Burmese Territory. It is difficult to foresee in what particular shape the next Civil disruption in Upper Burma may occur, but I should not anticipate that in any struggle for the throne there would be violence shown to British Officers. There certainly would be the danger of lawlessness among the people consequent on the conflict of authority, but this, it appears to me, is a kind of peril, which must be accepted in our intercouse with Native States. The question of course is one of degree, and I would say that the position of the Agent at Bhamo would not in my opinion be unduly hazardous.

5. In judging of this too, some thought must be given to the results that we hope to obtain by placing an Officer at Bhamo. Are they such as would justify risk and expense? I have already indicated to Government my opinion on these points. In a commercial aspect this line of traffic seems worthy of support. Imperial interests will be gained if we can establish a highway to the Western borders of China: and scientific enquiry is being directed to the tract of country—not very extensive after all—which intervenes between two such important markets as India and China. All these objects will be served by the presence of a British Officer at Bhamo. If trade has any tendency to flow by this old route, it will do so the more readily that the British Agent is there to protect the merchants. If the hitherto disunited condition of the authorities who hold the through route is to be changed into friendly co-operation, it

will be carried out, as it has been begun, by British Agency. If information is to be gathered regarding the head-waters of the Brahmapooter, the Yang-si-kiang, and the Irrawaddy our knowledge will be increased by the residence of a British Officer at Bhamo, the most central and the best adapted post from which to push enquiries.

6. Believing then in the advantage eventually to be gained from the establishment of a British Agent at Bhamo, and being of opinion that the difficulties in the way are not insurmountable I would, in reply to your query "whether " there is any English Officer in British Burma whom * * * " you could safely and conscientiously recommend for the " post," beg to nominate Captain G. A. Strover, Assistant Commissioner 1st Grade, at present Town Magistrate of Akyab. He is an Officer in whose judgment, discretion, and conciliatory disposition I have full confidence. I have also ascertained his willingness to undertake the duties of the appointment provided it be sanctioned.

7. With reference to the concluding portion of the fourth paragraph, in which you point out that the king must be consulted before any action is taken, and that his real opinion on the subject of the appointment of such an Agent must be ascertained, and that he must be informed that the Government of India only contemplate by the proposal the revival and development of trade, I would beg to remark that from the conversation I have recounted in a previous portion of this letter, it will be seen that His Majesty evidently contemplated our placing an Officer at Bhamo, and expressed his readiness to see his Officer co-operate with the British Agent. Indeed the Court and Ministers were well aware that the appointment of such an Agent would be the natural result of the late expedition to Momein, and when the objects and advantages of that expedition were discussed between the Burmese Officials and myself in 1867, while I was in Mandalay negotiating the last Treaty, there was no concealment of the prospective establishment of a British Officer at Bhamo. It will be seen from Captain Sladen's letter (copy attached) that the Burmese Government still profess to be actuated by the same desire to facilitate trade with China that the British Government is, but that unless we take steps to carry out our avowed intentions in the matter obstructions will be thrown in the way of inland commerce.

8. Doubtless the Court of Ava is half hearted in the matter. A lingering suspicion of our ulterior views will probably induce it to give the project but faint support, if it does not lead it to covert opposition. I think all this will the sooner disappear and be the more easily overcome by our steadily adhering to our intention, long ago announced and accepted by the King, of, as far as in us lies, developing the through traffic with China. It will be seen from letter No. 462 of the 12th May 1862, from the Secretary to the Government of India Foreign Department to the Chief Commissioner British Burma, that six years ago the attention of this Administration was directed to this subject by the Government of India, and the Chief Commissioner specially instructed to keep it in view in negotiating the Treaty of 1862. The importance of the question has increased rather than lessened during that period, and I should much regret to see our policy falter at the very time we have obtained information of its soundness. In accordance with your instructions, however, I shall communicate the wishes of Government to Captain Sladen, and request him to use his best endeavours to ascertain the real opinion of His Majesty the King on the subject of appointing a British Agent at Bhamo.

9. In reply to the last paragraph of your letter, I would beg to recommend that the pay of the Assistant Agent at Bhamo be Rupees 1,500 per mensem. It will be seen that Captain Sladen attaches considerable importance to the status of the Agent to be placed at Bhamo, and I agree with him that the pay of the appointment should be such as to enable the Agent fittingly to represent the British Government. As to his establishment I would suggest a guard consisting of:

1 Jemadar @ 50 .... Rs.	50	per mensem.
15 Privates @ 20 .... ,,	300	,,
4 Peons @ 20 .... ,,	80	,,
1 Burmese Writer @ 50 ... . ,,	50	,,

Total Rupees. 380 per mensem.
12

Per annum Rs. 5,760
Clothing for 16 men @ Rs. 13 ...... ,, 208

Total Rs...5,968 per annum.

and for the first year I would in addition to this allow a sum of Rs. 12,000 for contingencies, including the constructions of a house. The total charge would therefore be for the first twelve months say:

Pay of Assistant Political Agent	Rs.	18,000
Establishment	,,	6,000
Contingencies	,,	12,000
Total Rs.		36,000

and this amount I have included in the Provincial Budget for 1869-70. I would not recommend that the Guard should form part of the Police Department but that the Assistant Agent should select and enlist his own men from such classes as he thought best fitted for the duty.

10. I think the Assistant Agent should retain his position in the Commission and be "seconded" during his employment at Bhamo, at least until it is seen how far the duties of the appointment may suit the present nominee, our present measures being necessarily in some degree tentative.

---o---

No. 39-96.—From Colonel ALBERT FYTCHE, Chief Commissioner British Burma, Agent to His Excellency the Viceroy and Governor General to Captain SLADEN, Political Agent in the Territory of His Majesty the King of Burma, dated Rangoon, October 30th 1868.

I have the honor to enclose you herewith a copy of letter No. 1177 of 13th instant to my address, from the Secretary to the Government of India Foreign Department, being a reply to my letter No. 39-77 dated 19th ultimo (copy of which has been furnished you): and also copy of my letter of this day's date to Government regarding the appointment of an Assistant Political Agent at Bhamo.

2. Be so good as to take early steps regarding the disbursement of Rs. 500 to each of the families of the two Panthay officers, who were killed in escorting you to Momein. Mention again to the King of Burma the fact of an Assistant Political Agent being about to be stationed at Bhamo, and endeavour to ascertain the real opinion of His Majesty on the subject:—such are the instructions of His Excellency in Council, but it appears to me that the King

has already accepted the measure, and raised no objections to it.

No. 1413.—From W. S. SETON-KARR, Esq. Secretary to the Government of India to Colonel A. FYTCHE, Chief Commissioner of British Burmah,—dated Fort William, the 7th December, 1868.

I am directed to acknowledge the receipt of your letter dated 30th October last, No. 39-94, in which you reply to the question of the appointment of a British Agent at Bhamo.

2. His Excellency the Viceroy and Governor General in Council thinks it so important that there should be no risk of misapprehension on this question, that he will refrain from passing final or definite orders on the proposal until the King's sentiments shall have been ascertained, not by means of casual conversations, but by a distinct assent to the plan carefully explained to him, as one which requires a clear understanding, and a full approval on the part of His Majesty.

2. The expressions used in paragraph 8 of your letter, and the doubts thrown out by Captain Sladen in his 2nd paragraph, render it imperative that formal demand should be made and the King's assent be as formally given, before the appointment of an Agent can be settled.

3. You will therefore instruct Captain Sladen to ask for an audience of the King for this object, and to ascertain distinctly what His Majesty's views and wishes may be on the whole subject.

Pro 39-114.—From Colonel ALBERT FYTCHE, Chief Commissioner British Burma, and Agent to the Governor General,—to W. S. SETON KARR, Esq. Secretary to the Government of India Foreign Department,—dated Rangoon, January 11th, 1869.

I have the honor to submit to be laid before His Excellency the Viceroy and Governor General in Council copy of letter No. 229 dated 23rd December 1868 from Captain Sladen of in answer to my communication transmitting him copy of your despatch No. 1177 dated 13th October 1868

2. When this letter was written by Captain Sladen he had not received a copy of your letter No. 1413 dated 7th Ultimo to my address, which was forwarded him on 16th idem, with directions to carry out the instructions of His Excellency the Viceroy and Governor General in Council, as therein contained, with all convenient despatch. On receipt of Captain Sladen's reply to the latter communication it shall be at once submitted.

3. It is to be hoped that the several references that have been made to the King on this subject, will not tend to lead His Majesty to suppose that it is not the wish of His Excellency to post an Assistant Political Agent at Bhamo; or that the expediency of such a measure is not recognized.

———o———

No. 229.—From, Captain E. B. SLADEN, Political Agent, Mandalay, to Colonel ALBERT FYTCHE, Chief Commissioner British Burma and Agent to His Excellency the Viceroy and Governor General, dated Mandalay, the 23rd December 1868.

I have the honor to acknowledge the receipt of your letter, No. 39-96, of 30th with its enclosures, and to inform you in reply, that the amount sanctioned as compensation to the families of the Panthay officers who were killed whilst escorting me to Momein, shall be forwarded by the first safe opportunity.

2. In my several conversations with the King on the subject of establishing a British Agent at Bhamo, His Majesty has always rightly assumed that his formal consent to this measure had already been attained and instead of offering objections to the appointment or raising unnecessary misgivings, he has promised, on the appointment being made, to arrange that a good understanding shall be maintained between the incumbent (whoever he may be) and his own Governor of Bhamo.

3. I can well remember that, during the negotiations of the late treaty, the Burmese Government was of opinion that one of the first results of that treaty would be the location of British Agents, both at Bhamo and Menhla. It would be bad policy, I conceive, in the present case to disturb the impressions secured by treaty rights, by a

diffident enquiry into the risks attending the exercise of those rights.

4. If the question were now asked, whether His Majesty approved generally of the establishment of a British Agent at Bhamo, no amount of diplomacy in approaching the subject would conceal an implied diffidence, which must naturally suggest itself as involved in the question. The King would take advantage of our doubts and put forward serious objections, if by doing so he saw any reasonable hope (as he certainly would do) of retarding the appointment; or of even doing away with it altogether.

5. My own belief is that the personal risk of a residence at Bhamo would not be as imminent as those to which the Political Agent at Mandalay would be subjected in the event of a Rebellion, which, according Burmese History, always takes its rise or assumes its most hideous shape at the Royal capital.

6. But, setting aside risk altogether, it should be borne in mind that we have been at considerable pains to obtain from the Burmese Government the very important concession of appointing British Agents to reside at duty stations in Upper Burma: and it remains for us to decide as apart from the wishes or Policy of the King (who by the bye has already assented to the measure) whether the circumstances which now call for the services of the British Agent at Bhamo are not paramount to every other consideration or to the mere risk which must of a necessity be incurred by every European resident under Foreign Rule in an Asiatic State.

7. Judging by my own experiences on the late expedition into Yunan, I can only add as a supplementary remark to my letter No. 193 of 25th September last, that unless a British Agent is located at Bhamo in the person of an officer of standing and ability, the late expedition viâ Bhamo to Yunan may as well have never been undertaken, and overland trade with China will remain in abeyance as long as the Burmese Empire exists or the Burmese Government fancies that it is best serving its own interests by obstructing European progress, and refusing it the means of commercial extension through the comparatively insignificant tract of country known as Upper Burma.

No. 200.—From W. S. SETON KARR, Esqre.,—Secretary to the Government of India—to Colonel A. FYTCHE, Chief Commissioner of British Burma,—dated Fort William, the 8th February 1869.

I have the honor to acknowledge the receipt of your letter No. 39-114, dated 11th Ultimo, submitting a communication from Captain Sladen on the subject of the proposed appointment of an Assistant Political Agent at Bhamo.

2. In reply I am directed to inform you that the Viceroy and Governor in Council will await the receipt of your answer to the letter from this Department of the 7th December last, No. 1413, in which the views of the Government of India, and the course to be pursued, were clearly indicated, as well as the result of the reference which was to have been made to His Majesty the King of Burmah.

---o---

Pro 39-125.—From Colonel ALBERT FYTCHE, Chief Commissioner British Burma Agent to His Excellency the Viceroy and Governor General,—to W. S. SETON KARR, Esqre.,—Secretary to the Government of India Foreign Department,—dated Tavoy, February 12th, 1869.

Referring to your letter No. 1413 dated the 7th December 1868 in which I was informed that the Government of India desired that the wishes of His Majesty the King of Burma regarding the appointment of a British Agent at Bhamo should be distinctly and specifically ascertained, I have the honor, in continuation of my former correspondence on the subject, to submit for the information of His Excellency the Governor General and Viceroy in Council, copy of a letter No. 252 of 16th January from Captain Sladen Political Agent, Mandalay, in which he describes a special interview, held on the 11th January, with His Majesty the King with the view of ascertaining His Majesty's wishes on this matter.

2. It will be seen from this that His Majesty is quite willing that an Agent should be stationed at Bhamo. He naturally asked that a prudent officer should be sent, and with that proviso stated that "the appointment had his full consent and approval."

3. I would now repeat to the Supreme Government my conviction of the importance of at once acting in this long discussed matter, and so bringing to a legitimate conclusion—on this point at least—the commercial policy to-

wards Upper Burma which has guided our intercourse with the Court of Ava for years.

4. I beg again to bring to the notice of His Excellency the Governor General in Council, that when my predecessor Sir Arthur Phayre proceeded in 1862 to negotiate a Treaty with the Court of Ava, one of the main points he was directed by the Government of India to bear in mind was the development of through trade with China viâ Bhamo. He was directed to further the reopening of the commercial route to China viâ Bhamo, by a joint British and Burmese Mission. He was to provide for the passage of British or Asiatic Merchants by that route, and for their residence at Bhamo.

5. In obedience to those instructions Sir Arthur Phayre concluded a Treaty having as its sole object these important measures, and to obtain them we abolished our Frontier Duties which then amounted £60,000. Viewed as a mere matter of commercial policy, I believe, the abolition of these duties was a wise step. On the Burmese side a very heavy tax was levied, and it was hoped that the Court of Ava would gradually reduce the rates levied on their Frontier. This object was secured by my Treaty concluded with the Court of Ava in October 1867; and we need have no regret at the lapse of our Frontier Duty when we find that our Inland Trade with Upper Burma, which amounted to £1,129,00 in 1863-64 (the year our Duties were abolished,) has increased to £2,545.100 in the year 1867-68.

6. Still the wise policy which led to the Treaty of 1862 has been but faintly persisted in since that time. Sir Arthur Phayre reported to the Government of India in his letter of 21st November 1862, that the Treaty was expressly framed to provide for free passage of steamers on the Irrawaddy, and for the residence of Merchants at Bhamo, or elsewhere: and the King and his Ministers were fully prepared for their appearance.

7. Again in my Treaty of 1867, distinct provision was made for the appointment of a British Agent at Bhamo, or other places in Upper Burma where Duties were levied: and the intention of the British Government to carry out

this portion of the Treaty was most assuredly understood by the Court of Ava. On the same occasion opportunity was taken to gain the King's assent to the despatch of a British Expedition to reopen the route from Bhamo to China.

8. So much has been written of the importance of establishing a through traffic with Western China, that it is superfluous to go over the same ground. I have already expressed my strong opinion of the great value of such a measure in various communications with the Supreme Government. *The most immediately feasible route is undoubtedly viâ Bhamo*, and we may hope gradually to resuscitate and develope the valuable trade which formerly flowed by that channel. But to do this the presence of British Agent at Bhamo is, in my opinion, essential, and having in consideration the great commercial issue at stake—one which I am satisfied will year by year become of increasing Imperial importance—I would most strongly urge on His Excellency the Governor General in Council to give his assent to the appointment of a British Agent at Bhamo.

9. The detail measures requiring sanction, as to the pay of the Agent and his establishment, I have already submitted for the consideration of Government in my letter No. 39-94 dated 30th October 1868.

---o---

No. 252.—From Captain E. B. SLADEN, Political Agent, Mandalay, to Colonel ALBERT FYTCHE, C. S. I., Chief Commissioner of British Burma and Agent to the Governor General, Rangoon; dated Mandalay, the 16th January, 1869.

I have the honor to acknowledge the receipt of your letter No. 39-108 Foreign Department, dated 16th ultimo, and to inform you that on 11th instant I was admitted to a special audience with the King, for the purpose of explaining the nature of the Bhamo appointment, and of ascertaining His Majesty's views and wishes in their relation to the same subject.

2. During the interview I succeeded in making His Majesty conversant with all sides of the question; and begged that I might be favoured with a clear and distinct expression of His Majesty's opinion thereon, either then or

as soon as it might be convenient to admit me to another interview.

3. Somewhat to my surprise His Majesty seemed to have considered the matter, and to have already arrived at a definite decision on the subject of my interview. He replied almost immediately as follows:—

King.—I have no objection whatever to the Bhamo appointment. I shall not be sorry to hear that you have appointed an Agent at Bhamo, as well as at other duty stations in Burma (Toughoo and Menhla.) All I stipulate for is, that your Government will not send obstinate or intractable officers, who will be guided solely by their own opinion, without any regard to advice or reason.

Political Agent.—Your Majesty may rest assured that the British Government will be most careful in its selection of an officer to fill the Bhamo appointment. He will be a man of prudence and ability, with special qualifications for so responsible a position.

King.—In that case I have no misgivings. The appointment has my full consent and approval. When the officer arrives I wish you to introduce him to me, and I will then cause the attendance of the Governor of Bhamo. Between us we will arrange that the Governor and the British Agent shall understand each other, and be placed, as regards their mutual relations, on a sound and intelligible footing.

There is another point. I do not like the idea of English Steamers proceeding above Mandalay. The population generally may be led to believe that Burma is again invaded, and the steamer may get into difficulties.

Political Agent.—Your Majesty will do wrong, I think, to raise any question now, affecting the rights of British Steamers on the Irrawaddy. Those rights have already been secured by Treaty, and would not, in all probability, be relinquished without difference and misunderstanding. The difficulty, as regards popular opinion in your Majesty's dominions, may be avoided by a Royal proclamation on the first occasion that any English Steamer attempts the passage of the River north of Mandalay.

King.—Why should your Steamers wish to go to Bhamo? Does it not amount to the same thing if I make my steamers available for all cargo or goods that may pass between Bhamo and Mandalay.

Political Agent.—No, by no means; such an arrangement would interfere injuriously with the rights of owners shippers and consignees; to say nothing of the interests and and profits of trade. Besides, Treaty Rights cannot be easily lost sight of. It is my duty, I think, to advise your Majesty not to raise objections to the passage of English Steamers beyond the Capital. I am not in a position myself to recognize any such objections, when I find that they involve a breach of treaty stipulations. But if your Majesty wishes it, I will communicate what you have said to the Chief Commissioner of British Burma.

King.—No, I will take your advice: say nothing about the steamers. But I must not be blamed hereafter, if British steamers get into difficulties in navigating the Irrawaddy above my capital.

Political Agent.—Your Majesty has no reason to apprehend undue responsibility in this matter. All that we can reasonably expect, is the protection of a friendly Government and this protection your Majesty has agreed by treaty to extend to all British Traders within your Majestys dominions.

4. No further allusion was made during the interview to the Bhamo appointment, and my impression is that His Majesty is sincere at present in his desire to avoid all suspicion of indirect opposition, past or present, in the work of regenerating Overland Trade, viâ Bhamo, with South Western China. In fact I believe that he is fast recovering from the effects of certain evil influences which may have induced him, after my own departure for Bhamo, to view the Expedition with disfavour, and to try and defeat its main objects. Since the return of the expedition to Mandalay, it has been in my power to tender to His Majesty advice and information which, I am led to hope, has produced a reaction in favour of the establishment of a British Agency at Bhamo, and the furtherance of commercial enterprise in the direction of Southern China.

No. 359.—From W. S. SETON-KARR, Esq., Secretary to the Government of India, Foreign Department; to Colonel A. FYTCHE, C.S.I.; Chief Commissioner of British Burma; dated Fort William, the 15th March 1869.

I am directed by His Excellency the Viceroy and Governor-General of India in Council to acknowledge the receipt of your letter dated 12th ultimo, No. 39-125, and to state that, on the understanding now arrived at that the King of Burma is quite willing that an Agent should be appointed to Bhamo, His Excellency in Council will recommend the appointment to the Financial Department.

2. But His Excellency in Council would first wish you to report, after consulting Captain Sladen, the name or names of any Officer or Officers who possess the qualifications which the Government has a right to look for in the person who shall fill the proposed appointment. The Agent, it is almost unnecessary to urge on you, should be a man versed in the language and customs of Burma, and of acknowledged discretion, readiness, and tact.

3. His Excellency in Council is also disposed to think that 1,500 Rupees a month is too high a salary for such an appointment and that, at first, it would not be necessary to assign to the post more than 1,000 Rupees a month or 12,000 Rupees a year.

4. The Officer to be appointed might be styled Assistant Agent at Bhamo, and might be placed in subordination to the Political Agent at Mandalay, both Officers being, of course, under your supervision as Chief Commissioner.

5. The pay of the Political Agent at this latter place, I am to remark is only Rupees 1,500 a month.

No. 39-139.—Foreign Department: From Secretary to the Chief Commissioner, British Burma, Agent to His Excellency the Viceroy and Governor-General, to W. S. SETON-KARR, Esq., Secretary to the Government of India, Foreign Department; dated Rangoon, March 27th, 1869.

I am directed by the Chief Commissioner and Agent to the Governor-General to acknowledge the receipt of your letter No. 359 of 15th instant, and to request that the Chief Commissioner's letter No. 39-94 dated 30th October last, which contains in detail the information required may, be laid before the Right Hon'ble the Viceroy and Governor-General in

Council. A copy of this letter is enclosed for ready reference.

2. The Chief Commissioner, I am to say, consulted Captain Sladen long ago regarding the Officer to be nominated for the appointment of Assistant Political Agent at Bhamo and he fully concurs with General Fytche that Capt. Strover is eminently fitted for the post. An Officer placed in the important and responsible position which the Assistant Political Agent will be placed in at Bhamo, and completely cut off, too, from all European society and support, should be well paid. Captain Strover now draws Rupees 1,000 a month, is close on promotion, and it would not be worth his while proceeding to Bhamo on the salary mentioned in your letter under reply. If he does not accept the appointment, the Chief Commissioner has no other Officer here in a position to take the Office, who possesses the necessary qualifications for the post.

3. As stated in your Telegram just received, the pay of the Political Agent at Mandalay is Rupees 2,000 per mensem and not Rupees 1,500 as given in your letter.

4. A Schedule shewing the pay recommended for the salary of the Assistant Political Agent and his Establishment in para. 9 of the Chief Commissioner's letter above referred to, is annexed; as also copy of a Notification for publication in the *Gazette of India*, in the event of His Excellency thinking fit to appoint Captain Strover.

NOTIFICATION.

The Right Honorable the Viceroy and Governor-General of India in Council is pleased to appoint Captain G. A. Strover, Madras Staff Corps to be Assistant Political Agent at Bhamo in the territory of His Majesty the King of Burma, under article VI of the Treaty with His Majesty concluded on the 25th October 1867

SCHEDULE of the Proposed Establishment for the Office of Assistant Political Agent at Bhamo.

		Rs.	A.	P.
1	Assistant Political Agent	1,500	0	0
	Office Establishment.			
1	Burmese writer	50	0	0
	Personal Guard.			
1	Jemadar	50	0	0
15	Privates @ 20 each	300	0	0
4	Peons @ 20 each	80	0	0
	TOTAL	1,980	0	0

RANGOON, H. NELSON DAVIES, Major,
The 29th March 1869. *Secretary.*

No. 677.

GOVERNMENT OF INDIA
Financial Department.
SIMLA
The 28th May 1869.

Read an Extract from the Proceedings of Government in the Foreign Department (Political) No. 587, dated 30th April 1869, recommending sanction to the appointment of a British Agent at Bhamo, on a Salary of Rs. 1,200 per mensem with an Establishment at Rs. 480* monthly and a sum not exceeding Rs. 12,000 for contingencies including the construction or the purchase of a house.

*1 Burmese Writer	50
GUARD.	
1 Jemadar	50
15 Privates at 20	300
4 Peons at 20	80
	480

RESOLUTION.—The Governor General in Council is pleased to sanction the proposed charges, the salary of the Agent being subject to the approval of the Secretary of State.

ORDER.—Ordered, that the foregoing Resolution be sent to the Foreign Department and to the Accountant General, British Burma.

(SIGNED). R. H. HOLLINGBERY,
Assistant Secretary to the Government of India.

No. 791

Copy forwarded to the Chief Commissioner of British Burma, with reference to his Secretary's letter dated 27th March 1869 No. 39-139.

By Order &c.,

(SD). CHARLES GIRDLESTONE,
Officiating Under Secretary to the Government of India

SIMLA,
FOREIGN DEPARTMENT, (POLITICAL,)
The 8th June 1869.

www.ingramcontent.com/pod-product-compliance
Lightning Source LLC
Chambersburg PA
CBHW062125160426
43191CB00013B/2197